*"Britannia" Class 70005* John Milton *approaching the south portal of Ipswich tunnel with a London to Norwich express. To the left of the main line is Ipswich Loco Depot with the carriage and wagon repair shops at centre, beyond which can be seen the water softening tower, the original tank house, and the new concrete coaling hopper. This last sphinx-like structure enabled a coal wagon to be hauled to the top of the plant and the wagon's coal tipped into the hopper. A steam engine requiring coal would be set under the hopper, which was operated by the engine drivers and firemen themselves. In the distance are the houses of Wherstead Road, the river Orwell and Cliff Quay with the newly-built Power Station and its three chimneys (demolished 1994).* (Photo by Aubrey Frost, ABIPP, ARPS)

# IPSWICH ENGINES
# and
# IPSWICH MEN

*The story of Ipswich men, their engines and work taking them all over East Anglia and beyond, from early Victorian times to the present day*

Compiled and edited by
Jill Freestone and Richard W. Smith

**PUBLISHED BY THE OVER STOKE HISTORY GROUP**

*To the memory of
our respective fathers
Eric Pryke & Fred Smith*

First published 1998
This edition 1999

ISBN.......0 9532257 1 2

First published 1998

Copyright © J. Freestone & R.W. Smith

Published by The Over Stoke History Group
18 Luther Road
Ipswich IP2 8BN

Printed by Riverside Press Ltd., Units 14 & 15, Riverside Industrial Park, Rapier Street, Ipswich IP2 8JX

# Contents

Acknowledgements

Introduction

Foreword

A Railway Chronology

Page 3   Over Stoke
Arrival of the Eastern Union Railway  -  Ipswich tunnel  -  Royal visit  -   Stoke in the second half of the 19th Century  -  St Mary Stoke Church  -  Croft Street  -  Railway paddle steamers at Ipswich  -  The Stoke Bone Bed  -  Ransomes & Rapier  -  Clarke Gardens & Peppercorn Court

Page 21  Routes Worked by Ipswich Men
London to Norwich mainline  -  Road to the North  -  East Suffolk Line  -  The Hadleigh Branch  -  Manningtree to Harwich  -  Two sidings at Brantham  -  The Mid-Suffolk Light Railway  -  The Felixstowe Branch  -  Mellis to Eye - LNER promotional areas & outstations - The Griffin Wharf Branch and Dock Tramway  -  Marshalling yards and sidings  -  Single line working

Page 79  Engines, Trains, Excursions & Events
Titled trains  -  The Cromer Express / The Norfolk Coast Express  -  The North Continental / The Manchester  -  Specials  -  Rambles by rail  -  Removal specials  -  The breakdown train  -  The daily papers  -  The Royal Mail  -  The Hush-Hush  -  GNR Engine No. 1  -  Some Sandringham class locomotives  -  The Royal Show comes to Ipswich  -  EUR Centenary Exhibition  -  EUR 150 Anniversary

Page 117  Accidents
Causes and effects  -  The Westerfield explosion  -  Accident to the Cromer Express  -  The Witham collision

Page 131  Wartime
The railway during World War II  -  George Baker goes to war

Page 147  Railway Unions & Mutual Benefit Societies
Early days  -  ASLEF  -  ASLEF Women's Society -  NUR  -  GER Employees' Sick and Orphan Society  -  Local welfare funds

Page 165  Leisure
Early years of the Loco Club  -  British Railway Staff Association  -  Football teams  -  Ipswich & District BR Chrysanthemum Society

Page 175  Ipswich Men
Ipswich men  -  Trials and tribulations  -  Diary of a footplateman  -  Frederick Salmon  -  George Pinkney  -  William Goddard  -  Robert Ratcliffe  -  Three railway mayors of Ipswich  -  Ernie Gould  -  The Smith family  -  George Baker, Senior  -  Robert Goodchild  -  Ernie Payne  -  William and Gordon Barber  -  Alfred Alderton  -  George and Edward Deeks  -  Don Burton  -  Eric Pryke  -  James Gilbert  -  Fred Howard  -  Ivan Fletton  -  The men who kept the wheels turning  -  George Higgins - Sally Read

Epilogue

Appendix I  -  Renumbering
Appendix II  -  Wheel Notation
Appendix III  -  Seniority List

Sources and Further Reading

# Acknowledgements

Every book requires a title, and we thought long and hard before making our choice. At the back of our minds was an article entitled "Ipswich Engines and Ipswich Men" which was written by Ken Leighton in 1971 for the Ipswich and District Historical Transport Society. We felt this piece of writing aptly described the scope and direction of this book, and are therefore deeply indebted to Kenneth for allowing us to use his original title, and for permission to reprint his updated article as the opening text to the section headed "Ipswich Men". Thanks are also due to him for his helpful advice on many occasions.

We are deeply appreciative of the generosity of train-driver Kelvin Higgins in providing us with a wealth of material and photographs from his own collection, and allowing us to publish the Ipswich Seniority List (containing the names of nearly twelve hundred footplatemen) which he has so painstakingly compiled. Also for his contributions to the text of the book, including the epilogue.

To Ken Freestone, Jill's husband, thanks are due for sharing with us the story of a railway career, from a cleaner in LNER days to a driver of electrics just prior to privatisation. His help has proved invaluable regarding the day-to-day working of the railway, and he has patiently supplied the answers to numerous queries during the past two years.

Throughout this time, the help and support of Joan Smith, Richard's wife, has been of the utmost value.

Without Val Norrington, who "gently" persuaded us to start writing, the book would never have come about in the first place.

For their active support over a long period, we are grateful to fellow-members of the Over Stoke History Group, i.e. Helen and Alan Best, Bob Blastock, Kathy Hammond, Rev. Catherine Lack, Eileen Whymark and the late Leslie Gould.

We warmly thank Miss B. Ratcliffe for all her help and for allowing us to quote from her father's unpublished work, "The History of the Working Class Movement in Ipswich & District".

Special thanks are due to Robert Malster for all his advice and support, similarly to Hugh Moffat.

The late Percy Wilby, a railway employee and enthusiast, made several recordings of men recounting their railway careers and we were privileged to have access to those tapes.

We are grateful to so many people for kindly lending us their precious photographs to copy, and each one used is separately acknowledged in the relevant caption. Where it has proved impossible to find the name of the photographer, we mention the person who made the photograph available to us. If we have infringed any copyright, this was not our intention and we apologize. To those whose photographs we are unable to publish, owing to lack of space, we express our gratitude and we promise that the copies will be kept in the Over Stoke History Group's archive for future reference.

We wish to thank the following for their help; some answered a specific question but in many cases advice has been forthcoming on a variety of subjects: George Baker, David Barton, William Barton, Rita Benneworth, Richard Bird, the late Mr Chittock (Griffin Wharf), Graham & Edna Clarke (Chrysanthemum Society), Dave Cobbam, Mr & Mrs Emmerson, Reg Farrow, Mr W. Foulser, The Ipswich Building Society including Margaret Hancock (activities of the Freehold Land Society in Stoke), Derek Girling (Orwell & Levington), Rosemary Gitsham, Dick Glasgow, Ron Gooch (Cambridge Line), Neville Grant, Jean Halliday, John Keeble (Keeble's Siding, Brantham), Graham Kenworthy (Dock Tramway), Bob Markham and Peter Payne (Stoke Bone Bed), Tom Mole, Margaret Moore, Mr I. Mulley (TPO's), Russell Nunn, Richard Pinkney, Barbara Pye, Mr & Mrs F. Smy, Suffolk Record Office staff especially David Jones and Celia Cobbold, Mr & Mrs K. Tooke, and Don Turvey (Ransomes & Rapier).

For the information on the Scottish-East Anglian farming link we thank Mr A. M. Paterson, Simon Wallis, Mr & Mrs J. White, the Misses Wilson, BBC Radio Suffolk and EADT.

We are indebted to Eric Leggett for the use of his diary, which enabled us to chart his progress from cleaner to driver.

We have relied heavily on family memories for the section headed "Ipswich Men", and we expess our gratitude to the following: Graham Andrews (photographs taken at work), Gordon Barber, Doris Burton, Edward Deeks, Ivan Fletton, the Gilbert family, the Goddard family, Vic Goodchild, the Gould family, Fred Howard, Vera Lilley, Pat Ling, Ted Moyse, Mr & Mrs D. Taylor, Rhoda Taylor and Jennifer Witherley.

Compiling the final version of this book would not have been possible without the advice and support provided by David Armes, Claire Scott and all at Riverside Press in Ipswich, and our proof reader Philippa Gale who has helped us to avoid the many pit-falls encounted during the writing of the book.

The cost of publishing "Ipswich Engines and Ipswich Men" has been partly funded by an interest free loan, made available to us by the Suffolk Local History Council. For their support we offer the committee our sincere thanks.

Much of the book is based on memories told to us by ex-railwaymen. Memories do fade over the years however and while we have endeavoured to check our facts wherever possible, we apologize for any errors that may have crept into the text.

# Introduction

Memories of childhood may be extremely fickle, some standing out for no particular reason when viewed in retrospect over almost sixty years. Some remain as clear as ever, especially so with regard to one's parents. Picture Father coming home from work at any odd hour of day or night, unwashed and black with coal dust, hands so ingrained that only after a precious week's holiday did they regain their natural colour. Picture Mother packing cheese sandwiches and a bottle of cold tea - no milk - which when consumed on the footplate of a steam locomotive would truly be Nectar of the Gods. During the war years she would regularly be frantic with worry when enemy air raids caused disruption and what should have been a normal eight or nine hour shift stretched into sixteen, maybe twenty hours. Peaceful memories of walking with Mother on Gippeswyk Park, bordering the railway line and goods yard, in the hope of seeing Dad on "his" engine, even though he was the fireman!

We, the Editors of this book, are proud to share these and other recollections. Our respective fathers, Eric Pryke and Fred Smith, joined the LNER as engine cleaners at Croft Street Locomotive Depot in Ipswich during the 1920s. Great Eastern Railway traditions and practices were still fundamental to their working lives. The locomotives they worked on were pure Great Eastern and remained so for a brief period before the familiar types were diluted by engines from constituent companies of the new regime and the untried products of their Chief Mechanical Engineer filtered down from faraway works in Doncaster, Darlington and Gorton.

It was this background that helped persuade us to accept the challenge to put together an exhibition in 1996 as part of the 150th anniversary celebrations of the arrival of the railway in Ipswich; the Eastern Union Railway. We decided that the theme would be principally that of Ipswich railwaymen and their jobs, backed up by short historical and descriptive notes on aspects of their working lives, the trains they worked, and the routes over which they have moved trains across East Anglia for more than a century and a half. We began with the coming of the railway and its profound effect on Ipswich, particularly that part known as "Over Stoke", to the south-west of the town and approached over the River Orwell by Stoke Bridge. It was to Stoke that the Eastern Union came and built their station and workshops.

As Editors, we were conscious of the persuasive abilities of the more experienced and wiser folk who decreed that the broad content of the Exhibition should be published in book form, and this is the result in an expanded and more detailed semblance. Without that initial encouragement it would not have happened.

The original exhibition, under the auspices of the Over Stoke History Group, attracted much interest from railwaymen, particularly locomen, their relatives and descendants, many of whom have since provided us with information, photographs and personal treasures. Nevertheless we are aware that the book includes hardly any information on a host of railwaymen, such as platelayers, signalmen, shunters, porters, guards, booking clerks, fitters, and other people necessary for the smooth running of the railway. This was not at all intentional. It just happened that by far the greater number of visitors and contributors to the exhibition were connected in one way or another with life on the footplate, the obviously more visible side of the railway. As one visitor remarked, nobody took photographs of his father at work; he was a platelayer and worked almost permanent nights.

We have been privileged to receive contributions from many working and retired railwaymen who have been happy to help us record the local history of part of a national industry. Ipswich locomen have not shared in the well publicised exploits of the more spectacular East Coast Main Line. Instead they continued working, together with the fitters and labourers, in the often appalling conditions that existed at Croft Street before the modernisation of the Shed took place, this improvement happening ironically almost at the close of the steam era. We have attempted, with their help, to portray some of the railwaymen, their working lives and professional pride in the accomplishment of their duties in peace and in war, the light and shade of everyday work from steam to diesel and eventually to electrification and sophisticated radio electronic token block signalling.

We trust that this book will stand as a tribute to the generations of Suffolk men who have worked on the railway during the last 150 years, and can do no better than quote the highly respected Shed Master Richard Hardy. He wrote in his book "Steam in the Blood", when referring to his departure from Ipswich in 1952 having ninety-odd locomotives and some 450 men in his charge,

*".......I had worked with some of the finest of railwaymen, whose only aim was to do their best......"*

JILL FREESTONE & RICHARD SMITH
May 1998

# *Foreword*

Drive along Luther Road and over the mouth of the Stoke tunnel and you can look down on the site of the original Ipswich railway station, and the site of the railway's Motive Power Depot, otherwise known as the Loco. Go further on down Station Street — which never did lead to the station — and you see a fairly nondescript brick building used as a hall with, set into its wall, a large stone. On the stone, in stylish lettering, are the words Ipswich Loco Men's Club and Institute.

In these days of rapid change the stone serves as a reminder that Over Stoke was the railwaymen's suburb of Ipswich, inhabited by cleaners, firemen, drivers and others employed at the Loco or elsewhere on the Great Eastern or its successor, the London and North Eastern. What men they were!

The ordinary railway enthusiast knows of William Adams, James Holden and his son S.D. Holden, and the almost legendary Sir Nigel Gresley. Yet these great designers were by no means without fault; even the grand S69s, or B12s as they were known in LNER days, shedded at the Loco had their faults, as their crews knew only too well. It was the Loco men who had to overcome the faults and the quirks of the 1500s, employing their skill and their ingenuity to perform near-miracles.

Ken Leighton has written elsewhere of the preparations made by the driver and fireman of a 1500 that was to head "The Manchester" on its 232-mile run from Ipswich to the north-west, and to Liverpool. Those preparations included the loading of two pails, one filled with stones screened out of the loco sand (placed in the sandbox to be used when it was necessary to give the wheels extra grip) and the other filled with smaller screenings.

The larger stones were sprinkled on each layer of coal as the fireman built up a substantial fire at the beginning of the run. As the temperature built up to some 3000 degrees Fahrenheit the stones became molten globules, coating the firebars and preventing clinker fusing into a mass and adhering to the cast-iron grate. The smaller material only came into use as the heavily-laden train climbed towards the Pennines, when superb teamwork by driver and fireman resulted in the grit scouring out the sooted-up tubes, enabling the engine to complete its task.

A modification to a drain cock, carried out at the engine crew's expense, enabled the accumulated ash in the ashpan, that threatened to choke the draught, to be washed away on to the sleepers as the engine struggled on at perhaps 75 miles an hour towards Manchester.

Who knew of the subterfuges which these men resorted to, and paid for, in order to get "The Manchester" to its destination on time? Certainly not the Chief Mechanical Engineer or the General Manager, nor the passengers who snoozed or admired the scenery as the train made its apparently effortless way onward.

These were men for whom their work was their life; it was dirty, it was hard, it was sometimes gruelling and never comfortable. Yet these men took a pride in their work, and in completing it successfully against all odds.

The story of these men, of their work and of their lives richly deserves to be told. Jill Freestone and Richard Smith, both of them members of railway families, took on the task with enthusiasm; the exhibitions the Over Stoke History Group has held in recent years have attracted wide interest, and it is to be hoped that this book will be just as successful.

Jill and Richard are to be congratulated on completing the task they set themselves. Their forebears would approve of their dedication to that task.

ROBERT MALSTER
May 1998

# *A Railway Chronology*

**July 1844** - EUR obtains an Act of Parliament for construction of line from Ipswich to Colchester to link with the Eastern Counties Railway which had been carrying passengers between Colchester and London since March 1843.

**1845/6** - Construction of tunnel through Stoke Hill at Ipswich, providing link with Ipswich/Bury St Edmunds line being built by Ipswich and Bury Railway.

**June 1846** - Grand opening of EUR line between Ipswich and Colchester. Station situated in Croft Street.

**Jan 1847** - Newly completed Ipswich and Bury railway amalgamated with EUR.

**1847** - Griffin Wharf branch completed at Ipswich connecting Halifax Junction with the Dock.

**1847** - Bentley to Hadleigh line built by the EUR and the Hadleigh Junction Railway. This line was worked and later purchased by the EUR.

**1848** - Haughley to Finningham line opens (EUR).

**1849** - Finningham to Burston line opens (EUR).

**1849** - Burston to Norwich Victoria line opens (EUR).

**1851** - Opening of link at Trowse, Norfolk, enabling trains to use Norwich Thorpe Station with its important connections to Yarmouth, Ely, etc..

**1854** - EUR taken over by the Eastern Counties Railway.

**1860** - New Ipswich Station opened at far side of Stoke Hill.

**1862** - Formation of Great Eastern Railway.

**1900** - Westerfield Boiler Explosion.

**1906** - Formation of Ipswich Branch of ASLEF.

**1913** - Accident to Cromer Express.

**1923** - GER absorbed by London & North Eastern Railway.

**1932** - Passenger service withdrawn from Hadleigh Branch.

**1948** - LNER absorbed by British Railways.

**1950** - Witham collision.

**1952** - Closure of the Mid-Suffolk Light Railway, and withdrawal of passenger trains on Framlingham Branch.

**1953** - Modernisation of Ipswich Loco Depot, erection of coaling tower and engine shed.

**1955** - First diesel railcar runs on scheduled service between Ipswich & Norwich.

**1958** - First mainline diesel locomotives.

**1960** - Croft Street Loco Depot converted from steam to diesel working.

**1961** - Demolition of coaling tower at Loco Depot.

**1966** - Withdrawal of passenger trains on Aldeburgh Branch.

**1968** - Closure of Croft Street Loco Depot.

**1970** - Demolition of water softening tower at Loco Depot.

**1985** - Electric trains run between Liverpool Street and Ipswich.

**Nov 1993** - Act passed by Parliament allowing restructuring of the railway industry. Start of privatisation.

**1996** - EUR150 Celebrations held.

# *Over Stoke*

# Over Stoke

*Arrival of the Eastern Union Railway*

IN July, 1844, the Eastern Union Railway (EUR) obtained an Act of Parliament for the construction of a line from Ipswich to Colchester to link with the Eastern Counties Railway which had been carrying passengers between Colchester and London since March, 1843.

The site chosen for the EUR Ipswich terminus was at Stoke in the southern suburbs of the town. The area has always been referred to by local people as "Over Stoke" probably because one crossed "over" the River Orwell at Stoke Bridge to reach the small self-contained hamlet. It was described by one rector in the late eighteenth century as consisting mainly of farmland, and had changed very little by the time the railway came, the new station at Croft Street being surrounded largely by fields (see tithe map).

There have never been any fixed boundaries to the Over Stoke area which is made up of part of the parish of St Mary-at-Stoke (itself bordering on the villages of Wherstead, Belstead and Sproughton) and part of St Peter's parish. This latter part, consisting of land in the vicinity of New Cut West, Bell Lane and Great Whip Street, was originally the parish of St Augustine, with its church standing near the present Austin Street. St Augustine's Church was in use until the close of the fifteenth century when the land was then given to the Prior of St Peter's.

In the early part of the nineteenth century shipbuilding was a major industry on the banks of the Orwell at the southern end of Wherstead Road. A tide mill, later converted to steam, stood adjacent to Stoke Bridge. The area boasted five windmills by the early 1840s; two stood on Stoke Hill either side of the road leading to Belstead, two more were at Halifax close to Bourne Bridge, and one stood near the EUR terminus at Croft Street. Close to the last mentioned mill were the original premises (now demolished) of Stoke Green Baptist Chapel, which had been in existence since the late eighteenth century. Clearly shown on the 1840 tithe map is the brickfield owned and worked by James Thorndike, this site now occupied by the houses of Ashley Street, Pauline Street etc.. Men and women in Quaker costume were a familiar sight in the area, the Alexander family who lived at Goldrood, Belstead Road being especially prominent.

The initial plans for the proposed extension of the EUR line from Colchester show the line finishing at Bell Lane, in Stoke, further north than the final site chosen at Croft Street.

On the morning of the grand opening, 11th June 1846, a train consisting of thirteen open and closed carriages drawn by two engines, left Ipswich for Colchester. Peter Bruff was in charge of the engines, and the chairman was accompanied on the train by directors, shareholders and various prominent townspeople. They

*1920s view of Stoke Bridge linking the area known as Over Stoke (left of picture) with the town centre of Ipswich. A bridge existed here as early as AD 970, and there are numerous references in the town's records to repairs and charges for the use of the bridge, sometimes referred to as St Peter's Bridge. In April 1818 two of the arches of a stone bridge were swept away by flood waters and one of three men standing on the bridge was drowned. William Cubitt, chief engineer at Messrs. J. & R. Ransome, was responsible for the replacement cast-iron structure, the principle parts of which were probably made at an ironworks in Dudley (Staffs.) and shipped to Ipswich from Gainsborough (Lincs). Cubitt's bridge was supplanted by the present concrete structure in 1924/5. A second bridge was built alongside the existing one in 1983 to cope with increased road traffic. Until the opening of the Orwell Bridge in 1982, Stoke Bridge was the first bridge to span the river going upstream. Before Vernon Street was constructed in the latter half of the 19th century, the two main thoroughfares through Stoke from Wherstead Road were Great Whip Street and Bell Lane. For many years the former led directly to a ford adjacent to Stoke Bridge.*                    *(Postcard courtesy Richard W. Smith)*

# OVER STOKE

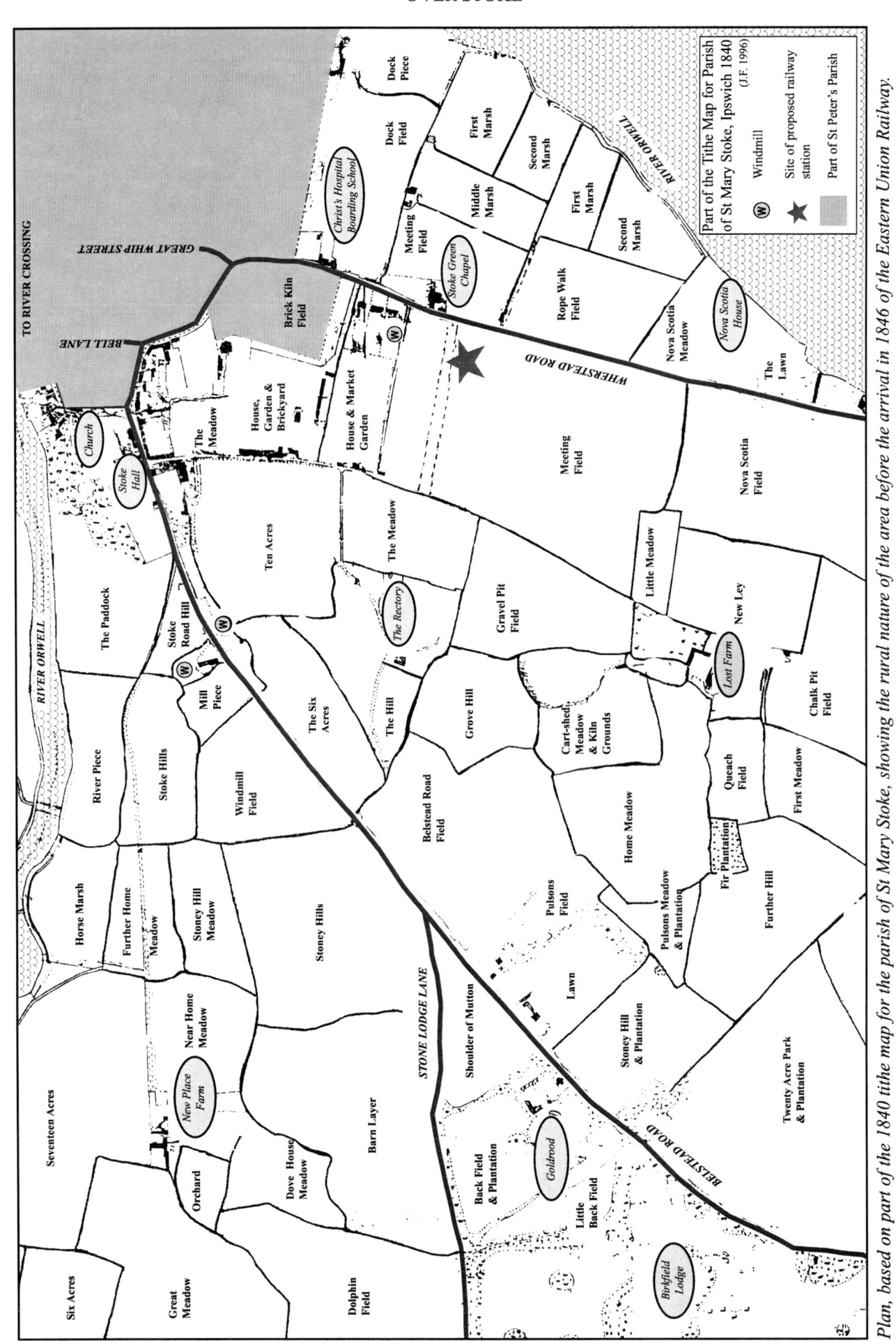

*Plan, based on part of the 1840 tithe map for the parish of St Mary Stoke, showing the rural nature of the area before the arrival in 1846 of the Eastern Union Railway.*

(Courtesy Jill Freestone)

OVER STOKE

*Part of White's 1867 map of Ipswich. A comparison with the tithe map shows the many changes that have been made in the Stoke area, due mainly to the coming of the railway.*
(Courtesy Suffolk Record Office)

were met at Colchester by a special train from London conveying more dignitaries. The two trains joined together and returned to Ipswich, passing under triumphal arches of flowers and flags. At the Croft Street station, a special stand had been built to seat the people awaiting the arrival of the train, which was welcomed by the sounds of bells ringing and guns firing.

A lunch was provided by the railway directors at Nova Scotia, Mr Charles Foote Gower's Wherstead Road residence, situated close to the river (see map). A small steamer, the River Queen was moored nearby, and a party made a trip to Harwich and back.

*Nova Scotia, the Gower family residence, where lunch was provided for the dignitaries attending the opening of the Eastern Union Railway. Charles Foote Gower's father, Richard Hall Gower (1768-1833), was formerly with the East India Company's naval service. The author of several works on seamanship, he was the inventor and commander of an experimental vessel, The Transit. He had moved to the riverside property in 1816 from Hertfordshire. Members of the Gower Family were prominent local benefactors, Elizabeth Gower giving the land on which was built St Etheldreda's Mission Church. Nova Scotia was demolished in 1937.* (Photo courtesy Gower Family Collection)

Later that day, two hundred gentlemen dined at the Ipswich Assembly Rooms, junior railway officers had dinner at the Golden Lion, sub-contractors at the Coach and Horses, and workmen at a tavern in Stoke. The townspeople were entertained by a balloon ascent, and a firework display took place at the Wet Dock. It was not until after midnight that a train took the London guests back to the Shoreditch terminal.

### Ipswich Tunnel

The tunnel through Stoke Hill was completed in 1846 shortly after the opening of the EUR station at Croft Street, providing a link with the Ipswich to Bury St Edmunds line under construction by the Ipswich and Bury Railway. Trains continued to reverse in and out of the Croft Street station at Halifax Junction however until the present station was built beyond the tunnel in 1860.

The tunnel, 361 yards in length, was probably the first in the country to be driven entirely on so sharp a curve. Young Peter Schuyler Bruff (c1811-1900), who had helped to plan and supervise the building of the Eastern Union Railway and became its resident engineer, was in charge of the tunnel construction. Bruff lived for a time in the Stoke area, his son, Peter John, being christened at St Mary-at-Stoke Church in July, 1845. Bruff later moved to Handford Lodge, close to the River Gipping. In addition to Ipswich tunnel, he was involved in many undertakings including the building of Chappel Viaduct and the development of the seaside resort of Walton in Essex. He also provided Ipswich with its first proper drainage system. Bruff has been called "the Brunel of the Eastern Counties" and fully deserves this title. He is buried in Ipswich Cemetery.

Many problems were encountered during the building of the tunnel, especially with the springs in Stoke Hill. A late 18th century map shows pipes conveying spring water from a reservoir or well in the grounds of Stoke Hall, adjacent to St Mary-at-Stoke Church, across the river near Stoke Bridge, to Key Street and Salt House Street. In 1850 the Eastern Union Railway Company was to offer for sale the "water works, springs and water heads" flowing from Stoke Hill.

Walter Goodchild, born in Stoke in 1840, related that building work on the tunnel was begun at the southern end, he himself as a small child living on the western side of Stoke Hill. The course of the tunnel disturbed the springs and affected the wells. His own family lost their water supply very early and for nearly twenty years afterwards all drinking water had to be carted from a distance until at last pipes were connected to the town supply. Not only was the water affected but the surface ground was shaken so that a cavity was opened, he relates, and the mill house had to be braced with timbers. This all took place at a spot which is now the entrance to Philip Road.

To this day, the springs still cause problems. Three shafts were sunk into Stoke Hill during the construction of the tunnel and after building work was completed they were filled with sand and gravel. In the late 1980s, when the line had been electrified, British Rail found that this loose-fill in the shafts was allowing water from the springs to leak into the tunnel. Railway engineers attempted to remedy the situation by drilling into the shafts and pumping a special mix of fly-ash (taken from power stations) and cement into them to consolidate the filling.

*Drilling and filling the middle tunnel shaft, Luther Road, November, 1987.*
(Photo by Leslie Gould)

Locating the shafts, which were nearly ten feet in diameter, posed a problem since they were not marked on any known map. A Cambridge company was therefore employed to take readings through the soil on top of the tunnel to establish the position of the disturbed earth marking the sites of the three shafts. Two shafts were found to be under the roadway at the top end of Luther Road, and the third was located in a garden in Chesham Road.

Work on stabilising the middle shaft was carried out in 1987, and the other two shafts were drilled and filled in January 1989.

Heaters have also been installed inside the tunnel to prevent ice forming in the winter months.

For many years, four cattle wagons were kept at the Croft Street end of the Loco Depot, to be used for the cleaning of the tunnel roof. While carrying out this work, the men stood on a flat walkway, built on top of the wagons.

*A Royal Visit*

In July, 1851, the year of the Great Exhibition and just five years after the opening of the Eastern Union Railway, plans were made for Prince Albert, husband of Queen Victoria, to arrive by train at Croft Street station in order to attend the 21st annual meeting of the British Association which was to be held in Ipswich. Peter Bruff was in charge of making arrangements for the journey with Station Master Mr Cole supervising.

The station building and nearby streets were decorated with flags, streamers and evergreens, in readiness for the Prince's visit. At Halifax Junction, a triumphal floral arch was erected between two signal posts and near the railway line leading to Griffin Wharf artillery men were ready to fire a royal salute. The station platform was carpeted and strewn with roses, as were passages leading to retiring rooms for the Prince and his party.

The rector of St Mary-at-Stoke, the Rev. S. Croft, was among many eminent people waiting to greet the Prince, the reception taking place in a marquee next to the platform.

Outside the station, horse-drawn carriages waited, including the Prince's own state carriage drawn by two fine bay horses, the coachmen and footmen dressed in liveries of scarlet and gold. A guard of honour was formed by the Queen's Bays, accompanied by the regimental band.

At 10.39 am a telegraph message announced that the royal train had passed Bentley Station and shortly afterwards the two-carriage train, pulled by an EUR engine displaying a royal coat of arms, approached the station. The Recorder, Mayor, Town Clerk, members of the Corporation and other eminent people took up their positions to receive the Prince.

As Prince Albert stepped on to the platform the Royal Standard was hoisted, the guard of honour presented arms, the band played 'God Save the Queen' and the cheers of the crowds gathered outside the station were drowned by the sound of guns firing the royal salute.

*The "new" Ipswich Station, opened in 1860, although the island platform was not built until 1883. Viewed here in 1957. The Station Hotel is on the right. Note the workmen on the station canopy. The engine and train waiting at Platform 2 are facing the direction of London. The carriage sidings area (immediate foreground, left) is known to railwaymen as the "foundout"*

(Photo courtesy Kelvin Higgins Collection)

### Stoke in the Second Half of the 19th Century

In 1841, the population of the parish of St Mary-at-Stoke was 992. Ten years later the number of inhabitants had more than doubled to 2,055. Most of this increase was due to the coming of the railway although the building of the nearby Wet Dock also had an effect. By 1891 the population had again doubled, 4,096 persons residing in the parish.

Obviously many new houses were required. The ruling that footplate men had to live near to the Croft Street Depot meant that many railway families required housing in the area, although the younger railway workers, coming into the town from the outlying villages, usually took lodgings. In addition, dock workers, barge skippers and mates, employees of the new engineering works of Ransomes & Rapier, all required somewhere to live.

Generally, the poorer type of house was built close to the river. As one approached higher ground, the housing became of better quality. Large substantial houses and mansions, for example Goldrood, Broadwater and Broughton Place, appeared along Belstead Road, many with views across the river estuary.

During the 1840s and 50s, many small cottages were built in Stoke, in courts, or in a row, on odd scraps of ground. These were called "single houses" and usually consisted of two rooms, having no back door or window so that it was impossible to obtain through-ventilation. It was quite usual to find a man and his wife with from five to eight children occupying this type of house.

The Ipswich Medical Officer of Health reported in 1870 that although great improvements had been made so far as drainage and sewerage were concerned, the same could not be said of Stoke, many parts of which remained in a bad state, more particularly the cottages and premises situated between Bell Lane, Stoke Street and Boars Head Lane.

A large proportion of inhabitants were supplied with

*Wherstead Road, between its junctions with Kenyon Street and Vaughan Street, looking towards the town. Note the track and overhead wires for the electric trams.* (Postcard courtesy Joan Peck)

pump water for drinking purposes but many of the back yards had a dirty and neglected appearance, with tumble-down and dilapidated outhouses, and rubbish lying about on ground that could have been cultivated with flowers and vegetables. In a room at 27 Boars Head Lane, a family was found living without a scrap of bedding or furniture.

Nearly sixty of these so-called single houses existed in Stoke in 1870, including twelve dwellings known as Railway Cottages, which were situated in a cramped narrow space, backing on to the Loco Depot, behind 144 to 166 Wherstead Road.

By 1874 parkland, for instance that belonging to Stoke Hall, had been sold and new streets and roads could be seen where formerly there was a well-wooded and picturesque view.

Many houses in Stoke bear a plaque on which, in addition to the date of building, are the letters FLS. These letters stand for the Ipswich and Suffolk Freehold Land Society (now the Ipswich Building Society). This local Society had an appreciable influence on the development of Stoke, as well as many other areas of Ipswich.

Founded in 1849, the Society introduced a balloting system in 1858, enabling members who were interested in purchasing one of the plots of land on offer, to have a wooden ball bearing their account number, placed in a ballot box at the time of the ballot. Members whose numbers were drawn were required to pay the agreed purchase price for the plot, albeit over a number of years.

In September 1899 a record ballot was held for twelve houses in Philip Road, Over Stoke. No less than 2,270 applications were received, and in the event, all twelve successful members hailed from Ipswich.

During the late nineteenth century the Freehold Land Society was involved in the development of housing in Burrell Road, Gippeswyk Road, Rectory, Philip, Luther and Martin Roads, Croft Street (see further) and Belstead Road. A later venture was the building of houses in Stoke Hall Road after the demolition of Stoke Hall.

By the turn of the century, many changes to the local scene had taken place, including the disappearance of two prominent buildings marked on White's map, the Blue Coat School and the Union Workhouse.

Since the early 1840s Christ's Hospital Boarding School for boys, (called the Blue Coat School on the maps) had occupied a large, ancient farm house, which was situated between Tyler Street and Purplett Street. This building had been demolished, and in its place now stood a small terrace of housing and shops. The figure of the blue coat scholar, which stood in a niche high up on one of the walls of the building, is still preserved however, in Ipswich Museum.

The Ipswich Union Workhouse, situated in Great Whip Street, had been closed and the premises put up for sale in 1899. The building had been erected in 1837, with room for about four hundred paupers of the Borough of Ipswich. The large red brick workhouse was divided into four wards with the governor's house in the centre. Soon rows of houses and a malting complex would occupy the site of the building and its grounds, the inmates having moved to a new institution at Heathfields, Woodbridge Road, in Ipswich.

Gone also by 1899 was the row of ancient houses overlooking the Canser, or raised footpath, in Stoke Street. On the site of the houses there now stood a Methodist Chapel, complete with balcony, known as the People's Hall.

Stoke Bathing Place, built jutting out into the tidal river in the early 1840s, was to remain in existence until the 1950s. It is remembered by generations of Ipswich boys as the place where they learned to swim; membership was restricted to men only, girls usually attending swimming lessons at Fore Street or St Matthew's Baths.

### *St Mary-at-Stoke Church - The Railway Church*

Situated on the south bank of the river, in an elevated position overlooking the town, and close to Stoke Bridge, the present St Mary-at-Stoke Church building dates back to medieval times although there has probably been a church on the site since at least the tenth century.

The churchyard was the setting for a murder in the fourteenth century, during the reign of Edward III. The victim, John Beneyt, was at vespers in the Church when an argument arose between him and one John Rodland. Together they went outside and were standing in the churchyard when John Rodland drew a knife and struck John Beneyt in the chest, killing him immediately.

National events touched upon Stoke and the Church in 1665, when several English seamen were buried in the churchyard. The men had been wounded during the sea battles between the English and the Dutch and were brought to Ipswich to recover from their injuries, but sadly some died in the town.

The Puritan, William Dowsing, visited the Church in January 1643. He noted in his journal:

*"Two crosses in wood, and two cherubims painted; and one inscription on brass with Ora pro nobis, etc."*

When William Spencer was buried in the churchyard in 1816, the following lines were inscribed on his tombstone:

*This world's a city full of crooked streets,*
*Death is the market place where all must meet,*
*Was life a merchandise that men could buy,*
*The rich would only live, the poor must die.*

In 1863, to cope with the increase in worshippers due mainly to the arrival of the railway, restoration work started on the Church, and a north transept was added. This was during the time of the Rev. Croft. The Church was greatly enlarged in 1870-2 when a new nave, chancel and south porch were added to the south side of the Church, the architect being William Butterfield. Gone now was the massive two-storey porch, with mock battlements surmounted by two pinnacles, which had dominated the entrance to the Church for so many years.

The registers of St Mary-at-Stoke Church reflect the varied occupations of the first railway workers living in the parish. As early as December 1845, the baptism is recorded of Grace Hawke, whose father was a railway labourer, also Mary Lucy Hawley, daughter of a railway sub-contractor. Between 1846 and 1850, the baptismal register notes the names of nearly forty children of railway employees. Many of these were sons or daughters of railway labourers, clerks, servants or porters. Other children's fathers included a railway smith, a railway contractor, and a gas fitter at the station. Three fathers were railway guards (from 1848 onwards) and three were engine drivers (1849 onwards).

In December, 1848, the register records the baptism of William Henry Telford Haslem, the baby son of a fitter at the station. Sadly William lost his mother Ann, aged twenty-seven, when he was only five months old, and he himself died before reaching his second birthday. Mentioned in the baptismal register for 1849 were the two daughters of Station Master Gideon Hatchwell, Laura aged six and Thomas aged three. (Hatchwell was killed in a tragic railway accident the following year.)

Two railway labourers, Thomas Wilson, aged twenty-two from St Peter's, and William Goode aged thirty-eight, were buried in the churchyard in 1846. Laid to rest there in 1851 was Thomas Truelove, aged thirty-eight, an Inspector of Police with the Eastern Union Railway.

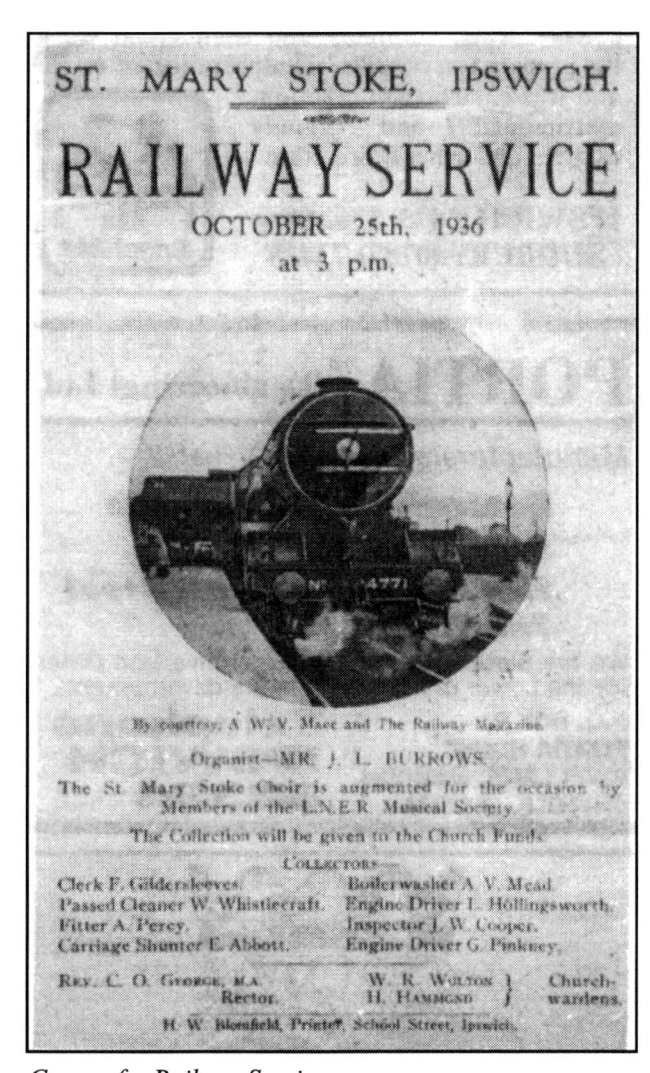

*Cover of a Railway Service programme.*

(Courtesy Canon Denis Yates)

The churchyard of St Mary-at-Stoke was closed for burials in 1855 except upon special leave granted by the Secretary of State. It had been decided that the overcrowding of graves in the burial grounds of the town was causing a health hazard, and therefore a new cemetery was opened to the north of Ipswich.

The Church of St Mary-at-Stoke has always been closely associated with the railway, even to the extent of being referred to as "The Railway Church" in an official guide to Ipswich churches published in 1927.

In the 1930s, a Railway Service was a regular item on the Church calendar, the event being held at least twice a year, in April and October. The church choir was joined by the LNER Musical Society, and railwaymen read the lessons and took the collection.

A replica of the GER armorial device now hangs on the north interior wall of the church, placed there by a former rector, Canon Denis Yates, to commemorate the many links between the railway and the parish. This crest, designed by Henry Parker of the carriage department when the GER was formed in 1862, can be used as a guide to the various counties through which the Great Eastern Railway ran. The crest, in a variety of sizes, appeared on coaching stock, many passenger tender engines, and also on the splashers of the Claud Hamilton 4-4-0s.

*Croft Street*

Croft Street, the approach road to the original Eastern Union Railway station terminus, and later the Loco Depot, was named after the Rev. Stephen Croft, rector of St Mary-at-Stoke Church from 1820 to 1868. The street is not the only one in Stoke to be named after a local rector. Bulstrode Road takes its name from Canon George Bulstrode, rector of the parish from 1880 to 1898.

From its junction at Wherstead Road, Croft Street runs

*The Great Eastern Railway armorial device. The arms are (clockwise from top left) Middlesex, Maldon (Essex), Ipswich (Suffolk), Norwich (Norfolk), Cambridge, Hertford, Northampton (possibly to represent the Soke of Peterborough) and Huntingdon. London takes pride of place at the hub of the device.*

(Photo by Aubrey Frost, ABIPP, ARPS)

steadily up hill to Rectory Road. With its small terraced housing and with at one time two public houses, it forms a good example of a typical Stoke street and as such merits a closer look.

Croft Street was part of a route frequently walked by railwaymen before the closure of the Loco Depot took place. Many footplate jobs entailed relieving other train crews at the present Ipswich Station or local Goods Yards. In these instances the driver and fireman would sign on at the Croft Street Depot and then walk by a prescribed route which included Croft Street, to where their turn of duty started. At the end of the job they were often faced with the same walk back. It was forbidden to walk through the tunnel, because of the obvious dangers, although this short cut would have eliminated the climb up the steep Stoke Hill. Some jobs required the men to initially take their engine light from the Loco Depot through to the Station. If they knew their shift was finishing there, then they would often take their bicycles with them on the engine so they could ride straight home from the Station on finishing work. This practice was unofficial, but management usually turned a blind eye.

The Great Eastern and the EUR Hotel, the two public houses previously mentioned, stand facing one another on opposite corners of Croft Street/Webb Street. Both public houses face the site of the original railway station and they each had stabling to accommodate the horses of travellers going to and from London using the newly introduced trains. Both later had a flourishing trade with the Loco Depot just across the road; drinking on duty was not frowned upon in earlier days.

The Great Eastern was formerly known as the Albert, The Royal Albert Inn, or, as shown on one map, The Halberd. It stood in Albert Street, which was an earlier name for Croft Street. Controversy has always existed as to whether the Great Eastern was named after the Great Eastern Railway or Brunel's steamship of the same name.

According to an advertisement appearing in the

*Croft Street, looking towards its junction with Wherstead Road. Photograph shows the unloading of a diesel storage tank for installation at the nearby Loco Depot, c1960.*
(Photo by R. Zagni)

Suffolk Chronicle, ratting took place at Mr J. Goodwin's Royal Albert Inn, one Monday evening in June 1850 between:

*"Mr Cresswell's dog Nelson, Mr Smith's dog Billy, and Mr Garnham's dog Pincher for £5 each, at fifty rats each. A good supply of rats for use."*

One does wonder how or where such a plentiful supply of rats was obtained.

The EUR Hotel, although named after the Eastern Union Railway, is always referred to by its initials. It was here that Peter Bruff entertained guests to supper after the marriage of his daughter, an event recorded in an Ipswich Journal of 1860.

The EUR Hotel was home to a lodge of the Royal Antediluvian Order of Buffaloes (RAOB) for many years. (There have been Buffs in Stoke since 1912.) The Stoke Flying Club for pigeon fanciers was also based at the EUR.

One popular landlord of the EUR Hotel was Mr George "Boggy" Willson. When he took over the establishment he sent out a card containing the following poem in an effort to attract customers:

*"If over Stoke you pass this way
and if in want of a drink you are,
George Willson will supply you well,
he keeps the EUR.
His ales are good, his whisky too,
and also is his porter,
So if you don't know of this house,
it's nearly time you oughta."*

The EUR Hotel was recently refurbished and renamed Crofts, but has now returned to its original name. Sadly the Great Eastern is at present (1998) boarded up and empty. There are two other public houses with railway connotations, the Stoke side of the river. One, the Railway Tavern in Burrell Road, closed in 1987 and was demolished. However the Station Hotel, standing adjacent to Princes Street Bridge and facing the Ipswich Railway Station forecourt, is still open.

The small St Mary Stoke Church of England Infants' School, which opened in 1880, was near the top end of Croft Street. The senior boys' and girls' departments were situated some distance away, in front of the Church, in Stoke Street, on what is now the church car park. The children of railwaymen living in the parish of St Mary-at-Stoke would mostly have attended either these church schools or Wherstead Road Board School. An additional church school existed for those families living in St Peter's parish but to reach this the children had to cross over Stoke Bridge as the school was situated the town side of the river. While Cubitt's bridge was still in existence, mothers were frightened at the thought of their children having to make this journey because of the volume of horse traffic using the narrow bridge.

Wilfred Brown, later to become foreman fitter at the Loco Depot, attended the small Croft Street Infant School when Miss Clarke, headmistress for thirty-four years, who died in 1921, was assisted by pupil teacher, Miss Haste. He remembers using slates for writing and drawing, and regular visits from the rector of St Mary-at-Stoke Church, Canon R. Tompson who was one of the school governors.

*View of Ipswich Loco Depot with the EUR Hotel in the distance. Note the high stacks of coal.* (Photo courtesy Richard Pinkney)

The St Mary Stoke Church Schools closed in the 1930s. In 1937 Wherstead Road School moved to new premises in Belstead Avenue, and became known as Stoke Junior Mixed Council School and Stoke Infants' Council School. Later it was called Luther Road School, and now (1998) it is referred to as Hillside Primary School.

The Freehold Land Society was involved in housing development in Croft Street. A ballot was held in 1889 for thirteen terrace houses at the top end of the street. Of the successful applicants, two were railway guards, a further two were listed as engine drivers and two more as engine fitters. It is uncertain whether these last four occupations were necessarily connected with the railway; the men could have been fitters with Ransomes and Rapier, for instance, and stationary engine drivers.

The Society also developed the site on which the windmill, worked by the Bruce family, originally stood on the corner of Croft Street and Wherstead Road, facing Stoke Green Chapel. The site was sold in 1882 and four houses fronting Wherstead Road and a corner shop were built. This small grocery shop was Barwells for many years, then run by Mr Grimes, followed in turn by Mr Beer. Then, like many local shops, it closed owing to the competition from the supermarkets, eventually re-opening for a time as an antique shop. The premises were later used by a travel firm.

## Two Railway Families of Croft Street

*Croft Street resident for many years, George Cork, born c 1840 the son of a shipwright. In 1851 the family was living "opposite the railway station", i.e. the original Croft Street terminus, and George spent the rest of his life in the area. He had started his railway service as a deck hand on the Great Eastern Railway Company's river steamers, but by 1861 he was a railway porter, and his address at this time was "Station Field". In 1871, now married, he was living at 2 Albert Street (the former name for Croft Street) and was a signalman at Halifax Junction, Ipswich, employed outdoors since the signals were worked from the ground with no cover. George Cork later became a relieving signalman but gave up this position in 1899 when almost sixty, owing to injuries received during shunting operations. He performed light work, probably at the new Ipswich Station, until his retirement, aged eighty, after sixty-two years service, when he was presented with a walking stick and a pocket wallet containing a substantial sum of money subscribed by members of the station staff. George Cork's two sons were employed by the railway.* (Photo and information courtesy Pat Waters, Mrs Dorothy Waters, Mrs S. Alderton and Bryan Green)

*Four generations of one family outside 82 Croft Street, c 1916. Seated is Maria Grimwood, nee Hazelton, born at Belstead in 1823. She married there Henry Grimwood, a shepherd, in 1847. Her daughter, Fanny, (standing), was born at Belstead in 1859. Fanny married Joseph Smith Goody, a railway porter, at Stoke Green Baptist Chapel in 1879. His father was a railway inspector. Fanny's son Joseph, who lived at 80 Croft Street, and whose father-in-law was an engine driver, is seen (left) with his young son Joe. It frequently happened that several members of one family worked for the railway. If a father or uncle, for instance, was a railway employee, this would often aid a young man when seeking a job with the railway company.*

(Photo & information courtesy Jean Austin & Tony Hale)

*Teaching staff pictured outside St Mary Stoke Infants' School, Croft Street, during the 1890s. Standing, Alice Cork (left), Miss Haste (right), seated (centre) headmistress Miss Clarke. Pupil teacher Alice Cork was born in 1874, the daughter of George Cork (see further photograph). The school log book mentions Emma Cork, an older sister, being at the school in 1898, so one of the two unknown young ladies may possibly be Emma.* (Photo courtesy Pat Waters)

On the opposite corner of Wherstead Road and Croft Street, facing the shop, was the railway garage. This originally housed the Great Eastern Railway's own buses which ran between Ipswich Station and Shotley from 1905 until 1920 except for a temporary break during World War I. Frederick Pallant, of Rectory Road in Stoke, was in charge as both driver and fitter. He had joined the GER in 1896 and served a seven-year apprenticeship in the loco sheds at Ipswich. The first buses in use were built by the GER at Stratford. Seats on the upper deck were open to the elements, the passengers being provided with waterproof sheets to pull over their knees in wet weather. The garage later became the maintenance depot for railway owned motor vehicles until its closure in 1964.

### Railway Paddle Steamers at Ipswich

The Great Eastern Railway Company inherited some early river steamers from its predecessor, the Eastern Counties Railway. The Company subsequently had built, at various yards, its own fleet of Continental ships to operate from Parkeston Quay. River steamers were also constructed for Woolwich Ferry on the Thames, and for the Ipswich to Harwich and Felixstowe services. Many of these carried on working for several years with the LNER.

The paddle steamers familiar at Ipswich, and particularly to Stoke residents, were the Orwell (1873), Norfolk I (1882), Suffolk (1895), Essex (1896) and the second Norfolk built in 1900. They all sailed to and from steamer piers constructed at New Cut East, and later along New Cut West. They were bunkered from the GER coal yard in Bright Street. An electric tramway, opened in November 1903, went down Bath Street to the river for the benefit of the steamer passengers.

For a few years prior to World War I the paddle steamers were joined by the sea-going Woolwich Belle. This was owned by Belle Steamers, having no connections with the railway.

The Essex was sold in 1913 but the Suffolk and Norfolk served until 1930 and were eventually broken up, bringing to an end a long era of popular railway river services on the Orwell.

During the 1930s the New Medway Steam Packet Company paddler City of Rochester provided a service from Ipswich to Clacton and return, with additional trips to the Cork Lightship or Harwich on some days, according to the tide. Again this service was unconnected with the railway, and it ceased in August 1939.

### The Stoke Bone Bed

Few train travellers through the tunnel at Ipswich realise that thousands of years ago crouching lions perhaps disturbed herds of red deer close to where the south portal now stands.

The bones of large animals are known to occur in the silt and mud deposits between Stoke Hill and Maidenhall. The first discoveries were made in 1846, when the tunnel was cut through Stoke Hill. The bones

*The premises, now demolished, which housed St Mary Stoke Church Schools in Stoke Street. Part of the building to the right, which originally had a thatched roof, was used as the Poor House for the parish before the Ipswich Union Workhouse was erected near Great Whip Street.* (Photo by Victor Goodchild)

*Boys of Wherstead Road School seen here in 1931 with teacher Mr Patmore (right). Left to right, top row: 1st boy Eric Birch (later a railway fitter); 7th, Bishop (driver's son). Second row down: 1st, Sid Reed (later a driver); 3rd, Charlie Brunning (driver's son, later a fireman and timekeeper). Third row: 3rd, Malcolm (killed on Stoke Bridge crossing by a tram engine); 6th, Laughlin (driver's son); 9th, Arthur Welton (driver's son); end right, Harold Saunders (driver's son). Bottom row: 1st, George Baker (driver's son); end right Jack French (son of signal fitter).* (Photo courtesy George Baker)

came from near the south end of the tunnel at a depth of eight to nine metres from the present ground surface. The finds, placed in Ipswich Museum, attracted the attention of Nina Layard (1853-1935). In 1908 she decided to try to relocate the bone bed where previously several baskets of elephant bones and teeth had been collected. This she successfully did but because of the fear of the bank slipping, no more was done until 1919 when the Loco Depot was extended by digging into the "cliff" in front of Croft Street. The railway company again gave Miss Layard permission to excavate, and most of the faunal remains in the Museum date to this period of collecting.

The deposit in which the bones are found is referred to as the "Stoke Bone Bed" and is the silt and mud of an ancient course of the River Orwell when it flowed at a higher level than at present. This was during the earlier part of the last interglacial period, about 120,000 years ago.

The next record of exposure of this bone bed is in 1948 when a small tunnel for a sewage pipe was being cut parallel to the railway line in the grounds of Hillside School. The tunnel was driven through the skulls of two mammoths, a bison skeleton and a rhinoceros astragalus.

In 1975 and 1976 further excavations were made, revealing, as before, bones of horse (plentiful), mammoth (mainly young animals), bison, red deer, giant deer, bear, lion, wolf, ox, birds, water vole and tortoise. The digging of sewage trenches, during the construction of Stoke High School at Maidenhall, revealed a concentration of bones which suggested that most of one animal was present. Upon investigation a large part of the skeleton of a young mammoth was excavated in the position where it had died. Most of the bones had moved slightly because of the action of the river currents. Nevertheless a complete articulated foot, together with another found close beside it, suggested that the beast had become stuck in the mud and drowned. The majority of bones found represented a young steppe mammoth, not a woolly mammoth.

A few flint flakes have been discovered which suggest that prehistoric hunters were in the vicinity, but no rich archeological site has yet been found.

Such discoveries have made this area a centre of geological research for over one hundred and fifty years.

*Part of an advertisement for Ransomes & Rapier's railway plant.*
(Courtesy Basil Gilbert)

### Ransomes & Rapier

In 1869 the firm of Ransomes & Rapier, taking over the existing engineering connections of Ransomes, Sims & Head, started to manufacture rail points and crossings at Waterside Works, alongside the River Orwell, in Stoke.

The firm was involved in the construction of China's first railway in 1874, although this was closed down by the Mandarins after having only a short life. Ransomes & Rapier continued with the design and manufacture of railway equipment, achieving a world-wide reputation for the production of turn-tables, traversers, buffer stops, loco hoists and breakdown cranes.

The firm employed a large number of men. Before the advent of the car, Wherstead Road used to be jammed with bicycles and pedestrians at the start or finish of a shift.

Ransomes & Rapier were heavily engaged in other spheres of engineering. Their sluice gates were to be found in most countries of the world, they were pioneers

*Locomotive turntable at Ipswich Loco Depot, built by Ransomes & Rapier in 1939. Picture shows Halifax Signal Box just left of centre background, and the line to Griffin Wharf leading off to the left. The London to Norwich mainline is at right. This turntable was powered by the locomotive's own vacuum system, whereas previously a turntable would have been operated manually by the driver and fireman.*

(Photo by Brian Leighton)

in the development of concrete-mixing plants, and they were heavily involved in the manufacture of small excavators, cranes and huge Walking Draglines. Unusual engineering jobs were also undertaken, the firm being responsible for the revolving stage at the London Coliseum, aircraft catapults for ships and the revolving restaurant on the Post Office Tower in London.

Sadly the firm of Ransomes & Rapier is no more, having been taken over by Robert Maxwell and closed down in 1987. A local newspaper mirrored the feelings of Stoke and Ipswich residents when it headlined an article on the firm's closure, "A Great Talent Gone to Waste - 118 Years of Care, Courage and History at an End".

### Peppercorn Court and Clarke Gardens

At the present time (1998) of writing, there are still reminders of the railway in Stoke. The Griffin Wharf line is in use once again, crossing the Wherstead Road at Black Bridge, near to the former Nova Scotia House where the Gower family once lived. The Croft Street Depot is largely deserted, although repairs to Freightliner wagons are carried out in the Carriage and Wagon Repair Shops next to the London to Norwich main line.

To date, nothing exists in the area to commemorate Peter Bruff, although the idea has been mooted to have an etched glass panel at Ipswich Station to celebrate his life and work. However, where Stoke Green Baptist Chapel and part of the engineering firms of Ransomes & Rapier and Cocksedges once stood, a small housing complex has been completed. Roads there have been named after famous locomotive designers, Peppercorn, Holden, Sinclair, Adams, Bromley, Johnson and Gresley. A garden, designed for the site of the former burial ground of the Baptist Chapel, and open to the public, has been given the name of Clarke Gardens. This is in memory of a long-time resident of Ipswich who helped to avoid a major train disaster at Soham Station during World War II. Mr H. G. Clarke was the guard of a munitions train which caught fire at the station.

Thus are memories of the railway, and its impact on local affairs for more than one hundred and fifty years, still living on - Over Stoke.

# Routes Worked by Ipswich Men

## London to Norwich Mainline

THE building of the railway line from London by the Eastern Counties Railway commenced in 1839 but ended four years later at Colchester owing to lack of funds. As related earlier in these pages, it was to be 1846 before the line finally arrived at Ipswich from Colchester, the link being built by the Eastern Union Railway. Until then, passengers wishing to travel to London, but without recourse to a private coach, had two options; a stage/mail coach journey via Colchester, Chelmsford, Ingatestone, Brentwood and Romford, or else a steam packet trip down the River Orwell, out to sea, and then up the Thames to land at one of London's many wharves, piers or quays.

At the start of the 1830s, with railways yet to make an appearance locally, the following coaches regularly left Ipswich for London, according to Pigot's Directory :

"The *Royal Mail* (from Norwich) and the Telegraph (from Yarmouth) call at the Mail Coach Office and Great White Horse Hotel, every night at ten. The *Old Blue* (from Saxmundham) calls at the Griffin and King's Head Inns, alternately, every morning at nine. The *Independent* from Haxell's Coach Office and Coach & Horses Inn, every morning at nine. The *Shannon* (from Halesworth) at half-past nine. The *Monarch* (from Norwich) calls at the White Hart Inn, St Lawrence Street, every night at half-past nine, and the *Star* (from Yarmouth) calls at the Great White Horse Hotel and Golden Lion Inn, every day at twelve."

For conveyance by water to London, the Suffolk & Norfolk Shipping Company's vessels set sail every Tuesday, Thursday and Saturday from Ipswich. The vessels of the Old Shipping Company left every Saturday, as did those of the Crown & Sceptre Shipping Company. The Ipswich Steam Packet, for passengers only, departed twice a week.

By 1844, White's Directory was giving details of coaches running from Ipswich to Colchester to meet the trains of the Eastern Counties Railway, now that the line from London to Colchester was open. Coaches included the *Quicksilver* at seven in the morning, the *Retaliator* (from Woodbridge) at twenty minutes to nine, the *Shannon* (from Halesworth) at half-past eleven, and the Norwich Day Coach at half past one, daily except Sunday. It was stated that "by these conveyances, passengers go from Ipswich to London in four and a half hours; and persons going by the *Quicksilver*, and returning the same day, have five hours in London."

At this time, with no direct railway link from London to Ipswich, the London-bound steam packets sailing from the town and calling at Harwich and Walton-on-the-Naze, included the *Orwell* (Captain S. Rackham), leaving at eight in the morning every Monday and Thursday and returning Tuesday and Friday, and the *Orion* (Captain R. Wheeler), departing every Tuesday and Friday mornings at eight and returning Thursday and Saturday. Omnibuses carried passengers to and from Woodbridge, Saxmundham, Yoxford, Stowmarket, etc. on the arrival and departure of the London steamers.

When in 1846 the railway eventually reached Ipswich and shortly afterwards was extended to Bury St Edmunds, the London coaches went into a decline. The guards on the mail coaches were fortunate however in that instead of becoming redundant, many of them found work in the dispatching of mail from railway stations, thus keeping their role as guardians of the Royal Mail.

In 1855, regular coaches were still running between Ipswich and Woodbridge (the *Shannon*), and Ipswich and Southwold (the *Old Blue*). These were soon to fade away however when the East Suffolk Line opened in 1859.

In spite of the spread of the railway in the region, the coastal steamers continued to operate. At one time, when the Eastern Union Railway was experiencing difficulties with the Eastern Counties Railway, the former company used its own vessels to convey goods between Ipswich and London. This was in addition to carrying those passengers who chose to make the seven-hour (weather and tides permitting) combined river and sea trip in preference to a shorter train journey. Perhaps the travellers enjoyed being able to stretch their legs on board the steamer, provided they were in no hurry.

### The London railway link from the 1840s onwards

In 1840 the temporary London terminus at Devonshire Street in Mile End, built for the Eastern Counties Railway, was replaced by an imposing station at Shoreditch which six years later was renamed Bishopsgate. There was little room for expansion and it soon proved inadequate to handle the increase in traffic. For many years the company examined different schemes, especially those designed to take the railway closer to the City of London, but not until the Great Eastern Railway developed Liverpool Street did anything happen. A few small rail-fed coal depots were opened on the approaches to Bishopsgate, one such being the Whitechapel Coal Depot in the late 1860s which became Spitalfields Goods Yard, known by generations of Ipswich enginemen.

The Great Eastern Railway was incorporated in 1862 and carried forward the aim of having a more convenient terminus. This was to be Liverpool Street, the rail approach to which was in a cutting with the main line diving under the Bishopsgate tracks just the London side of Bethnal Green station and ending up seventeen feet below ground level. This all conspired to make it difficult for departing steam engines to lift heavy trains out of the terminus, and enormous problems occurred for years with the bottleneck thus created.

The acquisition of the land required for the project meant that hundreds of small houses and tenement buildings of the worst slum areas of the East End were demolished. The landlords were compensated, but the manager of the GER, Mr Birt, reported afterwards that 7,000 people were displaced, many of whom had been moved out only a few years previously during land clearance for the construction of neighbouring Broad Street station. The dispossessed created even worse conditions nearby and slightly further eastwards, which coincidentally took them out of the City of London thus removing an enormous problem for the Corporation which had raised few objections to the scheme.

The west side of the new station was first to open in 1875 and the famous Trainshed has been very cleverly incorporated into the rebuilding of the station between 1985 and 1990. The east side, opened in 1894, was altered out of all recognition during the redevelopment. Completion of the whole station in that year also meant the culmination of the building of the London to Ipswich railway some fifty-five years after its commencement and the line has remained largely intact for over a century.

*Poster advertising steamer trips to London. Possibly referring to May 1845, as the* Orwell *had been involved in a collision a few months previous to this date, and it would therefore explain the "extensive repairs" the coastal steamer had just undergone.* (Courtesy Aubrey Frost, ABIPP, ARPS)

The opening of Liverpool Street Station meant that Bishopsgate was used only for goods traffic. It was completely rebuilt whilst remaining open for business and officially reopened in January 1881. The goods station carried on until 4th December 1964 when it was destroyed by fire with the loss of two lives. Spitalfields Goods Depot closed in November 1967.

To the north of Ipswich, in 1849, the Eastern Union Railway reached Norwich Victoria station via Haughley Junction (on the Ipswich to Bury St Edmunds line), Finningham, and Burston. A link with the Eastern Counties Railway at Trowse, just outside Norwich,

*An Eastern Union Railway Company's double-sided document, dated 1853, authorising the conveyance of one barrel of oil between London and Ipswich, aboard one of the coastal steamers run by the Ipswich Steam Navigation Company.*
*(Courtesy Mr Driver)*

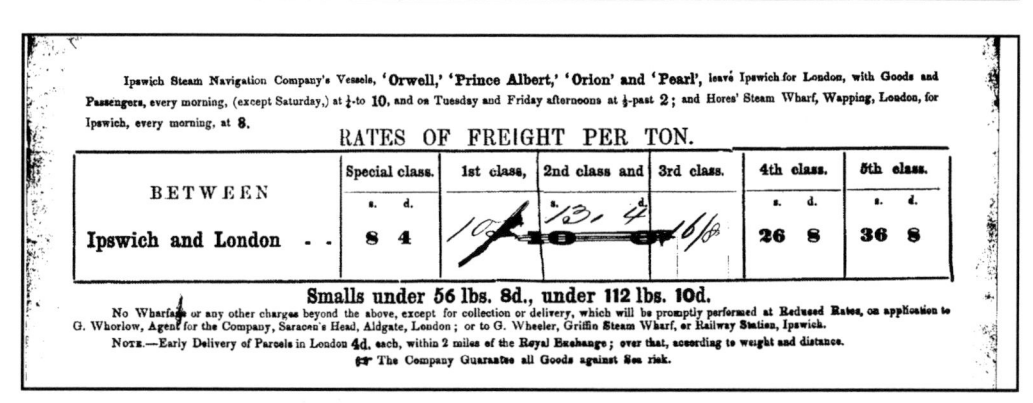

opened in 1851 providing access to Norwich Thorpe station but no EUR locomotive was allowed on to ECR metals. In 1854 the EUR was taken over by the ECR.

The ECR line from Shoreditch to Norwich, via Cambridge, Ely and Brandon, opened in 1845 but in later years the Ipswich route became the more favoured, being shorter at 115 miles compared to the alternative 123 miles via Cambridge. Norwich Victoria station remained in use for some stopping trains from Ipswich, before becoming a goods depot in 1916. It was used for coal trains only, in the 1970s, before complete closure.

The Eastern Union route in the 1950s was used by some of the fastest scheduled steam trains in the country, improving slightly with the advent of diesel haulage but revolutionised by electrification in the 1980s. Electric trains reached Ipswich in 1985 and Norwich in May 1987 and have operated to a timetable based on trains running at 100 mph.

Push-pull operation came in during the early 1990s saving time by removing the need for the locomotive to run round at the station to be at the front of the train for the return journey. The down trains are driven from a driver's compartment in the "last" carriage, the train being pushed by the engine to Norwich and hauled back to Liverpool Street. A far cry from the steam push-and-pull trains which shuttled between Yarmouth Southtown and Beccles and many other places powered by antiquated tank engines until the 1950s!

*Norwich "Britannia" Class No. 70010* Owen Glendower *climbing Belstead Bank in the 1950s. Ipswich Gasworks are visible on the horizon.* (Photo by Bob Rogers)

*4000 h.p. Class 86 electric locomotive hauling a push and pull Norwich to Liverpool Street set at 80 mph at the same location in August 1996.* (Photo by Richard W. Smith)

# Road to the North

SUBSEQUENT to the opening of the Ipswich and Bury St. Edmunds Railway in December 1846, the line was extended westwards by 1854 to meet the Cambridge to Newmarket line which had opened three years earlier. This latter superseded the original Newmarket railway linking the Eastern Counties Railway Company's London to Cambridge main line at Great Chesterford with Newmarket via Six Mile Bottom in 1848. As soon as the Cambridge connection was made in 1851 the original Great Chesterford line was abandoned proving that closures are not a new phenomenon.

The Eastern Counties Railway's main line through Cambridge to Ely and Norwich opened throughout by the end of 1845. A branch from Ely connected with the Great Northern Railway at Peterborough via March in 1847. The Ipswich to Newmarket line however did not have a direct connection with Ely until 1879 when the Newmarket to Ely line through Fordham and Soham was opened by the Great Eastern Railway. It incorporated the triangular junction on the Bury side of Newmarket Tunnel between Warren Hill, Snailwell and Chippenham allowing through trains from Ipswich to run direct to Peterborough.

Since its inception in 1862, the GER had focused its corporate eye on the potential coal traffic from the South Yorkshire and Nottinghamshire mines and even from further afield to London and East Anglia. From 1863 the company tried unsuccessfully to promote Parliamentary Bills to build various lines through Lincolnshire and had long negotiated with the Great Northern for running powers and joint ownership of proposed new lines. After years of wrangling, a Bill authorising joint ownership of railways linking St Ives, March, Spalding, Lincoln and Gainsborough with the GN main line south of Doncaster was successful and the Great Northern and Great Eastern Railways Joint Committee became a reality in 1879.

The direct line was opened in August 1882 and Great Eastern passenger trains began running from Liverpool Street through Cambridge to Doncaster and later to York, having gained running powers over the Great Northern and North Eastern metals. In 1885 a Boat Train was inaugurated between Harwich and Doncaster which was extended to York in 1892 with through coaches for Manchester and Liverpool. All these passenger trains were suspended during World War 1 and only the Boat Train reinstated, to be known as the *North Country Continental*. It was different in that the main section of the train went on to Manchester Central and Liverpool by way of Retford, Sheffield Victoria and Woodhead Tunnel. This route was made possible by agreement on running powers over the Manchester, Sheffield and Lincolnshire Railway later to become the Great Central Railway which was incorporated in 1897. The train left two coaches at March for Birmingham and the rest divided at Lincoln with the last section going on to Doncaster and York.

Various routes were used following electrification in the Sheffield and Manchester areas and the closure of the Woodhead route, and in 1973 the train was re-routed via Peterborough, Grantham, Nottingham and Sheffield. Accordingly, Lincoln and the GN & GE Joint Line saw the end of the Boat Train after 88 years in both directions.

Modern Sprinter diesel railcars were introduced on the service in May 1988 together with other new services to the Midlands and North West including Blackpool, apparently heralding a new era in rail travel from Ipswich and East Anglia. This was very short lived and within two or three years new long distance services commenced from Stansted Airport and all trains from Ipswich or Parkeston terminated at Peterborough. Thus ended over a century of service by a train which in its many manifestations had provided invaluable cross-country connections for countless holidaymakers, business people and servicemen, as well as for the Continental traveller arriving in the evening at Parkeston Quay to face a North Sea crossing and the uncertainties which lay beyond, having left the relative security, if not luxury, of the *North Country Continental*.

## The Cambridge Road
## The 1950s - A Passenger Remembers

One of the Editors clearly remembers regular journeys on the Ipswich to Cambridge line during his National Service, 1952-54. Weekends for him started midday Saturdays and the run home began at about 12.45 pm from Waterbeach station down the Ely line on a Norwich to Liverpool Street train via Cambridge, from where the 1.50 pm to Ipswich would leave from platform five. The timing of this latter train varied a little in the 1950s, starting at 1.45, 1.50 and 2.0 pm. The train was made up of very mixed stock. There could be an ex-Great Eastern coach with remnants of gas lighting still visible in the decorated roof, or an occasional clerestory

# ROUTES WORKED BY IPSWICH MEN

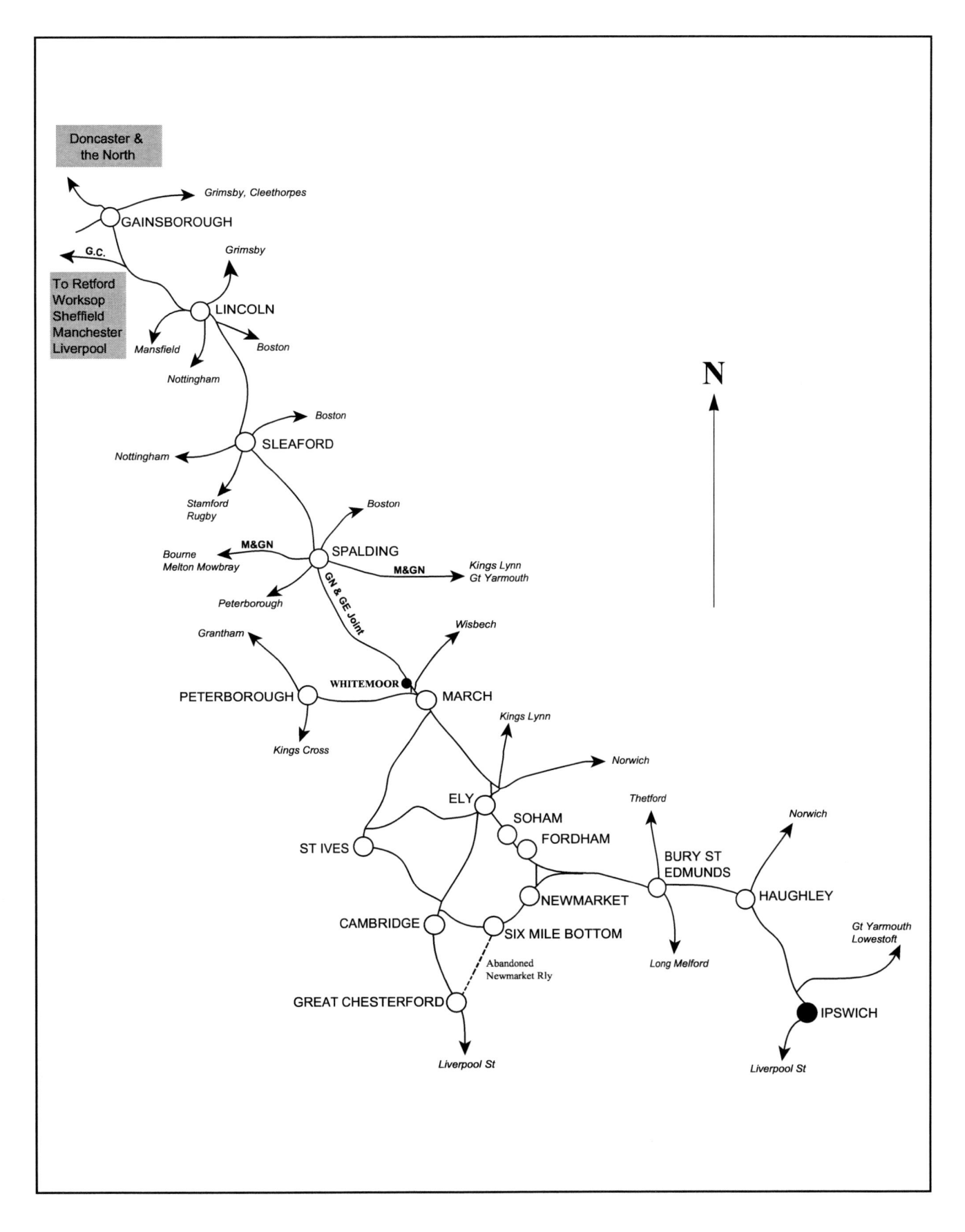

carriage of the same era, coupled to Gresley corridor coaches and the new B.R. steel carriages with unconnected corridors but sporting a toilet amidships. This particular job was one of only two Ipswich workings done by Cambridge men at that time.

The right-away was usually on time following the departure from number four platform of the Down Liverpool Street to Norwich train, booked to connect with it. The writer recalls that the Ipswich line trains did not have similar arrangements with trains off the former LNWR line from Bedford and Bletchley and a late arrival from that direction meant sprinting the entire length of the formidable platform only to see the Ipswich train gathering speed as it cleared the bay, and two hours to wait for the next! That particular service to Ipswich ran all stations to Stowmarket and at that time motive power was usually a "Claud Hamilton" 4-4-0 or a J15 0-6-0 often with another engine attached as far as Bury where it would be used on another working. Occasionally the engine was a J17 0-6-0 or an "Intermediate" 2-4-0, and briefly toward the end of the decade there would be a B12 4-6-0 then recently displaced by the Southend line electrification and soon to be superseded by the diesel multiple units. The train was well patronised by people returning home from Saturday morning work or shopping in Cambridge. Apart from a few passengers alighting at one or other of the three intermediate stations, the majority would leave the train at Newmarket.

Fulbourn was the first stop from which, at that period, it was possible to enjoy summer Sunday excursions to Hunstanton, picking up at stations via Newmarket, Fordham and Soham. Our next stop was at Six Mile Bottom where, before crossing the main London to Newmarket and Norwich road, it was just possible to see the trackbed of the original direct Newmarket line from Great Chesterford. Dullingham was next, one of those places reminding us of the old wartime cartoon depicting the off-duty American servicemen asking themselves, "Why didn't those guys build the church nearer the railway station?" Dullingham; carriage doors slamming shut, the squeak of the wicket gate as passengers left the platform to wait patiently by the level crossing where the locomotive

*The 2 pm Cambridge to Ipswich train, seen here on Saturday 19th July 1958, taking the sharp Newmarket Curve (complete with check rails) from the main Cambridge to Ely line. The locomotive is ex-LNER 4-6-0 No. 61575, one of the final batch of "1500s" built by Beyer, Peacock at Manchester.* (Photo by Richard W. Smith)

simmered away, the noise of the Westinghouse pump, the bird song, all these sounds allowing for just a minute or two a classic glimpse into the English countryside of the railway age. Suddenly the "pop" of the snifter valve and the opening of the regulator transformed the brief encounter with a world soon to be gone forever to a normal Saturday afternoon as we gathered speed and sped down the bank to Newmarket.

The remainder of the shoppers and workers alighted at Newmarket and a horsebox or two may have been detached. There were still railway shunting horses at work there then. Departure, passing the grand original station of 1848 which became the goods station, and the driver collecting the token for the single line through the tunnel.

Memories of the tunnel are of the loud exhaust from the engine and the echoing clank of the side rods. Emerging at Warren Hill, the signalman accepted the token and the train picked up speed over the junctions of the Newmarket triangle for the brief run to Kennet, joining the Ely line coming in on the left, close to the old Newmarket RAF airfield marked by the very short lineside telegraph poles; short to avoid collisions by aeroplanes. On to Higham and the dip in the road up on the high embankment where according to legend a

*The frontage of the original 1848 Newmarket Station, a Class 2 listed building, seen here October 1980 shortly before demolition in preparation for a new housing development. Described by Pevsner as "the most sumptuously Baroque station of the Early Victorian decades in England."*
(Photo by Richard W. Smith)

goods train parted with some of its trucks unintentionally and they wafted backwards and forwards until coming to rest quietly at the bottom of the dip and the guard, hitherto blissfully unaware of the situation, popped out to see why the train had stopped! Strangely enough several otherwise rational drivers and firemen were always a trifle apprehensive about that section, not far from the village of Barrow, especially at night.

Soon the train entered the station for Saxham and Risby, both settlements situated well away, one on either side of the Turnpike road. The smell of the nearby Calor Gas Depot marked the spot, "Stench" being the appropriate technical word for the familiar tang! And so to Bury St Edmunds where the goods yard was still busy on a Saturday afternoon and there was always time to admire the posters for farm machinery on the station wall during the lengthy stop, when the leading locomotive would be removed.

Leaving Bury at about 3.10 pm the next calls were at Thurston, Elmswell, Haughley and Stowmarket which was the last stop. From then on all hell was let loose as we roared through Needham Market and Claydon at a mile a minute and more until checked by signals at Ipswich and coming to rest in number one or two platform, always on time, one hour fifty minutes from Cambridge. Returning to Cambridge on the Sunday evening could be quite eventful. This journey commenced in august fashion by boarding the *Edinburgh* which left Ipswich at 6.35 pm on Sundays,

6.05 pm weekdays. This train had started from Colchester and so was usually on time. We passed Bramford village on the left, always looking idyllic with the river, church and cottages blending together in the summer evening sunshine or the lights in the old houses twinkling away in the winter darkness.

The train stopped at Stowmarket and Bury; passengers for the Cambridge line changed at Bury to join the all-stations Ipswich to Cambridge train which had left Ipswich half an hour before the *Edinburgh*. Bury station platform would be crowded as the express left and the Cambridge train, usually worked by a "Claud", made its way into the station from the old Long Melford branch where it had been waiting since its arrival at Bury.

If Bury station was crowded on a normal Sunday imagine it once a month when a day excursion from Liverpool Street to Bury via Cambridge would also be waiting to return. On these occasions both the Long Melford and the Thetford branches would be occupied. The London excursion would be the next to leave, and as it was fast to Cambridge everyone, excursionists and servicemen alike, piled in. As the third train in ten minutes left the same platform, those of us without a pressing engagement at the "Seat of Learning" or an immediate connection to make, could enjoy splendid isolation and an empty compartment for the rest of the trip, stopping at all stations to Cambridge.

Two firsts remain clear in this passenger's memory. One is of the sighting of mysterious lights in the autumn fields. They proved to be stubble fires as farmers were then turning to combine harvesters and for the next forty years burnt the straw and stubble left in the combine's wake.

The other memory is of one wet, blustery and very dark November evening on the crowded Cambridge train after leaving Newmarket. Slowly, making heavy going of getting up the bank to Dullingham, we eventually came to a stand. After a few false starts the guard ambled up to the engine and returned with the now legendary words "wet leaves on the line"! Probably the seven-foot wheels of the "Claud Hamiltons" did have difficulty with adhesion in those conditions with a heavy train. One hour behind time we crawled through the back of the goods yard at Cambridge having lost our path completely. Emerging the other side of Hills Road Bridge the train reversed into number three platform, the usual departure point for Up trains to Liverpool Street or Kings Cross.

National Service provided the railways with some useful passenger revenue and certainly saved several stations and some goods yards from being closed much sooner than they actually were. The RAF bases in East Anglia alone required daily goods deliveries to the nearest railway station of everything from barrack room furniture to nuts and bolts and aero-engines, all for collection by service vehicles.

## *Newmarket Tunnel*

This tunnel is situated on the Ipswich to Cambridge route, the Ipswich side of Newmarket. It is single line throughout, with a speed restriction of 40 mph. In steam days, the single-line token would be picked up at Warren Heath signal box and given up upon arrival at Newmarket. The reverse would apply when travelling from Cambridge to Ipswich.

The tunnel, 1,099 yards in length, was constructed in order that the railway would not interfere with the exercising of racehorses on Newmarket Heath. The line was dropped into a cutting and roofed over. To this day railway maintenance staff insist that it is possible to stand inside the tunnel and hear the sound of horses galloping on the turf above.

The tunnel is unique in that it has a restricted clearance and a dip in the middle. Travelling through it with a steam engine was always a very unpleasant experience. The dip meant that the train entered on a falling gradient and then faced a climb out. The tunnel's walls and roof were square, instead of the more normal rounded shape.

It was possible to put a hand out of the driving cab and touch the side of the tunnel, and there was only a foot or so clearance between the tunnel roof and the top of the loco's chimney. Great care had to be taken not to blow off steam whilst inside; any fireman who did so would be very unpopular with his driver. The engine would have to be worked fairly hard on the climb out and the resultant exhaust created havoc, making it impossible to hold a conversation on the footplate as the noise was so great. In addition, the cab would be filled with smoke and steam which resulted in the driver and his mate being unable to see one another. Breathing was difficult and often a driver, before entering the tunnel, would soak a handkerchief in cold water and tie it round his nose and mouth. In steam days the inside of the tunnel was never seen by loco crews and it was not until the advent of the diesel locomotive that it became apparent; not that there was much to see anyway!

A freight train, travelling from Cambridge to Ipswich, once ground to a halt in the tunnel, owing to the engine slipping and not being able to maintain enough speed to make the climb out. Driver Eric Pryke, mentioned elsewhere in this book, was requested by the local signalman to detach from his train at Chippenham Junction and take his engine into the tunnel to haul the train out.

The crew of the broken-down freight train were in grave danger of suffocating, as the tunnel filled with smoke and steam. The incident had a happy ending however, as everyone emerged safe and well although covered in soot and gasping for breath. The unfortunate fireman, Ron Bloom, black with grime from head to foot, did not get the sympathy he expected from the signalman, only a curt remark that the signalman hoped the fireman had brought the single-line token out with him. The freight train driver never lived the event down; Reg Greaves was a north countryman and when he first came to Ipswich Shed from Grimesthorpe had loudly declared that Suffolk men did not know what real tunnels and banks looked like; he had come from Sheffield and was accustomed to working over the steep Pennine gradients, together with the long associated tunnels. Becoming stuck in Newmarket Tunnel was a terrible humiliation after all those fine words!

## East Suffolk Line

WHAT is usually referred to as the East Suffolk Line was the end result of proposals acted upon during the 1850s by the Yarmouth & Haddiscoe Railway, the Halesworth, Beccles & Haddiscoe Railway, the Lowestoft & Beccles Railway, the East Suffolk Railway (Halesworth to Woodbridge), with branches to Leiston, Framlingham and Snape, and the Eastern Union Railway's branch from Ipswich to Woodbridge. These all came to fruition after several earlier schemes had failed to find backing. The line opened throughout on June 1st 1859, and the Leiston to Aldeburgh section in April 1860.

All the constituent companies had, by the time the line opened, been taken over by the Eastern Counties Railway, itself absorbed by the Great Eastern Railway Company on August 7th 1862. The Westerfield to Felixstowe branch was opened on May 1st 1877 by the Felixstowe Railway & Pier Company.

Apart from Ipswich there were locomotive depots at Yarmouth Southtown and Lowestoft, also small sheds at Framlingham, Aldeburgh and Felixstowe, although these last three were normally staffed only by a driver in charge plus another driver or acting driver, and two acting firemen with a cleaner who also coaled the engine. Holiday and sick relief would normally be covered by footplate staff from Ipswich who would find a space somewhere on the premises to sleep, such as a porter's room.

The East Suffolk was very familiar to Ipswich crews not only with ordinary passenger and goods traffic but also handling some of the fish trains from Lowestoft and Yarmouth, and the milk from Halesworth to Ilford which ran seven days a week. Grain and malt formed a large part of the goods carried; the maltings and cattle feed manufacturers were established at Snape, Halesworth, Beccles, Framlingham Woodbridge, Melton and later at Felixstowe.

These bulk commodities and seasonal traffic such as sugar beet and domestic coal helped keep some goods traffic in business into the 1960s and early '70s, whilst at Melton there was a short lived trade in the 1970s with trainloads of stone. Micklewright, the Melton coal merchant, still received coal by rail until about 1980 as part of the leasing arrangements for the coal yard land with British Rail. The only original branch to have survived is the Aldeburgh line as far as the Sizewell siding where nuclear waste is sent away by rail for disposal. The single line Felixstowe branch has become an important link with the Port of Felixstowe, and except for a connection between Trimley and the northern dock extension opened in 1983, remains largely as originally constructed.

The direct line from Beccles to Yarmouth Southtown via Aldeby and St Olaves closed to passenger traffic on 2nd November 1959. Sugar beet traffic from Aldeby to Cantley survived until 1965 by using the spur connecting the East Suffolk with the Lowestoft to Norwich line at Haddiscoe. A major item of expenditure on that line was the operation and maintenance of the swing bridges at Beccles and St Olaves.

As a result of this closure, Ipswich to Yarmouth trains left the old main line at Beccles for Lowestoft where they had to reverse and take the coastal route from Coke Ovens Junction in Lowestoft through Corton, Hopton and Gorleston to Yarmouth Southtown. This line was built by the GER in 1903 and operated jointly by the Great Eastern and the Midland & Great Northern Joint Railway under the auspices of the Norfolk & Suffolk Committee, itself authorised by Act of Parliament in 1898.

There were no expensive swing bridges along this track and in fact there were no level crossings in contrast to the rest of the old M&GN system on which they proliferated. Diesel railcars (DMUs) worked the stopping trains from Ipswich to Yarmouth and Ipswich drivers learned the alternative route. The few London to Yarmouth expresses, usually worked by "Britannia" Class locos, were taken on to Yarmouth by new Brush diesels and allowed four minutes for the changeover at Lowestoft. These trains were re-routed to Yarmouth Vauxhall via Norwich Thorpe in June 1962, and the Saturday holiday trains were diverted the following summer. Southtown goods depot finished January 1967, the station becoming an unstaffed paytrain halt for the DMUs and inevitably closure came on 4th May 1970.

Breydon Swing Bridge (near Southtown station) which closed in 1953, originally provided the link with Yarmouth Beach Station and the rest of the M.& G.N. system which closed on 28th January 1959 except for some goods traffic in central and west Norfolk.

The "Joint", as it was generally referred to by railwaymen, was always looked upon as a rival and viewed with suspicion by Great Eastern men including those at Ipswich. Clifford Emmerson, a fireman at Yarmouth Southtown in the late 1930s, experienced this phenomenon personally when his father, a "Joint" man based at Yarmouth Beach, obtained a locoman's cap for his son, this being of better quality than the current

LNER issue. It was not appreciated at Southtown; on its first outing it was removed from the fireman's head and pierced by a shunter's pole!

Great Eastern men were unimpressed by the apparent autocratic power wielded by Mr. William Marriott who, in 1881, joined the contractors building the line and in 1883 was appointed Engineer to the Eastern & Midlands Railway, one of the predecessors of the M&GN. He became Locomotive Superintendent in 1884, and was appointed Traffic Manager in 1919 before retiring in 1924. Mr Marriott, a very clever engineer and designer, was responsible for most of the infrastructure of the line, which included everything from concrete mileposts to Breydon Bridge, whilst simultaneously designing locomotives. He had served his engineering apprenticeship with Ransomes & Rapier Ltd. of Ipswich.

During the 1980s an important change occurred on the East Suffolk Line when radio electronic token block working (RETB) was introduced. The system enabled all trains between the stations of Westerfield and Oulton Broad South to be controlled by one signalman working from the signal box at Saxmundham. The original box there was stripped of its levers and instruments, and refurbished as a control centre.

All other signal boxes were dispensed with. The level crossings were converted to automatic operation worked by track circuits. The line, which had been double track throughout, was left double from Westerfield to Woodbridge; single from Woodbridge to Saxmundham; double again from Saxmundham to Halesworth, and finally single track once more from Halesworth to Oulton Broad South. This gave ample scope for trains to pass on route.

The system, although in use in Scotland, was unique in this area. Transmitting and receiving aerials were erected at strategic points. Diesel Multiple Units (DMUs), or railcars as perhaps they are better known, worked all passenger services and each driving cab was equipped with both radio receiver and transmitter to receive and send signals to the control centre at Saxmundham.

Before this a cloud had hung over the East Suffolk Line, and rumours of closure often arose owing to the vast expenditure required to maintain the stations, signal boxes, level crossings, etc. Under the new system, trains were run with conductor-guards, and the intermediate stations, with the exception of Saxmundham, became unstaffed halts. All freight traffic was stopped. Provision was made for the nuclear flasks to be transported from Sizewell by fitting two Class 37 diesel locomotives with radio equipment to enable them to haul these trains.

Initially, as with most innovations, teething problems were encountered but these were gradually eliminated. The railcars have since been phased out, to be replaced by the new sprinter type trains. The system now runs smoothly and financial savings must have been made.

## TRAVELLING BETWEEN IPSWICH AND LOWESTOFT USING RADIO ELECTRONIC TOKEN BLOCK WORKING

Upon leaving Ipswich, a train would be worked normally to Westerfield where it would come to a stand in the platform at a white board displaying the words "STOP - OBTAIN TOKEN". The driver would contact Saxmundham by means of a telephone handset installed in his cab and give his location. This was required because the Saxmundham controller did not have a visual track circuit picture of trains running in the system; he was however able to speak to individual drivers over the telephone by stating the radio number of the train he wished to contact.

The message could be heard by all drivers working in the system but would only be answered by the one whose number was given. This communication facility was designed for essential conversations only; any frivolity was frowned upon. All messages were recorded on tape at Saxmundham and kept for a specific period of time before being erased. Drivers were not expected to talk amongst themselves; everything had to go through the control centre at Saxmundham.

The driver now waiting at Westerfield would next give his train radio number (each unit had a different number) and also his train details, and ask to enter the system. He would then be asked by the Controller to press his "RECEIVE" button. This was one of two buttons on the console in front of him, the other being marked "SEND". Pressing this receive button enabled the electronic token to be sent from Saxmundham. The token would appear in a visual display on the console screen, showing the words "WESTERFIELD-WOODBRIDGE". The driver, after informing the controller that the token was received and displayed correctly, would then ask for, and receive, permission to pass the stop board and enter the section ahead.

*THE EAST SUFFOLK JUNCTION: The scene in the late 1960s as an excursion train, headed by the Flying Scotsman, takes the Norwich and Bury line towards Hadleigh Road Bridge. The centre two tracks formed the East Suffolk Line, and the diagonal lines led to and from both main lines to the Top Yard for goods traffic.* (Photo by Aubrey Frost, ABIPP, ARPS)

*The same view in 1997, with the signal box gone. The goods road has been singled, as has the East Suffolk Line. The recently vacated engineers' depot, at the far right, was the site used for the 1934 Royal Show traffic and for the naming of* The Suffolk Regiment *steam locomotive a year later. The 1946 exhibition celebrating the centenary of the EUR was also held there. (These events are covered in detail elsewhere in the book.) The small arch in the right-hand road bridge over the East Suffolk Line was for an approach to the sidings at the Manganese Bronze Ltd. works, where the firm used their own diesel shunters. The line was partly covered by the building of the GPO office block in the 1960s.*

(Photo by Richard W. Smith)

*Engine No. 61637* Thorpe Hall, *with the 3.53 pm fish train to Ipswich, passes Oulton Broad South on 16th June 1959. Although Ipswich men worked or relieved some fish trains and empties to and from Lowestoft or Yarmouth Southtown, the majority were worked by Lowestoft train crews.* (Photo by Richard W.Smith)

*12th May 1984 saw the final run of the Lowestoft through-train to and from Liverpool Street. Thereafter, all Lowestoft services terminated at Ipswich with passengers having to change there to the Norwich-London trains. A through-train is shown leaving Woodbridge during the final week of working. In the foreground is the track-bed of the former Melton Tramway.*
(Photo by Richard W.Smith)

Upon arrival at Woodbridge stop board, the driver would again contact Saxmundham. He would inform the controller that his train had arrived complete and he wished to return the Westerfield-Woodbridge token. The controller would instruct him to press his "SEND" button which enabled the token to be taken back, after which the driver's screen would go blank. The driver would inform the controller that the screen had blanked out correctly and that he now required a token from Woodbridge to Saxmundham, whereupon the same procedure as took place at Westerfield would occur.

The same procedure applied on arrival at Saxmundham, when a Saxmundham to Halesworth token would be required. Upon reaching Halesworth, the final token, displaying "HALESWORTH-OULTON BROAD SOUTH" would be obtained, to be returned on arrival at Oulton Broad South. Here the train left the system, as from Oulton Broad into Lowestoft, normal block working applied. On the return journey from Lowestoft to Ipswich the readings for the tokens would obviously be displayed on the screen in reverse, i.e. "OULTON BROAD SOUTH-HALESWORTH" etc..

In the event of a failure of the equipment for any reason, there was an emergency back-up system. At each of the four token stations was a telephone, enabling contact to be made with the controller at Saxmundham. If a driver found he was unable to transmit and/or receive a token, or to make contact with Saxmundham from his cab, then he would make use of these outside phones. The telephone cabinets were locked, the driver carrying a special key to open them.

Contained in the cabinets, in addition to the telephone, was a supply of "Authority Cards". These cards would be filled in by the driver at the controller's dictation with particulars of train times, radio number, etc., and also a special authority number. The controller would then give permission for the train to proceed between the two locations in which the failure occurred. At completion of duty these cards had to be handed to the station supervisor at Ipswich or Lowestoft.

The whole system was a completely new concept for the railcar drivers. For the first time in their careers they could contact the outside world without leaving their cabs. Any failure or mishap on the line could be instantly reported, without the necessity of using signal or lineside phones which often involved a long walk in cold or wet weather.

*The Snape Goods passing Playford on its way back to Ipswich.* (Photo by Bob Rogers)

## The Aldeburgh Branch

A BRANCH line from Saxmundham to Leiston was opened on 1st June 1859, reaching the coast at Aldeburgh the following April. There was considerable business to and from Richard Garrett's agricultural machinery works at Leiston, and some to Sizewell siding, plus the usual domestic coal and general goods to Aldeburgh, with a relatively small amount of fish outwards. Passenger traffic was steady and excursions ran to Aldeburgh in the summertime including the *Eastern Belle* Pullman train from London. The railway however did not make the same impact on Aldeburgh as it did on other resorts like Lowestoft, Felixstowe, Walton on the Naze or Clacton.

Thorpeness Halt opened in April 1914 and served the new, privately owned, holiday estate on which building had started in 1910 and was to continue for another twenty years. In 1953, to celebrate the Coronation, the pupils and staff of Northgate Grammar School for Girls, Ipswich, having assembled on the platform of Ipswich Station on the morning of June 4th, found that the destination of their mystery journey by special train was to be Thorpeness. The headmistress, Miss Appleton, wrote in the school's log book that Captain Ogilvie had placed the village of Thorpeness at the disposal of the school, lent the cricket ground and pavilion for a picnic and the workmen's hall for an entertainment.

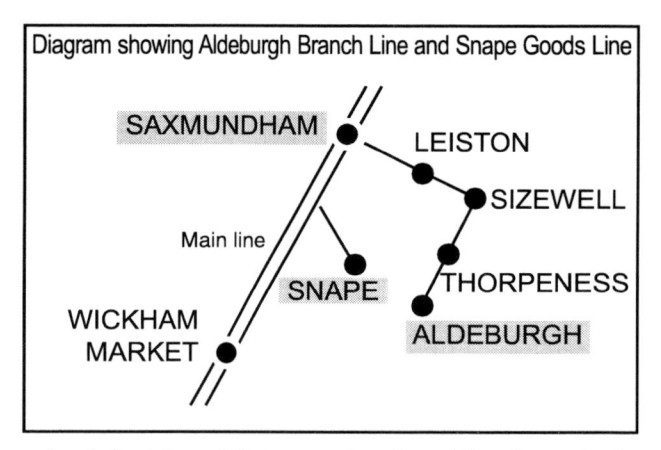

Thorpeness station booking-office and waiting-room consisted of old Great Eastern carriages which were never replaced by a proper building.

Passenger trains were withdrawn from the branch in September 1966 having been operated by Ipswich Diesel Multiple Units since 1956 when the branch engine-shed closed. Goods traffic had ceased in November 1959 at Aldeburgh, but lingered on for truckloads of coal to Leiston for a few more years. The branch has been retained as far as Sizewell however for special nuclear-waste trains to run from Sizewell Power Station.

*Thorpeness Halt in the 1950s, with the old Great Eastern carriages still forming the station buildings. The platform remained very tidy right to the end of its life, with good paintwork and neat firebuckets. Thorpeness enjoyed a quality clientele who arrived by train to play on the nearby golf course.*

(Photo by Bob Rogers)

*Sizewell Siding, the end of the line. Class 37 locomotive waits with the flask of nuclear waste from Sizewell Power Station.*
(Photo by Trevor Smith)

## The Framlingham Branch

LIFE on this branch line followed much the same pattern as on most country lines, the branch linking as it did the small town of Framlingham, plus the two villages of Parham and Marlesford, with the East Suffolk main line at Wickham Market, the station for which was actually in the parish of Campsea Ashe. Hacheston was served by a small halt but no platform, the guard on the train having a small step ladder for the use of passengers alighting or wishing to join the train there.

The grand opening at Framlingham, on 1st June 1859, coincided with the opening of the main line and heralded over sixty years of great railway activity and service to that part of Suffolk. Serious competition from both passenger and goods road transport then began affecting traffic in the 1920s and 30s, with the private motor car in the 1950s inflicting its toll, resulting in withdrawal of passenger trains on 3rd November 1952, although special beginning and end-of-term trains for Framlingham College continued until 1958. Complete closure of the line came on 19th April 1965.

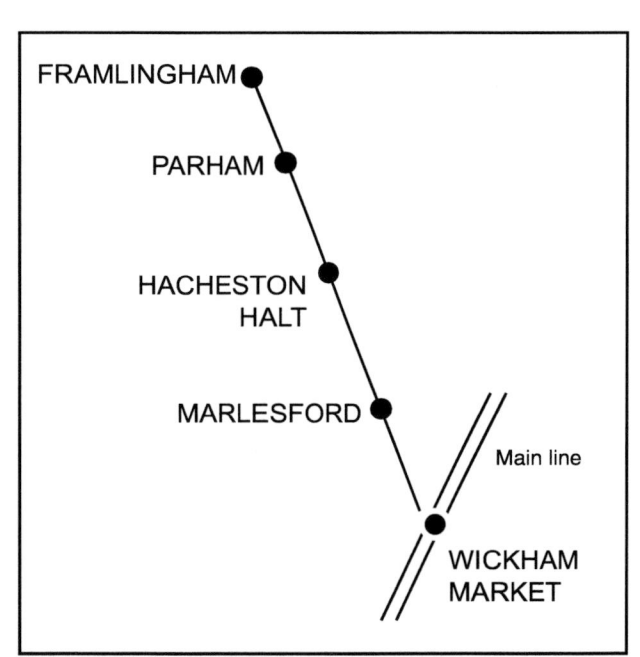

*The Up Daily Goods with J15 Class engine No. 65472 passing through Ford Crossing, Marlesford on 19th September 1959. The tower of Marlesford Church can be seen in the background.* (Photo by Richard W. Smith)

*A considerable traffic in grain helped to maintain the goods service to Framlingham for a few years longer than it might otherwise have lasted. The box vans were largely replaced by modern steel hopper wagons, which are seen in use here as the daily goods nears Framlingham.* (Photo by Richard W. Smith)

*Charlie Poacher, Harry Taylor (Ganger) and Jimmy Ling with Mr Messenger of Marlesford Station.*
(Photo courtesy Joy Clements)

The goods yards at Framlingham, Marlesford and Parham were busy with farm produce, corn, coal, and sugar beet. The nearby wartime airfield at Parham, officially named as Framlingham, brought the usual heavy increase in traffic to Parham from 1943-45. A pill-box was erected adjacent to the line at the Marlesford level crossing near the ford, and in this, during air-raids, the level-crossing keeper's family would be joined by several people from the village. Men of the American Airforce were a common sight during this time, walking along the track in twos and threes between their base at Parham, and Wickham Market. Another man who walked the line as opposed to riding it was the platelayer, Mr Clow, who made regular inspections of the track.

The Anglo-American Oil Company (later Esso) had small depots at Framlingham and Campsea Ashe, where British Petroleum also had a depot, whilst Shell Marketing Ltd. had one at Marlesford. All the depots were served by rail. The Campsea Ashe and Marlesford petrol depots closed in the 1920s. They were set up typically in the early 1900s using horse transport and mainly selling lamp-oil but as motor lorries became more reliable and the speed limit was raised above twelve miles per hour local distribution was possible by road from either Ipswich or Saxmundham.

*The station staff at Wickham Market (Campsea Ashe), the junction for the Framlingham branch. The station master, Mr Gibbs, is seated in the centre of the group with his black dog, which regularly travelled of its own accord to Framlingham and back in the guard's van of the branch train. Seated to Mr Gibbs' left is Thomas Elliot (1886 - 1959) who worked for the GER and LNER as a shunter, head shunter and guard. He lived for many years in Ranelagh Road, Ipswich.*

(Photo courtesy J. L. Elmer, grandson of Thomas Elliot)

*The last ordinary passenger train left Framlingham on 3rd November 1952. Seen on the footplate on that occasion are (left to right) Driver H. Double, Fireman A. Chittock and Driver J. Turner.* (Photo Kelvin Higgins Collection)

*Platelayers' trolley at Ford Crossing in the 1930s. Seated is Harry Taylor (Ganger), whose wife Florrie was the crossing keeper. Standing on trolley, right, is Charlie Poacher. Viewed looking towards Framlingham.*
(Photo courtesy Joy Clements, daughter of Harry and Florrie Taylor)

## Snape and Aldeburgh Bonus Trips

GOODS-train working on each of these branches used a long standing system of bonus payments which gave a financial incentive for the train crews to get the job done as quickly as possible. The trains started at fixed times from Ipswich goods yard but thereafter did not have a timetable to observe for shunting or running times. They were subject only to the effect of other trains using the same tracks and the instructions of the signalmen enroute. This enabled the East Suffolk main line to be cleared of these particular trains in good time and the engine would be available for other duties if required.

The bonus was calculated on the principle that the sooner the job was finished, the higher the payment would be. Delays caused by waiting for other trains to clear counted against the bonus, but the working was considered complete on arrival back at Ipswich goods yard. Any delay then encountered returning to the locomotive depot at Croft Street through the busy station and tunnel had no effect on the bonus.

The day commenced for the driver and fireman at 11.20 am by signing on at Croft Street. An hour was allowed for preparing the engine (always a J15 Class 0-6-0 because of the weight restriction on Snape bridge) and reading notices applicable to the route before moving through to the goods yard to collect the train ready for departure at 12.50 pm. The details above refer to the Snape bonus job in the early 1950s when the train went to Saxmundham, visiting Snape on the return journey to Ipswich. Starting in 1956 the Snape run included the daily Framlingham goods worked under bonus arrangements.

The Framlingham branch goods traffic was handled by some mixed passenger trains during the 1940s but when all passenger trains were withdrawn in 1952 a separate goods train ran daily. For the last four years of steam operation most goods traffic to and from intermediate stations between Ipswich and Saxmundham was handled by the Framlingham/Snape, or the Aldeburgh bonus trip which left Ipswich according to slightly varying timetabling between 7.00 and 7.30 am daily. The Snape traffic ceased on 4th March 1960 when J15 engine No. 65389 cleared the last trucks from Snape. This loco had worked the branch for several years and had been retained at Ipswich for that duty several months after steam working had officially ended at Ipswich.

*Engine No. 65389 and brake van arriving at Snape for the last time, on Friday 4th March 1960, to clear all the trucks from the yard.* (Photo by F. A. W. Smith)

Following closure of the Snape line, bonus working also ceased and Brush diesels worked the Framlingham and Aldeburgh branches. In 1964 they left Ipswich at 6.10 am for Woodbridge, Melton, Saxmundham and Leiston arriving back in Melton at 10.37 am. Departing for Framlingham at 10.50 am, they arrived there at 12.05 pm. Leaving Framlingham thirty five minutes later, the train returned to Melton, Woodbridge and Ipswich goods yard arriving there at 3.56 pm.

*The last train from Snape departing for Ipswich.* (Photo by F. A. W. Smith)

# The Hadleigh Branch

THE railway to Hadleigh from Bentley was opened in August 1847. A locomotive which was exchanged for a fresh engine from Ipswich every two or three weeks, and two sets of men were employed there until the passenger service was withdrawn in 1932. Thereafter the goods traffic was handled direct by Ipswich locomen and engines.

Once reliable motor bus services became established during the late 1920s, the road from Hadleigh to Ipswich, despite the tortuous bends, was by far a more direct and convenient route than the railway which required changing trains at Bentley. Consequently passenger services ended amid a whole range of cutbacks imposed by the LNER on branch lines where competitive road transport proved impossible to fight. Goods traffic though continued to Hadleigh with morning and afternoon trains until the late 1950s when only one train a day ran until complete closure in 1965. In addition to agricultural and coal traffic which always formed the bulk of the goods work on the Hadleigh branch, an ammunition depot still provided considerable traffic after the second world war and helped sustain the two trains a day for so long afterwards.

**RETIRED IPSWICH DRIVER KEN FREESTONE RECALLS THE WORKING OF THE BRANCH DURING THE EARLY 1950'S WHEN HE WAS A YOUNG FIREMAN.**

The Hadleigh Branch was worked on a two-shift basis by locomen from the local goods link (otherwise known as the "Old Man's Gang") at Ipswich. My mate at this time was Driver Fred Gosling who was nearing retirement. He had started his railway career in 1910 and later fought in the First World War at the Battle of the Somme where he suffered severe frostbite which affected his health in later life.

The type of locomotive used on the branch would sometimes be a J15 but more usually a J17 Class 0-6-0 goods engine.

On the morning shift we would leave Ipswich Goods Yard and first run to Bentley where we would unload any light parcel traffic at the station platform before moving the train over to the down side and into the goods yard.

The Bentley crossing keeper also acted as shunter and together with our guard dealt with the train, preparing it ready for the journey to Hadleigh.

Before leaving Bentley we would be handed the train "staff", a most important brass rod inscribed "Bentley/Hadleigh". This gave us permission to occupy the branch line and whilst in possession of this, we knew no other train would be permitted to enter our section. Attached to the staff were three keys, one each for the level crossings at Church Lane and Capel, and one key to unlock the siding points at Capel. Staff and keys would be handed to the signalman upon arrival back at Bentley later in the day.

On leaving Bentley we ran parallel to the main down London Line for approx. half a mile when we veered off to the left through some woods and then came to the pair of crossing gates across our line at Church Lane. These were padlocked and it was the fireman's duty to open these gates with the key recently acquired and after the train had passed through, the guard closed and locked them.

On a spring or summer's day, the job could be a real delight. We were in the heart of the countryside, well away from the main line with all its bustle and hurry, and with only ourselves to worry about. Church Lane was a very minor country road which was used very little. There was a crossing keeper's cottage which was very overgrown and inhabited by an elderly man who never appeared; at least I never saw him. He kept several chickens which would roam around at will, laying eggs anywhere.

While I waited for the train to pull through and the guard to lock the gates, I would have a quick glance around and often stepped back on to the engine with warm freshly laid eggs. With these, together with hazelnuts and other fruits in season, a week on the job could prove very profitable. Indeed, a driver's wife once remarked that she had made seven pounds of blackberry jam in just one week, using the berries her husband had picked. It was said the Hadleigh Branch engine was easily recognizable on its return to Ipswich as it would be festooned with bean-poles and pea-sticks and the footplate would be piled high with bags of goodies!

Chickens were not the only livestock to wander free at the Church Lane crossing; one train nearly killed a pig which had darted across the track in front of it.

After leaving Church Lane we ran a short distance to Capel St Mary which was originally a station in the days of the passenger service. The station house was still inhabited by a railwayman who was employed at Ipswich. He simply rented the accommodation and had no other responsibility regarding Capel. If we were required to go into the Goods Yard, we unlocked a ground points frame and let ourselves in and out, closing and locking the points after completion. We also opened and closed the road crossing gates as we had done at Church Lane. However these were a different proposition and a job I was never happy about. The gates opened across the main A12 trunk road from London to Yarmouth, which was busy even in those days. In winter time, coming back from Hadleigh on the afternoon late turn, it would be dark on arrival at Capel and sometimes foggy as well. The only illumination on these wide gates was a flickering red oil lamp which was not very obvious to approaching traffic. We did try to supplement this with a hand held engine headlamp with the red shade down, but this was far from satisfactory. The road was straight and traffic would be approaching at speed. There were several complaints about the danger at this crossing and I myself was always glad when the train was safely across and we were on our way.

The next call after leaving Capel would be at Raydon Wood. This again was a station in the days of the passenger service. It was manned by a railwayman I simply remember as Jim. The original Goods Yard was occupied by a coal merchant and we would sometimes shunt there or have parcel traffic for this location.

After leaving Raydon we passed through a heavily wooded area and shortly arrived at Hadleigh, or "Hadleigh Hole" as we called it owing to the fact that it was situated in a valley and was arrived at by a steep descent. Great care had to be exercised when running into Hadleigh Station which was a dead end terminus. The train was loose coupled, the only brakes available were those of the engine and the guard's van. After coming to a stand in the station and having a word with Herbert the shunter we would have our breakfast. There was a small Dickensian-type room in the station building containing an ancient gas-ring on which we could heat a kettle to make some tea. There was no comfort to be had in these old buildings so we sat on the engine to eat our food.

Breakfast finished, and back to work. We now had the yard to shunt but at the moment we were the wrong end of the train. There were no run-round facilities so we adopted an unorthodox means of achieving this by making use of the steep gradient out of the Station.

First we would push the train well up towards the top of the bank. The guard would then apply his van brake together with a few wagon brakes, and then release the engine which would draw forward into a siding. After the engine was clear, the points were replaced for the main line. The guard then carefully released his brakes and allowed gravity to do the work to get the train rolling. By operation of his van brake, he would let the train run down until it was well clear of the points enabling us to come out with the engine and couple up to the rear.

After an hour or so shunting the yard and sidings at Hadleigh we returned to Bentley. On arrival there we left the train and ran with the engine and guards van up the main line to Manningtree. We filled the tender with water at the station water crane and then shunted into the siding. This was the finish of the early turn. Our relief arrived on the up London and we returned passenger to Ipswich. We would do this by catching the Parkeston branch train to Mistley and after about half an hour wait, pick up the Parkeston-Peterborough train, arriving at Ipswich about 1.30 pm. We then walked from the Station back to the Loco Shed to book off, our day's turn of duty finished.

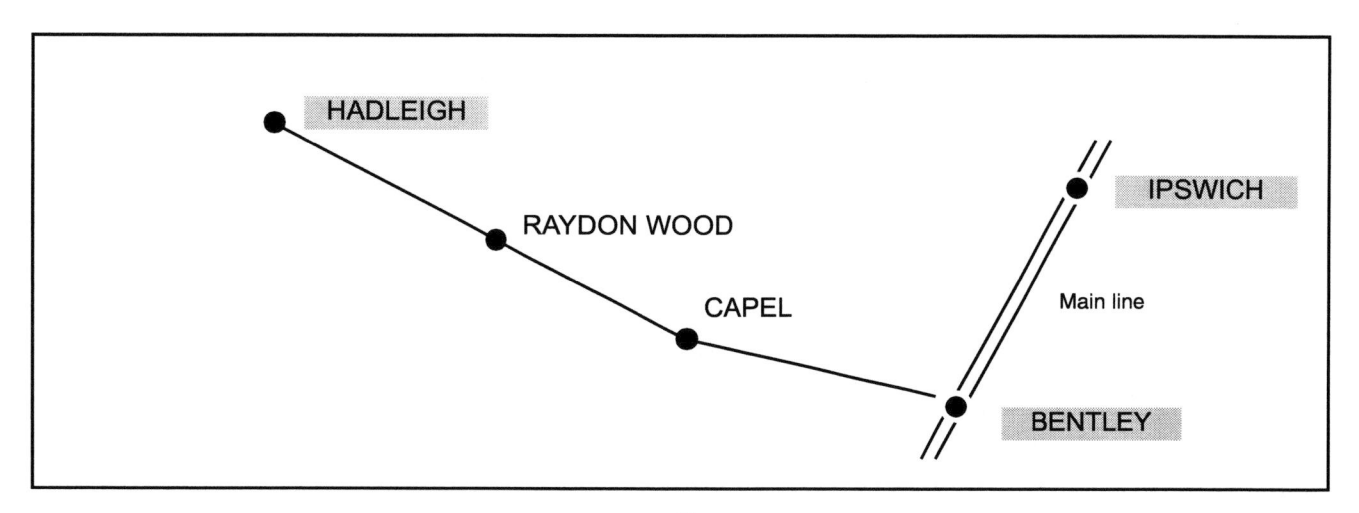

*Driver F. J. Grove, who worked the last ordinary passenger train to run on the Hadleigh Branch. Joining the GER as an office lad at Parkeston Loco Depot, he transferred to the footplate as a cleaner in 1884, eventually becoming a driver. He moved to Hadleigh in 1916 . On closure of the Shed there, he spent his last year of service at Ipswich from which Depot he retired in 1933, having completed just over forty-nine years on the footplate. He died aged eighty-two in 1950.*

(Photo courtesy Mr & Mrs D. Taylor)

*Enthusiasts' Specials, usually composed of open goods trucks and brake vans, sometimes travelled on the Hadleigh Branch, and one is pictured here on Good Friday 20th April 1962. As mentioned in the text, there was no run-round loop at Hadleigh, and the diesel locomotive is seen standing on an adjoining road (right) at the top of the gradient outside the yard area after being detached from the train it had propelled up the bank. The guard has released his brake, allowing the train to run down the bank into the yard, and the photograph shows him bringing the Special to rest, enabling the locomotive to follow the train down and couple-up ready for departure.*

(Photo by Richard W. Smith)

*Capel St Mary level crossing and station, on the main A12 road between Ipswich and Colchester, in 1959. The road had recently been widened to three lanes and it was here, on late winter afternoons, that the fireman had the unnerving experience of closing the gates against traffic with only the aid of an oil lamp. By the time the road was dualled, the railway had long since gone.*

(Photo by Aubrey Frost, ABIPP, ARPS)

## Manningtree to Harwich

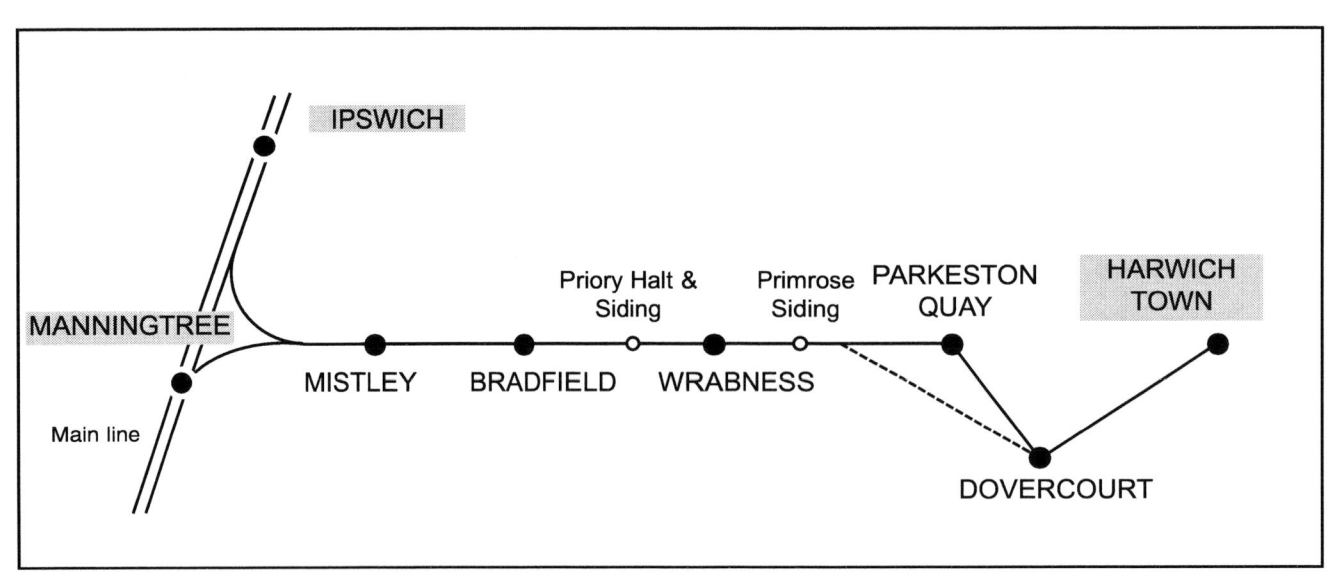

IN the manner of early nineteenth century railway proposals, the Harwich branch, perhaps more than most, was subject to the customary delays and financial problems associated with similar ventures of that era.

The Eastern Counties Railway had opened for traffic as far as Colchester by March 1843, but it was to be 1853 before the Eastern Union Railway started work on its branch line to Harwich from Manningtree on the Colchester to Ipswich main line. The EUR had been originally authorised to build the railway in 1847 but ironically was taken over by the ECR in January 1854 whilst the single line branch, just over eleven miles in length, opened for traffic in August of that year.

The Great Eastern Railway was incorporated in 1862 and connecting steamer services improved so much that the Company opened its own extensive quay on reclaimed land at Ray Island, two miles west of Harwich up the Stour estuary, in 1882. It was named Parkeston Quay, after the GER Chairman Charles Parkes, and became one of the most misspelled names in railway parlance e.g. Parkstone, Parkestone, a problem no longer relevant as it has now (officially anyway) become Harwich International. A new line from east of Wrabness was laid across the marshes to the new quay rejoining the original track at Dovercourt. The earlier line was lifted but the bridge crossing the latter, carrying the main road down to Parkeston, is still in existence, and much of the trackbed known as "The Hangings" became a popular footpath. The railway provided a new village of Company-owned houses, a large locomotive depot, marine workshops, a power station and a hotel.

The increase in traffic necessitated in 1882 the doubling of the track and the construction of a direct link to the Ipswich main line, known as the North Curve, avoiding Manningtree (see diagram). This new junction brought into being the Manningtree triangle, providing a useful means of turning a steam engine when there were problems with the turntable at Ipswich; the instruction to run to Mistley and turn was a familiar command to Ipswich men. In more recent times, after the removal of the turntables, visiting steam engines have been turned in this manner, also diesel locomotives when the controls at one end were faulty.

Intermediate stations were at Mistley, Bradfield, Wrabness, Parkeston Quay and Dovercourt. There was also Priory Halt between Bradfield and Wrabness, where a siding off the Up road led into some ballast workings, and Primrose Siding beyond Wrabness which served the Naval mine depot.

> **2.25 am Whitemoor to Parkeston.**
> To convey traffic for Bentley, Capel, Raydon Wood, Hadleigh, Mistley, Primrose Siding, Priory Siding, and Wrabness. Wagons for Hadleigh branch and Bentley are to be attached next engine and detached at Bentley. *From a 1940s Timetable Working Notes.*

From 1965, the only passenger stations remaining open were Mistley, Wrabness, Parkeston Quay, Dovercourt and Harwich. The sharply inclined approach to the sidings on Mistley Quay, which could cause adhesion problems in getting back to the main line, has been disused since the mid-1980s. The proposed railway from Mistley to Thorpe-le-Soken via Tendring, giving access to Clacton and Walton, never got beyond some earthworks through Mistley and a bridge under the main road to Bradfield but is marked on some tourist maps published in the 1890s.

There has always been a transfer of footplatemen between depots where vacancies arise and the possibilities of promotion to fireman or driver occur. None more so than in the Ipswich District with movements between Ipswich and Parkeston, and this is evident in some of the short biographies included in this book. Some local passenger and goods traffic on the Manningtree to Harwich Branch has always been shared by Ipswich men.

The Continental and ordinary passenger trains to and from Liverpool Street were manned by Parkeston or Stratford men. Most of the goods work was to Goodmayes, Spitalfields and Whitemoor although enginemen were relieved at Ipswich on some of the Whitemoor trains. The pattern did change over the years when, for example, during the 1940s, there were three Up and Down Whitemoor trains, one to Goodmayes, a 3.55 am train to Eye and 7.45 am to Saxmundham, apart from Ipswich and Bentley jobs.

The west end of Parkeston Quay was not wholly reclaimed and in the 1970s, spoil, carried by trains from all over East Anglia, was used to infill this marshy area. Ipswich and Parkeston men were often involved in the working of these trains. In recent years trade car traffic meant through workings for Parkeston men to Southall and subsequently to Didcot in the 1990s.

Harwich has long been a town of fluctuating fortunes, from the loss of mail contracts and dispersal of the associated ships away to the Thames and Humber in the 1830s, to the period following the first world war when the naval presence was greatly reduced and shipbuilding ceased.

Since the railway first came to Harwich, seamen, shore staff and train crews have been at the forefront of the changing fortunes affecting the whole of Harwich, Dovercourt and Parkeston. In recent years they have experienced the demise of the Train Ferry service in 1987, post-privatisation loss of former railway operated shipping services, the rise and fall of the container traffic in which so much infrastructure was invested, and run-down of the locomotive depot.

The withdrawal of the Train Ferries was a considerable blow resulting in the loss of jobs for many railway workers, including footplatemen, and has proved to be but a foretaste of another downturn in the fortunes of Harwich and its railway.

*Craven Diesel Multiple Unit (DMU) leaving Wrabness on the 5.11 pm (Sunday) Harwich to Manningtree service, 10th May 1959. This particular Sunday job started and finished at Ipswich and was worked by Ipswich men, on this occasion Driver Fred Smith.*

(Photo by Richard W. Smith)

*LNER Class J20 No. 64678 hauling wagons off the* Norfolk Ferry *on 6th June 1960. This engine was one of twenty-five similar locomotives built at Stratford Works between 1920-22. They were for some twenty years the most powerful 0-6-0 locomotives in Britain, their boilers being interchangeable with the 4-6-0 B12 "1500s". The Harwich to Zeebrugge train ferry service was opened on 24th April 1924, and the machinery, gantry, linkspan etc. were all brought from Southampton, where they had been used for service to France during the Great War.* (Photo by Richard W. Smith)

*MV Norfolk Ferry, built 1951 by John Brown, Clydebank, arriving at Harwich Train Ferry Pier on 17th June 1978. She was inbound from either Zeebrugge, the original train ferry port, or Dunkirk (for which service she had been modified in 1967). She was sold for scrap in 1982.*
(Photo by Richard W. Smith)

## Two sidings at Brantham

### Keeble's Siding

THE owners of Brantham Hall have had a long interest in the railway since its inception in the early 1840s. The Eastern Union Railway Directors were forced to divert their Colchester to Ipswich line 100 yards to the west by straightening an intended gentle curve to take the railway, although in cutting, further away from the Hall. The full story has been related in Hugh Moffat's book "East Anglia's First Railways".

During the twentieth century the Keeble family, who now owned the property and land, used the railway to its best advantage by the construction, c. 1914, of one of the relatively few private sidings to a farm. A trailing point from the Up main line, about one and a half miles from Manningtree, gave access to a siding approximately 200 yards long, serving a covered loading dock. This superseded a barge wharf in the saltings of the Stour estuary which had been used for sailing barges to load aggregate from a pit close to the site of the former Marsh Farm.

The ballast was transported to the wharf by a narrow gauge railway. The barges returned with the sweepings of London stables, including those of the railway, and Company horse brasses have turned up in the fields. Although the ballast proved less and less profitable, the family kept it going to assist local workers who otherwise would have become unemployed.

Farm produce was sent by rail principally to Spitalfields, the London market. Staff at Manningtree would be notified of the number of trucks required or ready for dispatch.

The accompanying transcriptions from the Working Timetable footnotes illustrate the methods of working traffic. Ipswich and Parkeston men were familiar with Keeble's siding which closed c. 1961.

### Brantham Siding

This siding, halfway between Keeble's Siding and Manningtree Station, was built for The British Xylonite Company (later BX Plastics Ltd. and now Wardle Storeys) situated on the banks of the River Stour near Catterwade.

In the early days of the firm, which came to the site in 1887, a truck-load of goods would be sent regularly from the siding to another factory at Homerton, East London, and, in later years, to Hale End. The Company considered that the railway truck was more economical, held more and was just as quick as sending a load direct by road using a van drawn by two horses.

The Ipswich to Liverpool Street main line ran straight through the centre of the Brantham Works, and once a spark from a passing steam engine found its way into one of the cowls of a paper-drying stove, causing the stove to blow up. Fortunately no one was badly hurt, although two men were inside the building at the time

For many years coal-trucks were regularly left at the siding to be unloaded by the Works' own men. When the type of side unloading truck then in use was taken out of service by British Rail about 1986, all coal for the Wardle Storeys' boilers, which burned about two tons of coal an hour, had to come by road because Brantham siding was unable to handle bottom unloading trucks.

---

**1.50 pm (SX)**
Ipswich-Goodmayes to convey empties ex-Bentley to Keeble's siding for next day loading. Time at Keeble's, arrive 2.35 pm, depart 2.50 (also to attach only at Brantham siding). Spitalfields traffic to be worked forward from Goodmayes by engine off 8.0 pm ex-Witham.

**5.45 pm (SX)**
Harwich-Bentley. Engine to be used at Manningtree to weigh wagons ex-Keeble's siding. Light engine, when required, to run to Bentley arrive 7.15 pm, depart 7.35 pm to Keeble's and Mistley, arrive 8.10 pm.

**4.0 pm (SO)**
Parkeston-Bentley, return Bentley depart 6.20 pm. To convey empties Bentley to Keeble's siding (6.25 pm-6.35 pm) for Monday's loading.

*Extract from timetable for 4th October 1943 - 30th April 1944.*

*Keeble's Siding in the 1950s. (Above) sugar beet for the local factory at Ipswich, (below) sacks of onions. Beyond the curve of the main line can be seen the factory chimneys of BX Plastics, now Wardle Storeys. This was the firm served by Brantham Siding.* (Photos courtesy Keeble Family Collection)

*Remains of Keeble's Siding, 20th July 1996. Dotted line below shows line of original siding.* (Photos courtesy Ken Freestone)

# The Mid-Suffolk Light Railway

THERE can be few people living in Suffolk and taking an interest in their county who are unaware of the existence, for almost half a century, of the Mid-Suffolk Light Railway which ran from Haughley to Laxfield.

The Light Railways Act of 1896 allowed the building, in rural areas, of railways which were not required to conform to the high standards of construction demanded by the Board of Trade for main line railways. Consequently these country branch lines needed less money for their construction. One of the reasons for the Act was the generally poor state of the agricultural economy of the 1880s and 1890s, and many lines were promoted throughout the country as a result.

Unfortunately by the time sufficient interest in individual schemes had been aroused, the necessary orders obtained, the money raised, the land bought, and finally the railway built, there remained only about fifteen years before second-hand lorries from the Great War came on the market to make inroads into the goods business. Buses soon followed, run in most cases by the local carrier, absorbing some of the passenger traffic. This meant only a few years of operation for the light railways before they were affected by far more serious competition than their previous rivals, the horse and cart.

Like the majority of new ventures since the dawn of railways the Mid-Suffolk quickly ran into money troubles and the original idea to connect Haughley with Halesworth and Westerfield ended at Laxfield. Work commenced in March 1902 at Haughley and Westerfield and the confidence shown by the extravagant ceremony of cutting the first sod on May 3rd belied the true state of the finances. A field adjacent to the GER station at Westerfield was the venue for over six hundred guests to enjoy an enormous banquet.

The line eventually opened for goods traffic on September 20th, 1904, and for passengers, four years later, on September 29th, 1908. The branch from Kenton to Westerfield reached the edge of Debenham but track laid to there was lifted during the Great War and the line through to Halesworth extended only as far as Cratfield and this was taken up at the same time after closure in 1912. Thus little more than nineteen miles survived instead of the proposed fifty. Livestock and agricultural traffic was considerable for several years and even the passenger service outlived some other Suffolk branch lines such as those to Eye and Hadleigh. Wartime brought additional military goods traffic in connection with the American airfields at Horham and Mendlesham.

Ipswich drivers and firemen relieved the local men for many years, sleeping in the station buildings at Laxfield. Amongst them were Tim Schofield, Tommy Mole, Ken Freestone, and Fred Smith. The last named locoman would cycle from Ipswich to Laxfield by way of Dennington at the start of his turn of duty because when he finished at Laxfield on the Saturday evening, there was no way of getting home other than using his bike.

Ipswich men soon became familiar with the idiosyncrasies of the railway including the ungated level crossings, and the milk churns full of drinking water to be dropped off at lineside houses during the summer. Joe Skinner from Ipswich, mentioned elsewhere in the book as a member of the Orwell Yacht Club, worked the line for some time towards the end, which came on July 26th, 1952 when Joe drove the last train with Jack Law as fireman. The track was completely lifted by April 1954, and the Mid-Suffolk passed into history. Since then however, in the 1990s, enthusiasts have laid a short length of line on the old trackbed near Brockford, rekindling a little of the history and atmosphere of the Mid-Suffolk Light Railway.

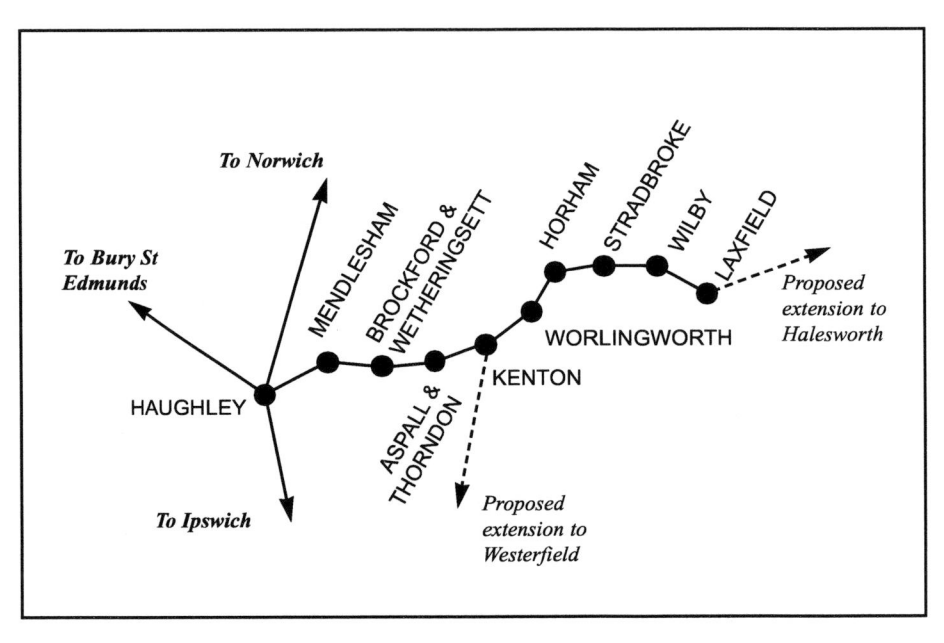

*Class J65 0-6-0T No. 7247 arriving at Laxfield in 1939. Built at Stratford Works in 1893 this was one of only five of the original twenty, light branch passenger engines, to survive until 1946.*
(Photo by Tom Mole of Ipswich, who was relief fireman at Laxfield at the time.)

*Above: The 11.15 am Haughley-Laxfield mixed train at the ungated Brown Street Crossing near Old Newton on 7th June 1952.* (Photo by Richard W. Smith)

*Left: Driver Joe Skinner arranging a wreath on the smokebox door of J15 No. 65447 at Haughley, ready for the last trip to Laxfield on Saturday 26th July 1952.*

(Photo Kelvin Higgins collection)

## The Felixstowe Branch

THE well known Colonel George Tomline of Orwell Park, Nacton, owned thousands of acres of land in the area between the Rivers Orwell and Deben and had strong ideas about developing Felixstowe as a seaside resort and port. Colonel Tomline and others promoted the Felixstowe Railway and Pier Company incorporated by Act of Parliament in July 1875. They proposed a railway to run from Westerfield Station to a pier at Felixstowe situated to the north of Landguard Fort and inside Harwich Harbour. The following year another act permitted the construction of a tidal basin.

The railway duly opened on May 1st 1877 and a further Act of July 1879 enabled the building of a dock, approach channel and additional railway lines in the area, also changing the Company's title to the Felixstowe Railway and Dock Company. The dock however was not opened until 1887. The railway meanwhile had run for two years using Company locomotives and rolling stock but in September 1879 the Great Eastern Railway, previously regarded by Colonel Tomline with intense disdain, began running the service, and later, on 5th July 1887, purchased the railway from the Company which changed its name again to Felixstowe Dock and Railway Company and retained the dock and sidings.

At that time there were intermediate stations only at Derby Road and Orwell (for the convenience of the residents of Orwell Park, i.e. George Tomline), and what later became Felixstowe Beach before reaching the terminus at the Pier. Trimley station was opened in May 1891. The opening of the fine Town station on July 1st 1898 was attended by the Chairman of the GER Lord Claud Hamilton. From then on the railway influence on the expansion of Felixstowe became very apparent.

Summer passenger traffic soared in the early 1900s with through trains and portions detached at Westerfield from Liverpool Street including a few non-stop trains from London to Felixstowe. The latter were made possible by the installation of the water troughs at Ipswich in 1897 for the benefit of the Norfolk Coast Express. The Great War intervened but the holiday excursion traffic built up again during the 1920s and 1930s resulting in some very intensive working especially on Bank Holidays. After the 1939-45 war, trade picked up quickly almost to pre-war levels for a few years including some weekend through trains and coaches from Liverpool Street into the early 1950s. Derby Road station, where some Felixstowe trains had actually started and finished, handled thousands of

*Felixstowe Town Station in the late 1950s. The long spacious platforms are intact, with a coal yard and goods shed to the right.* (Photo by Bob Rogers)

passengers from the north-eastern parts of Ipswich, and continued to do so until the late 1950s. A nearby private house with a large garden sported a sign offering bicycle storage for 3d a day until the mid-sixties.

The Pier station was closed in July 1951 and the Beach opened only for the summer seasons from November 1959 until permanent closure in 1967. DMUs first appeared on the branch in 1955 but their capacity was considered insufficient for regular service and the L1 2-6-4 tank engines continued until the end of steam for passenger work on 4th January 1959. Goods traffic had never been excessive and for many years a daily goods train from Ipswich to Felixstowe Dock sufficed. There were sidings at Derby Road, Orwell, Trimley, Felixstowe Town and the Dock where another siding served the RAF Station. The mainly American owned firm of Crane-Bennett Ltd. opened a factory on Nacton Heath and installed some private sidings linked to the branch in 1927, and Ransome Sims and Jefferies Ltd. were moving their works to an adjacent site from Ipswich Dock in the 1950s and put in private sidings. Goods services were lost from Westerfield and Trimley in 1964, and from both Felixstowe stations in December 1966.

## IPSWICH, DERBY ROAD AND FELIXSTOWE.
### Single Line between Westerfield and Felixstowe Town.

| Miles from Ipswich | DOWN WEEK DAYS | | 1 Gds. a.m. | 2 | 3 Gds. a.m. | 4 | Miles from Felixstowe | UP WEEK DAYS | | 5 Gds. p.m. | 6 Q Gds. p.m. | 7 Gds. 80 p.m. | 8 Gds. 8X p.m. |
|---|---|---|---|---|---|---|---|---|---|---|---|---|---|
| M. C. | | | | | | | M. C. | | | | | | |
| — | Ipswich | dep. | 5 45 | .... | 6 52 | .... | — | Felixstowe Town Ⓣ | dep. | .... | .... | 4 0 | 5 0 |
| 3 42 | Westerfield Ⓣ | arr. | 6 0 | — | — | — | 1 51 | Trimley Ⓣ | arr. | — | — | 4 5 | 5 10 |
| | | dep. | 6 10 | .... | 9 7 | .... | | | dep. | .... | .... | 4 15 | 5 20 |
| 6 7 | Derby Road Ⓣ | arr. | 6 20 | .... | 9 17 | — | 6 33 | Orwell Ⓣ | arr. | — | — | 4 22 | 5 35 |
| | | dep. | 6 36 | .... | .. | | | | dep. | — | — | 5 10 | 5 50 |
| 9 23 | Orwell Ⓣ | arr. | 6 46 | — | — | — | 9 49 | Derby Road Ⓣ | arr. | — | — | 5 20 | 6 0 |
| | | dep. | 6 57 | .... | .... | | | | dep. | 3 0 | 4 10 | 5 50 | 6 50 |
| 14 5 | Trimley Ⓣ | arr. | 7 7 | — | — | — | 12 14 | Westerfield Ⓣ | arr. | 3 10 | 4 20 | 6 0 | 7 0 |
| | | dep. | 7 20 | .... | .... | | | | dep. | 3 40 | 5 0 | 6 15 | 7 10 |
| 15 56 | Felixstowe Town Ⓣ | arr. | 7 25 | — | — | — | 15 56 | Ipswich | arr. | 3 55 | 5 15 | 6 30 | 7 25 |

1 To work not exceeding 12 wagons of Derby Road traffic. Engine and Men to make trips to Felixstowe Beach, Dock and Air Force Siding as required.
3 Engine to perform station shunting at Derby Road, Engine and brake to work a trip to Crane Bennett's Siding between Derby Road and Orwell.
5 When required, to start at 4.10 p.m.—See 6. To convey empty private owner's coal wagons only. To be made up at Ipswich Upper Yard to 50 and thence work to Sproughton Sdgs., depart 6.40 p.m. Sproughton arr. 6.45 p.m.
7 When required may start at 5.0 p.m. Control to arrange.   7 & 8  To detach Empty Private Owner's Wagons at Derby Road for clearance by 3.0 p.m. ex Derby Road, next day.
NOTE—Ipswich-Felixstowe Shed wagons to be forwarded by Passenger train

*Goods Timetable 1943 - 44*

During the 1950s, timetables were subject to a tight revision in order to benefit from the introduction of the "Britannia" locomotives on the main lines. Other workings were also affected, such as the Felixstowe branch where the new L1 tank engines had taken over from the old Great Eastern 2-4-2 tanks. Much to the drivers' irritation, half-minutes appeared in the working timetables, and the L1s were timed at 60 mph between stops where possible. This included the run down to Ipswich from Westerfield, for example, where the distant signal for the East Suffolk Junction had to be found by looking across the built up parts of the town, as the line curved to the left. This may have been all right in the daytime, when the signal could be found beyond the little spire of the Wesleyan Chapel on Bramford Road, but on murky evenings and at night, whilst travelling at a mile a minute, searching for an oil lamp suspended in the air amongst the glare of all the street lights of the Norwich and Bramford Roads gave cause for concern.

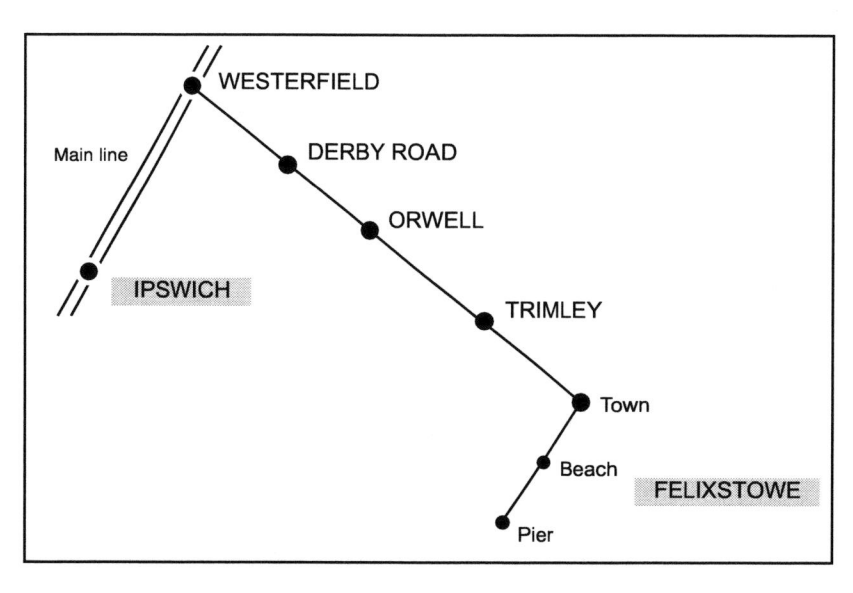

*Above: Ipswich to Felixstowe train, headed by L1 tank loco No. 67706, nearing Levington Bridge on 4th January 1959, the last day of steam working on the branch.* (Photo by Richard W.Smith)

*Below: Class 47 diesel locomotive hauling a Felixstowe-bound freightliner train at the same site in September 1982.* (Photo by Richard W.Smith)

## *The Container Revolution*

THE railways and removal men were pioneers of 20th century containerisation in the 1930s chiefly for door-to-door household removals, but a variety of containers were available for other goods. These were just large enough to fit on a four wheel lorry or Scammell trailer of the period but were eventually ousted by pantechnicon furniture vans, which like most road haulage vehicles developed as the regulations governing weights and speed of commercial vehicles changed, to the detriment of railway goods traffic. During the 1950s and 1960s smaller insulated containers were a familiar sight on the railway carrying Birds Eye frozen poultry and fish from the processing plant at Gt. Yarmouth.

The Container Revolution was begun in 1956 in the United States by a long-distance road haulier named Malcolm Maclean who acquired a shipping company and, by detaching the van bodies from 35ft road trailers, enabled them to be stacked one upon the other aboard ship or for storage on the quay side. Other American ship owners followed, using different sized non-interchangeable containers.

It quickly became obvious that standardisation was essential and the American Standards Association approved container size standards in 1961 which were adopted the following year by the International Standards Organisation (ISO). The approved size was, and still is, based on a cross-section of 8ft x 8ft and lengths of 10, 20, and 40ft. The standard box length was the 20 ft but in practice the 40ft container proved as useful. Therefore all 20 foot long containers world-wide are defined as Twenty Foot Equivalent Units, (T.E.U.), and a forty foot box represents two T.E.U.s.

Malcolm Maclean also utilised a system of container handling by means of a steel frame suspended from a shipboard or quay side crane with twist lock grips to engage precisely with matching sockets in the corner castings of each container. In the interests of world-wide standardisation Mr. Maclean allowed his patented twist locks to be made available freely throughout the world.

The container business came to Felixstowe in the mid 1960s as it did to all other ports, very quickly revolutionising road transport and railway freight operation. To start with some trains were run from Felixstowe to Parkeston Quay where they were re-marshalled into longer trains for other destinations, but direct trains began to operate and in April 1965 a weekly train to Kings Norton (Birmingham) commenced on Wednesdays only. In September 1964 a container train was booked Monday to Friday evenings from Ipswich Goods Yard to Cardiff via Cambridge, Bletchley and Oxford. Ipswich men worked the train to Cambridge where they were relieved by Cambridge men. This particular working was short lived because of the closure of the former London and North Western Railway connection between Bedford and Cambridge, the track being lifted in 1968. Ironically a high powered committee in the mid 1990s has sought ways of reinstating this important cross-country link. By the end of 1967 container trains or freightliners as they were known ran daily from Felixstowe to Kings Cross, Kings Norton and Prescot, increasing during the 1970s to Coatbridge, (Scotland), Liverpool and Manchester via Parkeston Quay.

On May 13th 1970 the original direct line to the Dock, lifted when the Town station was opened, was restored. This had the effect of leaving the Town station at the end of a short branch used only by passenger DMUs. The direct route did away with the requirement for locomotives to run round the train in the Town Station, although there had already been an exception to this practice during the 1960s when special trains, carrying cars for export, were worked to Felixstowe Dock.

Owing to the length of these trains, the run-round facility at Town station was inadequate. The trains were therefore run into the station and propelled (or pushed) under special working arrangements down to the Dock. There they were shunted into a special siding with a concrete ramp at the far end. The cars themselves were carried on long, low wagons between which were hinged metal plates which could be lowered to make a continuous run-off. A team of drivers would be waiting for the trains to arrive and they would start-up and drive the cars, one by one, off the trains and up the ramp to the parking area.

To serve the northern extensions to the Port of Felixstowe a new Freightliner Terminal was opened in 1983. It was linked to the original Felixstowe line by a new branch diverging just east of Trimley station.

*Two Class 37s, bound for Felixstowe Dock, seen at Trimley on 21st March 1994. The driver is giving up the tablet to the signalman. The nearest locomotive is fitted with a radio aerial (centre, front) for use when working to Sizewell on the East Suffolk Line.*

(Photo by Trevor Smith)

## Mellis to Eye

THE ancient and one-time relatively well-off borough of Eye was somehow neglected as transport facilities generally improved during the 18th and 19th centuries.

The turnpike road followed the course of the Roman road, a mile and a half to the west of the town. As early as 1825, Suffolk entered the railway age with an intriguing proposal to build a railway from Ipswich to Diss via Eye. This is referred to in detail by Hugh Moffat in his book, *East Anglia's First Railways*, but the line was never started. The prospectus of the Eastern Counties Railway, issued in 1834, revealed their proposed Ipswich to Norwich line passing through Debenham and Eye but by the time the ECR arrived at Colchester it was in financial difficulties and the Eastern Union Railway completed the project. The Norwich line however passed to the west, and it was not until April 1867 that the branch from Mellis to Eye was opened, being 2 miles and 64 chains in length.

The traffic was similar to other East Anglian country branch lines. Passengers found the new bus services of the 1920s more convenient however, thus hastening the withdrawal of passenger services in 1931. This was despite a Halt being established at Yaxley, plus Conductor Guards. Goods traffic declined rapidly in the '40s & '50s, but the branch survived until closure in July 1964.

The Shed was an outstation of Ipswich with the usual complement of one locomotive, two acting firemen and an acting driver under a driver-in-charge. Locomotives for maintenance or repair were sent to Ipswich. The men were relieved when necessary by Ipswich locomen, but the shed was closed on withdrawal of passenger services. One of the footplatemen, "Smiler" Weymouth, transferred to Ipswich.

Two goods trains a day sufficed through the 1940s, until only one was needed. Ipswich men did not work the trains regularly, as Parkeston and Norwich crews were involved. In the mid-1940s, for example, the first train of the day to Eye left Parkeston, worked by a J15, at 3.55 am. Mellis was first stop, except for taking water at Stowmarket, and the train arrived in Eye at 7.05 am, including 48 minutes shunting at Mellis. After leaving Eye at 9 am the crew were relieved at Stowmarket by Parkeston men, who would take the train on to Ipswich, arriving at 11.37 am.

They then worked engine and brake to Melton at twelve midday, to clear all loaded and empty trucks back to Ipswich by 2.40 pm. From there, engine and brake returned to Parkeston, the relieving men arriving back at 4.10 pm. Such were the normal complexities of timetabling a country goods service in the days of steam and plenty of business.

*Ivy (nee Jackaman), the mother of co-editor Richard Smith and granddaughter of a GER signalman at Stowmarket, had relatives living at Eye close to the station in Magdalen Street. She had happy memories of summer holidays spent there as a girl, and of travelling by train to Eye, changing at Mellis. Richard still has her souvenirs including the china shown here. This, one assumes, would have been delivered to Eye by train, perhaps from Staffordshire, and it certainly started its journey home to Ipswich, tenderly packed, along the Eye to Mellis line - "A Present from Eye".*

(Photo by Richard W. Smith)

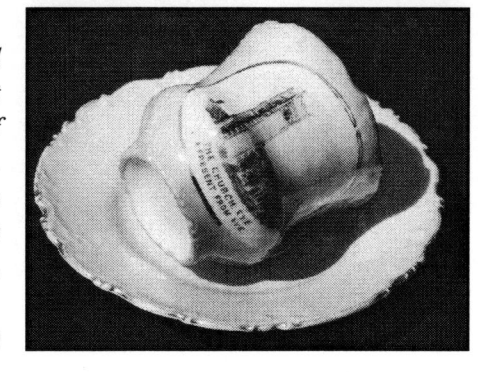

# LNER Promotional Areas for Drivers, Fireman & Cleaners 1925

SOUTHERN AREA - Area Number 1

| Depot | Out Station | Depot | Out Station |
|---|---|---|---|
| NORWICH | Yarmouth (Vauxhall) | CAMBRIDGE | Ely |
|  | Yarmouth (South Town) |  | Huntingdon East |
|  | Lowestoft |  | Saffron Walden |
|  | Beccles |  | Ramsey |
|  | Wells |  | Thaxted |
|  | Dereham |  | Bishops Stortford |
|  | Cromer |  |  |
|  | Swaffham | MARCH | -- -- |
| **IPSWICH** | **Hadleigh** | KINGS LYNN | Hunstanton |
|  | **Aldeburgh** |  | Wisbech |
|  | **Framlingham** |  | Stoke Ferry |
|  | **Eye** |  |  |
|  | **Stowmarket** | STRATFORD | Bethnal Green |
|  | **Parkeston** |  | Canning Town |
|  | **Felixstowe** |  | Millwall |
|  | **Bury** |  | Enfield Town |
|  | **Laxfield** |  | Wood Street |
|  |  |  | Palace Gates |
| COLCHESTER | Kelvedon |  | Epping |
|  | Clacton |  | Ongar |
|  | Walton-on-Naze |  | Hertford |
|  | Brightlingsea |  | Buntingford |
|  | Braintree |  | Southmister |
|  | Maldon |  | Wickford |
|  | Sudbury |  | Brentwood |
|  | Chelmsford |  | Southend |
|  | Halstead |  | Ilford |
|  | Haverhill |  | Romford |

# The Griffin Wharf Branch and Dock Tramway

IPSWICH Dock opened in 1842, the result of several years' debate on how best to improve the River Orwell for shipping, and the story of that time is well documented elsewhere. The coming of the Eastern Union Railway in 1846 transformed the original potential of the Dock by making it easily accessible to a large part of Suffolk and beyond as the railway expanded. Hitherto the Ipswich and Stowmarket Navigation (a waterway with locks, opened in 1793 using the River Gipping) had provided the only means of transporting bulk cargo into Mid-Suffolk. As with all land transport until the railway age, this method of moving goods was governed by the speed of the horse.

## The Griffin Wharf

The first connection made by the railway with the tidal river opened in 1847 when a branch from Halifax Junction, just outside the EUR station, bridged the Wherstead Road down to Griffin Wharf at the entrance to the New Cut. This was dug to divert the waters of the Gipping in preparation for the construction of the Dock out of a bend in the River Orwell. Initially the branch went only as far as Bright Street but was extended the entire length of New Cut West almost to Dock Street in 1898. The extension served R. & W. Paul's Stoke Maltings at the corner of Felaw Street, and the Ipswich Malting Company's big maltings at the far end where sidings ran the length of their yard. Pauls did not have a private siding and trucks were loaded or unloaded on a loop line on the roadway. Both had barley and coal inwards and malt out. No less than seventy-one trees, previously planted close to the water's edge over fifty years, were removed in the course of laying the extension. The branch also served the GER coal yard in Bright Street with coal for the river steamers, Ransomes and Rapiers, Cocksedges, and Eldred Watkins's cement and lime works. All these had their own sidings. Coal for the nearby Griffin Inn was delivered by a truck which was left on the railway line outside the front of the building, the coal then being unloaded and moved to a coal-shed in the back garden.

Ransomes and Rapier had an extensive rail network to all parts of its works and operated a steam and later a diesel shunting locomotive, well known as the *Biffer*.

Steam engines always had access to Griffin Wharf. Horses were used for shunting trucks beyond the point where locomotives were restricted, which was normally Bright Street, but the engines sometimes went as far as Felaw Street to Pauls' maltings. Otherwise horses served the whole of the extension to the Ipswich Malting Company's siding until tractors were available.

*A J15 engine No. 65459 seen crossing the Black Bridge over Wherstead Road, on 4th April 1959. The 0-6-0 engine, built at Stratford Works in 1906, is propelling a short goods train, including a train-ferry wagon, up from the Griffin Wharf to Halifax Junction.*
(Photo by Richard W. Smith)

*A Class 08 diesel-electric shunter on the Griffin Wharf in 1990. The main office buildings of the defunct Ransomes & Rapier Ltd. are to the left of the locomotive, and to the right is the rounded frontage of the former office of W. Christopherson Ltd., cattle food and corn merchants. Both premises were to be swept away shortly afterwards.*
(Photo by Richard W. Smith)

In 1973, the West Bank Terminal was opened by the Ipswich Port Authority, requiring a new siding to be laid into the Terminal to enable container traffic to become available to railway customers. One of the main users was the Cast Company who operated a feeder service to Zeebrugge for their North American box service from 1982 until 1992 when they withdrew from Ipswich, and thus rail traffic on the Griffin Wharf Branch ceased.

During July 1997 however, traffic resumed on the Griffin Wharf branch with the delivery of heavy steel pipes from north-eastern England for export to the USA. Brought down the East Coast Main Line from Hartlepool, the train, consisting of twenty container wagons adapted for pipe carrying, has arrived in Ipswich regularly. The Class 37 diesel locomotive hauling the train is manned by enginemen from Parkeston, the train being taken there for the final stage of its journey by drivers from March.

On arrival at Ipswich the train is split into two parts, each of ten wagons, which are taken down the branch separately by the same engine. The pipes are removed by a straddle carrier whilst the engine stays with the train, and are subsequently loaded on to "lash-lighters" berthed at the West Bank. These are then towed down the Orwell to Felixstowe for loading on to a Continental-bound barge-carrying ship, and transhipment to an American bound carrier.

The heavy diesel locomotive contrasts with previous motive power seen on the branch but the track was capable of carrying the very heavy machinery, including large steam railway break-down cranes, manufactured and sent from Ransomes & Rapier's Waterside Works.

*In July 1997, rail traffic resumed on the Griffin Wharf branch after a four-year lapse, as described in the text. Seen here, on 8th September 1997, is a Class 37 English Electric locomotive No. 37503 operated by English, Welsh & Scottish Railways.*
(Photo by Kenneth Freestone)

## Sketch map of Dock Tramway & Griffin Wharf Branch (not to scale)

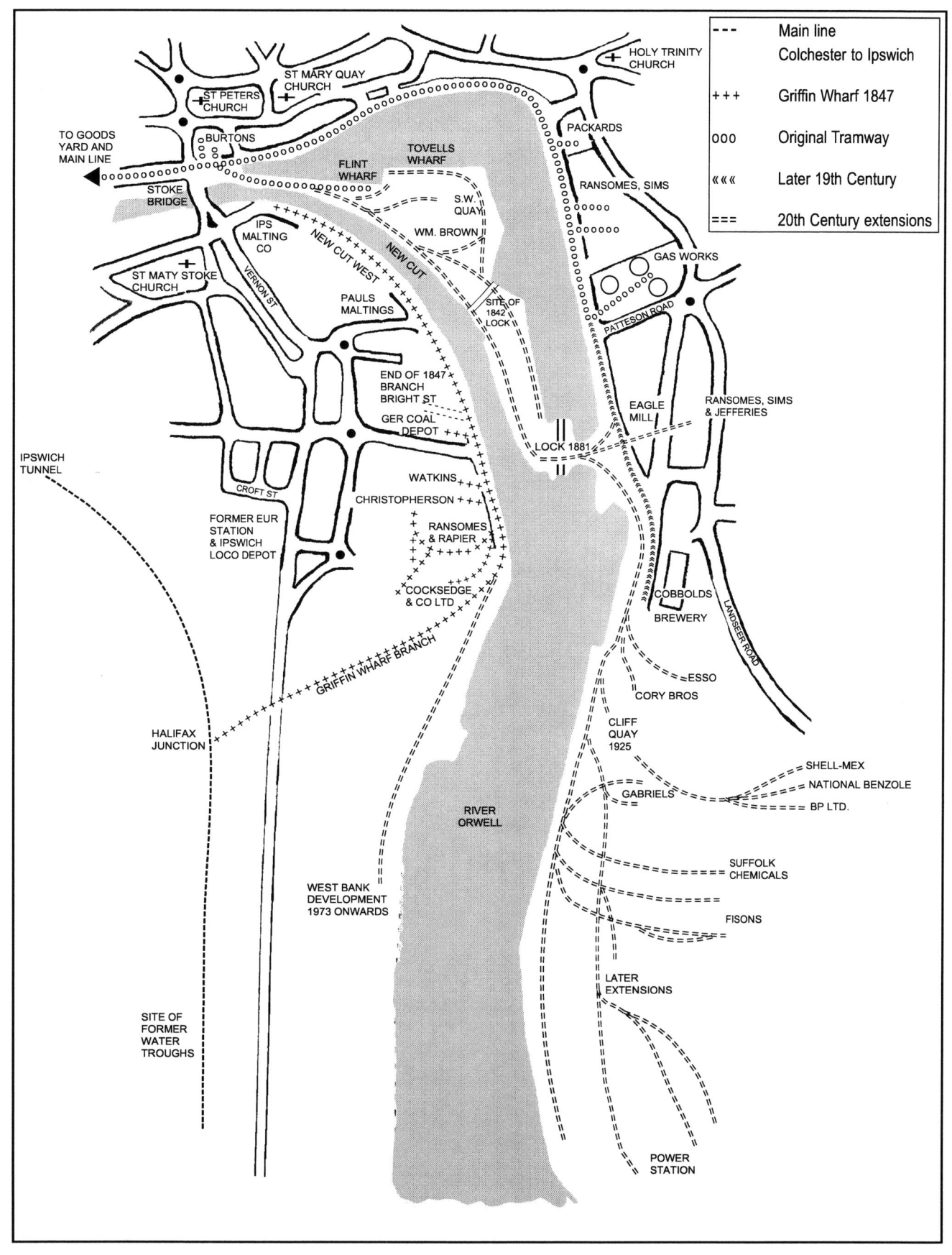

## The Dock Tramway

ON 27th October 1846 an agreement was reached between the Ipswich and Bury St Edmunds Railway Company and Mr William May, a provision merchant. This allowed the Company to build a railway track from the main line, approximately half a mile from the northern entrance to the tunnel, to St Peter's Wharf on the Orwell adjacent to Stoke Bridge. Mr May, who had premises on the site (later occupied for many years by Messrs. Burton, Son and Sanders) thus obtained a private siding along the quay, with a turntable and track into his building. Above all, the agreement allowed the railway access to Ipswich Dock.

By 1848, the Ipswich and Bury Railway had been absorbed into the EUR, John Chevallier Cobbold being Chairman of both companies. The single track approach to the Dock Tramway from the main line cut across what later became Ranelagh Road by means of a level crossing and then passed over the river. This route became extremely busy, linking as it did the Dock and the Lower Goods Yard alongside Commercial Road, with the Upper or Top Yard and the main line.

The Dock Tramway initially served the northern and eastern sides of the dock beyond the Old Custom House (the original headquarters of the Ipswich Dock Commission) and along past the corner at Coprolite Street as far as Patteson Road. There was also a siding to Flint Wharf which was owned by the railway, on the opposite side of the Dock to where Pauls later established their maltings on Smarts Wharf. Private sidings eventually served two other premises on St Peter's Dock (referred to in the agreement as St. Peter's Wharf), in addition to Packard's fertiliser works close to Coprolite Street, Ransomes, Sims and Jefferies Ltd., and the Gas Works.

Piecemeal expansion of the Dock Tramway continued with a branch along New Cut East to the Public Warehouse next to the original entrance lock. The line on the eastern side was extended beyond Patteson Road to Pauls' Maltings and Eagle Mill, and in 1901 to Cobbold's Cliff Brewery.

There were no additions on the Promenade side until the infilling of the old locks in 1902 enabled the tramway to be extended along New Cut East to the new lock which had opened in 1881. The South West Quay and the swing bridge were not opened until 1904 when at last a circle of the Dock road and railway was completed. Thereafter new sidings were put in on the site of the old branch dock opposite Ransomes, Sims and Jefferies and on Tovells Wharf opposite the Old Custom House, when the whole of that area was piled and developed in 1923-24.

The last major railway work was undertaken with the building of Cliff Quay outside the Dock, first used in May 1925. Sidings were laid to the Anglo-American Oil Co., Shell-Mex Ltd., B.P.Ltd., National Benzole Ltd., Gabriel Wade and English, the Suffolk Chemical Company, and in the early 1930s, to Fison, Packard and Prentice's new fertiliser factory. As Cliff Quay was extended, so the railway reached the post-war Ipswich Power Station which closed in 1983. A freightliner terminal was established in 1984 with road connections.

*One of the first Hunslet diesel shunting engines seen alongside the decaying Tram Shed at the Stoke Bridge end of Lower Yard together with one of the last tram engines. The Shed was used for the trams, saving a daily run to the Loco Depot for coaling, washing-out, cleaning etc.*
(Photo: Kelvin Higgins Collection)

*Tram engine, in LNER days, running light over the original swing bridge at the entrance lock. This bridge was replaced in 1949. The 1927 waterless gasholder was a prominent landmark until its demolition, c 1980.*

(Photo by R. G. Pratt)

New track had been put in to serve the Ipswich Grain Terminal in 1983 for 100 ton bulk grain wagons bringing in barley and malt to Cliff Quay from Scotland and the north of England. This had a very short lived career.

Traffic to the oil companies' depots ended by the late 1960s, and the timber and fertiliser work dwindled during the 1970s. Following closure of Fison's acid making plant, acid arrived at Cliff Quay in trainloads, this finishing when the entire works closed. All rail traffic on the original sections of the Dock Tramway ended in the early 1980s. Up until this time Pauls were still sending malt away from Albion Maltings. The Freightliners and grain trains stopped running to Cliff Quay, effectively marking the demise of the whole system by 1992, although the track to Cliff Quay remains in-situ at the time of writing (1997). The bridge carrying the branch over the river near Ranelagh Road was substantially rebuilt in 1995 at a time when the British Oxygen Company were discharging 100 ton tankers to road vehicles in the old Lower Yard. Ironically, this trade ceased after the costly rebuilding of the bridge.

## Dock Tramway Motive Power

Horses were used throughout the Dock Tramway from its beginnings until replaced by steam tram engines in 1889 following agreement with Ipswich Corporation to permit engines to work on public roads.

The Great Eastern Railway built two types of tram engines at Stratford Works. Designed by Mr Thomas Worsdell (Locomotive Superintendent 1882-85), the first ten 0-4-0 locomotives were built between 1882 and 1885 with inside cylinders and 3ft. 1in. diameter wheels. Twelve more were produced by Worsdell's successor James Holden from 1902 to 1921. They were of 0-6-0 wheel arrangement with outside cylinders and Walschaert's valve gear and were six inches longer than the 0-4-0s at 20ft. 8½in. over buffers. Both types were also used on the Wisbech and Upwell Tramway and on quay sides and public roads at Great Yarmouth, Lowestoft, and Colchester Hythe. They were all built with the characteristic wooden body to avoid frightening horses and fitted with sideguards or "skirts", cowcatchers and warning bells.

The very short wheel base of the tram engines was essential for working the tight curves of the dock tramway and if a conventional 0-6-0 tank engine had to be used, the side rods were removed from the leading axle allowing more play by effectively converting it to a 2-4-0.

The larger LNER 0-6-0 tank engine classes J66 and J67, built between 1886 and 1904, were used in the goods yards and along New Cut East to and from Cliff Quay.

Small Drewry and Hunslet diesel engines, complete for a time with cowcatchers and skirts, were in evidence from the early 1950s, and the first to work Cliff Quay was due to start on 5th May 1952. Thereafter steam disappeared from the Dock area and in the 1980s the more powerful British Rail 08 shunter handled the heavy grain and Freightliner trains.

*Flagman Jack Cuthbert stops road traffic along Bridge Street at Stoke Crossing, to allow a tram engine, driven by Vic Wroth (right), and train to pass from St Peter's Dock to the Lower Yard, during the early 1950s. Queues of vehicles could build up when long trains of wagons were marshalled in Lower Yard and shunted across the road, only to set back again before finally leaving for the Dock Tramway.* (Photo George Baker Collection)

*A Hunslet diesel shunter standing in Lower Yard, Dock end. Gazing out of the cab window is driver Tom Mole, who held various offices in the local branch of the ASLEF for thirty years or more.* (Photo Tom Mole Collection)

*Two views from Princes Street Bridge: Above: Looking east towards Stoke Bridge and Ipswich Dock, c 1950. Known as Lower Yard, but to Ipswich enginemen it was "Hell's Kitchen".* (Photo by Aubrey Frost, ABIPP, ARPS)
*Below: The same view taken in 1995 by Leslie Gould, lifelong friend of Aubrey Frost, and eldest son of driver Ernie Gould portrayed elsewhere in this book. Most of the land is now occupied by DIY and retail warehouses and only a few of the original railway lines remain.*

*Train of loaded vans tackling the gradient from Ranelagh Road level crossing to the Top Yard in 1954. The train is banked in the rear by the Lower Yard engine.* (Photo by R. Moore)

*British Oxygen Company's hundred-ton liquid-nitrogen tank wagons, seen 25th February 1992, working up across Ranelagh Road level crossing from the Lower Yard, where their contents had been off-loaded to BOC lorries.*
(Photo by Trevor Smith)

## Marshalling Yards and Sidings

**Top (Upper) Yard, Lower Yard and Ranelagh Road Sidings.**

THE Upper and Lower Yards received, transhipped, remarshalled and dispatched goods traffic at Ipswich. Originally it was the intention to extend the line passing over Ranelagh Road bridge (built c.1920) and provide access to the Lower Yard and Dock via a new river bridge, thus avoiding the existing river bridge and the Ranelagh Road level crossing (see map). Plans were drawn up but the LNER apparently abandoned the proposals and the crossing continued to cause road congestion at busy times. The existing river bridge was rebuilt in 1995 when the single timber pier in the river bed was replaced by substantial steel supports but the line has since been virtually unused (1998) except for occasional storage, although it may yet be utilized again if rail traffic returns to Cliff Quay. The road bridge was demolished in 1967.

One of the sidings on the Ranelagh Road site served a 1930s timber warehouse which was divided into sections and leased to various companies including Macfarlane Lang Biscuits, J. Lyons & Co., Swift & Co.(meat wholesalers), Boots Ltd. (chemists), and R. Silcock & Sons, (cattle feed manufacturers). In the 1950s and '60s, millions of bricks were unloaded in this yard, by hand from railway trucks to lorries, for Ipswich builders' merchants and hauliers J. H. Weavers Ltd.. Some of the land between the warehouse and the river was used by the railway engineering department as a tip for old sleepers etc., but the land was best known to the public as a venue for travelling circuses and funfairs until the 1980s when it was built over with retail warehouses and motor showrooms.

The carriage of livestock used to provide very useful revenue to the railway companies and all country stations and market towns had their own cattle pens. Those at Ipswich were situated on the approach to the Lower Yard between the river bridge and Princes Street Road bridge. They were very busy on Tuesday market days with the cattle, having started their train journey about 4.0 am from villages like Laxfield, being driven up Princes Street to the cattle market. Cattle trucks were usually marshalled next to the engine to enable the footplatemen to check at stops en route that no animals had fallen over. Road transport made inroads into the traffic during the late 1930s and livestock transport by train ceased in the 1960s.

**Sproughton Sidings**

Situated one and a half miles from the Upper Yard on the Down side of the Norwich line toward Bramford, Sproughton Sidings were established in the 1920s. A big thirty-five lever mainline signal box was installed to control a long goods loop and a run-round loop, which also gave access to the private sidings of the adjacent Sugar Beet Factory. The latter were separated from the

*Ranelagh Road skew bridge, about to be demolished in 1967. The right hand retaining wall is still in place. (1997)*
(Photo by Jack Keen)

# ROUTES WORKED BY IPSWICH MEN

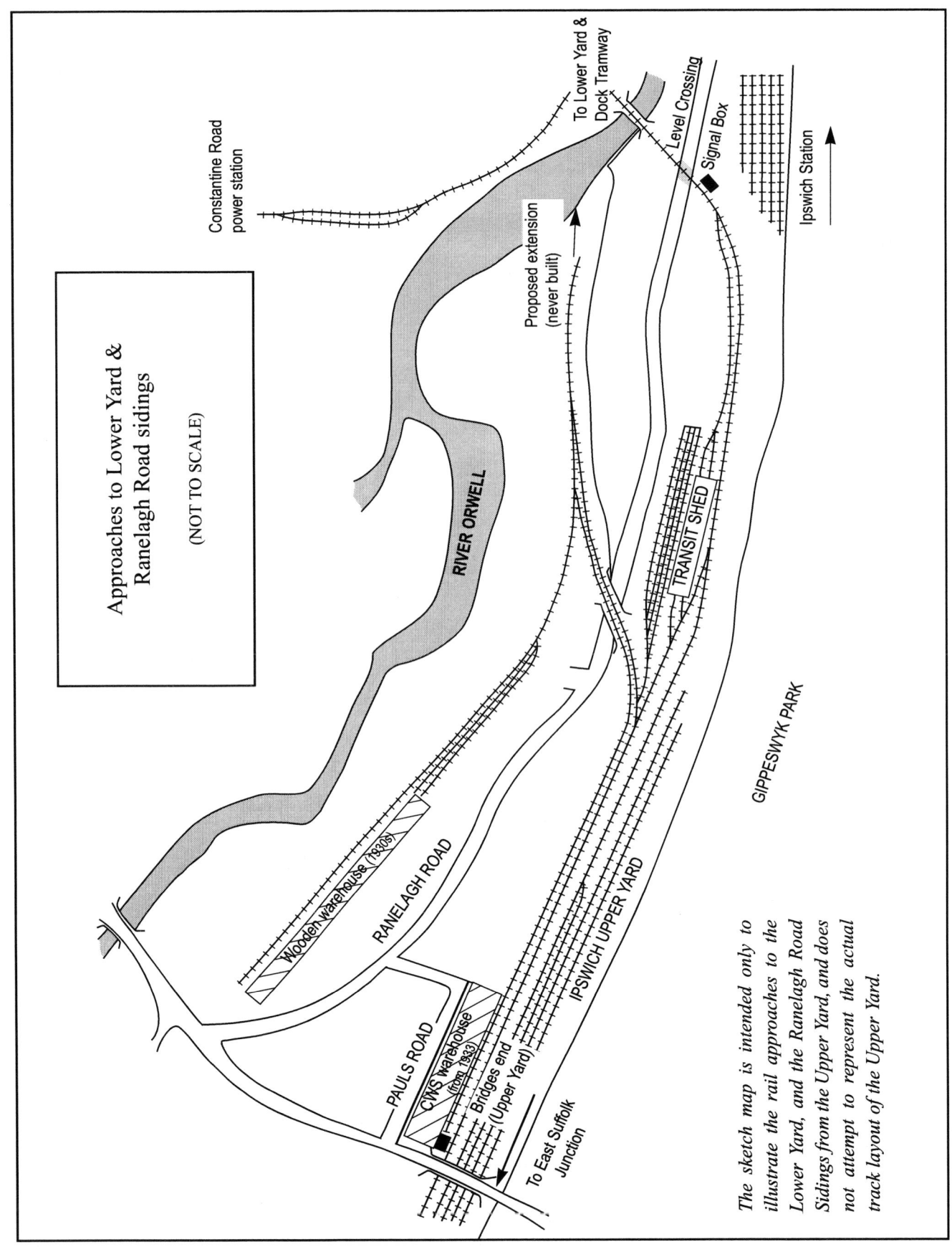

**Approaches to Lower Yard & Ranelagh Road sidings**

(NOT TO SCALE)

*The sketch map is intended only to illustrate the rail approaches to the Lower Yard, and the Ranelagh Road Sidings from the Upper Yard, and does not attempt to represent the actual track layout of the Upper Yard.*

railway-owned sidings and the mainline by a gate, and traffic was handled within the works by the factory's own locomotive. The sugar beet campaign tended to last from late September until February. It brought an enormous seasonal increase in traffic (and therefore revenue) to the railway, with the crop coming in from country goods yards, and pulp and refined sugar being sent away. In later years, some of the sugar went to Temple Mills via Cambridge, where a pilot driver would be provided, the Ipswich men not being familiar with the Cambridge to London road until the diesel era.

The railway-owned sidings at Sproughton were used to store empty wagons and carriages. Frequently a mainline train would be marshalled earlier at Ipswich and then taken to Sproughton to await departure time and its booked locomotive and crew. When the Ipswich yards were congested, which was quite normal until the 1950s and especially so during wartime, goods trains bound for Ipswich would be diverted at Sproughton, the engine would run through to Ipswich, and the train was collected later. During the 1940s some fifteen or sixteen trains a day were scheduled to depart from or arrive at Sproughton sidings, most of them to Whitemoor, including trains of up to fifty empty private-owner coal trucks returning to the north. By the 1960s however, the number was down to about three departures a day. By the 1980s the site was cleared and the A14 road bridge now crosses the mainline close to the site of the old signal box.

*The river bridge leading to the Lower Yard, seen in 1975. Ipswich Station is visible in the background.* (Photo by Richard W. Smith

### Goodmayes

At the end of the nineteenth century there was considerable congestion with goods traffic in East London, and therefore the marshalling yard at Goodmayes, situated nine miles from Liverpool Street, was developed by the GER between 1895 and 1911. The construction of Goodmayes yard went ahead with the quadrupling of the main line through the outer suburbs during that period. The passenger station at Goodmayes opened in 1901. Goods trains bound to London from East Anglia via the Colchester main line were sorted and remarshalled for dispatch to Bishopsgate, Spitalfields, or any of the other small yards in the London area or further afield.

For some fifty years Goodmayes remained a vital part of the London goods network but by the mid-1960s traditional methods of railway goods handling were fast disappearing as competition from road transport started to bite, with increased gross weights and higher speeds. Block container trains began running to and from new Freightliner Depots. Consequently the Up side closed about 1965 and the Down yard c 1971. The site was quickly redeveloped for housing, industrial and retail purposes.

### Temple Mills

A marshalling yard had been established by the GER about 1880 beside the Liverpool Street to Cambridge line close to Stratford. Additions over many years resulted in there being ten small yards and another five in the area. In 1954 British Railways began a massive redevelopment to concentrate the work of all the small yards to the main Temple Mills site between Stratford and Lea Bridge.

The main line was diverted from the centre of the site to the south, allowing room for the many reception, departure, brake van and engine roads. The hump area

*Remains of the Ipswich cattle pens.* (Photo by Richard W. Smith)

consisted of eight groups of six sidings equipped with automatically-controlled electro-pneumatic primary retarders which assessed the speed and weight of wagons and responded accordingly to slow the vehicles. Secondary retarders were also electro-pneumatically powered but manually operated for the final slowing. There was a complex telecommunications network including two-way radio between the control tower and the shunting engines, with a loudspeaker system allowing the tower operators to speak to shunters or anyone else throughout the site. During the first eighteen months after the redevelopment, one line, giving access from one end of the yard to the other, acquired the nickname "The Golden Mile". Due to the volume of traffic, engines were waiting longer than usual on this line while their trains were marshalled, resulting in late departures and subsequent overtime and extra money for the crews involved.

Temple Mills Yard still exists in a drastically reduced form and is used as a ballast yard operated by English Welsh & Scottish Railways. Ipswich men still run through on the way to Wembley and beyond.

## Whitemoor

The first fully mechanized marshalling yard in Britain had been high on the priorities of the LNER when the new yards were constructed at Whitemoor, a two mile stretch of flat fenland just beyond March station on the GN&GE Joint line to Lincoln. Their purpose was to speed up the flow of goods traffic using that route between the north of England, East Anglia and north east London, especially the thousands of loaded coal trucks moving south, and the corresponding numbers of empties returning northwards.

There were already some sorting sidings at March but the new yards were equipped for hump shunting, and modern hydraulic wagon-retarders were provided to slow the wagons as they ran by gravity into their appointed sidings. The Up yard opened in 1929 and the Down yard in 1933.

Due to the drastic transformation of freight services taking place in the 1960s and 1970s, the marshalling yards closed in stages during the 1980s. A section of the famous GN&GE Joint line between March and Spalding, which Whitemoor straddled, also shut. The area was cleared and a new purpose-built prison was erected on part of the site.

---

**WORKING OF LIVESTOCK TRAFFIC.**

Livestock traffic loaded at an Eastern Section station or exchanged to the Eastern Section at Temple Mills, Peterboro' East, Whitemoor or any other junction is to be dealt with as under:—

1. When 5 or more wagons and no suitable booked service is available, a special may be run.
2. When a special is run full use to be made of vacuum fitted vehicles, No. 1, +2 or No. 2 Braked times and conditions being observed.
3. When a booked train is used, the vacuum fitted vehicles should, when practicable, be made use of and the train run under No. 2 Braked times and conditions.
4. When less than 5 wagons either fitted or unfitted the best available transits to be arranged.

---

*Extract from a 1940s timetable working notes.*

## WORKING NOTES FOR FREIGHT TRAINS—continued.

### WEEKDAYS—continued.

**9.45 p.m. (SX) Witham to Ipswich.**

To convey all loaded and tranship wagons. Coal empties for via Whitemoor and Peterborough to be taken to Colchester for 12.55 a.m. Colchester to Whitemoor. Calls at Kelvedon to attach. To detach also at Colchester empties and unimportant traffic for Ipswich, which is to go forward by 1.20 a.m. Goodmayes to Ipswich. To be marshalled at Colchester with traffic for Norwich and beyond next engine.

**9.50 p.m. (SX) Whitemoor to Ipswich (Sproughton Siding).**

To be formed :—
>
> Engine
> Needham
> Claydon
> Bramford
> Sproughton
> Ipswich or East Suffolk line
> Brake

**9.50 p.m. (SO) Whitemoor to Chelmsford.**

To convey traffic for Witham and branches, and tranship wagons from Whitemoor for Witham.

**9.50 p.m. Colchester to Spitalfields.**

Calls at Witham to attach if necessary. On arrival at Goodmayes West, Colchester engine to be detached. Engine of 8.0 p.m. ex Witham to work train forward with all Bishopsgate and Spitalfields vegetable traffic from Goodmayes Yard received off 1.50 p.m. ex Ipswich, 1.50 p.m. ex Norwich, 8.0 p.m. ex Witham and 8.50 p.m. ex Southend. All Bishopsgate and Spitalfields traffic to be marshalled on brake.

**10.0 p.m. (SO) Ipswich to Whitemoor.**

To be marshalled—Engine, March and Wisbech Line, Peterboro', Whitemoor, Brake.

**10.0 p.m. (SX) Ipswich (Sproughton Sidings) to Peterboro E.**

To convey 50 empty Private Owners coal wagons only.

**11.40 p.m. (SX) Whitemoor to Ipswich.** To be worked by J 39 Class Engine, with water tank capacity of 4,200 gallons to enable the journey to be performed without stop en route for water. Load equivalent to 50 wagons of mineral, 4 of which are to be vacuum fitted and connected to engine. To convey East Suffolk Line traffic, load being made up with Ipswich proper traffic. Not to convey Stowmarket traffic.

*Extract from a 1940s timetable working notes included to show references to Sproughton Sidings and also to illustrate the complex instructions for the formation of working goods trains.*

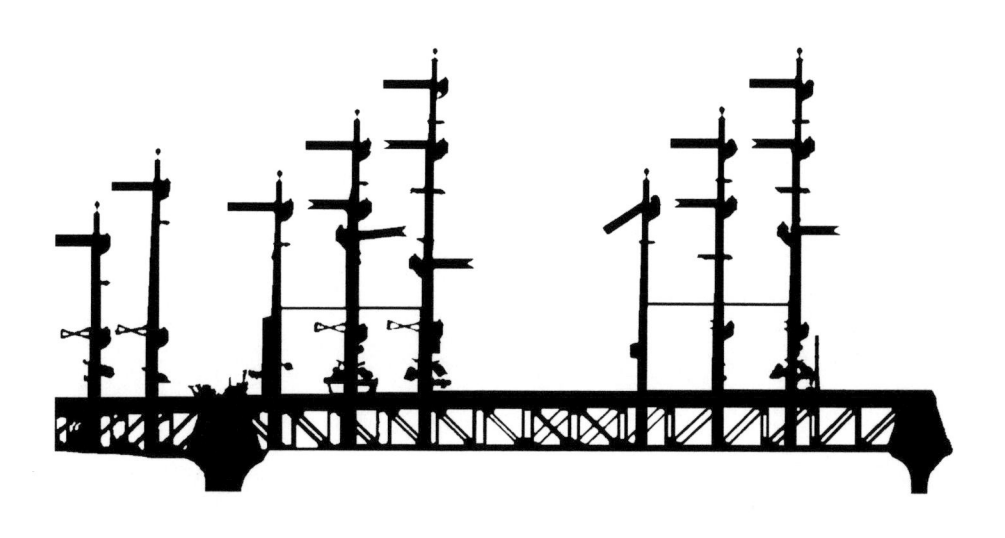

| 144 | LIST OF GOODS SHUNTING AND PILOT ENGINES—*continued*. |||||||
|---|---|---|---|---|---|---|---|
| STATION. | Description of Engine. | HOURS OF DUTY. |||| Total Hours Weekly | PARTICULARS OF WORK. |
| | | From | On | To | On | | |
| Ipswich | No. 1 | 5. 0 a.m. | Mondays | 10. 0 p.m. | Saturdays | 137 0 | Day and night. Lower yard shunting. |
| ,, | ,, 2 | 12.5 a.m. | Mondays | 6. 0 a.m. | Sundays | 149 55 | } Day and night. Upper yard shunting. |
| ,, | ,, 3 | 6. 0 a.m. | Mondays | 6. 0 ,, | ,, | 144 0 | |
| ,, | ,, 4 | 10.0 a.m. | Week-days | { 9. 0 p.m. / 4. 0 p.m. | Mondays to Fridays / Saturdays | 61 0 | Day only. Upper yard shunting. Griffin Wharf trips. |
| ,, Tram Eng | ,, 1 | 5. 0 a.m. | Week-days | 9. 0 p.m. | Week-days | 96 0 | |
| ,, ,, ,, | ,, 2 | { 7. 0 a.m. / 6. 0 a.m. | Mondays to Fridays Saturdays | 11. 0 p.m. 2. 0 ,, | Mondays to Fridays Saturdays | 88 0 | |
| , | ,, 3 | 10.0 a.m. | Week-days | 6. 0 p.m. | Week-days | 48 0 | Days, when required. |
| ,, | ,, 4 | 8. 0 a.m. | ,, | 4. 0 p.m. | ,, | 48 0 | ,, ,, |

*(Above) Extract from LNER working timetable, October to April 1943-44, showing the locomotive hours worked at the Ipswich Upper and Lower Goods Yards, Griffin Wharf and Dock.*

*(Below) BR working timetable, October to May 1968-69, revealing a drop in weekly shunting hours worked, due to the loss of goods traffic. Note also that the diesel shunting locomotives, having replaced steam and being by then fewer in number, were provided by Colchester Shed which was responsible for their maintenance.*

| BOOKED PILOTS AND SHUNTING ENGINES |||||  L83 |
|---|---|---|---|---|---|
| Station or Yard | Depot from which Engine provided | Number and Description of Pilot | Period required at Station or Yard | Particulars of Work ||
| Ipswich Upper Yard | Colchester | Station End (204 hp) | 00.01 Monday to 06.00 Saturday | Shunting as required. ||
| Ipswich Upper Yard | Colchester | Bridge End (204 hp) | 06.00 Monday to 06.00 Saturday | Shunting as required. ||
| Ipswich Lower Yard | Colchester | — (204 hp) | 05.00 Monday to 06.00 Saturday | Shunting as required. ||
| Ipswich Cliff Quay | Colchester | — (204 hp) | 10.00 to 18.00 SX | Shunting as required. ||
| Ipswich Wagon Shops | Colchester | — (204 hp) | 12.30 to 19.00 SX | Shunting as required ||

## Single Line Working
### A Plain Man's Guide

*SOME of the routes just described, especially branch lines, were single track. Ipswich footplatemen therefore had to have a knowledge of single line working when taking trains across these routes. Describing operations over single lines is difficult enough: indeed the whole subject can be a minefield and, not surprisingly, largely misunderstood by laymen.*

*The Editors hope that these short and greatly simplified notes will be of some interest to readers, and also contribute to the further appreciation of the duties of enginemen when adhering to the strict single line working regulations.*

*These notes could not have been included were it not for the professional help given by Signal Engineer William Barton, to whom we are indebted.*

Where a double line exists between two signal boxes each track can be dedicated to one direction of travel (e.g. Up and Down lines), and it is only necessary to prevent one train leaving the sending box before the preceding train has arrived at the receiving box to avoid accidents. Where only one single line exists, it has to be used by trains travelling in both directions so that not only "head to tail" collisions have to be prevented but "head on" ones as well.

An early method of achieving this was to regulate traffic by having only "one engine in steam" working on a specified length of railway. This proved impractical on busy routes however, so a "train staff" method was introduced. The "staff" was about twelve inches long, and made of metal or wood. The names of both signal boxes were embossed on the former, or inscribed on metal plates and screwed to the latter. If a train was not in possession of the staff, it could not proceed between the signal boxes named on the staff. The drawback with this method was that it required trains to alternate in each direction, in order to carry the staff backwards and forwards between the boxes.

This problem was solved by the use of metal "tickets". These were frequently metal discs of two or three inches in diameter. Signalman A would give the driver a ticket which authorised him to travel knowing that the train staff was being held at that particular box. Following trains would also be provided with a ticket if a train was not expected from the opposite direction. In this case, the last train in that direction would carry the train staff to the next box. Here Signalman B would give it to the driver of the train coming from the other direction, permitting his train to travel onwards and return the train staff to Signalman A. Again, if other trains were due in that direction, tickets would be given until the last train in the sequence collected the train staff. There could be about six such tickets for a particular section, and these were either padlocked to the train staff or placed in a locked container in the signal box. Sometimes a key was fashioned from the end of the staff which physically unlocked the signal lever protecting the single line as an additional safety measure.

The disadvantage of these methods was that they lacked flexibility with the train staff having eventually to travel in alternate directions. The train staff and ticket system required that the timetable had to be adhered to, and in the event of an out-of-turn working, the staff had to be conveyed to the appropriate end of the section either by a special light engine or taken by road.

Victorian engineers soon put their minds to improving the flexibility of single line working; there were far more miles of such sections than in modern times. Foremost in this field was Edward Tyer who was granted a patent in March 1878 for the "Tablet" method he had developed. His equipment for each signal box consisted of an electrically-locked magazine, holding up to twenty-four brass tablets each five inches in diameter and a half an inch thick, linked by a circuit connecting two machines together. The signalmen could communicate with each other using a bell and plunger system incorporated into the machine.

The method of working was as follows. With a train ready to depart, the signalman at the sending end would call the receiving box using an appropriate bell-code which, if all was well, would be repeated back to him. The bell plunger was held in by the receiving signalman after the last stroke to release the lock on the magazine at the sending box, enabling a tablet to be extracted. This process could be monitored by the receiving signalman by watching a galvanometer (an instrument for detecting electric currents) on his machine. Further bell signals caused an indicator to show 'Section Occupied'. Any attempt to extract more tablets would be unsuccessful until the original tablet had been replaced in either machine, which would also enable the section indicator to show clear. The tablet would be given to the driver who was then allowed to proceed.

Tyer's tablets could not be easily adapted to unlock subsidiary equipment, as could the older train staff, but this was overcome in 1889 when Messrs. Webb and Thompson produced their train staff machine which operated in a similar way to the Tyer's machine but held multiple copies of the old style train staff. Originally these Webb & Thompson machines used staffs two feet long but later on a miniature version was produced. When a signal box had more than one single line to deal with, as at a junction for instance, different rings or notches were marked on the staffs, thus allowing them to fit only in the machine dedicated to the single line section for which the staff was valid.

If the traffic in one direction was heavier than that in the other, tablets would build up at one end. This was corrected by a visit from the signal engineer, who would manually extract the excess and carry them to the other end to restore the balance. He would also be required to restore correct working should a tablet be lost or damaged. This would be done by removing another tablet and holding it under lock and key.

Various types of electric token and electric key token evolved and all were used in different situations to the same effect, that is, to prevent collisions on single lines. For example, in the 1940s, the Westerfield to Felixstowe line was controlled by electric token. The Bentley to Hadleigh branch was controlled by train staff without tickets and only worked by one engine in steam or two or more coupled together, as was the one mile, thirty-two chains, Snape Branch, where Snape Junction and Snape were designated train staff stations. The Haughley and Laxfield Light Railway was worked by split train staff where the staff was in two parts, one for the Haughley to Kenton Section, the other half for the Kenton to Laxfield Section. Both halves could be joined for the whole line which then constituted a single section. The single line section of the "Road to the North" between Soham and Ely Dock junction was electric key token controlled. The early concept that the "one engine in steam" rule alone would prevent accidents was soon supported by the train staff method as outlined above.

The tablet or ticket was usually given by the signalman to the driver, or more likely the fireman in steam days, in a pouch attached to a large metal "hoop" through which the engineman, or conversely the signalman at the other end of the section, could put their arm, with the train moving slowly by.

This procedure, shrouded in mystery, has been witnessed by thousands of passengers to whom it remained forever an enigma, although they realised it was connected somehow with the single line they were travelling over. The M&GN however, with over 100 miles of mostly mainline sections of single track, successfully erected delivery and receiving apparatus on the left side of the track, and equipped all their engines or tenders likewise (some on both sides to allow tender or bunker first operation). This reliable system permitted a higher speed for the actual exchange.

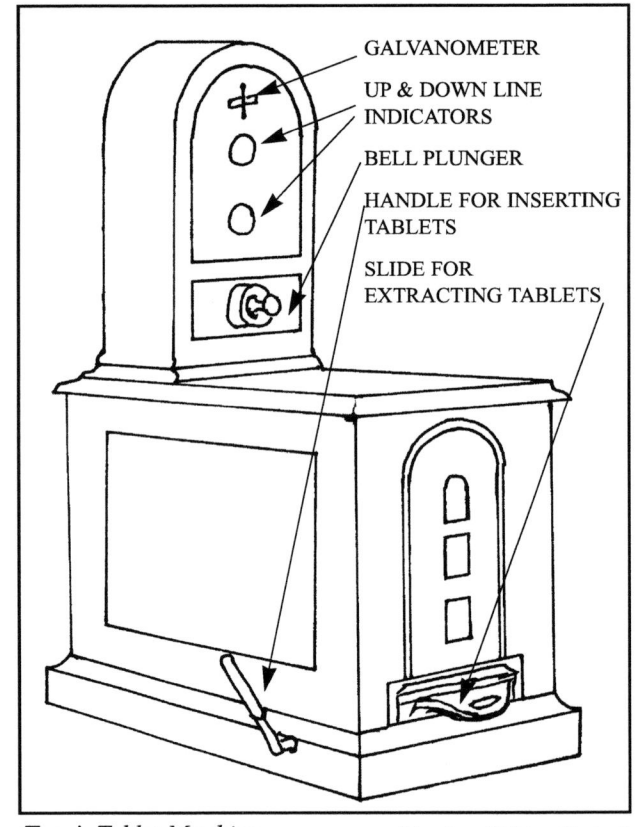

*Tyer's Tablet Machine* (Courtesy William Barton)

# Engines, Trains, Excursions & Events

## Titled Trains

IPSWICH, or for that matter East Anglia, did not experience the association with famous named trains enjoyed by many towns and cities in Britain. Some of the trains became almost legendary; for instance *The Flying Scotsman's* name had been in popular use since about 1862.

Well known names like *The Cornish Riviera Express* date from 1904 and *The Royal Scot*, *The Atlantic Coast Express* and *The Golden Arrow* appeared in the 1920s. Many of the services were restored after World War II but "naming" went out of fashion with British Rail for a time following dieselisation until a new generation of titles appeared, including *The European*, in the 1980s which made little impact and did not survive.

The summer season *Norfolk Coast Express* ended in 1914 and nothing similar appeared until June 1929 when the all-Pullman *Eastern Belle* started a six day summer service from Liverpool Street to a different coastal resort each day publicised by handbills and posters. Destinations included Felixstowe, Aldeburgh, Great Yarmouth and Cromer. On Sundays the train ran to Clacton as the *Clacton Belle*. It was not reinstated after the War finished in 1945. This was a popular train despite a Pullman supplement on a modest excursion fare, and was the only Pullman train in East Anglia to succeed.

*The East Anglian* appeared on 27th September 1937. Running Mondays to Fridays it left Norwich Thorpe at 11.55 am arriving at Liverpool Street at 2.10 pm including a four minute stop at Ipswich, returning at 6.40 pm. Speeds were modest, the highest start to stop timing requiring only an average 54.5 mph Ipswich to Norwich. Three minutes were cut from the timing the next year. Despite the relatively lower speeds in comparison with the LNER East Coast main line, two B17 engines were streamlined and named, No. 2859 becoming *East Anglian* and No. 2870 *City of London*. Engines and men were provided by Norwich Shed. The East Anglian was suspended during the war and the streamlined valances were removed and not replaced after the train was reinstated in October 1946.

New names appeared after 1945. *The Norfolkman* on 27th September 1948 left Liverpool Street at 9.30 am stopping at Ipswich, Norwich Thorpe, Wroxham, North Walsham, Gunton, Cromer Beach, West Runton and Sheringham. The original time taken for this train from Liverpool Street to Cromer was 3 hr 14 min, 19 minutes more than the *Norfolk Coast Express* achieved with its non-stop run to North Walsham. *The Norfolkman* however made five intermediate stops, including running into Norwich Thorpe station, making it a very creditable performance.

*The Broadsman* commenced running on the 5th June 1950, and by 1958 left Sheringham at 6.20 am, stopping at all stations to Norwich, then Diss, Stowmarket and Ipswich, arriving at Liverpool Street at 9.59 am. New "Britannia" pacific locomotives were allocated to the Norwich services in 1951, the first time that engines of this type had been permitted on the former Great Eastern system. The 3.30 pm Down *Broadsman* achieved fame in 1952 reaching Norwich in two hours. This was the first time that a train was timetabled to run start to stop at over 60 mph in Great Eastern territory. The 46.3 miles between Ipswich and Norwich was scheduled at 44 minutes requiring an average speed of 63.1 mph. By 1959 four trains a day maintained these timings

*Streamliner passing Halifax water troughs, Ipswich, en route for London. The houses of Wherstead Road are visible on the right of the photograph. The engine is B17 No. 2870* City of London, *introduced in 1937. The streamlining was removed in 1951. The engine later became No. 61670.*

(Photo courtesy Richard Pinkney)

The Easterling *seen here at Yarmouth Southtown with Ipswich men (left to right): Driver Ernie Wells, Driver George Gibbs and Fireman Alan Chittock.* (Photo courtesy K. Carr)

although, except for the *Broadsman,* London trains terminated at Norwich Thorpe. Continued improvements were made possible with the new 2000 hp diesel-electric locomotives which were able to sustain the "Britannia" timings with power to spare. Forty-five years on from the first *Broadsman,* headed by a steam engine, briefly becoming the fastest train in Britain by its highest average speed from Liverpool Street to Norwich, it is interesting to compare modern electric schedules. Now, in the 1990s, the *East Anglian* leaves London at 17.00 hrs, stops at Ipswich 58 minutes later for two minutes, and arrives in Norwich at 18.35 hrs. An improvement since 1952 of 25 minutes. The speed limit on the line has increased from 80 mph in the 1950s to 100 mph by the 1990s.

None of the titled trains mentioned, except for the *Norfolk Coast Express*, were normally worked by Ipswich locomotives or men, Stratford or Norwich Sheds supplying both. The radical timetable alterations of 1951, intended to make the most out of the new "Britannia" class 4-6-2 locomotives allocated to Norwich and Stratford, left Ipswich with Peterborough and Cambridge passenger jobs, but very little London work except from Yarmouth. The loss of work, though not critical, meant only just sufficient was left to occupy the two passenger links. The Ipswich Shed Master, Mr Hardy, argued firmly that Ipswich deserved more and succeeded in 1952 by gaining a Monday to Friday summer season train which had been started the previous year by Stratford.

*The Easterling* was first worked by Ipswich Shed at the start of the 1952 season. Driver Onkie Alderton (we have met him elsewhere in these pages) and his mate, left Ipswich with the 7.17 am to London. Leaving Liverpool Street at 11.03 am with *The Easterling*, they ran non-stop to Beccles where two coaches were detached for Lowestoft, then on to Yarmouth Southtown before returning passenger to Ipswich. The driver and fireman for the Up *Easterling* rode "on the cushions" to Yarmouth and left at 7.15 pm, stopping at Beccles for the Lowestoft coaches. Travelling non-stop from Beccles to Liverpool Street, the first train for many years not to stop at Ipswich, they returned to Ipswich, working the 11.15 pm Down. The engine for the initial trips was B17 No. 61668 *Bradford City*. Fresh from overhaul at Gorton Locomotive Works, it was standing in for Drivers Onkie Alderton's and Bill Barber's regular B1 No. 61055 which was in Stratford Works.

Other regular B1 4-6-0 engines used included 61201, 61253, 61058 and 61059 until the rebuilding of Ipswich Shed, started in 1953, caused numerous problems with regular manning and it was decided to keep a special B17 for the job, which was given the best of mechanical attention. By 1958 *The Easterling* was also being worked by a "Britannia" including No. 70036 *Boadicea*. The service, which was popular with Londoners, finished with the end of steam at Ipswich in 1959, and in November of that year the direct line from Beccles to Yarmouth Southtown closed.

*The European* replaced the Harwich to Manchester boat train in 1983, running daily except Sundays. It left Harwich at 7.17 am and arrived in Edinburgh at 5.11 pm after twenty-two scheduled stops including Manchester. Not only did the service cater for tourists arriving from the Continent and wishing to go to Scotland but also it was of benefit to local people travelling north who could now make the journey without the hassle of first going into and out of London.

*The Rhinelander*, running between Manchester and Harwich, replaced *The European* in 1987. A year later *The Lorelei* was introduced, a Blackpool-Sheffield-Harwich diesel-car service. The name was used in 1989 for a Birmingham and Liverpool to Harwich service, and also that year *The Britannia* ran between Harwich and Manchester.

---

### THE EAST ANGLIAN
#### NORWICH, IPSWICH AND LONDON (Liverpool Street)
**WEEKDAYS**

| am | pm |
|---|---|
| Norwich (Thorpe) ......dep 11 45 | London (Liverpool Street) .....dep 6 30 |
| **pm** | |
| Ipswich ...............arr 12 30 | Ipswich .....................arr 7 43 |
| .....................dep 12 32 | ...........................dep 7 46 |
| London (Liverpool Street) ..arr 1 45 | Norwich (Thorpe)................arr 8 30 |

Restaurant Car available

Seats can be reserved in advance on payment of a fee of 2s. 0d. per seat at London (Liverpool Street), Ipswich and Norwich (Thorpe) for journeys in either direction.

---

### THE BROADSMAN
#### SHERINGHAM, CROMER, NORWICH, IPSWICH AND LONDON (Liverpool Street)
**WEEKDAYS**

| am | pm |
|---|---|
| Sheringham ...........dep 6 20 | London (Liverpool Street) .....dep 3 30 |
| West Runton .............6 25 | Ipswich ....................arr 4 43 |
| Cromer (Beach) ..........6 38 | ..........................dep 4 46 |
| Gunton ..................6 53 | Norwich (Thorpe)..............5 30 |
| North Walsham (Main) ......7 1 | Salhouse.....................5 56 |
| Worstead ................7 7 | Wroxham......................6 3 |
| Wroxham .................7 15 | Worstead.....................6 3 |
| Salhouse ................7 23 | North Walsham (Main)..........6 19 |
| Norwich (Thorpe) .........7 45 | Gunton......................6 30 |
| Diss ....................8 9 | Cromer (Beach)...............6 44 |
| Stowmarket ..............8 27 | West Runton..................7 1 |
| Ipswich ................arr 8 42 | Sheringham..................7 5 |
| ..................dep 8 45 | |
| London (Liverpool Street) ....9A 59 | |

A On Mondays arrive 10 2 am.

Restaurant Car available between Cromer and London (Liverpool Street)

Passengers travelling from Liverpool Street, Sheringham and Cromer (Beach), also from Norwich to Ipswich and Liverpool Street and Ipswich to Liverpool Street, by this service can reserve seats in advance on payment of a fee of 2s. 0d. per seat

---

### THE NORFOLKMAN
#### LONDON (Liverpool Street), IPSWICH, NORWICH, CROMER and SHERINGHAM
**WEEKDAYS**

| am | pm |
|---|---|
| London (Liverpool Street) ..dep 9 30 | Sheringham ...........dep 4 25 |
| Ipswich ..............arr 10 43 | West Runton................4 30 |
| ...................dep 10 46 | Cromer (Beach)...............4 43 |
| Norwich (Thorpe) .......arr 11 30 | North Walsham (Main)..........5 5 |
| Wroxham ................12 5 | Worstead....................5 11 |
| North Walsham (Main) .....12 17 | Wroxham.....................5 19 |
| Gunton ................12 28 | Norwich (Thorpe)..............5 45 |
| Cromer (Beach) .........12 44 | Ipswich ....................arr 6 30 |
| West Runton ...........12 57 | ..........................dep 6 32 |
| Sheringham .............1 1 | London (Liverpool Street).......arr 7 45 |

Restaurant Car available between London (Liverpool Street) and Sheringham.

Passengers travelling from Liverpool Street, Sheringham and Cromer (Beach), also from Norwich to Ipswich and Liverpool Street and Ipswich to Liverpool Street, by this service can reserve seats in advance on payment of a fee of 2s. 0d. per seat

## ENGINES, TRAINS, EXCURSIONS & EVENTS

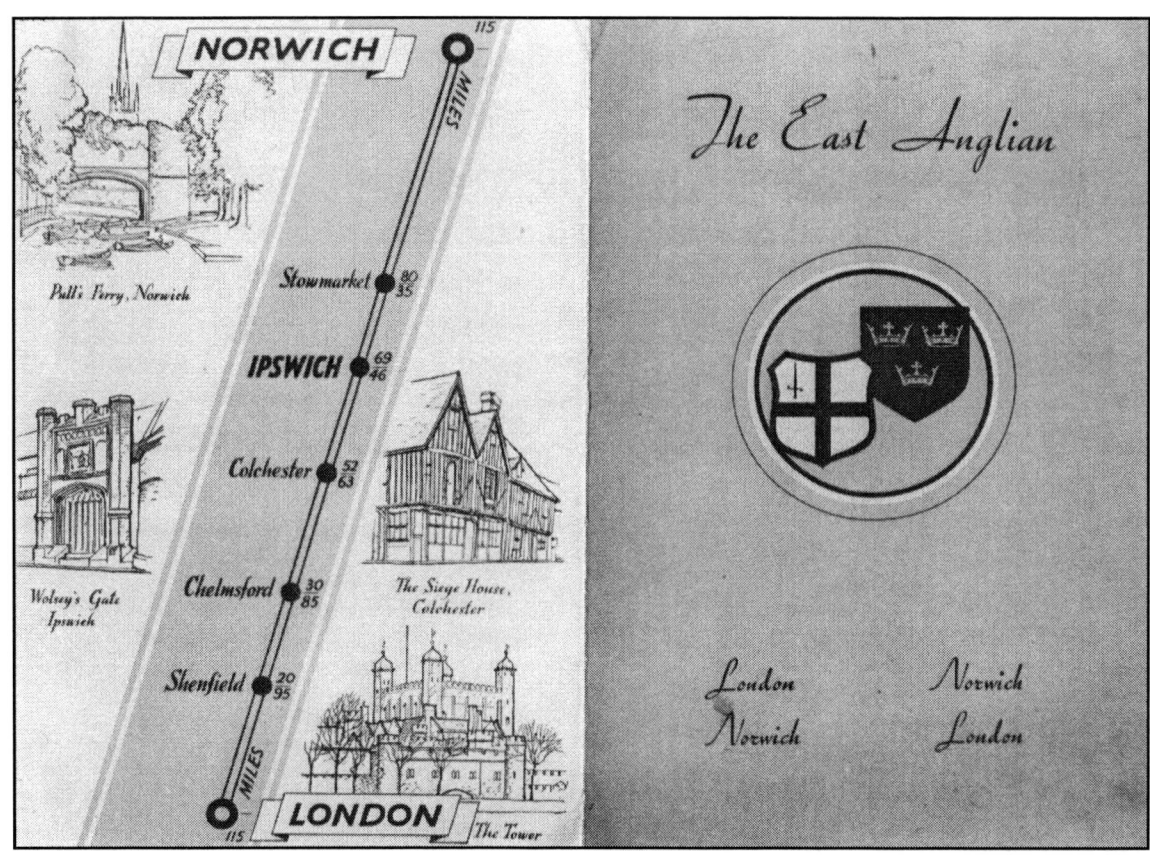

*Menu from* The East Anglian *(above) the cover (below) menu and drinks list.*    (Courtesy Richard Bird)

| | | | | | | | |
|---|---|---|---|---|---|---|---|
| **LUNCHEON 7/6** | | | | *Glass* | **SPIRITS** | | |
| | SHERRY | | | 2/6 | | | *Measure* |
| | APÉRITFS | | | | Brandy, Vieux Maison 30 years old | | 3/- |
| Soup | Gin and Lime, Orange or lemon | | | 2/3 | Brandy * * * | | 3/- |
| *Choice of* | Gin & Bitters | | | 2/- | Gin | | 2/- |
| Fish, Entrée, Joint or Cold meats | Gin and Vermouth, Noilly Prat or | | | | Rum | | 2/- |
| Vegetables | Martini | | | 2/6 | Whisky No 138 | | 2/6 |
| Sweet or Cheese | Vermouth, Noilly Prat or Martini | | | 1/6 | Whisky - Proprietary Brands | | 2/6 |
| Coffee 6d extra | | | | *Baby Bottle* | | | *Minature* |
| | Tomato Juice Cocktail | | | 1/- | Whisky - Proprietary Brands | | 5/- |
| | Pineapple Juice | | | 1/- | Gin | | 4/- |
| | BORDEAUX Red | | | | Rum | | 4/- |
| **DINNER 7/6** | | *Bott* | *½Bott* | *¼Bott* | | | |
| | Medoc | 10/6 | 5/6 | 3/- | **CORDIALS** | | |
| | Château Beychevelle, | | | | | | *Glass* |
| Soup | 1947 | 15/- | 8/- | - - | Lemon Juice | | 6d |
| *Choice of* | BORDEAUX White | | | | Lemon Squash | | 6d |
| Fish, Entrée, Joint or Cold meats | Graves | 10/6 | 5/6 | 3/- | Orange Squash | | 6d |
| Vegetables | Sauternes | 12/6 | 6/6 | - - | Grape Fruit Squash | | 6d |
| Sweet, Cheese or Savoury | BURGANDY Red | | | | | | |
| Coffee 6d extra | Mâcon | 10/6 | 5/6 | 3/- | **ALES, LAGER, ETC** | | |
| | Beaune | 15/- | 8/- | - - | | | *Bottle* |
| | CHAMPAGNE | | | | Bass and Worthington | | 1/6 |
| | Louis Roederer, | | | | Double Diamond | | 1/6 |
| *Children travelling at half fare are charged half price for table d'hôte meals* | 1945 | 47/6 | 24/6 | - - | Guinness | | 1/6 |
| *excepting Afternoon Tea* | Perrier Jouët, N.V. | - - | - - | 8/6 | Other Proprietary Ales | | 1/6 |
| | St. Marceaux, N.V. | 37/6 | 19/6 | - - | Whitbread's Pale Ale | | 1/3 |
| | ALSATIAN | | | | Othe Light Ales | | 1/3 |
| *The alternative dishes will be served as available* | Sylvaner | 16/- | 8/6 | - - | British Lager | | 1/6 |
| | SOUTH AFRICAN | | | | Imported Lager | | 1/8 |
| At Luncheon and Dinner | Paarl Amber Hock | 10/6 | 5/6 | 3/- | | | |
| cheese and biscuits may be served | PORT | | | *Glass* | **CIDER** | | |
| in addition to the Sweet for an | Very Fine Old | | | 3/- | | | *Bottle* |
| extra charge of 1/- | Fine Old Tawny | | | 2/6 | Cider | | 9d |
| | | | | | | | *Reputed Pint* |
| | LIQUEURS | | | *Liqueur Glass* | Champagne Cider | | 3/6 |
| It is particularly requested that a bill be obtained from the Conductor for all payments. In the general interest | Drambuie | | | 2/6 | | | |
| passengers are requested to refrain from smoking immediately before and during the service of meals. It | Van der Hum | | | 2/6 | **MINERALS** | | |
| will be appreciated if passengers will kindly bring any difficulty or lack of attention to the | Kümmel | | | 2/6 | | | *Splits* |
| notice of the Conductor in charge at the time of service. The British Transport Catering | Cointreau | | | 2/6 | Aerated Waters | Baby 6d | 7d |
| Services desire to render every possible service to passengers in the Restaurant Cars | Bénédictine | | | 2/6 | Sparkling Buxton | | 7d |
| and encourage efficiency in the service. They will be grateful if passengers will | Crème de Menthe | | | 2/6 | Apollinaris | Baby 6d | 7d |
| report any unusual service or attention on the part of the Restaurant | | | | *Minature* | Vichy Célestins | | 1/9 |
| Car staff to the British Transport Catering services, | Bénédictine | | | 3/9 | | | *Bottle* |
| St. Pancras Chambers. London, N.W.1 | Crème de Menthe | | | 4/6 | Ginger Beer | | 8d |
| | Boishümmel | | | 3/6 | | | |
| | Cherry Heering | | | 3/- | | | |

## ENGINES, TRAINS, EXCURSIONS & EVENTS

# *The Cromer Express / The Norfolk Coast Express*

*......The Great Eastern Station stands somewhat outside the town, and is perched upon the top of a hill, to which only a psalmist or a member of an Alpine club could do justice.........."* (E. L. AHRONS, referring to CROMER HIGH STATION)

THE Great Eastern line to Cromer, then just a village, opened in 1877. The area soon received attention from London journalists and acquired its sobriquet "Poppyland".

Mr Clement Scott of the 'Daily Telegraph' described Cromer as a perfect watering place, going on to write a poem which was set to music and became a popular ballad. He had found inspiration at Sidestrand, next to Overstrand, in a churchyard and church soon to be claimed by the restless waves of the North Sea. He, amongst others, captured the essence of North Norfolk in his writings and so encouraged the visitors to come to this beautiful part of East Anglia.

The GARDEN of SLEEP

*"On the grass of the cliff
At the edge of the steep
God planted a garden
A garden of sleep ........"*

The Grand Hotel opened in 1891 and the Metropole in 1894 to be followed shortly by visiting royalty. The up-market clientele thus enticed to Cromer encouraged the Great Eastern Railway in 1897 to provide a prestige summer-season train to run from London, Liverpool Street, non-stop to North Walsham and on to Cromer. The Down train left London on weekdays at 1.30 pm and the Up departed from Cromer at 1.0 pm. The 130 miles non-stop Down were covered in 2 hours 38 minutes, and the Up in 2 hours 39 minutes; the overall journey time to Cromer being 2 hours 55 minutes. Timings remained unchanged for the train's eighteen seasons but loadings nearly doubled from over 200 to 400 tons.

Additional branch lines opened, in 1898 from North Walsham to Mundesley, and in 1906 to Sheringham, connecting with the Midland and Great Northern Joint Railway which allowed through carriages to be added to the train for both destinations. In 1906 the *Cromer Express* was renamed, becoming *The Norfolk Coast Express* which was enhanced in 1907 by having all new corridor coaches. During the serious floods of 1912, when the main Ipswich to Norwich line was severed near Flordon, the *Norfolk Coast Express* was forced to

---

**THE NEW 1907 STOCK OF ALL BOGIE CORRIDOR CARRIAGES**

*To Cromer*
    Brake & 3rd class
    Two all 3rd class
    Restaurant Car 3rd class
    Kitchen car
    Restaurant car 1st class
    1st class carriage
    Brake

*To W. Runton & Sheringham*
    Composite 1st & 3rd class
    Brake & 3rd class

*To Mundesley & Overstrand*
    Composite 1st & 3rd class
    Brake & 3rd class

NOTE: The first class carriages were decorated in House of Lords morocco, the third class in red velvet. There were no second class carriages.

---

use the Forncett to Wymondham line, the train being reversed at Wymondham. The express train did not run again after the Great War; the 1914 season was its last.

Passengers were not lured to North Norfolk in the wake of all the publicity solely by way of the Great Eastern Railway. The Midland and Great Northern Joint Railway reached Cromer by way of Peterborough, Kings Lynn and Melton Constable in 1887, ten years after the GER arrived. Ironically the M&GN Beach station was situated much closer to the town and sea than the remote GER Cromer High which was nearly a mile away. The newcomer brought people in not only from the Midlands and the North but also from London (Kings Cross) via the Great Northern main line to Peterborough. The timings of the London trains varied from 3 hours 45 minutes to 4 hours 15 minutes and so did not provide serious competition with the Great Eastern time of 2 hours 55 minutes from Liverpool Street.

The eighteen years' summer workings of the prestige

*Cromer Expresses* was shared equally between Ipswich and Norwich Sheds. Each Shed had three of the six locomotives selected for that job. Those eighteen seasons spanned the finest years of locomotive development for the Great Eastern Railway. Four types of engines were used. The service started with six 2-2-2 single wheelers of which twenty-one were built at Stratford Works between 1889 and 1893. They were designed by GER Locomotive Superintendent James Holden who during this period had been experimenting with oil burning and some of these locomotives were converted from coal firing. In 1898 Mr. Holden produced ten 4-2-2 locomotives which were the last "singles" for the GER and like the 2-2-2s had 7ft diameter driving wheels. Some, if not all, of these were fitted for oil burning as were several of the 4-4-0 "Claud Hamilton" class which burst upon the scene in 1900 and carried on until 1912 with the Cromer Express. For the last two years of its existence, the new 4-6-0 engines, generally referred to as the "1500s" (being numbered in sequence from 1500), hauled the *Norfolk Coast Express* as it was now known.

The Ipswich and Norwich engines each had their own regular crews who worked the service every three weeks. Great professional pride was shown by the drivers and firemen of these trains.

MONDAY, WEDNESDAY, FRIDAY
*Ipswich men and locomotive.*
   10.0 am Ipswich to Liverpool Street
   1.30 pm Liverpool Street to Cromer
   5.30 pm Cromer to Norwich
   Rest at Norwich.
*Norwich men and locomotive*
   9.05 am Norwich to Cromer
   1.00 pm Cromer to Liverpool Street
   5.30 pm Liverpool Street to Ipswich
   Rest at Ipswich

TUESDAY, THURSDAY AND SATURDAY
*Turns reversed*

The 130 miles non-stop run from London to North Walsham required water for the locomotives to be scooped up at speed from open troughs laid between the rails. These were placed at Tivetshall and Ipswich. All main line passenger engines built after 1898 were fitted with water-scoops. The troughs at Ipswich were situated along the straight lengths of track at Halifax parallel with the Wherstead Road beyond the Black Bridge. Described by the "Great Eastern Railway Magazine" shortly after installation as water troughs *par excellence*, they were about 500 yards in length, 5 inches deep, and 18 inches broad. They were fed through 9 inch pipes from an elevated water-tank at the nearby Ipswich locomotive depot. Running into two cisterns (one for each trough - up and down roads) the flow from these into the troughs was controlled by quick-acting automatic buckets. Both the troughs at Ipswich and Tivetshall filled in less than five minutes after a train had passed over them. Cleaning out the Ipswich troughs was done on Sundays by staff from the locomotive depot, who used bass brooms. The troughs at Ipswich remained in use until the end of steam; water scooped at these meant not having to top up at the station, with the resulting saving in time.

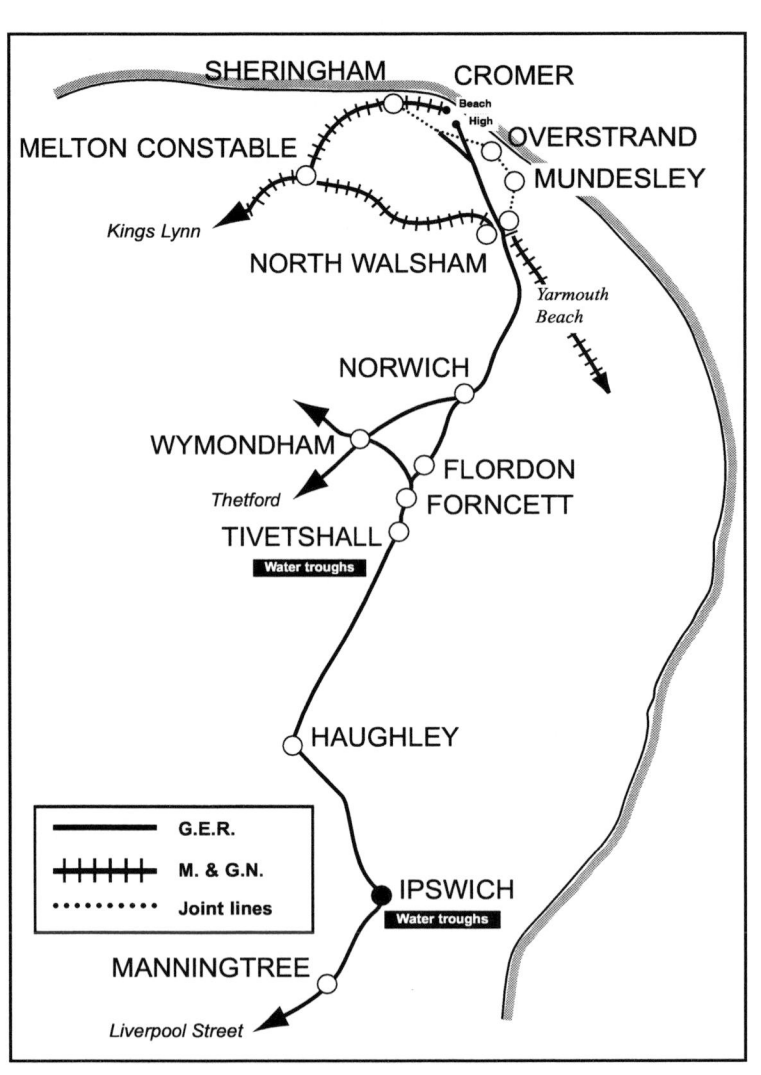

# The North Country Continental / The Manchester

*The Manchester bound* North Country Continental, *or* The Boat Train *as it was often referred to, departing from Platform 3 at Ipswich in 1928. The engine, No. 8555 LNER Class B12/1, was one of twenty built by William Beardmore & Co. Ltd. of Manchester in 1920-21. It was scrapped as BR No. 61555 at Stratford in October 1957.*

(Photo by Wally Newman, courtesy Richard Pinkney)

*THE Manchester*, as the *North Country Continental* was referred to by Ipswich footplatemen, started its journey at Parkeston Quay, leaving six days a week after the more prestigious Liverpool Street Boat trains had departed taking the passengers from the overnight steamers from Antwerp or Hook of Holland.

In the late 1920s, a Parkeston crew brought the train to Ipswich where they were relieved by local drivers and firemen who would take the train almost to Manchester. This somewhat unusual working was the longest regular turn on the Great Eastern section of the LNER, though enginemen at March in Cambridgeshire had a very wide route knowledge, regularly working to York and taking goods trains to London.

The journey from Ipswich into Yorkshire posed no great problems but from just beyond Sheffield began nearly nineteen miles of adverse gradients, from 1 in 100 to 1 in 135, followed by the three mile long Woodhead Tunnel, notorious because of its separate, twin single-line smoke-filled tunnels. The return twenty-one miles ascent out of Manchester was even more of an ordeal, including the 1 in 200 climb in the tunnel to the summit.

Prior to the Grouping in 1923 the Great Central and Great Eastern Railways were jointly responsible for the train being worked by as many as six engines en-route. Changes were made when both companies became part of the LNER and in 1925, Parkeston and Ipswich B12 1500 engines ran through to Lincoln. May 16th 1927 was the date when through running began between Ipswich and Manchester and back. Outward trips for both Ipswich and Gorton (Manchester) men and locomotives were on Mondays, Wednesdays and Fridays, the respective return trips after lodging were on Tuesdays, Thursdays and Saturdays. Ipswich crews booked on at 6.30 am to prepare the engine and left Ipswich for Manchester shortly after 8.0 am. They originally worked through to Manchester Central but to effect economies they were later relieved at Guide Bridge, on the outskirts of the City, within their eight hour shift, to rest at the Gorton Hostel. The next day they would work a stopping passenger train into Manchester Central from Guide Bridge before leaving for Ipswich at about 3.05 pm. (Times did vary slightly.) This meant that Ipswich men spent about twenty-one hours off duty away, whilst the Gorton crews booked off

*Manchester Central in the 1930s. Ipswich engine, Class B17 No. 2820* Clumber, *waiting to back on to the* North Country Continental *for the return trip over the Pennines to Ipswich with fireman William Barber and either Driver George Pinkney, or Driver Charlie Cross, in charge. The locomotive was built at the LNER Darlington Works in 1930, and scrapped at Stratford in January 1960.*

(Photo courtesy Gordon Barber)

for only nine hours in Ipswich, usually lodging at 18 Croft Street, just outside the locomotive depot.

Due to stringent limits on dimensions and weight on the original Great Eastern section, the only suitable locomotives available were of the B12, 4-6-0 1500 class. One of these, No. 8561, successfully worked a heavy thirteen-coach train of Canadian-bound emigrants in April 1927 through to Liverpool, regarded as a trial run. The fireman, Frank Cocksedge, referred to the experience in the 1970 edition of the Ipswich & District Historical Transport Society Handbook. He and the driver, Jack Pack, learned some time later that a train consisting of over eight coaches should have been double-headed from Sheffield through Woodhead Tunnel to Manchester! The first engines allocated to the Manchester job at Ipswich were No. 8561 (Driver J Pack, Fireman Harry Church) and No. 8535, (Driver George Pinkney, Fireman Ernie Payne); No. 8557 going to Gorton. The Gorton engine had a permanent crew which eventually caused dissent. Great Central footplatemen did not at that time operate a Seniority Scheme which the former Great Eastern men adhered to strictly and which certainly provided a fairer system for promotion.

The B12s worked the North Country Continental over the two-hundred and fifteen mile run for eighteen months. In December 1928 the Gresley designed B17 "Sandringham" 4-6-0 class locos replaced the B12s. There were a number of problems with the first batch of the new engines requiring, in some cases, several months work to rectify. The 1500s reappeared during 1930 but from then on, the B17s held sway until September 1939 when the train was suspended. The train was reinstated after the Second World War, but not the lodging turns. Before this, relief was afforded to the drivers and firemen when in 1936 another batch of B17s, the "Footballers" came out with a tender capacity of 7 tons of coal instead of the 4 tons on the earlier locos of both B12 and B17 classes. The original tender size, which had been governed by the restrictions referred to earlier on the Great Eastern and by now being eased, was only just sufficient to allow the engines to get to Manchester without coaling. Water was taken at the scheduled passenger stops.

**HARWICH (Parkeston Quay), IPSWICH BURY ST. EDMUNDS, ELY, LINCOLN, SHEFFIELD, MANCHESTER AND LIVERPOOL**

**WEEKDAYS**

| | A am | | B pm |
|---|---|---|---|
| | | Liverpool (Central) .... dep | 1 15 |
| Harwich (Parkeston Quay) .... dep | 8 C0 | manchester (Central) .... " | 2 15 |
| Ipswich .... " | 8 36 | Guide Bridge .... " | 2 43 |
| Bury St. Edmunds .... " | 9 12 | Sheffield (Victoria) .... " | 3 30 |
| Ely .... " | 9 54 | Worksop .... " | 3 59 |
| March .... " | 10 20 | Lincoln (Central) .... arr | 4 41 |
| Spalding (Town) .... " | 10 47 | .... dep | 4 48 |
| Lincoln (Central) .... arr | 11 36 | Sleaford .... arr | 5 17 |
| .... dep | 11 43 | Spalding (Town) .... " | 5 50 |
| | pm | March .... " | 6 21 |
| Sheffield (Victoria) .... arr | 12 52 | Ely .... " | 6 53 |
| Guide Bridge .... " | 1 40 | Bury St. Edmunds .... " | 7 31 |
| Manchester (Central) .... " | 2 4 | Ipswich .... " | 8 8 |
| Liverpool (Central) .... " | 3 0 | Harwich (Parkeston Quay) .... " | 8C40 |
| | | Dovercourt BAy .... " | 8 51 |
| | | Harwich (Town) .... " | 8 53 |

A—Restaurant Car from Harwich (Parkeston Quay) to Sheffield (Victoria)

B—Restaurant Car from Sheffield (Victoria) to Harwich (Town)

C—These trains will connect with the night steamer sailing from Harwich (Parkeston Quay) to the Hook of Holland and with the steamer arriving Harwich (Parkeston Quay) from the Hook of Holland.

Passengers travelling from Harwich (Parkeston Quay), Liverpool (Central), Manchester (Central) (dep. 2 15 pm) and Sheffield (Victoria) (dep. 3 30 pm) can reserve seats in advance on payment of a fee of 2s. 0d. per seat.

*Timetable advertising The Boat Train during the 1950s.*

## Specials

TRAINS not listed in the passenger or goods working timetables were referred to, in railway parlance, as "Specials". The term covered a variety of trains, running both locally and nationally, one from as far afield as Scotland as will be seen later.

Circuses frequently hired special trains to transport their animals and equipment between venues. When a circus was booked to appear at Ipswich, for instance, the animals would often be paraded through the streets after the special train was unloaded at the siding adjacent to number one platform at Ipswich Station. Parents and children would gather on the pavements to see the procession. Driver George Baker can recall working such a train from Felixstowe to Ipswich at a speed of only 30 mph in order not to alarm the circus animals aboard.

In the 1950s the Household Cavalry, with their horses and equipment, arrived at Ipswich Station by special train, to make an appearance at the Suffolk Show. Again, many people lined the route from the station to watch them pass.

Specials ran on the Framlingham Branch to take the boys of Framlingham College to and from Liverpool Street at holiday times. H.M.S. Ganges also had a Christmas-leave special, the boys first travelling by bus to Ipswich Station from their base at Shotley. One such train for the Ganges boys ran to Newcastle on Tuesday, 13th December 1960. The details for the special were as follows:

|  |  |  | Passengers detrain | Remaining on train |
|---|---|---|---|---|
| Ipswich | dep. | 6.58 am | - | 544 |
| Ely | arr | 8.25 am | 16 | 528 |
| March | arr | 8.57 am | 35 | 493 |
| Spalding | arr | 9.32 am | 21 | 472 |
| Sleaford | arr | 10.02 am | 77 | 395 |
| Lincoln | arr | 10.36 am | 52 | 343 |
| Doncaster | arr | 11.38 am | 100 | 243 |
| York | arr | 12.25 pm | 38 | 205 |
| Darlington | arr | 1.30 pm | 47 | 158 |
| Newcastle | arr | 2.25 pm | 158 | - |

Richard "Dickie" Bird, who had transferred from the footplate grade at Ipswich to become a restaurant car attendant, recalled light refreshments being available on the train including tea, coffee and minerals, plus bridge rolls with butter and sausage. No alcoholic drinks (including cider) were allowed to be served on the trip. A good sale was expected for the hot dogs at 1/3d each. The restaurant car staff had duty passes and were required to return by passenger train, leaving Newcastle at 3.57 pm and arriving at Kings Cross at 9.20 pm. They then caught the 10.40 pm train from Liverpool Street, and finally reached Ipswich at 12.30 am.

A pre-war special train which Richard Bird remembers was an Eastern Counties Special to Aintree for the Grand National, on Friday, 24th March 1939. Breakfast was served on the train, consisting of grapefruit or porridge and cream; kippers or fried Dover sole; bacon and eggs with grilled tomatoes and sausage; preserves and tea or coffee. The covers to the menus in those days usually featured reproductions of watercolours by well-known artists, for example Greta Bridge, Teesdale by W. Russell Flint, R.A., or a view of Lavenham by Rowland Hilder.

Another special, recalled by Richard Bird, left Ipswich at 5.14 pm for Stratford on 2nd August 1957 to enable people to visit the Searchlight Tattoo at White City. This train arrived back at Ipswich at 1.44 am the following morning.

A week-end holiday special, advertised as a "Treasure Island Tour", was run by British Railways to Oban in Scotland, in June 1965. The excursion included a trip on *R.M.S Lochfyne*. The train left Colchester at 5.32 pm on the Friday, calling at Ipswich, Bury, Ely, March, Peterborough, Grantham, Newark, Retford, Doncaster, York, Newcastle, Edinburgh and Cowlairs, finally arriving at Oban on Saturday morning at 7.55 am. It left Oban the same evening at 8.30 pm, arriving back at Ipswich just after midday on the Sunday. Breakfast was served on the train at 4.00 am, 5.00 am and 6.00 am, with forty-two persons being served at each sitting. The Buffet Car was open continuously each night.

Bank Holiday specials and cheap excursions have always been popular with the travelling public. In 1906 the Great Eastern Railway published a large poster detailing the Company's additional trains and altered arrangements for the August Bank Holiday. A midnight train was advertised to leave London for Ipswich, Norwich (Thorpe), Yarmouth (Southtown) and Lowestoft, calling at many stations on the way, for the convenience of passengers who were unable to leave the City earlier on the Saturday. The same day, the 8.15 am Horse Box and Carriage Truck Train from Ipswich ran to Bishopsgate Goods Station instead of the usual

*A railway enthusiasts' special on a tour of Ipswich Docks in August 1968. The trip, arranged by the Ipswich Land Transport Society, started at the Locomotive Depot at Croft Street. There, over fifty enthusiasts clambered aboard five British Rail brake vans and were shunted around the Ipswich Dock Commission's rail installations, including the Griffin Wharf, on a tour lasting three hours. The railwaymen standing in front of the Drewry shunting engine at Cliff Quay are (left to right): Ken Freestone, Colin Smith, Inspector ?, and Kenny Carr.* (Photo courtesy Freestone Family Collection)

Liverpool Street destination. The Railway Company also stated that on the Bank Holiday Monday, horses and private carriages would NOT be conveyed by the 8.25 or the 8.45 am trains out of Liverpool Street.

On Good Friday 1912, three special excursion trains ran to Felixstowe and numerous special cheap tickets were issued for all kinds of sporting events taking place.

The Football Specials of later years were not popular with footplatemen or guards, owing to the rowdy behaviour of some supporters. On one occasion West Ham supporters, travelling on a special to watch their team in action at Ipswich, brought the train to a halt four times before reaching Ingatestone, by pulling the communication cord.

The driver of the diesel locomotive was slightly upset that day, anyway, as normally he and his secondman were booked to return to Ipswich as passengers. Here they were however, having to work this special home instead. The train ground to a halt once more just outside Chelmsford as the communication cord was again pulled. Enough was enough. Driver Ted Clarke got down from his locomotive and strode through the carriages of the train. The supporters were informed by him in no uncertain terms that he did not care whether or not they watched their team play football that day but he was determined to be home in time for his dinner. If the train was halted once more, he told them, he would shunt it into the nearest siding and leave it there, he himself catching the next train to Ipswich.

He knew of course that he would not be allowed to carry out this threat, but it had the desired effect. The rest of the journey was uneventful until the train was running into number four platform at Ipswich Station when the brakes went on again. There was another wait while the guard reset the brakes to allow the train to drag into the platform, but Driver Clarke was home in time for his dinner.

Flying Scotsman, *then owned by Alan Pegler, heads a special train away from Ipswich, following a round trip from Kings Cross, Cambridge and Norwich, on May 17th 1969. Seen here near Claydon, on its return to Cambridge via Newmarket, with an Ipswich pilotman on the engine for this section. Concern had been expressed about the approved weight restrictions, due to under-line culverts, being officially ignored. The engine had paid a visit to Ipswich the previous September, when it headed a steam special to Derbyshire.* (Photo by Richard W. Smith)

*"If £5 you can afford,*
*Try your strength upon this cord.*
*If £5 you cannot pay,*
*Wait until another day."*

(LNER Magazine, July 1935)

# Rambles by Rail

IN addition to the "special" trains intended for the tourist, steam enthusiast and so on, ramblers, golfers, anglers and yachtsmen were not forgotten by the railways. Cheap fares were available to enable them to make use of the leisure facilities in the area, both on the coast and inland.

Yachtsmen were able to travel on Friday afternoons to Burnham on Crouch, for example, go sailing for the weekend and leave their yacht at Maldon, Brightlingsea, Ipswich, Woodbridge or Aldeburgh on Sunday evening to return another weekend. Local boatmen kept an eye on the yacht and there was the added freedom of not having to return to one's parked car.

In the 1930s, for the benefit of the keen rambler, sixteen LNER rambling guides were published, price 6d. Available from booksellers and LNER Agencies, the guides were advertised at railway stations with posters entreating passengers to "ask for the guide covering the district you require" together with the slogan "It's quicker by rail."

The following description of a ramble, between Orwell and Woodbridge, is taken from one of these guides; "Rambles in Suffolk" by Bernard Reeves. The guide states that a Walking Tour Ticket is available every day by any train from Ipswich to Orwell Station price 1/4d, or issued from Colchester price 3/4d for a 3rd class return.

Intending walkers were advised when making arrangements for the ramble that one member of the party should be deputed to watch the tide as it is only possible to cross the River Deben at Waldringfield when the tide is in. At low tide the mud on each side is

*Left: Front cover of guide. A map of LNER lines and associated bus companies of the Eastern Counties was inserted at the back of the book. Other titles in the series covered rambles in Essex, Norfolk, Yorkshire, Hertfordshire and Buckinghamshire. Right: GER advertisement, appearing in the 1904 "Suffolk County Handbook & Official Directory", referring to cheap fares for tourists, golfers, anglers and yachtsmen. The advertisement also refers to the Great Eastern Hotel at Liverpool Street, opened in 1884, and to the Harwich to the Hook of Holland service for which the GER held the contract for the Royal Mail.*

*The station approach and Stationmaster's house at Orwell Station - the start of the LNER ramble.* (Photo courtesy D. Girling)

impassable. They were told to study the tide table, and plan the ramble for a day on which high tide fell soon after midday, or about teatime.

### ROUTE 5 - ORWELL TO WOODBRIDGE

"On leaving Orwell Station approach, bear left along the road to the first opening on the left. Turn in here and keep left at the fork just inside. Go straight on, over the field beside the wood to a piece of rough ground with trees and broom. On the far side is a gate with a notice, "No Path Here.". Do not cross this ground, but turn right along the edge of the wood. The path becomes a lane and drops down hill (with the decoy ponds behind the fence on the left) to a junction of several ways at a house. Turn left to the two gates and go through the right hand one into the field. Keep straight ahead until you cross a ditch; there bear right to a stile in the corner. Go over the second stile beyond the strip of ground and follow the path to the left up the broken ground.

At the road turn left, over the railway bridge and the main road to the little wood. Skirt the far side of this and strike across the bracken to the tumuli. Beyond them, in the far corner of the two hedges, is the beginning of a path. It runs right along the hedge, though often unmarked save for the gaps in the cross-hedges, to the road. Cross the road to the path between the trees. This leads right along a little valley which is so overgrown that the path is often indiscernible, but there is a gate at the end. Through this turn right.

If you prefer easier walking do not go along the path between the trees, but turn right along the road and you will find a path on the left which runs parallel to the valley and comes out on the same lane. Turn right. Keep straight on past Kirton Hall to a gate. Take the path on the right of the gate, go through another gate, over the stile and straight across the fields to Kirton. (4 miles)

Cross the road and go down by the Co-operative store to the church and round the bend. On the right a footpath goes off sharply to the right across a field, to another road. Turn right and go through the park gates and through the farm yard ahead. In the yard turn right and through the first gate is a path cutting diagonally down to a house. Here go right and to the top of the lane in front. You will see the path leading down over the top of the creek. Follow it and keep straight on into Hemley. (6 miles)

Turn left and take the first on the right past the church. At Hemley Hall take the road on the right out of the yard and keep on to the footpath on the right past Waldringfield church. At the end turn right to the river and quay at Waldringfield. (8 miles)

From Stonner Point follow the lane to the cross-roads a mile inland. Here turn left and at Brickkiln Farm keep left to the path at the left hand corner of the wood. On the road beyond turn left then right. At the top of this road turn left into the "courtyard" at the end of which is a path on the right. Once on this keep straight ahead, over the road, and it will bring you to Woodbridge Ferry. (11½ miles)

If the state of the tide prevents a crossing at Waldringfield the pleasantest alternative is to return up the road from the Quay and when the main road turns right, keep on over the heath. Bear to the right, but do not leave the track for the road which you cross near a cross-roads. Make for the wood which lies to the right of the aerodrome and, skirting its left-hand side, come to the main road. From this point strike across the heath to the corner of the big wood beside the other main road half a mile ahead. There is a track, but the map shows how easily you may miss it. A few yards from the corner of this wood a lane runs to a farm beyond which is a stream. On the far side take the path to the left and on reaching the road turn right for Little Bealings Station. (12 miles)"

More than sixty years after the publication of the

*Orwell Station at the time of its closure in 1959.* (Photo courtesy D. Girling)

LNER "Rambles in Suffolk", Doug Harper, a keen walker for over fifty years, has made the following observations.

Apart from the fact that Orwell and Bealings Stations have long closed, it would not be too difficult in the 1990s to walk the route just described, allowing for some diversions. There is a slight alteration to the route through the Orwell Park Estate, and also where the footpath crosses what was farmland at Levington and the modern A14, before reaching Kirton. From there, most of the paths on the western side of the River Deben are still usable through Hemley and Waldringfield until one reaches Martlesham and the areas now covered principally by BT and the Tesco Superstore and car parks. Once the A1214 (the old A12) is crossed, it is still possible to find the path to Bealings.

On the eastern side of the river the ancient footpaths from Stonner Point to the Sutton ferry landing are largely intact but of course the ferries have long since gone, although the Woodbridge to Sutton ferry survived until the 1970s. Another LNER ramble, beginning at Wickham Market and finishing at Saxmundham and extended to nineteen miles by way of Aldeburgh, similarly used a ferry, now extinct, between Sudbourne and Slaughden Quay.

*Special ramblers' trains ran on into the 1960s in Suffolk. On Sunday June 4th 1961, the last publicly advertised passenger train ran to Lavenham, for instance, with a ramblers' excursion from London. (There was to be a privately hired passenger train bringing guests to a wedding shortly after this ramblers' special, but the scheduled passenger service on that branch had ceased on April 10th of that year.) The ramblers' special started from Liverpool Street at 9.42 am, calling at Stratford, Ilford and Romford, and ran via Marks Tey and Long Melford, arriving at Lavenham at 11.55 am. It continued as a privately-hired train to Bury St Edmunds at 2.00 pm, with photographic stops at Cockfield and Welnetham, arriving back in Lavenham at 5.15 pm. The train is seen here, on a peaceful and sunny June evening, waiting to depart at 6.00 pm for London, complete with "THE LAST TRAIN" headboard and accompanied by the sound of Lavenham church bells and the Salvation Army band playing in the Market Place.* (Photo by Richard W. Smith)

"Remember that, generally speaking, you can only be run over by an engine once in a lifetime."
(GER accident prevention notice)

## *Removal Specials*
### The Scottish - East Anglian Farming Link

TOWARDS the end of the 19th century there began a trek by some farmers and their families from the Borders and Lowlands of Scotland to East Anglia and in particular Suffolk and Essex, the numbers peaking during the 1920s and 1930s.

In some cases the families and all the farm livestock and implements were transported by special train hired by the farmer for the long journey south. Others sold up completely and the family travelled by normal passenger train.

At the turn of the century one branch of the Drummond family moved to the Duke of Grafton's Park Farm at Barningham in North Suffolk. In that instance the women and children probably came by train but the men drove the farm horses and wagons loaded with the machinery, furniture and other belongings down from Scotby near Carlisle. The 270 odd miles were covered in nine days, Mr Drummond senior riding ahead on horseback to find overnight accommodation.

Many Suffolk farms which had been arable changed to dairy or beef production by this influx from Scotland. Amongst those families making their home in Suffolk were the Jacks, Kerrs, Patersons, Whites and Wilsons.

**THE WILSON FAMILY.**

In 1919, James Wilson brought his wife and four children to White House Farm, Dallinghoo from Strathaven, Lanarkshire in Scotland by passenger train. Travelling with them were a dog, some cats and a few hens. They brought no farm machinery with them, and their furniture had been sent ahead by train. Mother had packed their belongings into wooden barrels, nailed down the lids and attached a list of the contents, thus making everything easy to find on arrival at their new home. The farm in Scotland was one mile from a small town and the neighbours were very sorry to see the family depart. Several friends and relations travelled on the train with them as far as Glasgow to wave them good-bye. Sadly, little Jessie Wilson arrived in Suffolk with a badly injured finger, having caught it in a train door. The family finally arived at Woodbridge Station where a friendly Suffolk neighbour met them.

It was hard to make a living from the farm. Mrs Wilson would frequently be heard to ask while shopping, "Have you nothing cheaper?" At one stage Mr Wilson threatened to sell the cattle and buy a dog and keep sheep but his wife pleaded the case of the poor wives and children of his sacked farm workers if he should follow this idea through and so he relented and struggled on. Suffolk farmers' wives were sometimes thought of as "ladies" with a high social standing but Mrs Wilson and her daughters were not afraid of hard work, milking the cows and toiling for long hours on the farm. They were among the first in the area to have a Simplex milking machine. Daughter Jeanie remembers visiting the Royal Show at Ipswich in 1934 where her father purchased a Canadian Beatty washing machine. This appliance, powered by a Lister engine, made light work of laundering the heavy shirts of the menfolk. The family had possessed a bathroom in Scotland but enjoyed no such luxury in Suffolk. Similarly, there had been tarmac roads in Scotland but around the farm at Dallinghoo were only gravel roads.

Mr Wilson went back to Scotland every year to buy cattle. Usually about twenty Ayrshires were purchased and sent back to Suffolk by train in cattle wagons. Beef cattle were put to graze on marshes at Aldeburgh, Trimley, and Higham and the family would walk the animals along the roads to their destinations. Milk would be taken in churns by horse and cart to Wickham Market Station where it was sent by train to Ilford. Robert, the son, would unload the milk-churns while his sister Jessie held the horse's head.

Jessie Wilson later became a teacher at Laxfield. To reach the school, she would be dropped off in the morning by her father at Framlingham, and then cycle the seven miles to reach Laxfield. Coming home at night involved cycling the whole distance back to the farm.

In 1936 the Wilson family moved to Fir Tree Farm close to what is now the Chantry Estate, Ipswich, which two years previously had been the site of the Royal Show. In 1970 the family bought the farm at Dallinghoo when it was put up for sale and returned to their old home.

**THE WHITE FAMILY**

It was in 1960 that Jim White and his family decided to move the entire contents of their farm from Doune in the lowlands of Scotland to Framsden in Suffolk.

Jim White came from a farming family; at one stage grandfather, uncle and father all worked on the same farm. His father, who served four years in France during the first World War, had been a horseman for several years before starting farming on his own in 1926. Jim moved with his parents to the farm at Doune in 1941, and when his father retired in 1957, Jim took over the

*Young Jim and Elizabeth White seen in the yard at Kirkton Farm with the Pickford's van which brought the gear and packing materials required for loading the family's household effects into the BR furniture container.*

(Photo courtesy White Family Collection)

tenancy of the 84-acre farm. Jim's wife Janet had worked at a cotton mill in a nearby village during the Second World War, before her marriage. Her father had been a woodcutter.

It was not long before Jim White decided that he wanted a bigger farm with better land to enable him to grow crops, in addition to keeping a dairy herd, and he looked to England in order to fulfil his aim. The soil of the Doune farm was very poor; every spring, two whole days would be spent gathering stones off the fields intended for cereal growing. After a shower of rain, when the ground dried out, stones the size of a fist would make their appearance. The climate was very wet in the Doune area; the total annual rainfall of forty-six inches was twice that of Suffolk.

The tenancy of Red House Farm, Framsden, part of the Helmingham Estate, was advertised at this time in The Farmer's Weekly, the previous tenant having met a tragic death earlier that year. Jim and his wife came in October 1959 to view the 184-acre farm, and they paid another visit to Suffolk in November to be interviewed by Lord and Lady Tollemache. Jim was the successful one of three applicants, another of his neighbouring farmers in Scotland also being in the running for the tenancy.

At the time of the move to England Jim and Janet had a daughter Elizabeth, aged thirteen, and a son Jim (junior), aged ten. Jim's sister and brother-in-law decided to accompany him to England with their family including an eight-year-old daughter Elizabeth. Jim's elderly mother-in-law Granny Stevenson was concerned that if she moved to Suffolk then she would be unable to be buried in Scotland. Jim promised however that he would take her body back to Scotland for burial, and he kept his promise after her sudden death later at Framsden.

The decision was taken to move the entire farm livestock, implements, household goods etc. to Suffolk by train. Jim White asked at Doune railway station for an estimate and after an inspection, a price of £500 was quoted for the journey from Doune Station to Stowmarket Station. (Although Westerfield Station was nearer to Framsden, it did not have the unloading facilities required.) The price was to include everything necessary for the move and the railway took care of all the organisation. Transport was arranged for the animals in cattle trucks for the two miles between the farm and Doune Station, also at the other end between Stowmarket Station and Framsden. The furniture and household effects were packed into containers (two for the White family and one for the sister's family) by the removal firm Pickfords on the Friday and Saturday preceding the move, leaving the families only the bare essentials for the weekend. The families were not allowed to pack for themselves as their belongings would not then have been insured.

The move itself took place on Monday, February 29th, 1960. Two weeks before, a rail strike occurred and the local papers ran the headline, "WILL RAIL STRIKE STOP A FARM FLITTING?" Fortunately everything was settled before the great day arrived. Three or four local farmers helped load the train. Flat wagons had been left in a siding at Doune Station ready for loading at the farmer's leisure, and tractor, trailers, binder, muck spreader, ploughs, and family car, were chained down on these. The cows were milked at lunch time instead of the usual time of 4.00 pm and then taken to the station. Fifty head of livestock were to make the journey, six to eight cows travelling in a cattle truck. Yearlings were placed in one wagon, two-year olds in another. No horses or sheep were transported but a bull travelled in a special pen and two dogs, a collie and a retriever, were tied up in the guard's van. The loaded train left Doune Station in the late afternoon, the families well stocked with sandwiches and thermos flasks for the long journey through the night.

A short half-hour stop was made just south of Edinburgh, then the train was given a clear road through to March with no stops apart from those required for crew or locomotive changes. On arrival at March, farmer White was asked if he wanted to give the animals any water to drink. At 9.00 am the next morning the train arrived at Stowmarket Station, to be greeted by TV cameras and presenter Dick Joyce. The unusual event was a feature on the local six o'clock news that evening.

Taxis were laid on to take the families from Stowmarket to Framsden where the farmhouse was warm with fires already lit. Cattle lorries, hired from Hatchers of Framlingham, were waiting to take the cattle to the farm, and the containers were brought to the front door of the house and unpacked by Pickfords. When Jim White returned to the station from Framsden he found the railway staff had already unloaded his car from the train, and one of the dogs had been freed from the guard's van. The railwaymen told him they were afraid to approach the second dog, but Jim laughed and informed them that they had let loose the wrong dog; the other dog was the docile one in spite of its manner!

Several trips were made between the farm and the station that day with only one mishap, when Jim White lost his way and finished up at Cretingham. The young man who had been managing the farm before Jim took over the tenancy, agreed to fetch the tractor from the

*Newspaper report of the move, and photograph of the loading of fifty pedigree Ayrshires. (Stirk is an ancient name for yearling cattle.)*
(Courtesy White Family Collection)

station later in the day but then had second thoughts saying he was unsure of the route. Although he possessed a motor bike he had never been to Stowmarket (just fifteen miles away) preferring to visit the town of Ipswich for shopping or a night out.

Jim White brought with him on the train enough animal feed to last for a day or two. Many commercial travellers turned up at the farm during the next few weeks however, hopeful of obtaining contracts to supply Jim's agricultural needs.

Everything therefore went well throughout the journey, thanks to the forethought and organisation put into the task by the railway. The children soon settled in at the local school and Janet (Nettie) was kept so busy that she had no time to worry about the rights and wrongs of making the move from Scotland. It was she who milked all the cows at the farm using a milking machine.

Jim White stayed at Red House Farm until his retirement in October 1986, just short of his sixty-fifth birthday. He still has his Scottish accent, although many Suffolk words creep into his conversation especially when he is discussing farming.

## ENGINES, TRAINS, EXCURSIONS & EVENTS

*The late afternoon departure of special train No. 434 from Doune in Perthshire, to Stowmarket, Suffolk. Ex-LMS Stanier "Black Five" 4-6-0 pictured ready to haul the train to Edinburgh. Doune was on the Dunblane to Oban branch of the Caledonian Railway, eight miles north of Stirling. The branch opened in 1880. In September 1965, however, the line between Dunblane and Crianlarich, where it passed beneath, and connected with, the North British line to Fort William, was closed because of landslides. These occurred less than two months before the line was due to shut in any case, closure notices having already been posted.* (Photo courtesy White Family Collection)

*The local newspaper evidently enjoyed the occasion, providing a cartoon version of events.*
(Courtesy White Family Collection)

# The Breakdown Train

THE breakdown train, only seen in abnormal circumstances, was kept at the Ipswich Loco Depot where it was always stocked and provisioned ready for use at short notice. It consisted of a breakdown crane and vans that were specially adapted to carry stores and workshop equipment. A further van provided accommodation for the staff.

On board the train were hydraulic jacks, acetylene cutting gear, wire hawsers, timber for packing and skids for use in sliding vehicles back on to the rails after a derailment. The riding van for the men carried a supply of tinned foods and vegetables, and blankets in which to sleep on the occasions when long hours were worked. Ladders and steps, for use in a disaster, were also to hand. Specially selected and trained men, who normally worked in the fitting shops, would man the train. In charge of the train crew in the 1950s was Stan Stiff. Upon receiving news of a mishap or derailment, the men were expected to leave their normal activities immediately and man the train in readiness for departure. In the meantime a locomotive, with driver, fireman and guard, would be hastily arranged.

The nature and location of the accident would be known before leaving the depot and if only a minor mishap had occurred, which did not affect the main line, the urgency was not so great. If a main line blockage was involved however, then the utmost speed was required; the train would be given top priority to reach the scene of the problem and it would display an express passenger headcode of one disc or lamp above each buffer. The breakdown train not going to clear the main line would run as a slow passenger with one disc or lamp at the top of the smokebox. It would be given no particular preference, running between normal booked passenger trains.

Most derailments and collisions occurred in shunting yards and depots, and were of a comparatively minor nature, although they could often give a breakdown crew a few headaches. A simple straightforward derailment would normally be dealt with by the use of timber packing and hydraulic jacks.

Occasionally however a mishap would occur which blocked either one or both main lines and this would create many additional problems coupled with the need to restore normal working as soon as possible. Very often the services of a crane would be required, and in cases where the Ipswich crane was not powerful enough, a larger crane from Stratford or Cambridge would be brought in.

The breakdown train was essential for the smooth running of the extensive yards, depots and sidings throughout the region. Frequent mishaps occurred, these often resulting in the anguished cry, "Call out the breakdown!".

*Gathered round the breakdown crane at Ipswich, from left: crane driver Cyril Hayward, engine driver Frank Gill and Stan Stiff with Cyril giving an action replay of a goal from the previous day's football match.* (Photo by Kenneth Leighton)

## ENGINES, TRAINS, EXCURSIONS & EVENTS

*The steam breakdown crane (above) at Ipswich Loco Depot, 1966. Built at Stratford Works in 1910, legend has it that during the First World War the crane was sent to France where it received a small shell hole that was never repaired.*

*At the rear of the crane is the new carriage heating vehicle containing two oil-fired boilers for providing steam heating for carriages standing overnight in the station sidings. (Empty coaching stock was preheated ready for the diesel locomotive to take the train out.) This operation became necessary after the withdrawal of nearly all steam engines except for about sixteen retained for use specially for steam heating purposes around the Eastern Region. The last of these steam engines at Ipswich is seen in the photo below. Former B1 4-6-0 engine No. 61059, with couplings removed, became Departmental No. 17 in 1963 specifically for use in train heating. The engine was sent for scrap shortly after the photograph was taken in April 1966, more than six years after steam had officially disappeared from Ipswich. To the left of the engine is the sand hopper, used for filling sand boxes on steam engines. When wheel slip occurred in bad rail conditions, especially in autumn with leaves on the line, the driver would operate the steam-sanding gear to sprinkle sand on the rails in order to obtain better wheel adhesion. This method could not be used with diesel locomotives however, for fear of sand being blown into the traction motors.*

(Photos Richard W. Smith)

# The Daily Papers
## The Newspaper Trains

NEWSPAPER trains, generally referred to as the "Papers" by railwaymen, were special trains of vans hired by the national newspaper proprietors. Each train usually had an unadvertised passenger coach or composite brake attached for the benefit of railwaymen and newspaper men going home or on duty.

Occasionally ordinary fare-paying passengers were carried at the discretion of the guard, such as servicemen or others who had missed their overnight connections with the last train out of Liverpool Street. These paper trains were run at passenger speeds and, like the mail trains, signalmen were not expected to slow or stop them without good reason. Many a poor goods train crew, already running late and struggling to get home, would cringe upon hearing the dreaded words, shouted from some outlying signal box, "Shunt for the Papers!"

At Ipswich station, following the departure of the Up Peterborough Mail at about 2.0 am, there was a two hour lull in the intensive twenty-four hour cycle of work apart from an occasional through goods train until the arrival of the "Papers". The newspaper wholesalers would be waiting to clear the Ipswich vans and take the papers to their warehouse for sorting into bundles for distribution to the newsagents. Stratford men would continue with the main section of the train to Norwich, and Ipswich crews would take the East Suffolk and Bury St Edmunds portions forward. A van had already been detached at Manningtree for the Harwich branch.

Provincial newspapers delivered their publications to Ipswich or Norwich stations and put them aboard the first available passenger train, the guard putting them out at the appropriate station. The continuing improvement in road transport from the 1950s meant that newspaper trains did not have to stop at so many stations and there was no longer any need for early morning goods trains to stop and take bundles of papers to stations on country branches, as may be seen in the accompanying notes.

The legendary "Power of the Press" manifested itself not only in the capital but also in the provinces, as illustrated by the following tale told by Robert Malster concerning a certain Samuel Sleigh, a colourful and robust member of the East Anglian Daily Times staff, which he joined in 1881.

Stranded in deepest Essex when on one of his reporting assignments, Sam Sleigh made his way to the nearest railway station to inquire at what time the 6.15 from Liverpool Street stopped there. Told that it did not stop at that station, Sleigh retorted, "You'd better stop it for me. How do you think I'm going to get back to Ipswich - I am Sleigh of the Anglian!"

Properly impressed, the porter telegraphed Liverpool Street to tell them that Sam Sleigh of the Anglian was requesting that the 6.15 make an unscheduled stop. On that day only, the 6.15 stopped at a minor station somewhere down in Essex. The exact details are not recorded but the incident became a part of journalistic legend in East Anglia and was included in an account of the newspaper's history in the East Anglian Daily Times centenary supplement in 1974.

The drastic changes in the newspaper industry, as the motorways spread their tentacles across the country, eventually spelled the end, in the 1980s, of the largely unseen and unsung "Paper Trains".

**Below are details from some GOODS working timetable notes of the 1940s. Comparison of these with the page opposite, shows how growth in road transport affected the workings of Paper Trains in the 1960s.**

| | |
|---|---|
| 3.30 am | Ipswich to Colchester to call at Ipswich Station and pick up newspapers for the Manningtree and Harwich branch. |
| 4.18 am | Colchester to Whitemoor (via Sudbury, Lavenham and Bury) to pick up at Marks Tey the Sudbury newspaper van ex-3.20 am Liverpool Street for forward working on the 6.35 Sudbury-Cambridge passenger train. Papers for Chappel and the Colne Valley line from the 3.20 am ex-Liverpool Street to be transferred to the Brake. To call at Bures and Long Melford to put out papers. |
| 4.40 am | Manningtree to Harwich to call at Mistley and Dovercourt Bay to leave papers. |

**WORKING TIMETABLE, 6th March 1967 to 5th May 1968, for NEWSPAPER TRAINS**

**Liverpool Street to Ipswich, Norwich and branches - other paper trains from Liverpool Street worked the Cambridge to Norwich and Southend Victoria lines with limited advertised passenger facilities.**

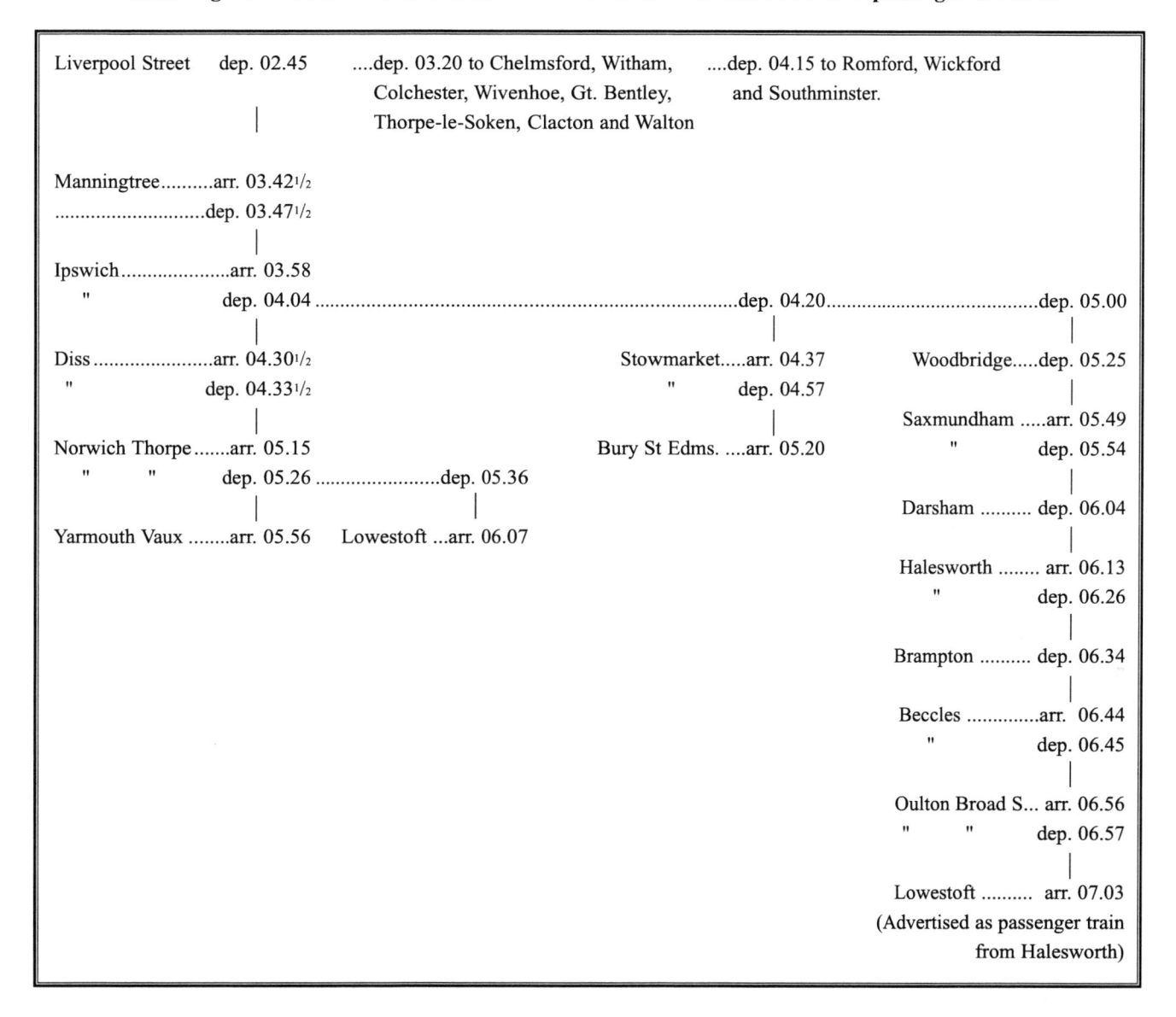

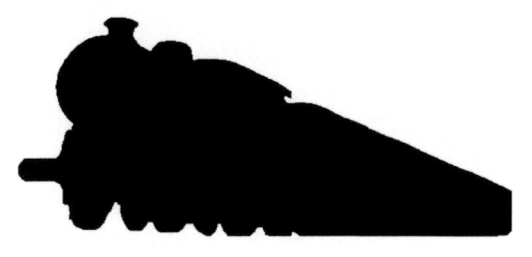

| | | |
|---|---|---|
| Liverpool Street   dep. 02.45 | ....dep. 03.20 to Chelmsford, Witham, Colchester, Wivenhoe, Gt. Bentley, Thorpe-le-Soken, Clacton and Walton | ....dep. 04.15 to Romford, Wickford and Southminster. |

Manningtree..........arr. 03.42½
..........................dep. 03.47½

Ipswich.................arr. 03.58
  "                dep. 04.04 ..................................................dep. 04.20..............................dep. 05.00

Diss......................arr. 04.30½                    Stowmarket.....arr. 04.37          Woodbridge.....dep. 05.25
  "                dep. 04.33½                         "           dep. 04.57
                                                                                            Saxmundham .....arr. 05.49
Norwich Thorpe.......arr. 05.15              Bury St Edms. .....arr. 05.20          "             dep. 05.54
  "     "       dep. 05.26 ...............dep. 05.36
                                                                                            Darsham .......... dep. 06.04
Yarmouth Vaux ........arr. 05.56    Lowestoft ...arr. 06.07
                                                                                            Halesworth ........ arr. 06.13
                                                                                              "             dep. 06.26

                                                                                            Brampton .......... dep. 06.34

                                                                                            Beccles .............arr. 06.44
                                                                                              "             dep. 06.45

                                                                                            Oulton Broad S... arr. 06.56
                                                                                              "    "       dep. 06.57

                                                                                            Lowestoft .......... arr. 07.03
                                                                                            (Advertised as passenger train from Halesworth)

ENGINES, TRAINS, EXCURSIONS & EVENTS

# The Royal Mail

THE regular running of mail carriages, tenders and trains from Ipswich, started in 1858 with the introduction of a mail Sorting Tender which was withdrawn on economic grounds in 1869, but re-introduced in 1872. Bag Tenders arrived at night from Norwich and Lowestoft and were added to the Sorting Tender for travelling to London. Each Tender was in the charge of a "Mail Messenger" with the rank of Postman, who received and delivered sealed bags of letters at stops en-route.

A trip for the Sorting Tender consisted of the "Day Up" and "Night Down" on trains leaving Ipswich at 3.23 pm and returning from Liverpool Street at 8.20 pm. The other trip left at 1.05 am and returned from Liverpool Street at 5.0 am. A stationary carriage at Ipswich was normally placed in the "dock" near Number One platform between 11.0 pm and 1.0 am. It was manned by four clerks to handle cross-post mail, enabling it to connect with the night departure. Parcels were dealt with on the ground floor of the large GPO building across the way in Burrell Road between 9.0 pm and 1.0 am. This facility ended in 1923 with the opening of the new Sorting Office at the Old Cattle Market.

The Ipswich mail train from 3rd March 1929 became the Ipswich Travelling Post Office (TPO), and was extended to Norwich in May 1931. The East Anglian TPO was inaugurated when the Norwich Sorting tender, which had run via Cambridge and Ely and included a section serving Kings Lynn, was diverted through Ipswich on the same date in 1929. The Kings Lynn portion (later discontinued) and, from October 1949, a Peterborough section, were attached and detached at Haughley.

These arrangements for the Up and Down East Anglian TPO remained, except for the war years, with only minor alterations until 1966. After that the dividing and joining of the train took place at Ipswich instead of in the relative remoteness of Haughley as a consequence of tightened security following what became known as the Great Train Robbery, when the Up Special TPO from Aberdeen to Euston was stopped south of Linslade in Buckinghamshire in the early hours of 8th August 1963 and robbed of over 2 million pounds in used bank-notes. Two-way radio was fitted to the TPO vehicles, enabling them to keep in contact with the police forces as the trains crossed county boundaries. An Ipswich police presence was established at Ipswich Station when the TPO was due.

*Allocated to Ipswich for the Royal Mail trains, a 4-2-2 "Bromley Single" No. 609, stands at Croft Street. Designed by Massey Bromley, Great Eastern Locomotive Superintendent 1878-81, No 609 was built in 1882 by William Kitson of Leeds. (Kitson had held the same post of Superintendent earlier in 1865-66.) It was one of a class of twenty express passenger engines which were short-lived, all having been withdrawn by 1893. Note the brazier, beside the water crane, used for preventing the water freezing in cold weather. It was known as a "devil" by railwaymen.*

(Photo courtesy Ken Leighton)

**The Ipswich Sorting Tender**
*(Left to right) Messrs Dawdry, Airey, Kedgley and Moore with the Norwich Mail Messenger demonstrating the apparatus used for dropping and collecting mailbags at speed. The GER coat of arms is emblazoned on the side of the van. A gas jet for heating the wax used for sealing the mailbags was installed inside the sorting tender and the chimney of this can be seen just above Mr Dawdry's head. Below: The interior was fitted out in mahogany, and lit by incandescent gas burners.* (Photos courtesy H. E. Wilton's Collection)

*A Royal Mail van, on contract hire from F. W. Canham, seen on Ipswich railway station forecourt 15th June 1914. Canham's yard was in St Matthews Street, and the firm was well known for the hire of horses and carriages to private patrons, besides carts and vans to commercial users. The large brick building, in the background in Burrell Road, was used by the GPO for sorting parcels and for many years as the Post Office Engineers' stores.* (Photo courtesy Mrs Pat Brown)

The Up Norwich to Liverpool Street TPO's final stop at Ipswich was on 11th May 1990 which was also the last time that the TPOs incorporated passenger coaches and henceforth ran as dedicated postal trains. The Peterborough section was also discontinued from the same date. Mail trains ceased using Liverpool Street Station on the night of Friday 27th September 1996. On Monday 30th, the Royal Mail Depot at Willesden opened for handling London mail trains to and from all parts of the country. This applied to the Ipswich and Norwich mail trains, and from that date one train left Norwich at 19.50, stopping at Ipswich at 20.30 for eleven minutes. The next left Norwich at 21.59 non-stop to Willesden. The return workings departed from Willesden at 23.15, stopped at Ipswich for ten minutes at 01.09 and arrived in Norwich at 02.07. The second down train left Willesden to reach Ipswich at 02.02, Diss at 02.35 and Norwich at 03.05.

**Timetable of the Up Postal Norwich to Liverpool Street March 6th 1967 - May 5th 1968**

| | | |
|---|---|---|
| Dep. | Norwich | 18.40 |
| Arr. | Diss | 19.00 |
| Dep. | " | 19.02 |
| Arr. | Stowmarket | 19.16½ |
| Dep. | " " | 19.19½ |
| Arr. | Ipswich | 19.36 |
| Dep. | " " | 19.43 |
| Arr. | Manningtree | M |
| Dep. | " " | Pass 19.52½ |
| Arr. | Colchester | 20.03 |
| Dep. | " " | 20.06 |
| Arr. | Witham | M |
| Dep. | " " | Pass 20.17½ |
| Arr. | Chelmsford | M |
| Dep. | " " | Pass 20.30 |
| Arr. | Liverpool Street | 21.07 |

**M** *Mails delivered or received at lineside apparatus*

*The Norwich to London Up TPO approaching Ipswich station at 7.45 pm on 25th July 1960. Hauled by British Railways standard 4-6-2 "Britannia" Class locomotive No. 70001,* **Lord Hurcomb.** (Photo by Richard W. Smith)

*Class 86 electric locomotive No. 86238 moves off into the tunnel with the early evening Norwich to London TPO during the last week of the train stopping at Ipswich (11th May 1990). The return Down working however did still call at Ipswich. The long-standing Peterborough Mail, departure time 23.10 (time varied), which attached a later Norwich portion at Ipswich, was also discontinued on the same date.*

(Photo by Richard W. Smith)

*Photograph taken at 00.46 hrs. on Saturday 28th September 1996 on Platform Two at Ipswich Station. It shows the arrival of the first of the two postal trains which that night had departed from Liverpool Street for the final time. The new Royal Mail Terminal at Willesden would come into use the following Monday, 30th September 1996.*

(Photo by William Barton)

## Timetable of the Down Postal, Liverpool Street to Norwich & Peterborough via Ipswich

### June 15th 1964 - June 12th 1965

Dep. Liverpool Street......22.50

Arr. Chelmsford..........23.21
Dep. "    "   ..........23.27

Arr. Witham............23.40½
Dep. "    ............23.41½

Arr. Colchester..........23.58½
Dep. "    ..........00.05

Arr. Ipswich............00.24
Dep. "    ............00.40

Arr. Stowmarket..........00.53½
Dep. "    ..........00.58½

Arr. Haughley Junc......01.03

Dep. Haughley Junc......01.18        Dep. Haughley Junc......01.45
Arr. Bury..............01.36        Arr. Diss..............01.58½
Dep. "  ..............01.42        Dep. "  ..............02.03½

Dep. Fordham...........02.14        Arr. Norwich...........02.26
Arr. Ely...............02.30
Dep. "  ...............02.37

Arr. March.............02.58
Dep. "  .............03.06

Arr. Peterborough East...03.30
Dep. "       "    ...03.45

Arr. Peterborough North..03.50

## Timetable of the Up Postal, Norwich & Peterborough to Liverpool Street via Ipswich

### June 15th 1964 - June 12th 1965

Dep. Peterborough East (SX)....23.00           Dep. Norwich...........23.40

Arr. March.............23.21                    Arr. Tivetshall........23.59
Dep. "  .............23.30                    Dep. "    ............24.00

Arr. Ely...............23.50                    Arr. Diss..............00.07½
Dep. "  ...............00.00                    Dep. "  ..............00.14½

Dep. Fordham...........00.22

Arr. Bury..............00.47
Dep. "  ..............00.58

Arr. Haughley Junc......01.17                   Arr. Haughley Junc......00.36

Dep. Haughley Junc......01.40

Arr. Stowmarket.........01.44
Dep. "    ..........01.47

Arr. Ipswich...........02.01
Dep. "  ...........02.11

Arr. Colchester.........02.30
Dep. "    ..........02.37

Arr. Chelmsford.........03.03
Dep. "    ..........03.09

Arr. Romford...........03.30
Dep. "  ...........03.34

Arr. Liverpool Street....03.55

ENGINES, TRAINS, EXCURSIONS & EVENTS

# *The Hush-Hush*
## Steam Locomotive No, 10000

*The* Hush-Hush *seen emerging from the tunnel on a visit to Ipswich Station, probably in 1932.* (Pryke Family Collection)

DURING the 1930s, several railway exhibitions were held in the region during which newly designed engines and rolling stock were put on display. One such exhibition, held at Ipswich in 1932, included water-tube boilered 4-6-4 engine No. 10000, the *Hush-Hush*. The futuristic looking locomotive was a regular guest at railway exhibitions at this time.

Designed by Nigel Gresley, the engine was completed at Darlington in 1929 after five years of development under conditions of secrecy, hence its nickname. The design met with several problems. The engine was found to be unreliable in traffic and spent much of its time in workshops and store or attending exhibitions. The locomotive was rebuilt in 1937, and lasted until 1959, although the boiler itself was in stationary use at Darlington until 1965.

**RAILWAY EXHIBITION**
AT
**IPSWICH**

IN AID OF
EAST SUFFOLK & IPSWICH HOSPITAL
AND RAILWAYMEN'S CHARITIES

Saturday & Sunday, 30th April & 1st May
9 a.m. to 9 p.m. each day

THE EXHIBITION WILL INCLUDE

Engine No. 10000, 4-Cylinder High Pressure Compound
Flying Scotsman Corridor Pacific Engine 4476 *Royal Lancer*
Enginemen's Instruction Vans containing
working models
Electric Restaurant Car Set   Sleeping Car (First Class)
Pullman Car (First Class)    Sleeping Car (Third Class)
Pullman Car (Third Class)    Milk Tank
70-ton or 110-ton Wagon      Banana Van
Large Steel Containers

ADMISSION: Adults **6d.**   Children **3d.** (Under 16)

Cheap Rail Tickets from certain Stations
For Particulars see handbills at Stations

*Right: Poster for a railway exhibition at Ipswich in 1932. The Hush-Hush is pictured in the top corner.*
(Courtesy Richard Pinkney)

# GNR Engine No. 1

DURING 1938, amid considerable publicity, the LNER introduced two completely new trains for the Flying Scotsman service, and also set about restoring GNR engine No. 1 and refurbishing a train of seven six-wheeled carriages. The idea of a replica train was enthusiastically approved by Sir Nigel Gresley (he was knighted in 1936) who readily authorised the overhaul of the engine at Doncaster.

Engine No. 1 had been built in 1870 for express passenger work to the design of Patrick Stirling, Locomotive Engineer to the GNR from 1866 until his death in 1895 at the age of seventy-five. This engine, first of the "Stirling eight-foot singles" had driving wheels 8ft. 1in. in diameter and a front bogie. Fifty-three such 4-2-2 engines were built, with some minor variations.

The restored train was so popular that it continued to provide excursions until the end of 1938 to various stations in LNER territory, including Ipswich, Cambridge and Norwich.

GNR engine No. 1 was preserved and is on static display in the National Railway Museum at York.

*Right: A close-up of the 8ft. 1in. driving wheel of GNR engine No. 1.* (Photo courtesy Richard Pinkney)

*GNR engine No. 1 is seen here standing at No. 2 platform at Ipswich Station in October 1938.* (Photo courtesy Richard Pinkney)

## Some "Sandringham" Class Locomotives

MANY B17 "Sandringham" class 4-6-0 steam engines were named after famous castles, halls and stately homes located within LNER territory. Others took the names of regiments, for instance *Lincolnshire Regiment* No. 2805 (later renumbered 61605) and *The Suffolk Regiment* No. 2845 (renumbered 61645).

This latter engine, although originally intended to bear the name *Gilwell Park*, was ceremoniously named by the Colonel of the Suffolk Regiment, Major-General Sir John Ponsonby in honour of the Regiment's 250th anniversary. The event took place on Saturday, 22nd June 1935, at the Hadleigh Road "Show Ground Station" (later to become the Permanent Way Depot) at Ipswich.

The Regiment was represented by many ex-soldiers, serving members and officers. Members of the public present included Lord Woodbridge, High Steward of Ipswich; Sir John Ganzoni, MP for Ipswich and the Mayor and Aldermen of the Town. LNER officials attending included Mr William Whitelaw, Chairman of the Company and Mr H. N. Gresley, Chief Mechanical Engineer.

Mr Whitelaw expressed the hope that the sight of the locomotive travelling through the County would help to inspire the same ideals as were represented in the great traditions of the regiment whose name it bore. Sir John Ponsonby, with an appropriate speech, unveiled the nameplate of the engine, and followed it with an inspection of the locomotive.

The engine was then used to haul a special train to Bury St Edmunds, the home of the Suffolk Regiment. The driver on this occasion was Ernest Nathan Brown, aged forty-six, who had served in the 4th Battalion of the Suffolk Regiment during the First World War. The fireman was William Harry Mutimer, aged thirty-nine, who had fought in the 2nd and 7th Battalions of the Regiment at that terrible time.

At Bury, on behalf of the Regiment, Sir John Ponsonby placed plaques bearing the regimental badge on the locomotive. He later presented souvenirs to Driver Brown and Fireman Mutimer.

Several "Sandringham" class locomotives were given the names of prominent English football teams. On these B17s, a brass replica football was displayed under the nameplate on the driving wheel splasher each side of the engine. The locomotives were referred to as the "Footballers", and mention is made elsewhere in the book regarding their use on the North Country Continental. A little tale has come to light involving one of these engines, *Leicester City*; a steamy romance, you might say, in fact.

Clifford Emmerson was a locomotive fireman at

*"Sandringham" class Engine No. 2845* Suffolk Regiment *pictured at the naming ceremony at Hadleigh Road, Ipswich.*
(Photo courtesy Richard Pinkney)

Yarmouth Southtown in the early nineteen-forties to the mid-fifties. For about five years he worked the Yarmouth to Liverpool Street express trains using B17 "Footballers" and B12s.

Living near the railway embankment in Thompson Road, Ipswich at this time was a young lady who moved there with her father after being bombed out during the War. Maureen Cole often waved to the trains as they sped past her window and soon it became a regular occurrence for Clifford to give a toot on the engine whistle and wave back, in spite of the neighbours' complaints about the noise. One day Maureen was able to talk to Clifford when she saw him and his engine while she was cycling in Gippeswyk Park alongside the railway. The next day at teatime, when Clifford and his driver ran into Ipswich Station from London, there was Maureen waiting at the end of the platform with a bottle of Cobbold beer.

From then onwards Clifford's driver, Joe Taylor, would always give the brass football, on their engine No. 61665 *Leicester City*, a special polish while they were waiting at Woodbridge Station during the trip to Liverpool Street. Later, Maureen would be asked if the football was gleaming bright enough as the express sped past her home at Thompson Road. The romance blossomed, and Maureen and Clifford Emmerson have now been happily married for many years.

*Above: Clifford Emmerson (right) with his driver, Joe Taylor, pictured at Woodbridge.*

(Photo courtesy C. Emmerson)

*Below: "Footballer" engine No. 61649* Sheffield United. *The brass replica football can clearly be seen under the nameplate. On the framing are (left to right): A. Maskell (fitter's mate), C. Rudland (fitter), G. Elliston (fitter), E. Waldridge (fitter), I. Fletton (apprentice fitter), R. Goodchild (fitter's mate), R. Clarke (fitter's mate).*

(Photo courtesy Ivan Fletton)

## The Royal Show Comes to Ipswich

IN 1934 Ipswich had the great honour to host the 93rd Royal Show of England, held from Tuesday July 3rd to Saturday July 7th on land now occupied by part of the Chantry Estate. The Show was described at the time as being the most comprehensive exhibition of its kind in the world.

On display were more than sixty different pedigree breeds of horses, cattle, sheep and pigs, besides goats and poultry. Agricultural machinery and implements were exhibited, and daily parades took place in the Grand Ring. The services of more than one hundred judges were necessary to make the awards. The Flower Show, held at the same time, was hailed as standing next in importance to the great Chelsea Flower Show.

The so-called Show Ground Station near Hadleigh Road, Ipswich (where the naming ceremony for *The Suffolk Regiment* locomotive would take place a year later in 1935) was specially constructed by the LNER for the purpose of unloading stock and implements bound for the Royal Show site just a few hundred yards away.

The material removed during the construction of the unloading station was conveyed by train to Parkeston where it was used in the building of Parkeston Quay West. Unfortunately some of the earth shifted included that belonging to allotments cultivated by railwaymen on the top of the former embankment.

The souvenir of the Royal Show, issued by the Ipswich Industrial Development Association with official backing, proudly proclaimed Ipswich to be the industrial capital of East Anglia and announced that:

*"a good service of restaurant car trains is available, while from early morn to late in the evening, breakfast, tea and dinner trains run between London and Ipswich from Liverpool Street, where there is the Company's admirably managed hotel [The Great Eastern]. Here it is possible to stay at night and spend whole days in Ipswich with an evening available for London entertainments."*

Continental visitors were not forgotten. The LNER's steamship services were available from the Hook of Holland, Antwerp and Zeebrugge.

*"The Company's well-equipped miniature "liners," the acme of comfort, and excellent as regards catering, afford an opportunity to visitors of spending a long day in the Show from early morning to late in the evening and by using the night service either way to be away from home for only a day. There is no doubt these services will commend themselves to intending visitors from the Netherlands, Belgium and beyond."*

The LNER arranged reduced fare facilities from Antwerp or Zeebrugge through to Ipswich and back. Available also was the Zeeland Shipping Company's day service from Flushing to Harwich, again with special fares obtainable. The service from Denmark, from Esbjerg to Harwich, provided a means of getting to Ipswich for Danish agriculturists, whose interest in British agriculture and its livestock shows was, according to the souvenir, "by no means remote."

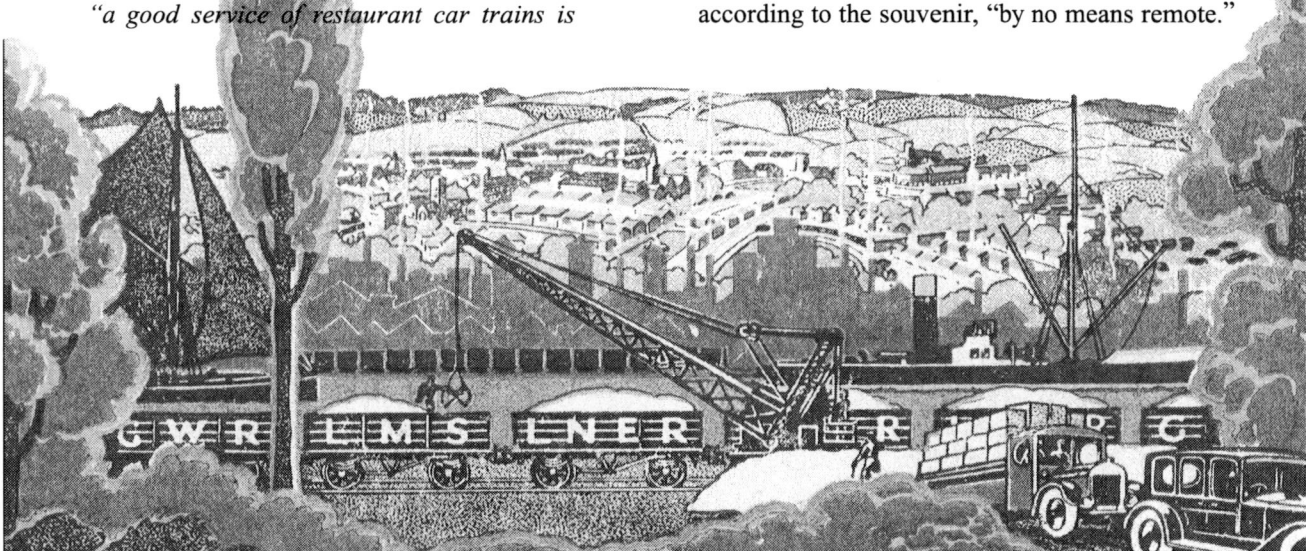

*Geo. Westrip's design for the back cover of the official souvenir of the Royal Show, 1934.* (Pryke Family Collection)

# *EUR Centenary Exhibition*

IN 1946, on June 14th, 15th and 16th, an exhibition was held at Ipswich to celebrate the centenary of the opening of the Eastern Union Railway between Ipswich and Colchester.

The event was held on land between the Hadleigh Road and London Road bridges, where previously, in 1935, the naming ceremony for *The Suffolk Regiment* had taken place. The land later became the Permanent Way Depot.

Only twelve vehicles were on display, due to lack of space and the fact that the Second World War had finished only the previous year. The exhibition souvenir stated however that it was hoped those exhibits which were available would be of interest and give some idea of the progress made in the LNER region during the past one hundred years.

## EXHIBITS

**First-class coach** built in 1851 by the Eastern Counties Railway, and typical of the period.

**Steel-panelled corridor coach** containing three third-class compartments with seating accommodation for eighteen passengers and a brake van to carry three tons. Ten of these coaches had been built at York that year for the LNER main line service.

**Steel-panelled corridor coach** containing six first-class compartments. Eleven coaches of this type had been built at York that year, for LNER main line service.

**Signalling instructional van** used for the training of signal and telegraph staff.

**Museum coach** containing replicas of old illustrations, old railway timetables, coats of arms, a six-foot model of a Great Eastern Railway locomotive, and other illustrated material.

**Road/rail demountable milk tank** used for express conveyance of milk from the country to London and large provincial towns. Tank hygienically lined with highly polished stainless steel. Milk cooled down to between 36°-38° Fahrenheit before dispatch, and insulated tank held milk to within a degree or so of that temperature during transit. Tank had capacity of 2,000 gallons, and was cleaned and sterilised between each journey.

**Modern fruit van** fitted with louvre ventilators at each end and torpedo air-extractors in the roof. Vacuum braked. Used for fruit during fruit season and general merchandise during remainder of year.

**Diesel-electric shunting locomotive No. 8000.** Four of these locomotives had been built by the LNER and were in use on shunting duties in big marshalling yards.

**Mixed Traffic Steam Tank Locomotive No. 9000.** First locomotive to be completed under the LNER Five Year Plan for 1,000 new engines. Designed for hauling passenger, goods or coal trains.

**Mixed Traffic Steam Locomotive No. 1003.** 400 of the 1,000 new LNER locomotives built during the following five years would be of this type, known as the "Antelope" Class; officially Class B1.

**Mechanical Horse and Trailer.** Three wheeled articulated unit and semi-trailer. This type of vehicle, of which the LNER had 2,000, was primarily produced as an alternative to horse cartage. It embodied all the advantages of interchangeability of the live horse with any number of horse-drawn vehicles, and extraordinary manoeuvrability with the motor's speed instead of that of the horse.

**Express Parcels Collection and Delivery Van**, typical of over 500 in service with the LNER at the time.

ENGINES, TRAINS, EXCURSIONS & EVENTS

# *EUR 150th Anniversary*

*Three steam engines on display at the former Croft Street Motive Power Depot, 15th and 16th June 1996. Left to right: 0-6-2T No. 7999 from the East Anglian Railway Museum at Chappel, 2-4-0 "Intermediate" Class ex-Great Eastern No. 490 from Bressingham Steam Museum, 4-6-0 B12 No. 8572 from the North Norfolk Railway. Modern diesel locomotives and rolling stock were also on display, together with trade stands, refreshment stalls etc.. A free bus link operated to Ipswich Railway Station and local car parks.* (Photo by Jill Freestone)

*4-6-2 No. 70000 Britannia at Ipswich Station during the weekend celebrations. The steam engine hauled special passenger trains to and from Bury St Edmunds.*
(Photo by Russell Whymark)

To celebrate the 150th anniversary of the coming to Ipswich of the Eastern Union Railway

**The Railway Correspondence & Travel Society**
*and*
**The Over Stoke History Group**

present a

RAILWAY
**Exhibition**

A tribute to the generations of local men employed on the Railway during the last 150 years

**Ipswich Museum**
**High Street**

**Tuesday 2nd April - Saturday 1st June**

**Open 10am to 5pm Tuesday to Saturday**
**(excluding Good Friday)**

*Poster advertising an exhibition, linked to the EUR 150 celebrations, at Ipswich Museum. (The opening day of the exhibition coincided with the abolishment of admission charges at the Museum.) It was involvement in this exhibition which inspired the editors to compile this book.* (Poster by Jill Freestone and David Barton)

## ENGINES, TRAINS, EXCURSIONS & EVENTS

*The Mayor of Ipswich, Councillor Philip Smart, waving away a London-bound train at Ipswich on 11th June 1996 at 10.46 am, which was almost the time that the first train had left Ipswich for London exactly 150 years previously. The oil lamp, held by the Mayor, was issued to Robert Taylor, Foreman of Engines at Ipswich, who drove the leading locomotive of that first train.*

(Photo by Jill Freestone)

*The old method and the new - a modern track maintenance machine on display at the Loco Depot at Croft Street during the weekend celebrations and inset, a group of platelayers at Ipswich in the late 1920s.*

(Photos courtesy Joy Clements and Russell Whymark)

# *Accidents*

## Causes and Effects

RAILWAYS in East Anglia have been relatively free of major accidents associated with great loss of life but during the earlier days of railway construction, lives were lost in the primitive conditions which were all too prevalent in civil engineering of the time.

Ten men were killed during the construction of the Eastern Union Railway's line between Colchester and Ipswich alone, and many more were seriously injured. A tombstone in the south porch of Ely Cathedral in memory of two men, William Pickering aged thirty years and Richard Edger aged twenty-four, who died on 24th December 1845 in a railway accident near Thetford, bears witness to what was happening throughout the country as earthworks collapsed, and moving trains and wagons inflicted their toll. The verse, entitled "The Spiritual Railway", inscribed on the Ely memorial, reflected the awesome impact which railways and the coming of steam engines were having.

> *"The Line to heaven by Christ was made*
> *With Heavenly truth the Rails are laid*
> *From Earth to Heaven the Line extends*
> *To Life Eternal where it ends*
> *Repentance is the Station then*
> *Where Passengers are taken in.*
> *No Fees for them is there to pay*
> *For Jesus is himself the way*
> *God's Word is the first Engineer*
> *It points the way to Heaven so dear.*
> *Through tunnels dark and dreary here*
> *It does the way to Glory steer.*
> *God's Love the Fire, His Truth the Steam,*
> *Which drives the Engine and the Train,*
> *All you who would to Glory ride,*
> *Must come to Christ, in him abide*
> *In First and Second, and Third Class,*
> *Repentance, Faith and Holiness,*
> *You must the way to Glory gain*
> *Or you with Christ will not remain.*
> *Come then poor Sinners, now's the time*
> *At any Station on the Line.*
> *If you'll repent and turn from sin*
> *The Train will stop and take you in."*

During the early days of train operation four wheeled 0-4-0 or 2-2-0 locomotives, weighing only ten or eleven tons, were usual and achieved a reputation for very unsteady running. In little more than the year taken to open the line from Shoreditch to Brentwood, two engines had come off the track killing both drivers and firemen. The second, which derailed going down Brentwood Bank, also killed a passenger and a Government enquiry was set up to examine the technical arguments over the suitability of four wheeled engines. The Eastern Counties Railway was still ordering similar locos in 1842 but by 1845 2-2-2s were in service, which in reality meant locomotives were being built with three axles. The wheel arrangements varied from 2-2-2 to 2-4-0 and 4-2-0 and in 1846 six-coupled 0-6-0 engines appeared, all requiring longer frames and boilers thus enhancing their stability at speed.

On September 1st 1905, a near 70 mph derailment occurred at Witham when all fourteen coaches of a Down express from Liverpool Street to Cromer left the rails after a permanent way gang had loosened a fastening in a cross-over which they had not had time to make good. Five coaches demolished the porters' and ticket collectors' rooms on the down island platform, killing a porter. One first class coach caught fire due to escaping gas and another turned over and broke up, eight passengers being killed.

The consequences of many accidents were made far worse by outbreaks of fire caused by the introduction of gas lighting in carriages. Such occurred twice on the Settle and Carlisle railway; a collision at Hawes Junction on Christmas Eve 1910 when nine passengers died, and another at Ais Gill in 1913 where a further fourteen were killed and thirty-eight injured. Igniting gas caused many more deaths than would have been the case. In May 1915, Quintinshill, ten miles north of Carlisle, was the scene of the worst disaster in British railway history when five trains including a troop train were involved. In two of the trains ten passengers were killed but on the troop train at least 215 men died and another 191 were injured. The gas, ignited from the locomotive, caused a fire which burned for a day and a night. The wooden carriages telescoped one into another. The investigating officer urged abolition of gas lighting and pressed for steel construction of rolling stock. Only seven months later a triple crash at St. Bedes near Jarrow resulted in fire with eighteen dead and a further eighty-one injured.

As a result of these terrible accidents, all within the space of ten years, the Inspectors called for gas lighting to be abolished, the adoption of track circuiting (invented in the USA in 1872 and used there during the following thirty years but not in Britain), and the use of steel coaches which eventually came about several

# The train now standing in Croft-street

THERE was quite a fuss when a train stopped in Croft-street, Ipswich, yesterday. But that's not surprising because it arrived via a brick wall, a telegraph pole and a fence. One minute all was peaceful in the little row of terrace houses, then there it was . . . diesel shunter No. D8221, parked a few feet from the front doors. Before long a crowd of railwaymen from the loco depot on the other side of the fence had come to see where there engine got to after it crashed through a set of buffers. No one was hurt.

*The scene at Croft Street, Ipswich, in November 1963, after a Paxman diesel locomotive from the Depot had crashed through the buffer stops and into the street. This was not the first time that such an incident had occurred. A steam engine had ended up in almost the same situation early one morning during the 1950s when it burst through the fence, the sound of the crash rudely awakening the inhabitants of the nearby houses.* (Courtesy Evening Star)

decades later along with improved couplings to prevent telescoping. Electricity had already been introduced on the railways to create inter-locking signals with lever frame and block instruments, but human error still prevailed.

On New Year's Day 1915, the driver of a morning train from Clacton to Liverpool Street approaching Ilford failed to see the distant and home signals set at danger. A train from Gidea Park to London was crossing from the slow to the through line ahead of the express. The Clacton train hit the other on the cross-over, seriously damaging six carriages. Ten passengers were killed and about 500 were injured to some degree. In this case the Inspector recommended additional warning if a driver misses a distant signal. The distant signal assumed even more significance where high-speed running was normal.

The London and North Eastern Railway announced in 1924 new coaches with electric lighting and cooking facilities to reduce the risk of fire. In 1927, exterior steel panelling appeared but all-steel coaches were not commonplace in ex-LNER areas until after nationalisation. A kitchen car with an anthracite range but retaining electric grills was introduced in 1937 and became standard LNER equipment because of the load on the carriage dynamos and lack of battery charging points in some carriage sidings.

An example of another type of frequent accident, caused by one train running into vehicles derailed from the adjacent track, occurred at Shenfield in 1964. On 10th February the 11.50 pm Liverpool Street to Ipswich passenger train collided with a derailed goods train at

## ACCIDENTS

*Two breakdown cranes, from March and London, in action on the main line at Bentley (between Ipswich and Manningtree) on July 31st 1971. Both lines were blocked when a freight train ran into the back of another that was stationary at the time. One locomotive was flung off the track and several trucks were derailed. Fortunately no one was injured although the Ipswich driver (Harry Whitman) and the guard of the following train were taken to hospital and treated for shock. The two trains involved were the 1.00 am Colchester to Whitemoor carrying empty coal wagons, and a train of empty oil tanks going to North Walsham. The crash caused a delay in the distribution of national newspapers in Ipswich.*
(Photo by Tony Ray, courtesy Evening Star)

Shenfield. A signalman heard the noise of the wagons coming off the track and set the signals to danger for the passenger train which was then passing. By then the driver had seen the wreckage strewn in front of his train and braked hard but could not stop in time. Six trucks had come off the rails, some carrying Birds Eye containers holding frozen poultry. Another held a £5,000 consignment of cash from the Gt. Yarmouth branch of the Midland Bank for their City of London Bank. Poultry and cash covered the track but most if not all the coins were recovered and locked in the Shenfield Stationmaster's office. The police had been waiting at Spitalfields to guard the money on arrival there.

The cab of the diesel engine hauling the passenger train was severely damaged and driver Charles Talbot of Ipswich was trapped for some time and received injuries to his arm but was allowed home after treatment at Harold Wood Hospital. His secondman Peter Mulley, also from Ipswich, was badly shaken but not seriously hurt. The main up and down lines were badly damaged and blocked for about thirty-six hours.

Locomotive boiler explosions fortunately became a rare event after bad experiences in the early years of steam engines led to better engineering and more reliable safeguards. Things improved after 1870 when the Board of Trade insisted on more frequent and thorough boiler inspections. Hydraulic tests of 100 lb p.s.i. in excess of normal boiler pressure became the rule. The manufacture of boilers benefited by the development and use of rolled steel sheets, a great improvement on the wrought iron plates previously used by the boilermakers.

As boilers became safer it was the construction and maintenance of safety valves, boiler water gauges and sight-glasses that deserved more attention. Human error and a degree of carelessness in design and subsequent use still caused horrific accidents, similar to the Westerfield explosion in 1900, described in detail later. The LNER was free of this type of accident with its own locomotives and maintained a good record from the Company's inception to the end of steam working. During the war however, some USA built 2-8-0 engines worked on the LNER, including Ipswich. There were problems with reading and testing the water gauges. The spindles on the three water gauge test cocks could prove difficult to turn giving the impression they were open as required, and there were no diagonal black stripes backing the single sight-glass, customary on the LNER, making it very difficult to establish exactly where the water level was, especially in the dark.

This was the situation that contributed to three explosions due to low water levels in the boilers of the American locomotives. One of these incidents happened to the engine of an Ipswich to Whitemoor goods train at Thurston on 12th January 1944 at 12.40 am. A severe explosion on USA engine No. 2363 forced the firebox crown sheet down three feet and blew the firebox door off, striking and seriously injuring the driver. The fireman survived but was blown off the engine suffering considerable bruising and burns. The cause was a combination of problems mentioned above. Driver W. Nicholls, in hospital afterwards for several months, was held to blame because not enough care was taken in checking the water level in the boiler. This was undoubtedly justified, but if the equipment provided had acknowledged problems, then how much more difficult it must have been coping with them on a dark January night with the noise and motion of the moving train. Without anyone at the controls the train passed through Thurston station and rolled to a standstill on an incline beyond, literally having run out of steam.

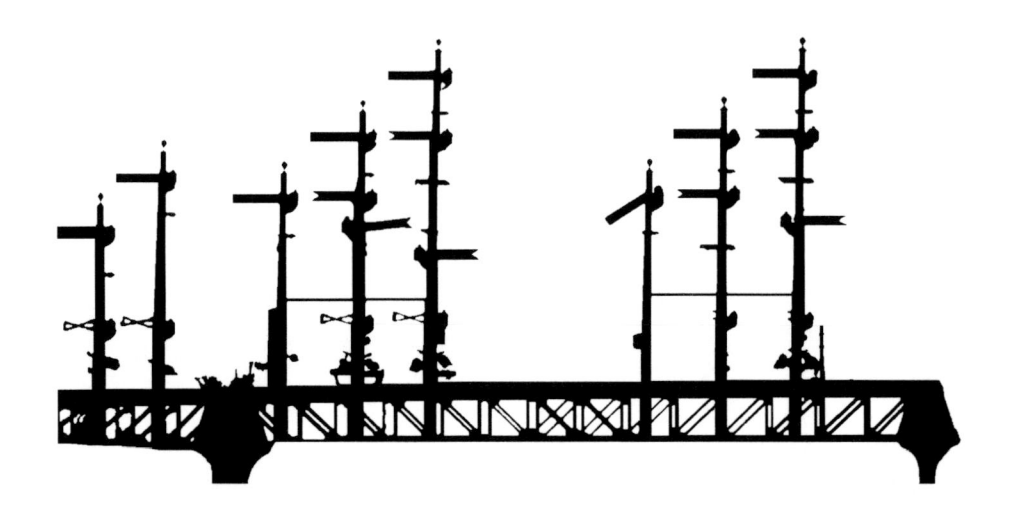

## The Westerfield Explosion
### 25th September 1900

ON September 25th 1900, at 8.45 am, a goods train from Ipswich to Felixstowe stopped at the Westerfield down home signal just on the Ipswich side of the level crossing. The locomotive No. 522, GER class Y14 (later LNER class J15) had been completed at Stratford Works in September 1899.

Shortly after stopping, the engine was torn apart by a violent explosion which threw the boiler 40 yards forwards, over the public road, to bounce back on the track and end up on the down platform. The driver, John Barnard aged sixty-six, and his fireman, William MacDonald aged thirty-four, both of Ipswich, were killed.

The engine had been in service at Ipswich for a year and there had been forty-one reports of leaks at the firebox stay ends and serious damage was found to the firebox one month prior to the accident. After the accident it was found that the left hand side of the firebox had collapsed. The weakened ends of the stays, which were of bronze (this alloy apparently being used experimentally instead of copper), caused problems as the firebox expanded, hence the reported leaks. And because the engine was still relatively new, repairs were made to rectify the leaks only, without consideration of more serious and sinister damage taking place.

The official report largely blamed the boiler foreman at Ipswich but this could possibly be regarded as unfair because no instructions on the maintenance or inspection of the new bronze stays had been issued by Mr J. Holden, the GER Locomotive Superintendent, whose invention they were.

*The headstones in Ipswich Cemetery at the graves of Driver John Barnard and Fireman William Macdonald, both killed in the Westerfield boiler explosion. John Barnard's son William was later fatally injured when the Norfolk Coast Express that he was driving, collided with a light engine at Colchester in 1913.* (Photos by Richard W. Smith)

# ACCIDENTS

*GER Y14 locomotive No. 522 standing on the Ipswich side of Westerfield level crossing following the explosion.*
(Photo courtesy K. G. Leighton Collection)

*The boiler, having come to rest on the down platform 40 yards further on.*
(Photo courtesy K. G. Leighton Collection)

*The scene at Westerfield level crossing after the explosion.*
(Photo courtesy Kelvin Higgins Collection)

## Accident to The Cromer Express
Colchester, 12th July 1913

AT 2.58 pm, on a perfect summer Saturday afternoon, the 1.00 pm express from Cromer to Liverpool Street collided with a light engine at the London end of the Colchester Up platform. This engine, a 2-4-0 'Intermediate' No. 471, had been waiting on the main line for ten minutes to reverse via a cross-over to the Down line which was occupied by another train.

Unfortunately, by the time the line was clear the signalman had forgotten the waiting locomotive despite the fact that it was in full view from the signal box only fifty yards away. He accepted the Cromer train and lowered the signals protecting the light engine. The curve of the line through the station restricted the view ahead from an approaching Up train and the express driver only saw the obstruction when he was half way through the station and travelling at the 40 mph limit imposed there. He instantly closed the regulator and applied the brakes.

The driver of the light engine, realising what had happened, sent his fireman to the signal box, released the brakes and applied steam to reduce the inevitable impact but the engine was pushed 283 yards along the track, the driver receiving serious injuries.

The engine of the express, 4-6-0 No. 1506, remained on the track for another 145 yards before turning over and ending up lying across the Down line. The driver William Barnard and fireman Sidney Keeble, both of Ipswich Shed, and the guard travelling in the leading van, were killed.

The shock and distress experienced by the railway community of Stoke is reflected in the obituary notice published in the parish magazine of St Mary-at-Stoke Church at that dreadful time:

*"A sudden gloom fell upon Stoke when the news arrived that in a railway collision, near Colchester, two of the three killed were our own parishioners, Driver William Harry Barnard and Fireman Sydney Keeble. The mother of the latter, who lives at Bramford, seemed to hear her son calling her in her sleep, at the very time of the accident. How mysterious are these cords of sympathy, these wireless messages from mind to mind and heart to heart. There are bonds invisible, but none the less real.*

*There is no place where earth's sorrows*
*Are more felt than up in Heaven.*

*The Father pities his children. The sorrowful sighing of the desolate, the cry of the oppressed and the tempted - these find an echo in the Human Heart of Him who bears our griefs and carries our sorrows. His alone is our refuge and strength, and into His keeping we commit the souls of those so suddenly called away."*

# ACCIDENTS

*The aftermath of the crash.* (Photo courtesy Pat Ling)

*Fireman Sidney Keeble's funeral procession at Ipswich, seen here about to move off along Wherstead Road, near to its junction with Rapier Street.* (Photo courtesy Robert Malster)

# ACCIDENTS

*The grave of Driver William Barnard (left) in Ipswich Cemetery, and that of Fireman Sidney Keeble (right) in Bramford Churchyard. The guard killed in the collision, George Henry Burdett, was buried in the Rosary Cemetery at Norwich.*

(Photos by Richard W. Smith)

## The Witham Collision
### 7th March 1950

MARCH 7th, 1950, is indelibly marked in the history of Ipswich Loco. This was when the 11.00 pm Up mail and passenger train from Peterborough to Liverpool Street overran signals and collided with the rear of the 7.45 pm goods train from Whitemoor to Witham in fog near Witham at eleven minutes past three in the early morning.

The mail train engine was Class B1 4-6-0 No. 61057. Its train comprised one 4-wheeled van and nine bogie vehicles weighing about 425 tons. The driver and fireman, both from Ipswich, relieved their colleagues at Ipswich Station, leaving late owing partly to misty conditions encountered on the way from Peterborough. By the time the train left Colchester it was running twenty minutes late.

The goods train involved was composed of 34 loaded wagons plus a 20 ton brake-van and was hauled by a 2-8-0 locomotive.

The engine of the express struck the goods brake-van, veered to the left and came to rest in soft ground beside the track 100 yards beyond the point of impact. The brake-van underframe was found between the engine and its tender. The next seven wagons were destroyed and another fourteen badly damaged. The first van of the mail train was wrecked but the buckeye couplings held and no other coaches overturned or telescoped.

The goods guard A. F. Balls and young fireman W. "Spot" Haggar of the mail train were both killed. The driver* of the express was badly injured and about seven passengers and postal staff were slightly hurt.

The official inquiry reported that the signalman should have called out fogmen in the patchy, though worsening, foggy conditions. The probable cause of the accident however was failure by the express driver to fully observe signals at Rivenhall and that he was travelling too fast.

As in all terrible accidents, fate had taken a hand. Ipswich engine No 61057 was not originally intended for the Up Mail that particular morning. Indeed it was the regular engine of Driver S. Hall and Fireman A. Talbot, but because of problems with the engine's electrical system it was decided to send the loco to Stratford for expert attention. The quickest and most convenient method of achieving this was to work the 2.02 am Mail up to London and finish up at Stratford.

Driver G. Wright and Fireman E. Smith were on Loco Duties that morning and they backed on to the train. The express driver had made his way to Ipswich Station from the Loco Depot alone because his mate Fireman Haggar was late. On relieving Messrs. Wright and Smith, he mentioned that Fireman Smith would have to come with him because his regular fireman had not turned up. Shortly afterwards Fireman Haggar arrived to begin that fateful journey.

*The Ipswich express driver's name is omitted out of respect for his family's privacy.

*"Spot" Haggar, later fatally injured in the Witham Crash, seen here with fellow Ipswich locomen. Left to right: Stan Chapman, Dusty Miller, W. Haggar.* (Photo courtesy Kelvin Higgins Collection)

## ACCIDENTS

*Engine No. 1057, later to be involved in the Witham crash, seen when new at Ipswich Loco Depot on 1st October 1946. The tank house and water column are in the background, right. Looking out of one of the engine-shed windows is Michael Collyer. The Nominated Gang commenced in September 1946, and the two sets of men "nominated" for working this particular engine at the time were Driver George Viney and Fireman Bob Brown, and Driver Harry Theobald with his fireman Ron Lockwood.* (Photo by Norman Glover)

*Photographs of 61057 after the locomotive was recovered and placed in the siding at Witham to await removal.*
(Photos courtesy Eric Pryke Collection)

# *Wartime*

## The Railway during World War II

"The lines behind the lines" - wartime railway slogan

ON 1st September 1939, the Government took control over the big four railway companies and London Transport, in addition to six other smaller joint and independent light railways including some dock railways, on behalf of the Ministry of Transport (changed to Ministry of War Transport in 1941). This was accomplished by an Order issued under the Emergency Powers (Defence) Act, 1939. The Railway Executive was appointed by the Minister to give directions under that Order.

A daily Central Inter-Company Operating Officers' Conference was set up to meet every morning by means of a special telephone link. Immediate decisions were taken affecting all priority movements of passenger and goods traffic including the allocation of routes, manpower and motive power. Thus the ever increasing demand for troop, munitions and fuel trains by liaison with Movement and Transport Officers from the Services, was maintained alongside the everyday requirements for food, mail, coal, agricultural produce and ordinary passenger needs.

A Central Wagon Control was established to regulate over one and a quarter million railway wagons including the 600,000 trucks requisitioned from 4,000 different private owners, plus over 400,000 wagon sheets and ropes together with 17,000 odd railway containers; all had to be strictly controlled. At stipulated times of the day, stationmasters or other officials gave estimates of particular types of wagon required for loading the next day.

Large numbers of ordinary passenger trains were cancelled at the outbreak of war due to the obvious uncertainty of events such as heavy bombing by the enemy which was widely expected but did not happen until summer 1940. The railborne evacuation of schoolchildren from cities and south-east coastal towns and ports commenced on 1st September, followed by the transport to France of the British Expeditionary Force. The train cancellations resulted in a very slack period for railwaymen after the initial flurry of activity and notices were put up inviting footplatemen to volunteer for the army, the railway making up the difference in their pay. At the same time there were rumours, unfounded as it happened, that the locomotive depot at Parkeston would close and the staff move to Ipswich. This worried the young passed-cleaners and firemen because the seniority of so many of the Parkeston men might put the jobs of junior Ipswich men in jeopardy. Consequently a few did join up. The job was not at the time a reserved occupation which it subsequently became. Acting-Fireman Tom Mole had been conscripted in July 1939, ostensibly for six months, in the first batch of conscripts aged twenty to twenty-one. By the end of 1939 during the period of the so-called "phoney war", passenger services were largely restored and work built up quickly. Staff who had previously left railway employment were contacted and offered work. Tom Mole, who had been posted to Dover with a Royal Artillery anti-aircraft battery was released and returned to work in March 1940. He went into the passenger link and recalls

*L Company, 9th Battalion, Home Guard, all LNER railwaymen from the Ipswich area. Front row, 3rd from left W. Lacey (locoman); 7th W. Newman (locoman). Second row, 3rd from left E. Rivers (list clerk); 7th E. Payne (locoman). Third row, 6th from left D. Burton (locoman); 7th J. Skinner (locoman). Several Wagon Shop staff are also included in the photograph.* (Photo courtesy Mrs J. Witherley, and names courtesy Eric Leggett)

working troop trains to or from Olympia (Kensington) and on one occasion went through to Weybourne on the M&GN Joint line where there was a large military camp.

Traffic increased considerably throughout East Anglia thereafter because of troop movements plus the growth of ordinary goods and passenger traffic due to petrol rationing affecting road transport. The drive to increase farm production created congestion in country goods yards. Between May 1940 and 1944 deep-sea and coastal tankers were prevented from using the southern North Sea because of enemy action and petroleum products were brought from West Coast ports by rail to existing oil installations such as Ipswich. A newly installed pipeline system spread across England connecting with strategically placed government fuel storage depots equipped with railway sidings, mainly for aviation fuel for the RAF. Such was the case at Claydon just outside Ipswich. Petrol trains were very unpopular during air raids and retired driver Ron Manning recalled a not uncommon event in these circumstances of being held in a siding for nearly two hours at Bentley with a train of empty tanks for Cliff Quay, Ipswich.

During this time, with the blackout in force, a fireman would try to build up his fire as much as possible at the start of a trip, to prevent the firebox door having to be opened while out on the track with enemy planes around to spot the glow. Attempts were made to shroud the cabs of the locomotives but this made conditions on the footplate unbearable as the heat was unable to escape. Railwaymen were instructed how to immobilize their engines in the event of an invasion but fortunately the question of whether or not they could commit such an act against their lovingly maintained charges was never put to the test.

Airfield construction, especially after the arrival of the USAAF, used train loads of rubble from London's bomb damaged buildings. Cement and bricks were sent to the nearest siding convenient to remote airfield sites, to be followed by vast quantities of equipment, bombs, ammunition and fuel along small branch lines like the Mid-Suffolk, the Waveney Valley line, the Eye, Hadleigh and Framlingham branches. Much of it was hauled by Victorian and Edwardian locomotives from Ipswich and other loco depots in East Anglia, with drivers taking on pilotmen when proceeding over unfamiliar routes made all the more unfamiliar by the blackout. The latter caused considerable problems at depots like Croft Street where in 1944, enginemen were drawing attention to the amount of time lost when leaving the depot, due to the difficulty of trying to locate their locomotives in the darkness at the start of their shift. Engines were unknowingly being blocked in and then perhaps had to be turned.

*Engine driver Bob Ratcliffe, with his grandson, outside the air raid shelter in the garden of his Martin Road home.* (Photo courtesy Ratcliffe Family Collection)

Congestion on all railways was severe. Ordinary passengers were packed into long trains often without corridor facilities and suffered interminable delays while troop trains or train loads of bombs took precedence. At Ipswich, a train of goods wagons hauled by a tram engine could take eight hours to reach the Top Yard from Ipswich Dock, via Lower Yard and Ranelagh Road level crossing, due to the sheer numbers of wagons everywhere.

Compulsory firewatching by enginemen at Croft Street and Derby Road Station was the source of much irritation considering the round the clock uncertainties of their normal hours of work. Additional food rations of meat, cheese, tea and sugar were available to footplatemen, and there were extra clothing coupons and

*Air raid warden Bob Ratcliffe (driver) at his home in Martin Road, Ipswich.* (Photos courtesy Ratcliffe Family Collection)

soap rations. It should be remembered that locomen went home as black as coal miners before modernisation of the Depot in the mid-1950s. Permits had to be obtained to buy alarm clocks; calling men for duty by knocking on front doors in the early hours was still the rule and was not abolished until 1951. In July 1942 the locomotivemen's job was no longer a reserved occupation and they became liable to call-up subject to the age limit. Drivers reaching retirement age at sixty-five were given the opportunity to stay on and those awaiting promotion in accordance with their seniority were duly registered as promoted and received the pay rate to which they would have been entitled. At Ipswich, for example, Driver D. Humphreys stayed on until 1942, although he had reached retirement age in 1940.

The Loco Depot at Croft Street was remarkably unscathed by the bombs dropped on the town of Ipswich. One bomb left a large crater on Luther Road School playing field, very close to the railway line and tunnel, in May 1941. Other bombs were dropped on Griffin Wharf, New Cut West and Ranelagh Road Sidings.

Fatalities occurred when bombs fell on the nearby firm of Ransomes and Rapier, and nine people lost their lives and a number were injured when three houses were totally destroyed in Seymour Road, Over Stoke, during an early morning bombing raid in March 1945.

Out on the line there were perhaps a dozen incidents in East Anglia of trains being shot at by enemy aircraft. In January 1941 the 1.03 pm passenger train from Liverpool Street to Ipswich, Driver Stan Mills, was bombed and machine-gunned at Colchester, the guard receiving fatal injuries. Fireman "Spud" Murphy's train was shot at in daylight in June 1943 shortly after a bomb was dropped near Bentley Station, the fireman receiving slight injuries.

During the bombing of London, traffic on the Ipswich line was frequently interrupted and long delays in returning home were sometimes eased by diverting trains, caught on the wrong side of any disruption, to the already congested Liverpool Street - Cambridge line. This enabled trains to regain the main line by using the Bishops Stortford-Braintree-Witham branch, or by way of Cambridge and Bury St. Edmunds. One of the most

*The locomotive of the 8.45 pm, Liverpool Street to Harwich passenger train, in the bomb crater near Shenfield.*
(Photo LNER)

serious incidents of that kind occurred at 9.45 pm on the 3rd March 1943 when the locomotive of the 8.45 pm Liverpool Street to Harwich passenger train fell into a hole blown in the embankment between Shenfield and Ingatestone. The tender mounted the engine and some carriages were derailed. Bombs had been falling in the area and a motorist on the nearby A12 road saw that the line had been cut and stopped at Shenfield station to warn staff. Unfortunately the train had been allowed to proceed with caution, bearing in mind that it was totally dark and the chance of seeing the damage to the line from the footplate was remote. Only one passenger and the guard were hurt but Driver William Greenfield and his fireman Arthur Barratt, both of Parkeston, were killed. Subsequently, Mr W. Thorne, Member of Parliament for Plaistow, questioned the Parliamentary Secretary for War Transport about the incident. Mr P. Noel-Baker replied that the authority given to allow the train to proceed was an error of judgement and the train should have been held until examination of the line was complete. He said that regulations had not been strict enough but they had since been tightened up to prevent a similar occurrence.

Acting-driver Ernie Dunnett had joined the GER as a cleaner in 1914 and was firing on the North Country Continental prior to its suspension when he was put with Driver Rumsey, then in the Old Man's Gang, on the Station shunting engine and local goods work. He was aware of the rumours about Parkeston men coming to Ipswich and he and Percy Burrows decided to join the army in response to the notice posted at the Shed stating drivers were required and offering twelve shillings a day. They were told they would have "a wonderful time" and advised to go. After passing a medical they were sent to the Longmoor Military Railway at Liss in Hampshire. There they were given uniforms and inoculations ready for service abroad. Ernie and Percy however, being qualified drivers, were kept in this

*The Battery Headquarters' despatch rider, F Warburton, seated on an "Ariel" motor cycle beside the vans used as living accommodation for the gun crews in Orwell station yard, August 1941. Mr Warburton later married an Ipswich girl he met in the Shepherd and Dog Public House at Nacton.* (Photograph courtesy Derek Girling)

country as Royal Engineers, First Class Instructors, Ernie eventually gaining promotion to sergeant and Percy to corporal.

In the aftermath of the return from Dunkirk and the likelihood of invasion by the enemy, Ernie was sent to Canterbury from where he marched to Woodchurch just south of Ashford and close to the Romney Marshes. There was no railway at Woodchurch but they were billeted in a large house and were digging trenches, without leave, for nearly four months. Senior drivers were sent to Ashford for road learning in the area, clambering aboard locomotives in full army uniform with rifles and tin hats and giving the impression they were about to take over from the Southern Railwaymen; they did not receive overalls until a month later. Ernie Dunnett spent the rest of the war in charge of six engines at Canterbury locomotive depot. After the war, while on duty, Ernie spotted an Ashford driver going home from holiday at Gt. Yarmouth. During his time at Ashford, Ernie had met this driver who had welcomed him onto his footplate, so Ernie gave him a reciprocal trip to Ipswich on his engine.

Two heavy railway mounted guns were placed close to Levington and Nacton on the Felixstowe Branch, between November 1940 and November 1942, as part of the coastal defences against the expected German invasion. One was situated on a purpose built siding within a barn-like shed, the movable top half of which was mounted on rails which extended from one end sufficiently to allow the gun to be cleared for action. This was situated next to the level crossing on the lane leading to Stratton Hall.

The other was based in Orwell goods yard and when required for practice firing, a locomotive hauled it through Levington railway bridge where another siding had been installed between the railway and the main road, concealed in a small wood. The Orwell Stationmaster, Mr Fred Girling, with the key to the siding, accompanied the gun on these forays which were organised at night and he remained until practice was completed and the gun returned to Orwell Station. One effect of these nocturnal activities was that ceilings were brought down in some nearby cottages during the firing of the gun.

The guns were assembled by the Elswick Ordnance Company using First World War type 12 inch guns with a maximum range of nearly eight miles which resulted in the field of fire extending beyond the position of the Cork Light vessel off Felixstowe. The gun barrels were 225.3 inches (5.715m) long, the shells were 750 pounders and the entire assembly weighed 76 tons. They were operated by men of the 9th Super Heavy Regiment, Royal Artillery, who used converted railway goods vans in Orwell Station Yard as living quarters.

*Above: One of the Nacton/Levington railway guns swung at 90° to the track. Note the 12 inch shell suspended from the loading crane and the concrete anchorage blocks to which the gun was attached by steel hawsers when being fired.*

(Photo Courtsey Derek Girling)

*Below: The gun shed near Stratton Hall level crossing, referred to in the text, photographed in 1986.*

(Photo by Richard W. Smith)

## George Baker goes to war

GEORGE Baker, junior, joined the LNER in 1936 as a cleaner at Ipswich loco like his father, George Baker, senior, before him. George junior spent eighteen months of his cleaning time at Aldeburgh. He was called up for military service in April 1940 and after basic training spent eight or nine months "keeping his hand in" on the LMS lines around Crewe before joining the Royal Engineers' Longmoor Military Railway for driver training, where he spent a further five months on the permanent staff.

In September 1941 George's railway operating company boarded the *SS Duchess of Richmond*, a converted liner belonging appropriately to the Canadian Pacific Railway Company. Bound for Bombay in convoy by way of Freetown and Durban, the company transferred to the troopship *Devonshire* at Bombay for the passage to Basrah in Iraq, arriving there on December 5th. From there they were taken to Ahwaz in Iran (Persia) and set up quarters in the local railway club.

The name of Persia was officially changed to Iran in 1935 although the name Persia has remained in common usage in the West. During the 1930s, the Shah was industrialising the country and to expedite this, he promoted the very costly Trans-Iranian Railway which opened in August 1938, linking Bandar Shapur at the head of the Persian Gulf with Bandar Shah on the Caspian Sea coast, via Tehran.

Germany developed strong trading links in this period, displacing Russia as Iran's main trading partner. By 1941 over 2000 German "technicians" were organised into Fifth Column cells which also included hundreds of Iranian students educated in Germany.

British protests to the Shah went unheeded. On 22nd June 1941 Germany invaded Russia bringing threat of invasion from the North whilst the Iranians prevaricated. Inevitably the Allies invaded on 25th August when two divisions of the British Indian Army entered Iran despite the Shah's earlier proclamation of neutrality. At Abadan the landing of Indian troops was resisted but casualties were few and resistance ceased on 28th by order of the Iranian Government.

The Allied force moved northward to Tehran where, on their approach on 16th September the Shah abdicated and went into exile being succeeded by his 22 year old son. In January 1942 the Allied presence was formalised by a tripartite agreement by Iran, Britain and the USSR. Shortly after the invasion the Allies decreed that the Trans-Iranian Railway should become a vital alternative to the dangerous Arctic Convoy route which carried aid to Russia via Murmansk.

This was the background to the arrival in Iran of the British Army's Railway Operating Companies and how George Baker and his colleagues found themselves working the erstwhile prestigious Trans-Iranian Railway. Tanks, ammunition, food, medical supplies and spares were loaded at Bandar Shapur for the 70 mile run to Ahwaz for re-marshalling into local destinations, or for Russia. George was a member of No. 190 Railway

*George Baker (extreme right) in Iran with some of his colleagues of No. 190 Railway Operating Company, Royal Engineers. The other three are (left to right): Len Scott who came from Hull, Colin Butt and Abbey Rainer who later became a driver at Shrewsbury.* (Photo courtesy George Baker)

*Two Stanier Class 8F locomotives double heading a train north of Andimeshk, in the mountains.*

(Photo courtesy George Baker)

Operating Company, Royal Engineers, comprising some 380 men including 58 locomotive drivers and 60 firemen. There were three Operating Companies, 190, 192 and 153, plus workshop, stores and construction companies. In overall charge as Director of Transportation was Brigadier Sir Godfrey Rhodes who had hitherto been running the Kenya and Uganda Railways.

Locomotives already there included a Beyer-Peacock 2-8-0, German built 2-8-0s and 2-10-0s and later on an American 2-8-2 appeared. New engines were imperative and in September 1941 the first of over 140 British 2-8-0 locomotives arrived at Abadan. These were originally designed for the LMS by their Chief Mechanical Engineer from 1932 to 1944, Sir William Stanier, F.R.S. and were adopted by the War Office as standard for service overseas.

The railway terminus was fifty miles east of Abadan at Bandar Shapur but the only heavy-lift crane capable of unloading the engines was that built in 1939 (amongst controversy as to its real usefulness) for the Anglo-Iranian Oil Co. Ltd. at Abadan. The crane, with a capacity of 200 tons, and named "Akvan" (White Giant), lifted the locomotives and tenders into Company barges fitted with rails to be towed the sixty odd miles up the River Karun to Ahwaz. Here a 100 ton electrically-driven derrick was erected to unload the engines but such was its consumption, the local electricity supply had to be cut off when the crane was in use.

Twelve thousand tons of cargo and equipment were moved north from Bandar Shapur weekly to Tehran by British drivers and taken forward by Russians. Spares and knocked-down American Mack lorries for assembling, were delivered to a big supply base about seventy miles north of Ahwaz at Andimeshk where summer temperatures reached 130°F. 1,600 railway wagons, prepared at Ashford, Kent from components made by all four British railway company workshops, were despatched in crates and assembled in Iran. From Bandar Shapur to Andimeshk single Stanier 2-8-0s hauled 850 tons. Beyond there into the mountains the limit was 350 tons, or the trains were double-headed and pushed by a banker.

Except for the first twenty locomotives to arrive, which burned coal and were quickly converted, all motive power was oil-fired. The railway handled only the heaviest freight and special consignments such as the seventy miles length of coiled undersea cable the Russians needed to lay under the Caspian Sea. All the rest, including oil, travelled north along arduous desert and mountain roads in convoys of lorries.

The British-worked section of the line totalled 576 miles. The railway line from Ahwaz to Khorramshahr, north of Abadan on the Shatt-al-Arab waterway opened in August 1942, and when the Americans arrived later in 1942 they established a huge Aid to Russia Base at Khorramshahr. The 711 Railway Battalion USA brought their own locomotives, over 140 of which were discharged at Abadan, again by "Akvan" the 200 ton crane, which also served to unload vast numbers of Boston bombers and Thunderbolt fighters when the United States Air Force arrived. This was besides enormous amounts of spares and equipment including snow ploughs and lawn mowers to cut non-existent grass!

The Americans took over the running of the Trans-Iranian Railway from the Royal Engineers and George Baker left Iran with a part of his Company for Iraq. They travelled from Basrah to Baghdad in February 1943 on the metre gauge railway and proceeded to work 250 miles of that line from Baghdad to Mosul with goods and passenger trains.

In September 1943 after a few weeks rest and re-training in Beirut, George and his colleagues found themselves in Sicily and Italy from where they advanced northwards with the Army and in July 1945 they crossed into Southern Austria and were based at St Vite near Klagenfurt.

This part of Austria known as Carinthia is famous as a tourist and holiday region, just north of the Italian and Yugoslavian border. Few present-day visitors even know of, let alone understand, the horrors that were enacted in that beautiful countryside during 1945 and continuing after the end of the war. George Baker and his Company became embroiled in the events unfolding before them, at first unwittingly, then powerless to avoid involvement.

In 1944, prior to the Normandy landings, it was reported that huge numbers of Russians were being drafted in to fight with the German army in France. Many of these were originally opposed to Stalin and the Soviet Union and had joined the German army to fight against Stalin.

Thousands more however had been taken prisoner when Russia was invaded, most of whom were put to work in German uniformed labour battalions where cruelty prevailed and food was scarce. As the tide of war

*An accident involving a collision between an 8F and one of the pre-war German 2-8-0s used by the Allies on the railway.*

(Photo courtesy George Baker)

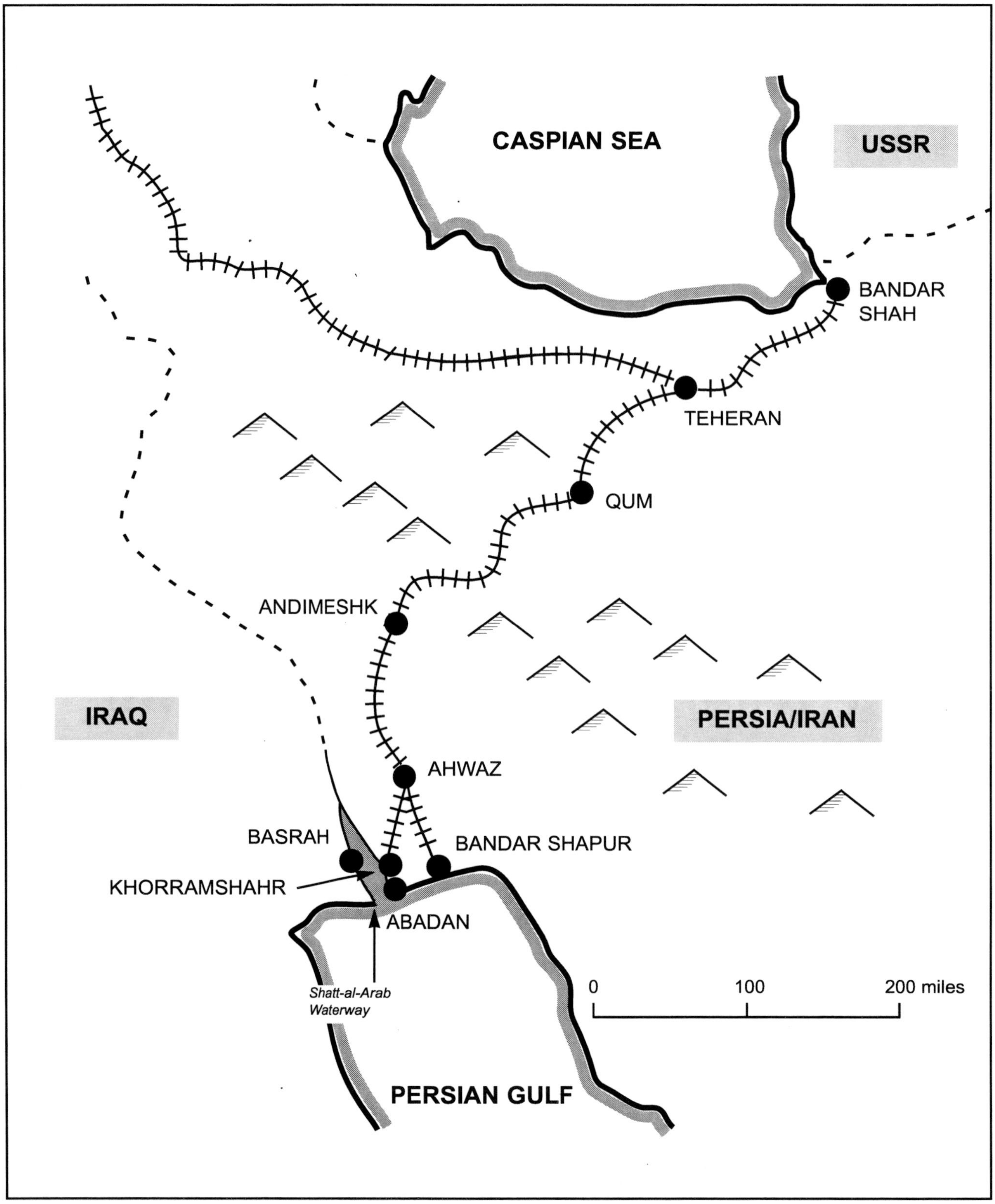
CASPIAN SEA
USSR
BANDAR SHAH
TEHERAN
QUM
ANDIMESHK
IRAQ
PERSIA/IRAN
AHWAZ
BASRAH
BANDAR SHAPUR
KHORRAMSHAHR
ABADAN
Shatt-al-Arab Waterway
0
100
200 miles
PERSIAN GULF

turned these people were directed to handling arms and active service, or they faced being shot. Enormous numbers of them in German uniforms were captured by, or surrendered to, the Allies. They were sent to P.o.W. camps in Britain and North America.

The situation became extremely delicate and within days of the Normandy landings, the British Government was contemplating the fact that the Soviet Union had the right to deal with its own citizens many of whom were considered to be traitors. At the Yalta Conference of February 1945 Britain and the USA agreed to compulsory repatriation of all Soviet citizens and during the first six months of 1945 over 30,000 were transported home by sea from Hull and Liverpool to Murmansk or Odessa on the Black Sea.

Many committed or attempted suicide. On the Continent they were herded on to trains. The former Russian prisoners misguidedly held on to the hope that Britain would never send anybody home against their will, let alone by force to almost certain death, but this was already happening. The fact that they were captured wearing German uniform swayed opinion and there was little sympathy for their plight.

In Southern Austria 20,000 Cossacks and civilian refugees with children were camped awaiting forced repatriation from the British held sector into the Russian sector at Judenburg. This started on May 28th 1945 when about 1,500 officers were deliberately misled into thinking they were going to attend a conference where they would be taken by convoy, to return that same evening. Many were suspicious and suicides and escapes were attempted though others still trusted the British because of their inherent politeness.

The contradictory replies given through interpreters to the British escort at the handover convinced the latter that all was not well but everything went ahead and it became apparent that within a few days the Cossack officers would be handed over to the Security Police and their fate sealed. Back in the camps the Cossacks asked why their officers had not returned and were met with British evasiveness. Henceforth the deportation went ahead by road and rail with the use of force, and suicides

*A British streamlined 4-6-2 built by Robert Stephenson & Co. Ltd..*
(Photo courtesy George Baker)

and escapes continued. Forced repatriation officially ceased at the end of August but confusion over policies reigned and the political and moral ramifications of the whole nightmare would continue and be brought home to a wider public with the opening of the secret files thirty years later and the publication of "The Last Secret" by Nicholas Bethell, together with a BBC television film based on the book shown in November 1975.

George Baker and his colleagues drove the trains on the last stretch to Judenburg and at first were not aware of the true nature of events taking place, assuming that the Russians were going home. George was driving a banking engine to assist the trains in the hills and it was not until the engine crew of one of the train locomotives saw or heard evidence of what was happening and told their mates on returning, that the enormity of what was occurring became clear. Naturally as soldiers first, and railwaymen second, they could do nothing to change things. The army was carrying out the policies of the British Foreign Office and the Allies, following the unfortunate Yalta agreement and was acting under the direct orders of the British High Command. One of the few Members of Parliament to question the Government about the conduct of the repatriation by the British was coincidentally the Member for Ipswich, Mr R. R. Stokes, who raised the matter at least three times in the House of Commons.

Coming home in May 1946 George returned to the Locomotive Depot in Croft Street as a fireman and in September he was appointed to the "Nominated Gang" where men were allocated to a single engine whenever possible. He was Vic Saunder's mate on B1 Class 1059, and gained promotion to acting driver in February 1947 in the midst of one of the worst winters of the century.

George was passed for driving by Chief Inspector Jenkins who had been on the footplate of Mallard when she gained the world speed record for steam in 1938. George was then transferred to the Shunting Relief Link which consisted of three shifts on "Bridges" (London Road end of Top Yard), three shifts Lower Yard, engine preparation and disposal and other relief duties. About thirty crews were thus occupied in that link and another job covered by them was working the extra summer service trains to Felixstowe.

George Baker was promoted to Driver in 1955. From 1948 to 1980 he was assistant secretary of the Mutual Improvement Classes. The Chairman was Charlie Kape, a great character and engineman. As mentioned elsewhere in the book, these long-standing instructional classes were unpaid, and though held on the railway premises, received little encouragement, but in steam days the railways got their staff trained "on the cheap".

In June 1958 George was selected to become the first main line diesel locomotive driving instructor at Ipswich which required attendance at an eight week course at the Ilford Training School on the English Electric Type 4 2000 hp and Brush Type 2 1250 hp diesel-electric locomotives. As other types came into service he went back to Ilford for week long courses on North British Types 1 and 2, the BR Sulzer, English Electric Class 37 and the BR Class 47.

In 1964 George returned to driving in the goods link to Temple Mills, Whitemoor and local goods. Three years later came the move to the passenger link with regular work to Liverpool Street, Norwich and Peterborough. After a number of older drivers retired, some before the age of sixty-five, George transferred to the railcar link in 1973, staying there until he himself retired at sixty-five after forty-six years rewarding railway service.

*Ipswich drivers at the Sulzer Works in Switzerland. This was an unofficial visit for which the men paid their own expenses. (In the 1960s British Railways built some main line diesels powered by Sulzer engines. Some of these locomotives were based at Ipswich.) Left to right: Ernie Buroughes, Eric Hazell, Frankie Gill, George Baker, Herbert Stanley, Reg Greaves, Reg Richardson, Peter Mulley, Jack Percy (fitter), Jack Catchpole, Cyril Broad, Ron Bloom, Glen Griffiths.*

(Photo courtesy George Baker)

*Instructor George Baker with a diesel conversion course on a North British Locomotive Company engine. Left to right: George Baker, Joe Skeels, Ernie Leah and Cyril Broad.*

(Photo courtesy George Baker)

*One of the first Brush "toffee apple" main line diesels, on loan from Stratford for driver training, seen at Yarmouth Southtown with empty coaching stock, having been on a training run from Ipswich. Left to right: Reg Thompson, "Pussy" Catton, "Daddy" Frost, Tim Schofield, Eric Hazell, George Baker and Billy Gardiner. In cab is Jack "Hambone" Leaning.*

(Photo by Jimmy James)

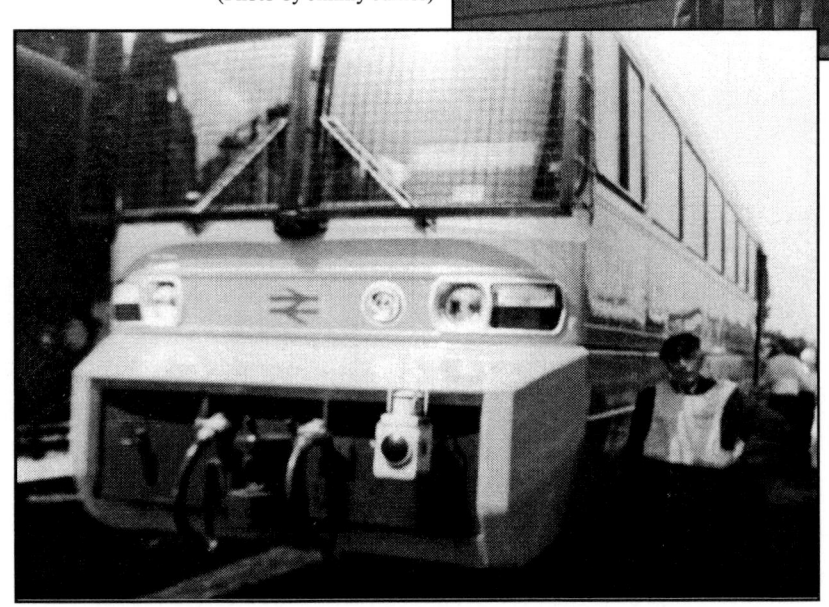

*George Baker standing beside the experimental rail-bus developed jointly by the BR Derby Works and Leyland Buses in the early 1980s. Test runs were made, mainly on the East Suffolk Line, by George Baker and John Barnby. It had also been to Boston USA for trials. There stones were thrown at it by children, hence the protective grill fitted to the windows. Although not in itself successful, it paved the way for the new generation of Sprinter trains.*

(Photo courtesy George Baker)

# Railway Unions & Mutual Benefit Societies

# Early Days

WHEN the Eastern Union Railway first arrived in the area there were no organisations representing the railwaymen; no doubt this was largely due to the absence of any large industrial enterprise and the very low wages paid to the agricultural workers at the time.

One of the first local railway disputes to occur was during the building of the tunnel at Ipswich. An extract from Robert Ratcliffe's "The History of the Working Class Movement in Ipswich" describes the event:

> "Whilst the work was in progress the men engaged on the construction of the tunnel became dissatisfied with their working conditions, and on Monday, April 6th, 1846, the men who could not work because of the weather assembled on the Cornhill. About two hundred in number met to discuss their grievances, one of which was the low wages paid ...... As it was feared that an outbreak of violence might take place, shops were closed and the police were sent for; the magistrates also appeared on the scene. Aided by a sub-contractor, the police succeeded in calming the angry feelings of the men who dispersed during the evening and resumed work the next day."

Three years later, in 1849, a Mutual Benefit Society was established for the railwaymen. According to John Glyde, writing in his book "The Moral, Social, and Religious Condition of Ipswich", this society's plan differed from that of any other club that he knew of in the town and neighbourhood.

Everyone in the employment of the railway company was required to join the society, either as a benefit or an honorary member. The funds were raised by the payments of the members, the subscriptions of honorary members, and the fines which were imposed for negligence of duty, disobedience of orders and so on while in the company's service.

The board of directors very liberally made a donation of one hundred pounds to the funds, although it was evident that without a large influx of honorary subscriptions it would be impossible to maintain the promises made. Medical attendance was guaranteed to all the members.

The benefit members were divided into four classes:

| CLASS | WEEKLY PAYMENT | SICKNESS WEEKLY BENEFIT | DEATH BENEFIT |
|---|---|---|---|
| First | 2d | 5s | £3 |
| Second | 3d | 7s 6d | £4 10s |
| Third | 4d | 10s | £6 |
| Fourth | 6d | 15s | £9 |

An institution of this character was invaluable, owing to the high risk a railway employee ran of incurring an accident, which would otherwise result in the injured worker having to resort to begging.

Another early friendly society was The Railway Officers' and Servants' Association, founded in 1861. It provided annuities for members permanently incapacitated for work, and relief by "money allowances" in cases of sickness, and also at the death of Members and their Widows. Orphan children were provided for until the age of fourteen, and relief was granted in special cases of distress and necessity.

Railway employees could join one or more of the funds and did not forfeit benefits by leaving the railway service, provided they resided in the United Kingdom. The Association was still going strong in 1909, with some Great Eastern Railway employees locally as members. At that date it had paid out more than £210,000 since its inception.

The first appearance of a railwaymen's union in Ipswich was in 1874 when a branch of the General Railway Workers Union was formed. No actual membership figures are available, yet from the balance sheet of that year which showed £7 16s 6d as entrance fees, it is evident that a large number of members were enrolled. In 1876 the membership was returned as sixty, but by 1878 the number had dropped to thirty-three. It appears that soon after this the branch went out of existence.

At about this time a branch of the Amalgamated Society of Railway Servants was formed, and their meeting place was the Great Eastern Railway Hotel in Commercial Road. Mr J. Goody took an active part in the Society which, in the event, did not last long and the railwaymen were unorganised for some time with the exception of a few drivers and firemen who were members of the Enginemen's Society, a union catering for employees of the Great Eastern Railway. The headquarters was at Stratford but there was no local branch. During 1892 a branch of the Amalgamated Society was reformed. Their meeting place was at the Vernon Arms on the corner of Vernon Street and Little Whip Street, Over Stoke, and Mr C. Bewley, the Secretary, with the help of Mr F. J. Ellis of the T.A. carried on for some time and the branch made steady progress. Eventually Mr W. Lovett became Secretary but the branch later lapsed.

On September 24th 1892, the trade unions in Ipswich held a big recruiting demonstration in a meadow adjacent to the grounds of Oak Hill and Stoke Rectory, by the kind permission of Mr Daniel Ford Goddard and Canon Bulstrode respectively. The latter was Rector of St Mary-at-Stoke Church and Mr Ford Goddard was Engineer and Secretary to the Ipswich Gas Light Company, following his father and grandfather in those posts. He had recently been Mayor of Ipswich and was returned as a Member of Parliament in 1895, a position he held for nearly 24 years. He received a Knighthood in 1907, becoming a Privy Councillor in 1916. His family home, Oak Hill off Belstead Road, eventually became a part of St Josephs College but now stands empty.

Thus these two liberally minded men lent their land for the mass meeting which had assembled at St Margarets Green at 3.00 pm before marching to Stoke led by a band. Railway unions were amongst the dozen or more organisations taking part. Mr Ford Goddard, supported by Canon Bulstrode, addressed the meeting and appealed for all to do as much as possible to increase the membership of their respective Trade Unions.

*Watch-fob badge of the Amalgamated Society of Railway Servants.*
(Courtesy Deeks Family Collection)

*Canon George Bulstrode, Rector of St Mary-at-Stoke, who supported the drive in 1892 for increased membership of the trade unions.*

(Photo courtesy Elizabeth Youngs)

*Sir Daniel Ford Goddard of Oak Hill*

(Photo courtesy Over Stoke History Group)

*St Mary-at-Stoke Rectory and grounds. Part of the building still stands at the junction of Belstead Avenue and Maidenhall Approach. This photograph was taken c 1904 by the then curate, the Rev N. Raper.*

(Photo courtesy Over Stoke History Group)

# GREAT EASTERN RAILWAY.

### LOCOMOTIVE, CARRIAGE AND WAGON DEPARTMENT.

### REGULATIONS REGARDING THE EMPLOYMENT OF ENGINEMEN, Etc., TO COME INTO OPERATION ON THE 1st JANUARY, 1909.

**HOURS -**

On week-days ten hours shall constitute a day's work, and overtime will be paid for every completed quarter of an hour at the rate of eight hours per day.

From the previous midnight, to midnight on Sundays, Christmas Days and Good Fridays, 6 hours and 40 minutes shall constitute a day's work, and for every completed subsequent 10 minutes 1/40th of a day's wages will be paid.

Time shall be computed from signing on duty to leaving engines.

Short and long days will not be averaged, but each day will be paid for separately. A full day's pay will be given in those cases where only a partial day's work is performed in working trains.

As far as practicable not less than 9 hours shall elapse from the finish of one day's work to the commencement of another.

**WAGES -**

Men will be considered in the London District when they are stationed at places not more than 15 miles from Liverpool Street.

Payment for trips run will be discontinued, but rates will vary (daily if necessary) according to the importance of the work performed.

One rate only will be paid to Drivers for one turn of duty and will be that which is paid for the most important work in that turn.

Certified Firemen and Cleaners acting as Drivers or Firemen respectively, will be paid special rates for the actual time they are so engaged

**DRIVERS' RATES -**

1st year - 5s. 6d. per day.
2nd year - 6s. per day. (unless engaged on work specially rated at 5s 6d.)
3rd year and after, as follows :-

MAIN LINE, CROSS COUNTRY, AND OTHER PASSENGER TRAINS NOT SPECIALLY ARRANGED FOR ELSEWHERE.

|  | London District. Per day. s. d. | Other Districts. Per day. s. d. |
|---|---|---|
| When working:- |  |  |
| Trains booked to run 300 passenger train miles during one turn of duty | 8  0 | 7  6 |
| Trains booked to run 175 passenger train miles in 10 hours, the longest non-stop booked run of which is at least 70 miles | 8  0 | 7  6 |
| Trains booked to run 225 passenger train miles during one turn of duty | 7  6 | 7  0 |
| Trains booked to run less than 225 passenger train miles during one turn of duty | 7  0 | 6  6 |

**SMALL BRANCHES.** *[List only includes those branches likely to be worked by Ipswich Men - Editor]*

When working on the following branches trains booked to run:-

|  | Per day. s. d. |
|---|---|
| 100 train miles | 6  6 |
| Under 100 train miles | 6  0 |

Manningtree and Harwich.   Mellis and Eye.   Bentley and Hadleigh.
Framlingham Branch.   Aldeburgh Branch.   Ipswich and Felixstowe.

**FIREMEN'S RATES -**

|  | London District. Per day. s. d. | Other Districts. Per day. s. d. |
|---|---|---|
| Cleaners when acting as Firemen | 3  6 | 3  3 |
| Firemen, 1st year | 3  9 | 3  3 |
| "    2nd year | 4  0 | 3  6 |
| "    3rd year | 4  3 | 4  0 |
| "    4th year | 4  6 | 4  3 |
| "    6th year | 4  9 | ....... |
| When certified*, or when firing to Drivers on |  |  |
| 8s. 0d. work (London District) | 5  0 | 4  6 |
| 7s. 6d. work (Other Districts) | 5  0 | 4  6 |
| When certified & whilst actually engaged driving | 5  6 | 5  3 |
| Turning | 5  3 | 5  0 |

* Certificates will be given to Firemen properly qualified, as occasion requires.

**LODGING ALLOWANCES**

Men lodging away from their home station will be paid 2s..6d.each for each period of rest. If required to remain in the same lodgings 20 hours or more 5s.expenses each will be allowed. Half these amounts will be allowed to men lodging in the Dormitory

**HOLIDAYS.**

Payment for holidays will be discontinued.

**CLOTHING.**

Drivers and Firemen will be provided with a top coat once a year.

*S.D.HOLDEN,*
*Locomotive Superintendent.*
*30th October 1908.*

*Extracts from rates of pay and conditions as laid down by Mr Stephen Dewar Holden in 1908. He had just succeeded to the post of Locomotive Superintendent on the retirement of his father, James Holden. Note that a ten hour day is standard, Monday to Saturday, and paid holidays are discontinued.*

(Courtesy Rosemary Gitsham)

# The Associated Society of Locomotive Engineers & Firemen

THE Associated Society of Locomotive Engineers and Firemen (ASLEF) was formed in 1880 specifically for footplate men. Several attempts to form a branch in Ipswich failed until 1906 when one was at last established. The first meeting was held in the old Museum rooms on Sunday April 29th and was attended by Mr R. Thurtle and Mr W. Clarke, Chairman and Secretary respectively of the Stratford branch, and also by the ASLEF National Organiser, Mr H. Parfitt.

Thirteen drivers and firemen and one cleaner joined and at the following Sunday's meeting another six men enlisted, making twenty in all, which was sufficient to form a local branch. Mr E. Howe became Chairman and Mr H. Percy Secretary and they were supported by six committee members.

It was at the conclusion of business at their first Sunday meeting that the members found they had been accidentally locked in, having to escape one at a time through a Museum window, much to everyone's amusement.

Their next few meetings were held at the Station Street Institute, but from January 13th 1907 their meeting place was the EUR Hotel in Croft Street until in 1927 they moved to the Loco Club premises in Rectory Road. The Loco Club remained the meeting place until 1971. Then the Branch moved to the British Rail Staff Association (BRSA) premises close to Ipswich Station, thereafter to the Labour Club from 1979 to 1985, then briefly to the Railway Tavern and the Station Hotel, returning to the BRSA in 1986.

Landmarks for the ASLEF included the agreement on the eight-hour day which came into being on 1st February 1919. This breakthrough meant that the long hours worked at Ipswich and similar places came to an end. For others, especially on the Scottish railways, there were reductions of between eighteen and twenty-four hours a week to the hitherto compulsory hours worked, with all the attendant hardship and accidents caused by fatigue. The forty-four hour week was not achieved until October 4th 1947, and the forty-hour week commenced in February 1966.

The eight-hour day agreement however was between the Union and the Government, who retained control of the railways after the armistice, and it did not deal with national standardisation of wages and conditions of railwaymen.

In fact, satisfactory new terms on these matters, agreed in 1919 with ASLEF, were not offered to the National Union of Railwaymen (NUR) which led to a nine day strike of nearly all railwaymen from September 26th 1919. After this the government conceded the guaranteed week excluding Sundays, with overtime rates of pay, one week's holiday and twelve hours' rest between booked turns of duty.

At Ipswich, a public meeting had been arranged by the Trades Council at the Public Hall on October 5th, the day the strike finished. During this meeting it was rumoured that the strike was settled, but no official confirmation had been received. It was not until the evening that a brief telegram was read from the unions telling their members to return to work immediately, and

---

**THE FOURTEEN LOCOMEN WHO FORMED THE IPSWICH BRANCH OF THE ASLEF ON SUNDAY, APRIL 29TH, 1906**

(Note the addresses are in the Stoke area, in close proximity to the Loco Depot, this being a requirement for many years.)

| | |
|---|---|
| Edward Howe | 43 Croft Street |
| Edgar Button | 119 Rectory Road |
| Robert Dalby | Croft Street |
| William Nunn | 49 Rectory Road |
| George Pinkney (Sen) | 36 Rectory Road |
| Charles Pinkney (Jun) | 36 Rectory Road |
| Harry Pizzey | Wherstead Road |
| Thomas Cook | Martin Road |
| Christopher Downing | 72 Croft Street |
| Ernest Osbourne | Croft Street |
| Richard Fenning | 30 Croft Street |
| Sidney Haggar | 4 Rectory Road |
| Frederick Button | |
| Hervey Percy | 119 Rectory Road |

**Vol. 61 No. 1     JANUARY, 1948     PRICE 2ᴅ**

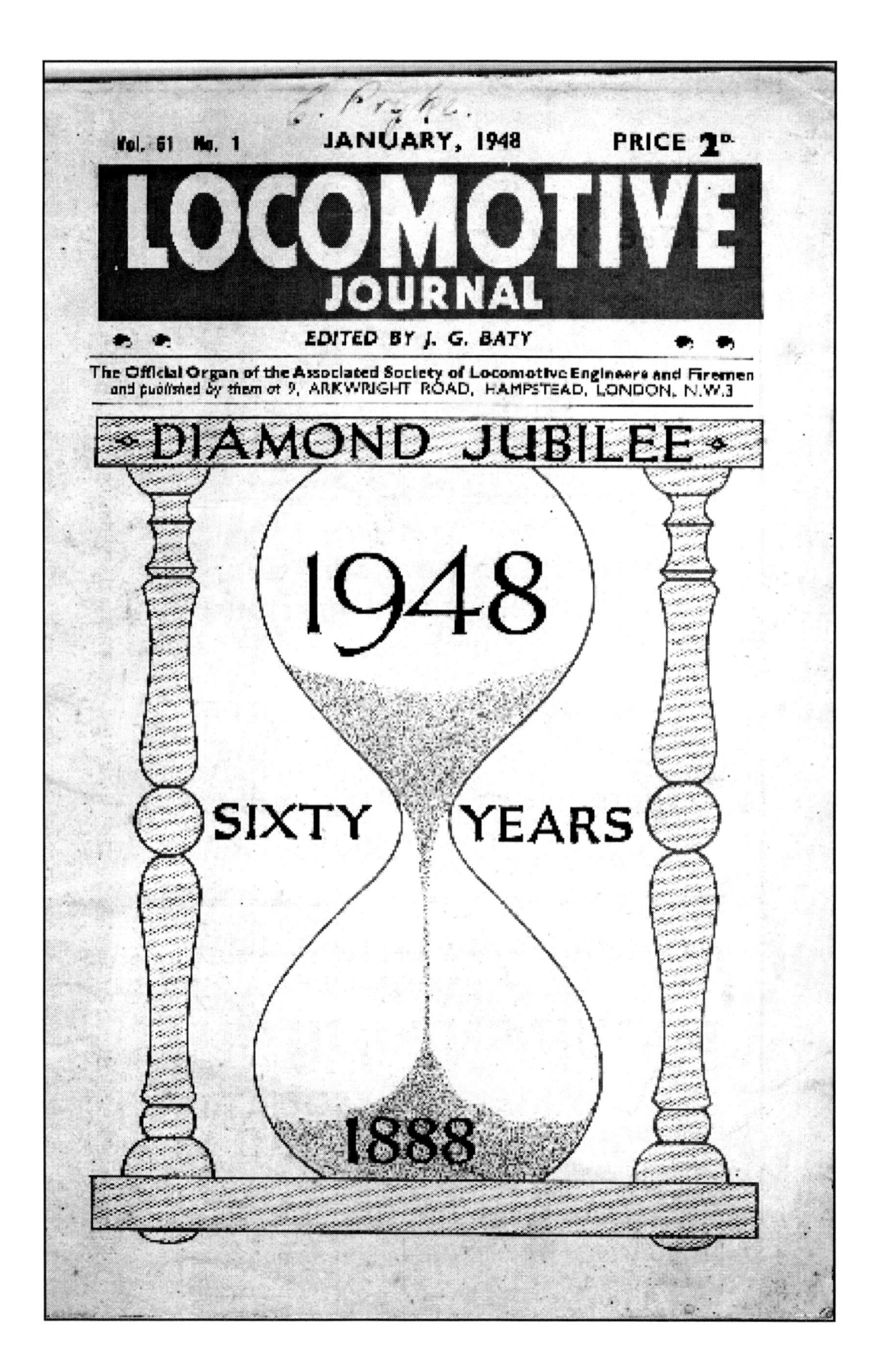

# LOCOMOTIVE JOURNAL

*EDITED BY J. G. BATY*

The Official Organ of the Associated Society of Locomotive Engineers and Firemen and published by them at 9, ARKWRIGHT ROAD, HAMPSTEAD, LONDON, N.W.3

### • DIAMOND JUBILEE •

**1948**

**SIXTY YEARS**

**1888**

that there were satisfactory terms for everybody. Inspector Firman of Ipswich Borough Police went to the Public Hall with a phone message from the Union's Headquarters, asking for a party of strikers to go by car to inform all stations around Ipswich that the strike was over and to ask everyone to report for duty the next day. Unfortunately the strikers got lost in the Halesworth area, and did not arrive back at Ipswich until 5.30 am the next morning.

In 1923 there were indications that the goodwill, which had existed between the ASLEF and the NUR during the 1919 strike, was fading. In the same year the railway companies demanded drastic revisions to the locomen's conditions of service, and then refused to consider the union's counter proposals.

In fact the companies were making an attack on the economic standards of footplatemen secured by the ASLEF in the 1919 strike. The companies were in a good financial position and had no just reason to threaten a reduction in earnings. The case went to the National Wages Board, whose findings were not acceptable to the ASLEF and a strike duly commenced on January 20th 1924.

Although the ASLEF had supported the NUR in the 1919 struggle on behalf of all grades of railway workers, this time the NUR advised all its members to remain at work, despite the fact that some of those members were footplatemen. After further negotiations, the strike was called off on January 29th, the railway companies conceding the point that the union did not have to accept the findings of the National Wages Board. The relationship between the ASLEF and the NUR had been badly damaged however, and numbers of footplatemen who had been members of the NUR left that union.

The complex General Strike of 1926, referred to by the unions as the National Strike, began on May 4th. The coal owners were to cut the miners' wages in response to Prime Minister Stanley Baldwin's call that "All workers have got to take reductions in wages." The miners went on strike and were locked out.

The TUC General Council called out the transport workers, engineers, shipyards, builders and printers a week afterwards in a very uncoordinated manner. The strike was called off on May 12th, the miners being left on their own, some remaining on strike until November, a fact which left many trade unionists forever embittered. This applied especially to railwaymen; although Ipswich was a long way from the coalfields, train crews were, by the very nature of their jobs, heavily involved in the working of coal traffic and its consumption. The government had long been preparing strike-breaking measures and in spite of near 100% support amongst other workers called out, the collapse was inevitable.

In 1955 the ASLEF Executive Council authorised a strike, not supported by the NUR, in defence principally of the footplatemens' traditional differential which had been eroded considerably in favour of other grades. The strike began on Sunday 29th May and ended 14th June after the Transport Commission conceded the case. The Ipswich branch had supported the action but deplored the fact that there had not been a prior ballot of the membership.

1982 was a year of unrest on the railways. January and February saw ASLEF members on strike for two days each week. NUR members went on strike at the end of June that same year, and during a two-week national strike, called at the beginning of July, ASLEF members were threatened with the termination of their employment by the railway if they did not return to work.

The day to day business of the branch, which met monthly, consisted of working arrangements at Ipswich affecting rosters, links and seniority. Most of the relevant comments were passed on to the Local Departmental Committee (LDC) where they were discussed with the Shedmaster. Delegates were elected annually to other bodies such as the Ipswich Labour Party and the Trades Council, and support was given to individual members to become Town Councillors.

At one branch meeting, Driver C. English, one time mayor, queried the small number of J.P.s in Ipswich. He referred to a proposal made some years previously for the appointment to this position of fellow driver (and future mayor) Robert Ratcliffe, who had come top of the poll, but up to that time (1942) had not been made a J.P..

Occasional meetings would be attended by the national Organising Secretary of the day. These were men of vision and wide experience and had all started as cleaners moving up the footplatemen's line of promotion.

Such a man of foresight was Albert Hallworth, who was later to become General Secretary between 1956 and 1960. At a branch meeting in November 1946 he vehemently warned against apathy and called upon everyone to help improve the drivers' status, especially looking ahead to inevitable electrification with single manning and redundancy problems. This had already happened with London Transport and on the Continent where many drivers were classed as tram drivers.

It would be another forty years before the full impact was felt at Ipswich, although at the time Albert Hallworth spoke, only fifteen years remained before the introduction of diesel motive power, which few in the 1940s had really considered a possibility.

One unique event, occurring in Norfolk, with which the Ipswich Branch became associated, was the well known Burston School Strike, which started in 1914 and ended in 1939, making it the longest strike in British history.

The children at the school went on strike, with the approval of their parents and most of the villagers, to support the much respected and warm-hearted teachers Mr and Mrs Higdon who had been unjustly dismissed. The local establishment, including the parson and squire, had not taken kindly to the Higdons' active support for the Agricultural Workers Union seeking recognition in the area, and consequently the couple were dismissed, and evicted from their home.

After three years' schooling in a disused carpenter's shed by Mr and Mrs Higdon, a new school was built on the Green with the proceeds of a national appeal, mainly from trade union branches all over the country. The names of the donors are inscribed on the walls of the new school and in 1988 the Ipswich ASLEF Branch placed the original branch minute book, including references to the appeal, in the school that now houses an exhibition recalling those events.

*Pictured after an L.D.C. Meeting in 1951 are (left to right) Bert Coleman, Arthur Brooks, Fred Newby, Fred Thorpe and Ernie Payne.*
(Photo courtesy Eric Leggett)

## Railmen on both sides of the table

● Sixty-five retired members of ASLEF attended a reunion dinner at the Locomotive and Workingmen's Social Club, Rectory Road, Ipswich, last night. This is the first time the re-union has been held for Ipswich retired members, and it is planned to make it an annual event. The evening was financed by fund-raising activities among active members.

*Retired ASLEF members' dinner at Loco Club, Rectory Road, Ipswich, in 1973. Top (left to right): E. Skeels, F. Gunther, L. Birch, A. Brooks, V. Benham, W. Leonard, B. Studd, L. Eley, E. Burton, C. Cape.*
*Bottom (left to right): A. Pettingale, F. Nock, R. Tricker, T. Dakin, E. Heffer, G. Gibbs, ? , E. Payne, C. Newman, H. Gayfer.* (Photos courtesy "Evening Star")

## RAILWAY UNIONS & MUTUAL BENEFIT SOCIETIES

*ASLEF General Secretary Ray Buckton (third left), at the annual dinner of retired members of the Ipswich branch, in 1975. Left to right: E. Leah, W. Leonard, R. Buckton, G. Hawes, E. Clarke, R. Bloomfield, F. Howard, E. Leggett and E. Smith.*
(Photo courtesy "Evening Star")

*Ipswich Branch Chairman Kelvin Higgins pictured at Union Headquarters in London with ASLEF General Secretary Derek Fullick.*

(Photo courtesy Kelvin Higgins Collection)

*Minutes of an ASLEF branch meeting (held at the EUR Hotel, Croft Street, Ipswich) during which a letter was read from the Burston School Strikers, appealing for assistance in their "fight against the tyranny of the country squire and parson".*

(Courtesy ASLEF, Ipswich Branch)

# RAILWAY UNIONS & MUTUAL BENEFIT SOCIETIES

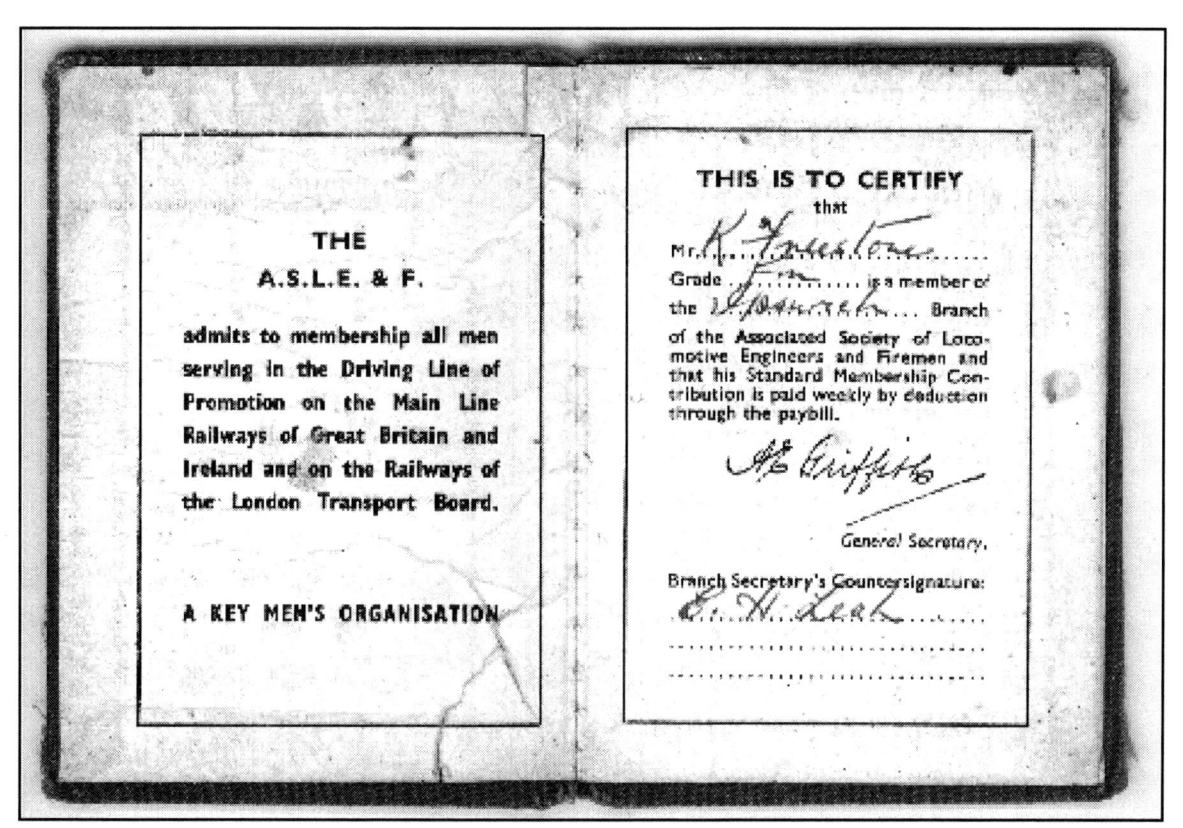

*Pages from union membership booklet.* (Freestone Family Collection)

# ASLEF Women's Society

SOON after the Locomen's strike in January 1924, a women's section of the Associated Society of Locomotive Engineers and Firemen was formed in Ipswich, comprising the wives of members of that Union. Although the section lapsed, it did play a part in the founding of the Loco Club in Rectory Road, Ipswich.

*The Ipswich section of the ASLEF Women's Society seen here at Great Yarmouth in 1926. Gordon Barber, later to become an engine driver, is sitting on his mother's lap (centre).* (Photo courtesy Gordon Barber)

## The National Union of Railwaymen

SHORTLY after the 1911 Railway Strike, The Amalgamated Society of Railway Servants (formed in 1871), the United Signalmen's and Pointsmen's Union, and the General Railway Workers' Union, endeavoured to bring about one union for all railwaymen. The Associated Society of Locomotive Engineers and Firemen, and the Railway Clerks' Association turned the idea down. However, the three first-named unions amalgamated in 1912 to become the National Union of Railwaymen (NUR).

In Ipswich, a few members of these unions opened a branch of the NUR, the Chairman elected being Mr W. Kisby and Secretary Mr J. B. Girling. Twenty-three men joined at the opening meeting, and in the first year membership had grown to 346. The numbers continued to increase and by 1916 the Union considered it desirable to have its own meeting place. After prolonged negotiations and searching for a suitable venue, premises in Bolton Lane were purchased in 1917 to become the local headquarters for the NUR, later opening as a social club as well.

In his book "History of the Working Class Movement in Ipswich" Robert Ratcliffe relates how a member of the National Union of Railwaymen attempted to help a railwayman facing eviction. During and after the First World War, the interests of tenants were closely watched by a committee of the Ipswich Trades Council. Under the Rent Restriction Act then in force, tenants could not be evicted from their houses unless alternative accommodation was provided for them.

One case that came before the committee was that of railwayman Mr J. Schofield, who rented a house in Stoke at 105 Rectory Road. The owner wanted the house for his own use and alternative accommodation had been found for the tenant. He, however, objected to the move on the grounds that his wife was ill in bed and the dwelling offered was not suitable. The owner had been granted possession on the last Tuesday of July 1919, from twelve noon.

The tenant contacted the secretary of the Trades Council, Mr T. Bird, who with Councillor Jackson sought an interview with the Chief Constable in an effort to get the order postponed. NUR member Mr A. I. Curl

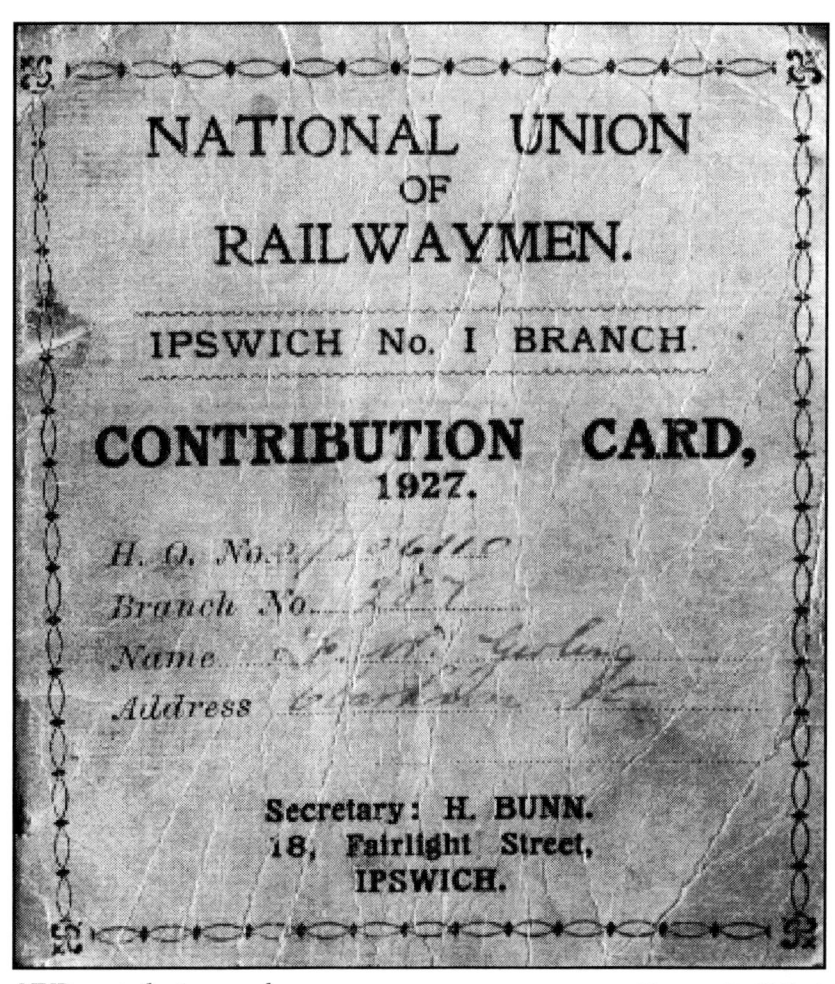

*NUR contribution card cover.* (Courtesy D. Girling)

accompanied them to the Police Station where Superintendent Firman granted them an interview. When they saw the Chief Constable later, he informed them that he had instructions that must be carried out. On hearing this statement Mr Curl told the police that if the tenant's furniture was turned out on to the street it could lead to a railway strike, and he would certainly use his influence to make sure this happened.

On the Tuesday in question, a special court sat at 10.00 am when the case was again considered. After listening to the deputation and the tenant's solicitor, the bench retired. On returning, they asked the deputation to agree to allow the tenant's furniture to be stored in a building at Stoke Rectory for a week to enable the owner to move into his house and for the other house to be cleaned. This was agreed.

It was now 11.30 am. The deputation went to inform Mr Schofield of their efforts on his behalf, and the findings of the special court. A crowd of railwaymen had assembled at the house, ready to render any assistance possible to the tenant about to be evicted. When however they learned of the arrangements made they took no further part in the case.

Mr Schofield, realising that nothing else could be done, thanked the deputation for their help and left the house by the time stipulated. The incident was now closed, apart from the tenant's wife making several rude remarks to the deputation; she obviously did not share her husband's view that everything possible had been done on their behalf.

In 1931 the National Union of Railwaymen held their annual conference in Ipswich, at the Co-operative Hall in Carr Street, from the 5th to the 11th of July. In due course two more Ipswich branches were formed. The original, or No. 1 Branch, catered for most grades and skills of railwaymen, typically station staff, platelayers, shunters, guards, signalmen, goods porters, and most 'outside' railway workers. No. 2 Branch represented supervisory staff and No. 3 Branch included wagon shop fitters and carpenters, and locomotive fitters and engineers.

Engine drivers and firemen in East Anglia were usually ASLEF members; only a handful were NUR members at any one time.

From the mid-1960s to the late 1990s, modernisation, rationalisation, and privatisation have meant continuous reduction in the work force throughout the industry and a drastic decline in membership for all railway unions. NUR branches at country depots and stations, such as at Bury St Edmunds, folded and the remaining members transferred to Ipswich where, by the 1980s, only No. 1 Branch survived. During the ten years up to the time of writing (1997) the number of members dropped from about seven hundred to only two hundred and fifty.

In 1990 members of the National Union of Railwaymen were balloted on a proposal to merge with the National Union of Seamen. The latter had experienced legal and financial problems resulting from a dispute and conflict with new trade union law. Both unions had suffered serious membership loss and the proposal was accepted. The NUR and NUS lost their separate identities and emerged as the Rail Maritime and Transport Union (RMT).

# Great Eastern Railway Employees' Sick and Orphan Society

THE Society was established in 1903 and registered in London as No. 970 under the Friendly Societies Act of 1896. The Society's registered office was at Liverpool Street Station.

The objects of the Society were to provide, by means of voluntary subscriptions and donations from the Company and others, relief for members during incapacity caused by sickness, accident, or other bodily or mental infirmity. Payments were made on the death of a member for the maintenance of his children aged 15 or under, or for funeral expenses of a member's wife. The Company by Deed Poll in 1903 undertook to donate half-yearly a sum equivalent to an aggregate of twopence for every member's weekly contribution to the Society funds.

Qualification for membership allowed all male employees of the Company (from 1923 the Great Eastern Section of the LNER), aged 16-34 and in sound health, to join. Four classes of membership were available, that is A, B, C & D. In 1936 for example, weekly contributions were 1/1d to 1/5d depending on age for class A down to 8d to 10d weekly for Class D. Sick pay benefits were respectively 20/-, 16/-, 12/- and 8/- for 26 weeks and half of these amounts for the remainder of such illness.

Accident pay was 17/- a week for 26 weeks and half pay for a further 78 weeks for all classes, the weekly accident contribution was the same (2d) for all classes and age groups. Payments on the death of a member were respectively £25, £20, £15 and £10, and for a member's wife the benefits were £7.10s, £6, £4.10s and £3. Weekly payments on the death of a child born in wedlock and under the age of 15 ranged from 3/6d for one child, 5/- for two, and up to 9/6d for six or more children. The benefit was usually paid to the member's widow or an appointed guardian.

All claims for benefit had to be supported by a doctor's written certificate duly certified by the station master, supervisor, foreman or chief of department. As with most conditions imposed by similar organisations, Rule 14 governing receipt of sick or accident benefit was rigorously applied. "No such member shall quit his home without leaving word where he may be found, or travel more than ten miles from home, or enter a public house or place of public amusement, or be absent from home between 7.00 pm & 8.00 am from 25th September to 25th March, or between 9.00 pm and 8.00 am from 26th March until 24th September." These restrictions had to be observed strictly and were backed up by sick visitors, appointed by the secretary, who were empowered to visit any member in receipt of allowances.

The Committee contributed to hospitals or other institutions an annual sum of up to £50 to secure for the members of the Society the benefits of such hospitals etc.

Many changes have naturally been made over the years, contributions and benefits have been continuously revised whilst some of the older scales have long been closed to new entrants. The conditions applying to those members in receipt of benefit have been relaxed. The member today "shall refrain from behaviour calculated to retard recovery and shall not leave his place of residence without leaving word where he may be found nor travel more than ten miles from his residence without requesting consent of the Society" and so on.

The Sick & Orphan Society was extremely popular as were similar Friendly Societies that met vital needs prior to the advent of the National Health Service and the Welfare State in 1948. It is remarkable that the Society has remained in favour, and indeed survived, for almost a century.

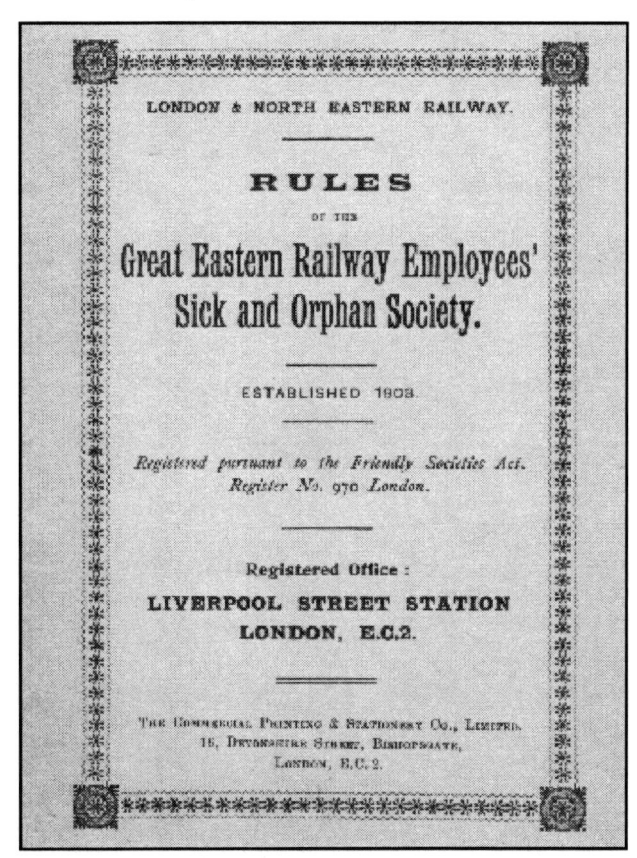

*Cover of rule book for the Sick and Orphan Society*

# Local Welfare Funds

THE Ipswich Locomotive Department's Mutual Aid Fund was an example of a fund run by local trade unionists to assist locomen in cases of hardship. The contribution cards were printed in Ipswich and the actual contributions were only sixpence (2½p) per week, even in the late 1960s. Few, however, of the younger men joined, and the fund ceased when the Ipswich Locomotive Depot closed in 1968.

The Great Eastern Sick Fund, despite its title, was another locally-run, old established scheme for locomen and station staff at Ipswich, with a collector at Croft Street and another at the station. There were some 200 members during the 1950s, but again it was wound up following a decline in membership and the eventual closure of the "Loco".

Branch funds were customarily organised by most ASLEF union branches, supported by voluntary additional contributions, and were available to members in all kinds of financial need at the discretion of the branch committee.

These funds were indicative of the experiences of earlier generations before the almost forgotten impact that the Welfare State made in 1948. Improved trade union agreements, including sick pay, and more recently salaried status, all combined to render the local benefit funds superfluous and hence their eventual demise. That so many existed and survived for so many years reflects the awareness of the locomen to the needs and hardships of their workmates, and the willingness of many to take on the thankless task of collecting subscriptions.

While by no means unique within industry, railway footplate staff traditionally looked after their own. It came from years of hard graft, acquired skills and loyalty, usually only noticed by the public when speed records were broken miles away from East Anglia, or a long simmering dispute with a one-time autocratic management ended in a disruption of service to make headlines in the newspapers.

The following quotations are taken from "A Handy Book of Information", published in 1909 by The Railway Officers' and Servants' Association (see earlier). The small booklet was noted as being both useful and interesting to railwaymen.

*"Railway Men and their Duty - It is an admitted and indisputable fact that Railway men are always ready to, and often do, make great sacrifices at the call of duty. They take great risks fearlessly, and often endanger both life and limb in the performance of their duty to their employers and the travelling public; yet there are numbers who from want of a little thought neglect their duty to themselves, their wives and children."*

*"Not once, or twice, in our rough-island story,*
*The path of Duty was the way to Glory."*
*........Tennyson.*

*"Evil is wrought by want of thought, as well as want of heart."*

*"Leave not to chance that which foresight may provide for, or care prevent."*

*"The first years of man must make provision for the last."*

*"Old age comes on apace. Spare when young to spend when old."*

# *Leisure*

## Early years of the Loco Club

Taken from *"History of the Working Class Movement in Ipswich"* by Robert Ratcliffe

SOON after the loco men's strike in January 1924, a Women's section of the Associated Society of Locomotive Engineers and Firemen was formed in Ipswich, comprising the wives of members of that union.

On February 10th 1925, they held a social evening at St Peter's Church Hall in St Peter's Street, and a most enjoyable time was spent, the idea of having a permanent home of their own being considered at this gathering. Little further developed until May 5th, the same year, when a special meeting of the ASLEF was held at the EUR Hotel in Croft Street to go thoroughly into the question.

At this meeting a Club Committee was formed, Mr A. J. Hatch being elected Chairman and Mr C. W. English, Secretary. The Committee soon got to work and leaflets were distributed among union members inviting them to take up shares in the new club. £75 was taken up in the first six weeks and a plot of land in Ipswich, at the top of Station Street and Rectory Road, was chosen as the ideal spot for the club. Negotiations were opened with the owner who wanted £100 for it, but eventually it was purchased for £50.

On June 14th 1925 a special meeting of loan members was held and Messrs. C. W. Hatch and G. H. Pinkney were appointed trustees. At this meeting Mr English resigned the secretaryship and Mr Hatch was appointed in his place.

Nothing much developed until March 5th 1926 when the Club Scheme Committee was put on a more businesslike footing. Up to now Mr Hatch had had the dual position of Secretary and Chairman, but at this meeting Mr H. Percy was appointed Chairman. The Secretary reported upon an interview he had had with an architect for the erection of a permanent building which he estimated would cost £2,569.

This was considered to be out of the question, and further quotations from other firms were asked for, one from Mr Read at £650 being eventually accepted. Loans from members had now reached approximately £300 but still more money was required, so a loan of £500 was obtained from the Freehold Land Society, and the order for the erection of club premises was placed with Mr Read on May 10th 1927. The building was completed and duly furnished, exhausting all monies received except 5/8d, which princely sum was the amount of capital on hand when a month's supply of stock was ordered with obligation to pay for it by January 15th, 1928.

The Club was opened on November 27th 1927, but the only people to turn up were the president and secretary. Even Mr A. Fisher, who had promised to act as steward at the opening, failed to arrive, so the secretary acted as steward and the total takings on this occasion amounted to 5d from the two members present. But a start had been made and the custom grew bit by bit. For some time the work of the steward was carried on by Messrs. T. Latter, N. Dickerson, D. Burton and V. Trenter on a voluntary basis. Later on others came forward and helped with the work. On April 29th 1929 Mr C. Moss was engaged as full time steward and carried on with this work for several years.

At first only members of the ASLEF had been allowed to join the Club, but at the time of appointing a full time steward, it was agreed to invite the public to become members.

At a committee meeting held on April 19th 1929, it was decided to purchase two old cottages adjoining the Club, which were in a very bad state, just being slum property. Negotiations opened, and the properties were purchased, and eventually pulled down ready for extension of the Club. During January 1930 Mr I. Cobbold presented the Club with a billiard table, and plans were drawn up for building a billiard room, which was done eventually by direct labour at a cost of £200.

At a committee meeting held on January 1st 1933, it was decided to go all out for a permanent building, plans being drawn up and the new Club being erected by Messrs. Gower and Robinson at a cost of £1,770. The new building was opened on Saturday February 3rd 1934. It was soon well patronised and within ten years all loans had been cleared off, and there was a comfortable bank balance in hand to cover all stock holders.

LEISURE

No. 19                                                                                    £ 2-0-0

## THE IPSWICH LOCOMOTIVEMEN'S CLUB AND INSTITUTE LIMITED

INCORPORATED UNDER THE INDUSTRIAL AND PROVIDENT SOCIETIES ACTS, 1893 and 1913.
REGISTERED No. 10619 R. SUFFOLK.

**This is to Certify** that the Ipswich Locomotivemen's Club and Institute Limited is indebted to ......Mr Robt Goodchild...... of ......Rectory Road Ipswich...... in the principal sum of ......Two...... Pounds receipt of which is hereby acknowledged, advanced as a loan to the said Club and Institute, upon the condition that Interest at the rate of ..35/-.. per cent. per annum is paid to the order of the above-mentioned Lender half-yearly on January 1st and July 1st and upon the conditions contained in No. 20 of the Rules of the said Club and Institute.

**Signed** for and on behalf of the said Club and Institute the ......first...... day of ......January...... 1933.

REGISTERED OFFICE:
STATION STREET,
IPSWICH.

G. H. Pinkney  } Members of
T. E. Latter   } Committee.

O. J. Walet ......Secretary.

*Locoman Robert Goodchild's loan-receipt from the Loco Club. It is dated 1st January 1933, the day on which the committee decided to erect a permanent building to house the Club.* (Courtesy Victor Goodchild)

# British Railways Staff Association

*The official programme for the opening of the branch premises in Willoughby Road, near to Ipswich Station, on Thursday, 11th November 1954. The railway helped with the funding of the BRSA.* (Courtesy Kelvin Higgins Collection)

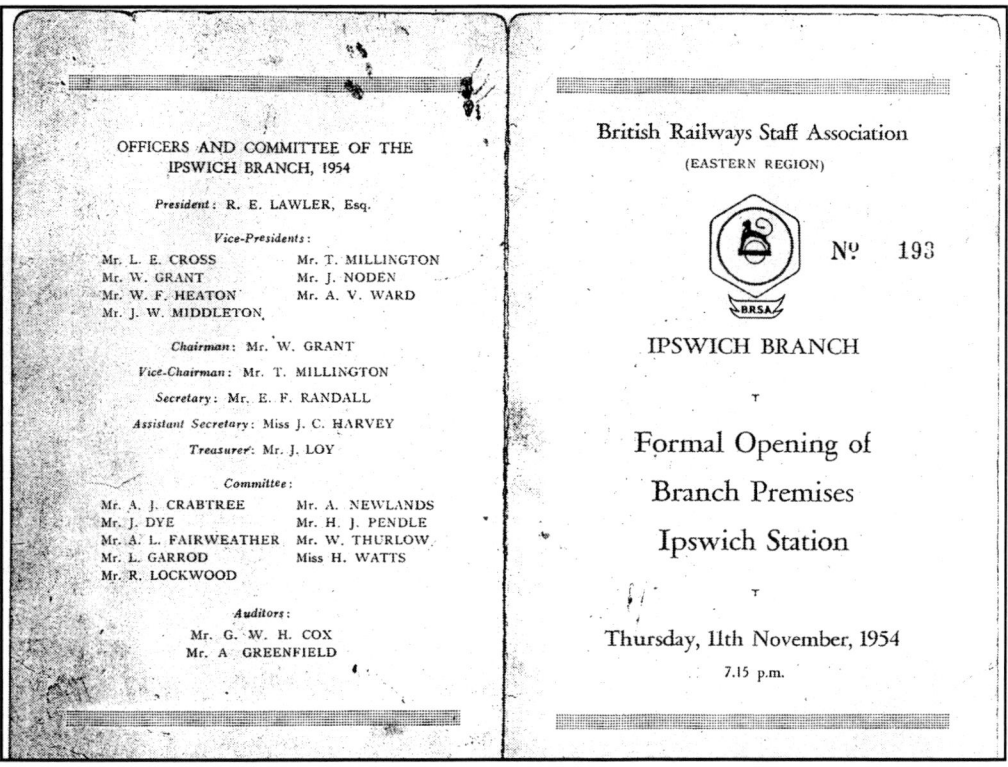

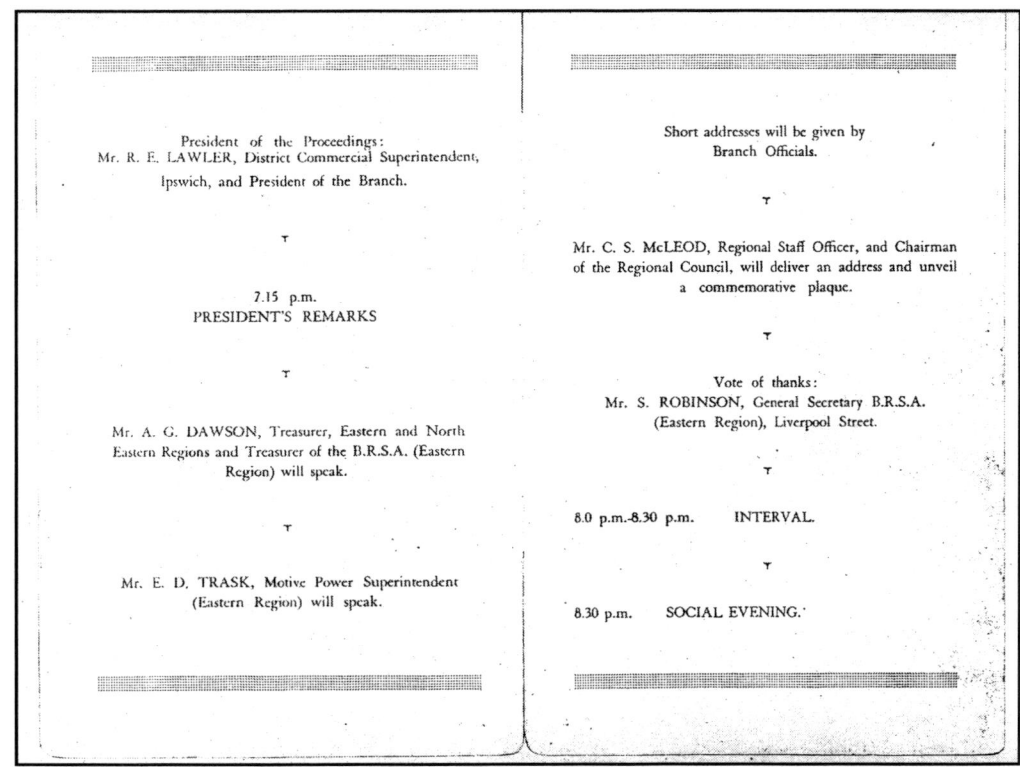

---

**OFFICERS AND COMMITTEE OF THE IPSWICH BRANCH, 1954**

President: R. E. LAWLER, Esq.

Vice-Presidents:
- Mr. L. E. CROSS
- Mr. W. GRANT
- Mr. W. F. HEATON
- Mr. J. W. MIDDLETON
- Mr. T. MILLINGTON
- Mr. J. NODEN
- Mr. A. V. WARD

Chairman: Mr. W. GRANT
Vice-Chairman: Mr. T. MILLINGTON
Secretary: Mr. E. F. RANDALL
Assistant Secretary: Miss J. C. HARVEY
Treasurer: Mr. J. LOY

Committee:
- Mr. A. J. CRABTREE
- Mr. J. DYE
- Mr. A. L. FAIRWEATHER
- Mr. L. GARROD
- Mr. R. LOCKWOOD
- Mr. A. NEWLANDS
- Mr. H. J. PENDLE
- Mr. W. THURLOW
- Miss H. WATTS

Auditors:
- Mr. G. W. H. COX
- Mr. A. GREENFIELD

---

**British Railways Staff Association**
(EASTERN REGION)

N⁰ 193

**IPSWICH BRANCH**

Formal Opening of
Branch Premises
Ipswich Station

Thursday, 11th November, 1954

7.15 p.m.

---

President of the Proceedings:
Mr. R. E. LAWLER, District Commercial Superintendent, Ipswich, and President of the Branch.

7.15 p.m.
PRESIDENT'S REMARKS

Mr. A. G. DAWSON, Treasurer, Eastern and North Eastern Regions and Treasurer of the B.R.S.A. (Eastern Region) will speak.

Mr. E. D. TRASK, Motive Power Superintendent (Eastern Region) will speak.

---

Short addresses will be given by Branch Officials.

Mr. C. S. McLEOD, Regional Staff Officer, and Chairman of the Regional Council, will deliver an address and unveil a commemorative plaque.

Vote of thanks:
Mr. S. ROBINSON, General Secretary B.R.S.A. (Eastern Region), Liverpool Street.

8.0 p.m.–8.30 p.m.    INTERVAL.

8.30 p.m.    SOCIAL EVENING.

LEISURE

## *Football Teams*

*Great Eastern Railway football team, 1917, pictured at Ipswich Railway Station; the tunnel portal can be seen in background at right. The team's home ground was at Stone Lodge Lane in Ipswich and their pavillion was an old railway coach. Meetings were held at the Reaper's Inn in Stoke Street.* (Photo Ken Leighton Collection)

*Another picture of the Great Eastern Railway football team. They played in black and amber in the Ipswich and District League Division One. Back row (left to right): Clow, Stannard, Bloomfield, Munnings, A. Durrell, Grundy, Bloomfield. Front row: F. Strange, Bert Orvis, Lionel Turner, A. Warren and King.*
(Photo and names courtesy W. Foulser)

*Railway football team, 1963. Standing (left to right):R. Pearce, G.Higgins, B. Bradbrook, R. Page, Pryke, P. Davey, C. Brame. Sitting: C. Minns, Ward, A. Morley, T. Brown, C. Waters.* (Photo Kelvin Higgins Collection)

*I. F. C. Railfreight football team, 1992. Squad made up of Ipswich drivers, trainmen and shunters. Back row (left to right): A. Clouting, A. Holland (manager), K. Higgins, G. Edwards, A. Fowkes, G. Cox, R. Medows. Front row: J. Orvis, M. Bradbrook, R. Burman, A. Derret, C. Leonard. Missing from the picture were S. Szcespansksi (Spanner) and C. Legget.* (Photo by Mrs K. Higgins)

## The Ipswich & District British Railways (Eastern Region) Chrysanthemum Society

THE Ipswich & District British Railways Chrysanthemum Society was formed in August 1951 after notices were posted inviting all members of Eastern Region staff, interested in the cultivation of quality chrysanthemum blooms, to attend a meeting at the Old Social Club, Ipswich Station.

Officers elected at that first meeting were:

| | |
|---|---|
| VICE PRESIDENTS | Richard Hardy (Loco Shed Master), Ernest Payne (Driver), G. Hawes (Driver), S. W. Bailey (Inspector). |
| CHAIRMAN | Wallace Rose |
| SECRETARY | E. Clarke (Driver) |
| SHOW SECRETARY | W. Versey |
| TREASURER | B. Nicholls |
| AUDITORS | Alderman A. Cook, A Towler (Driver). |
| COMMITTEE | Mrs Rose, Mrs Williamson, Messrs. Meehan, Spurling, Hawes, Waspe, Topple, Foulser, Williamson. |

The aims of the Society were "to try to develop good fellowship and happy contacts, arrange lectures, and assist beginners to learn the arts and crafts of chrysanthemum culture."

The annual subscription for each member was two shillings, and a retired railwayman or a member's wife paid one shilling. It was agreed at the meeting to hold a chrysanthemum show on November 17th and 18th at the Social Club, Willoughby Road, Ipswich.

At the next general meeting, Mr W. Foulser presented a challenge cup to the Society, and the Show Secretary, Mr W. Versey, reported that encouraging assistance had been given by local traders in supplying special prizes, including the promise of a challenge cup by Mr A. J. Sneezum. The Secretary, Ted Clarke, said that membership was increasing daily and now stood at seventy. Members were also informed that Messrs. Cramphorn Ltd. allowed a 10% discount on purchases of gardening requisites from its branches.

The chrysanthemum show, held as planned in November, was opened by Mrs Bunny Haskell, daughter of Mr R. E. Lawler (District Commercial

*The scene at St Mary Stoke Parish Hall during the Society's Chrysanthemum Show in November 1952. In the background (centre) is a map, made from flower petals, depicting the Eastern Region railway network.*

(Photo courtesy W. Foulser)

Superintendent and President of the Society). There were 175 entries, and by this time membership numbered 100. The judges were Mr S. Nunn (Deputy Park Superintendent, Chantry Park), and Mr H. Harwood (Co-operative Nurseries).

Mr Nunn, speaking also on behalf of his fellow judge, said the quality and number of the blooms surprised them, having regard to the fact that the Society was only twelve weeks old, and added that some of the blooms were up to national standard.

Winner of the A. J. Sneezum Cup was Mr C. Edwards of Lowestoft, while the National Chrysanthemum Society award of merit and the Foulser Challenge Cup went to Mr E. Clarke.

November chrysanthemum shows continued to be held during the 1950s, some taking place at St Mary Stoke Parish Hall in Luther Road, Ipswich, and later, in 1959 for instance, at the Art Gallery, High Street. Although an intended early chrysanthemum and dahlia show was cancelled for September 1952 owing to the low number of entries, similar shows went ahead in the years that followed. The Society later changed its name to The British Railways and Ipswich and District Chrysanthemum and Dahlia Society. Sadly, the Society is no longer in existence.

*Society members at their 1954 Chrysanthemum Show. (Left to right): W. Foulser, E. Clarke, N. Spurling and W. Gardiner. Behind them is a replica smoke-box door of* The East Anglian, *worked in flower petals.*

(Photo courtesy G. Clarke)

# *Ipswich Men*

# Ipswich Men

by Kenneth Leighton

IN bygone days when a new railway came into being, our Victorian forefathers took great pains to record the event in minute detail. Every aspect was scrutinized with tireless energy. The livery of the coaches, the finery of the passengers, the band, the banquet; all were written up with gusto. The locomotive, usually referred to as "the fiery steed", was watched warily, and every hiss of steam or belch of smoke dramatically described.

Very rarely did the central figure, the driver, get even a passing mention in the closely printed account of the great doings of the day. Our local Eastern Union Railway was a fortunate exception to this rule, for we are told that the inaugural train of thirteen vehicles drawn by the 2-2-2 tender engines No. 1 *Colchester* and No. 2 *Ipswich*, left Ipswich at 10.30 am on 11th June 1846 for Colchester, the leading engine being driven by Mr Robert Taylor, Foreman of Engines at Ipswich Croft Street Depot.

Sadly, at this point the pattern that was to dominate the official railway mind into our time was set, for the reporter of 1846 stated that "the second engine was in the charge of a trusted driver". This laid down the British practice; the drivers of our railway locomotives were trusted, respected, but anonymous. Apart from the few who worked for companies that emblazoned the driver's name on the cab side or front plate of his regular engine, the greater mass of loco men over the years were nameless Olympians who could be seen gazing benevolently down from the steamy fastness of their cabs at terminal stations, or very briefly glimpsed as they peered ahead from the "fiery steeds" in full flight across the countryside.

Very often tragedy broke the wall of anonymity as in 1900 when the boiler of a Y14, 0-6-0 goods engine No. 522 of the GER exploded at Westerfield with great violence and catapulted her Ipswich crew into eternity. Today they are still remembered; Driver Barnard and Fireman MacDonald, two men lifted from the nameless

*One of the earliest surviving photographs of an Ipswich engine and men. 0-6-0 Class 477 No. 526 was one of fifty engines built during 1871-73. This engine was the last of the class and was built by the Yorkshire Engine Company. All had been withdrawn by 1902. They were designed by Locomotive Superintendent Samuel W. Johnson, who had left the GER in 1873 for a similar post with the Midland Railway. The photograph was taken near Halifax Junction and the fireman at the extreme right was Mr Everett.* (Photo courtesy Kenneth Leighton.)

*Resplendent No. 1877, one of the first forty-one "Claud Hamilton" 4-4-0s, as originally built with a round topped firebox. No. 1877 was new in 1902 and it is quite likely that this photograph dates from that time. The locomotive, as British Railways No. 62528, was withdrawn in 1951. The only person identified in the picture is Fireman Bert Carter, sixth from left, who lived at 6 Croft Street, later moving to Hadleigh. He became a driver but died in 1931 aged forty-nine.*
(Photo courtesy W. Carter, son of Bert Carter)

mass by a great and terrible gout of steam.

The next Ipswich men to achieve public fame did so in far happier circumstances. In 1911 a very young GER man, C. J. Allen, wanted material for an article in the GER Magazine. This was gathered with the blessings of the senior Great Eastern management and the article was printed as "On the Footplate, A Trip on the Norfolk Coast Express". In the years prior to the Great War the *Norfolk Coast Express* was the crack express of the Great Eastern Railway and the honour of providing engines and men for the working was shared days about by Ipswich and Norwich Depots. The job was an arduous one. It meant hauling a train weighing between 350 and 400 tons from Liverpool Street to North Walsham, 130 miles in 158 minutes, with a non-superheated engine weighing only 50 tons.

On the day of Mr Allen's trip, Ipswich held the reins and at the head of a magnificent rake of Great Eastern Bogies stood engine No. 1809 of the famous "Claud Hamilton" class of 4-4-0's. At this time the Ipswich *Norfolk Coast Express* crews and engines were hand picked for the job. As a result the most extraordinary feats of power and speed were being coaxed from the relatively small engines. Mr Allen had hit upon a star engine and a crack crew, Driver Arthur Cage and Fireman Cross, for on that day no less than five minutes were slashed off the booked time for the run.

Arthur Cage or "Chuffy" as he was known, was a stocky gentleman with a Captain Kettle beard and a taste for hard running. For years he struck sparks from Great Eastern metals and then spent the last few years of his railway career quietly working the Aldeburgh branch.

The magnificent work done with the *Norfolk Coast Express* prompted C. J. Allen to publish in the February 1912 issue of the GER magazine a table of the best runs of 1911 achieved with that prestigious train.

After a span of sixty years the list of engines and men reads now like a roll of honour, and raises visions of Driver Cage and his contemporaries with their elegant blue engines going hell for leather from London to North Norfolk with a flair and style that still makes the pulse quicken. Coleman and Strutt on No. 1874, Barnard and Frost on 1813, Sadler and Dennent on 1812, Storey and Barnard on 1823, Pinkney and Barnard on 1816 and Lincoln and Last with 1815. All men who gave a lifetime to the GER and in some cases sent their sons to give another lifetime to the LNER and British Railways.

Driver George Lincoln ran 1815 for years and when the new S69 Class (the 1500s) of 4-6-0s came out in 1912, Ipswich received a batch to cope with the heavier trains. Mr Lincoln took No. 1518 and worked the newcomer with the same skill and verve that he had displayed with his old "Claud Hamilton" 4-4-0. But 1518 bit the hand that drove her and gave her driver the worst moment of his career. Descending Belstead Bank at speed one day the great S69 developed an uneasy lurching gait and even as George's hand flew to the brake there came a loud crack and the driving axle broke under him. Mercifully, in the grip of the brake blocks the wheels kept to gauge and the engine held the road, being brought safely to a stand; even so the memory of that wild shuddering ride stayed with Driver Lincoln to the end of his days.

Another of the 1500s went to Bill Barnard and Sid Keeble of Ipswich Shed. Today faded photographs of them are treasured showing the great engine proud and full chested at the tunnel end of No. 2 platform at Ipswich. Steam simmers from the safety valves and the summer sun of 1912 gleams on the immaculate metal and paintwork. The old Great Eastern express headcode graces the front end with a great dignity. Sid Keeble stands on the raised part of the running plate clasping the hand rail. Nearer the smokebox Driver Barnard stands holding his badge of office; a polished oil feeder. Both men radiate pride in their calling and in their new mount. Within a few short months the next summer's sun shone on that proud trio for the last time as 1506 bore herself and her crew to a terrible and untimely end in the Colchester smash of 1913.

And so it went on. Engines and men changed, the "Clauds" and "Super Clauds", the 1500s, the 2800 "Sandringhams" and the B1 4-6-0s came and went. The young fire-eating speed merchants slowly grew old and grey and had to retire. Younger men stepped up into the driver's place until they too became old and grey and left the footplate for a small pension. Most had passed an entire career unknown to the millions of souls they had carried in safety over untold miles.

Some are with us still, some now exist in memory or faded photographs. All of them would scorn any suggestion of hero worship or public recognition, yet what a band they were! The last of the old style enginemen like Billy Mutimer with an impish sense of fun; Ernest Payne, the gentleman and polished ex-World War 1 army officer; Frank Cocksedge, precise, scientific, immaculate; and George Hawes who addressed everyone regardless of rank as "Boy John". That is except for the Shed Master who as a mark of respect was on one memorable occasion addressed as "My Dear"!

These are just a few of that great company of men who saw the end of steam at Ipswich and the birth of the diesel era.

Today, Ipswich men still blast a path across the

*Great Eastern Class S69 No. 1562, built at Stratford in 1920. The four old-timers on the footplate have not been identified.*  (Photo Kelvin Higgins Collection)

length and breadth of East Anglia in machines that would stagger the old timers. Their glazed and heated cabs insulate them from the passengers far more than the open cab of the steam engine did. The modern driver carries on the traditions of skill, trust and pride in the job established over long years by his many predecessors. He also preserves the tradition of anonymity and in his privacy is well content, for by and large, he is a modest man.

*Since this piece was written in 1971 for the handbook of the Ipswich and District Historical Transport Society drastic changes have overtaken our railways. The great Depot which had started from such small beginnings at Croft Street in 1846 had closed in 1968 but in 1971 was still intact. Today, except for one small fragment, the old Depot has been swept away. A few marks on the weed strewn ground serve as a reminder of the positions of the old buildings that made up the Shed that was known in BR days as 32B. Its engines and men have all gone and the small facility at Ipswich Station handles a much diminished workload.*

*Although the job is smaller, the quality of Ipswich enginemen remains at the same high level it has known for the last 150 years.*

*The intervening years have seen the passing of all the men named in this piece. Once the footpaths of Stoke echoed around the clock to the tramp of their footsteps as they trod the well worn way from Croft Street to the "New" station to relieve incoming crews. Hours later they would make the steep weary climb up Willoughby Hill on route to the "shed" to book off.*

*Their tread in the dark hours must have woken many who heard the footfall and subdued murmur of the voices of men returning tired from a trip to Whitemoor, Goodmayes or Temple Mills. Turning over and drifting off again the sleeper knew their passing meant all was well with the world outside.*

*Now they have all gone. Croft Street and Rectory Road know them no longer. The hobnails and quiet voices have moved into history and our world is not the same without them.*

**Kenneth G. Leighton 1996.**

*S69 engine No. 1519, built at Stratford in 1913. The photograph was taken one Sunday morning at Ipswich Loco Depot c 1919. The only person known is Bob Tyrell, on ground, wearing a cloth cap.* (Photo courtesy David Cobley)

*Great Eastern engine No. 1529 (LNER No. 8529) pictured at Ipswich Loco Depot in the late 1920s. Engine built at Stratford Works in 1914. On boiler (left to right): Jumbo Robinson, Toby Waterman, Ginger Knock and Jim Talbot. On framing: Vic Wroth, ?, Bob Tricker, Tom Noble, Bob Fenning, E. Barber, S. Eley, Bill Dale, Wilf Taylor, Val Carter, Frank Peachey and Ron Manning. On Ground, Philip Jay.* (Photo courtesy Mrs Howard, names by Bill Foulser)

*Pictured late 1920s (left to right, at back) Percy Coates, ?, Jack Baldwin. (Front), ?, George Gummerson, Bert Tweed, ?, Bob Stiff, Eric Pryke, Don Dutton and Tim Schofield with foot on pipe.* (Eric Pryke Collection)

## Trials and Tribulations

From cleaner to mainline driver, by Ken Freestone

I STARTED my railway career at Ipswich Loco Depot in October 1947 after passing an intelligence test and a medical examination requiring good eyesight and colour vision, for entrance to the footplate grade which I had decided upon.

The line of promotion in this grade was engine cleaner, passed cleaner/acting fireman, fireman, passed fireman/acting driver, and finally driver, but as I was to find out, it could take several years before the status of a main line driver was achieved. In fact, at some small depots, it was possible for a man to reach retirement age without ever becoming a regular driver.

The change-over from steam to diesel operation on main lines started about 1959, so for twelve years, apart from two years National Service with the RAF, I was engaged entirely with work involving steam engines. Eventually as a "secondman" and then a driver I progressed to diesel and electric working but I look back on those early steam years as the most interesting and satisfying of my railway career.

I have always felt that a railway fireman never received the full recognition he deserved. His was a skilful and demanding occupation requiring a great deal of physical effort. The top express engine drivers of the day could not have achieved all they did without the constant supply of steam and water provided by the fireman. The majority of these drivers would be the first to admit this fact, having been firemen themselves.

This supply of steam was often only achieved after overcoming many adversities, for example low grade coal, poor steaming engines, or even the fireman himself could sometimes be at fault. Correct firing of a railway engine was an art in itself. The fire had to be kept right at all times and this was not as easy as it may sound. Some of the engines were overdue for repairs and were very rough riding. Attempting to carefully place every shovelful of coal whilst on the footplate of one of these engines was a very difficult task. When running at speed with a white-hot fire, the glare was of such intensity that the actual fire could not be seen and each shovelful had to be placed by experience. Fireboxes of different types of engines varied considerably in their dimensions and this had to be continuously in the fireman's mind as he fed his fire.

It must be evident therefore that a fireman's job did not consist of throwing a few pieces of coal on to the fire now and again, and having a rest in between. On a heavy main line express passenger or freight train the fireman would be occupied practically the whole running time.

Obviously a passed cleaner just starting firing duties would not be expected to perform this type of work as he would not have the necessary experience. He would start by being booked with drivers on shed duties, shunting yard engines, branch work, and short-trip local goods work. During this period he would be expected to learn all he could from the driver and any friendly fireman he was acquainted with.

Apart from a few exceptions I found that much could be gained from these men. They were willing to impart their knowledge and experience gained over the years, provided they realised you were keen and interested in the job. Railway work was similar to many other occupations in those days; there was no tuition as such and one had to learn as one went along.

Many of the young cleaners studied books on locomotive technology which they bought themselves but railway engines could not be worked solely by reading a book; practical knowledge and experience were invaluable. There was an organization known as the Mutual Improvement Class (MIC) which was run on a volunteer basis by experienced drivers or acting drivers who were willing to devote a few of their leisure hours to help any aspiring young locoman wishing to expand his knowledge.

These were usually held on Sunday mornings to enable as many as possible to attend. In addition to the theory aspect, models were available to demonstrate the movements of the pistons, valves, connecting rods, and link motion, and by operating these models it could be shown how the presence of steam in the cylinders was used to impart power to the driving wheels in forward and reverse motion. When firemen were promoted to driving duties, they were required to pass a rigorous theory test requiring extensive knowledge of the locomotive, and rules and regulations, in addition to demonstrating their practical knowledge. If promotion moves were known to be in the offing, then the numbers of men attending the classes would increase dramatically.

Occasionally we would go for a trip on the main line in our own time after finding a friendly driver and fireman who were willing to allow us to travel on the footplate with them. Once underway the fireman would hand over his shovel with a "come on then, let's see what you can do!" This was an ideal way to gain insight into main line work and I learnt much from this. Also, in our early days as cleaners, we had ample opportunity to learn the more technical details of the locomotive. As engine cleaners we were considered to be veritable maids of all work and would be utilized by the running shed foreman to fulfil a myriad of tasks. Any boilerwasher, tube-cleaner, steam-raiser, fitter, storekeeper etc., who found himself without the services of his regular mate, would apply to the foreman who would then detail a cleaner to assist him. This did not always go down very well with us as we considered ourselves to be members of the elite footplate grade and looked upon this type of work as rather below us.

That was the law of the day however and I found that by assisting these other grades a great deal could be learnt of work that normally we would not come into contact with. Another duty that the foreman would sometimes hand out to us was "calling up" men who were on early morning turns and this would involve cycling to these men's homes and banging loudly on their doors or windows to make sure they were up and ready for work. We always tried when on cleaning duties to get an engine situated as far as possible from the running shed foreman's office in the main shed, since if one of these jobs cropped up the foreman would usually grab the nearest cleaner and delegate him for it. The foremen in those days were Clem Hollingsworth, Sid Moyes, "Ninety" Burrows, and Tammy Gooch.

We were fortunate that Ipswich at that time had a large variety of jobs. In addition to the main line, the Ipswich shed was also responsible for several local branch lines. More than 90 locomotives were based at the Depot, appearing in all shapes and sizes, from the lowly little tank shunting engine to the mighty B1s. A large amount of shed work took place at the Depot including coaling, watering, turning, preparation and disposal, in addition to the outside shunting yards and main line jobs, and this work required the efforts of many drivers and fireman. Any aspiring young locoman therefore was ideally placed to make his way from the early less demanding stages through to the ultimate main line express work.

Here was I therefore, on the bottom rung of the ladder and starting my career as a rookie engine cleaner with the LNER at Ipswich two months before my sixteenth birthday, having been born in the town in December 1931. Owing to the fact that my father was an RAF serviceman, my early years were rather disruptive. We left Ipswich when he was posted to the RAF Station at Feltwell, where we lived in married quarters and I started at the local village school. We returned to Ipswich when my father was posted abroad, shortly before the start of World War II. I finished my schooling at Tower Ramparts School, leaving at the age of fourteen and starting my working career at a small jobbing printers in January 1946. I was employed as an apprentice compositor and I found the job interesting but became increasingly disillusioned by the small amount of time I was actually employed on typesetting.

Being the "boy" at this small firm, I had to do all the errands, sweep the floor, make the tea, clean the press rollers, fold, cut and perform a host of other mundane tasks. I was quite resigned to this at first but as time went on and there was no improvement, I entered my second year with the thought that perhaps I was not cut out to be a printer. My mind was finally made up when one day the boss confided to us that he was considering allocating a part of the yard to keeping pigs. As I could visualize the task of chief pig-keeper being added to my list of jobs, I decided there and then to say good-bye to a printing career and to look for pastures new.

I now began to take an interest in the job vacancies section of the local evening newspaper, becoming an avid reader of its columns. One night, in the late summer of 1947, there appeared an advertisement for engine cleaners at the loco depot at Wherstead Road. At this time I was living Over Stoke in Purplett Street, not far from the Depot. My uncle Eddie Goodchild was a driver, and his son, my cousin Ray, had just started on the footplate, so this encouraged me further to consider replying to the advertisement, although receiving much well-intentioned advice against the idea, I must admit.

I had never suffered from the "every boy wants to be an engine driver" affliction, but in my youthful enthusiasm, I saw this job as a means to break out and see the world outside. Apart from an occasional train journey to Lowestoft to visit my paternal grandparents, I had travelled very little, being restricted by the war years. This job would enable me to travel and get paid for it. I threw caution to the wind, applied for the position and was accepted. Cleaners were employed at the Loco Depot on a twenty-four hour basis with three shifts of 6am-2pm, 2pm-10pm, and 10pm-6am. In my case, as I was only fifteen years of age, I was not allowed to work the night shift until I reached the age of sixteen, two months later.

And so at 6 o'clock on Monday morning the 13th of October, 1947, I presented myself at the Croft Street entrance to commence my first day as a railwayman, or perhaps I should say boy!

Just inside the entrance gate was the timekeeper's hut. The timekeeper was Charlie Brunning, an ex-locoman who had been badly injured during war service abroad, and was unable to resume his footplate duties. The back wall of the hut was festooned with rows and rows of oval brass discs, each stamped "London and North Eastern Railway" and with a number in the centre. There was also a large clock. I informed him that this was my first day of employment and he handed me one of the discs with the number 242. Before giving this to me however he carefully checked the clock as if I had been five minutes late I would have been cut a quarter of an hour off my eight hours.

*Brass check issued to footplatemen, literally to check if on duty. The hole at the top enabled the timekeeper to hang the disc on the appropriate peg*
(Courtsey Richard Pinkney)

The brass discs were called checks and had to be kept carefully during the time one was on duty and handed back to the time keeper when leaving off work. They were also used for receiving wages which were paid on Fridays, being shown to the pay clerk who would check the number and hand out a small round tin containing notes and loose change. After checking and agreeing the amount, the money was removed and the tin handed back. If there was any dispute a shortage form had to be submitted which would be examined later and any genuine discrepancies put right the following week.

My check number 242 would be mine until I gained promotion when I would receive a fresh check and number. It was said that when a man was promoted to fireman or driver then he had "got his check".

Now, in proud possession of my new check I made my way to the loco sheds, where I was to report to the cleaner foreman. Between the Croft Street entrance and the sheds there was a vast area given over to coal stacks. I had never seen so much coal in my life. Over to the right was another large area taken up by the carriage and wagon repair shops. These extended to the main London Line. Hardly a square foot of land appeared to be wasted.

Ipswich loco depot at that period was a very compact, intensely worked area. There was activity all round the clock and the place never seemed to rest. The buildings and working conditions were Victorian with no sign of any modernisation at all. Everywhere was badly lit and very dangerous at night and in bad visibility. Surveying the gloomy engine sheds, the thought went through my mind of "dark satanic mills" as I weighed up my new working environment.

The cleaner foreman's office was a tiny dark cubby-hole off one side of the main engine shed. The enginemen's signing-on lobby, foreman's office and mess room were also located in this range of outbuildings. The shed itself was dark, open at both ends, and with only two tracks housing no more than six locomotives. Apart from the repair shops, this was the only sheltered accommodation for engines. All maintenance and running repair work was dealt with outside exposed to the elements. I always had great admiration for the men who worked under such primitive and unpleasant conditions. It could be very dangerous and accidents did occur. Fortunately there was a fine body of men well trained in first aid who dealt admirably with any case until medical help could be obtained.

The two tracks that ran through the shed were given names, the origins of which no one appeared to know. They were called the "Express" and the "Bay". Most of the other tracks outside were also named. A few which spring to mind are Ballast Road, Potters Road, Back Hadleigh, Straight Hadleigh, Table road, Tender Road, Tar Road, Main, Straight, Drop Pit, Coal Road, and Lower Shed. There was one long road which ran from Halifax Junction, next to the main line, almost to the mouth of the tunnel. This had various leads off into the loco shed, fitting shops and carriage and wagon shops, and was known as the "Bury Up". The name probably goes back to the time of the Eastern Union Railway when trains for Bury St Edmunds left from here, the site of the original station.

I stood that morning, therefore, in the old shed and awaited my instructions from the foreman cleaner. There were several of us, including one young chap who like myself had just started that day. His name was Ted Rands and he came from Shotley. I became friendly with him until the time we both left in 1950 for National

Service. He did not return to the railway and I never saw him again.

The foreman formed us into groups and gave us each a can of paraffin, a metal scraper, and some cotton waste and cloths, and told us the number of the engine we were to clean. My group or gang were allocated an engine which stood just inside the shed at the London end. This engine, I later learnt, was a 4-4-0 "Claud Hamilton" passenger engine.

Being new to the job I was of course given the dirtiest task, being told by the others to do the "top framings". This was the footplate which ran both sides of the boiler from cab to front buffer beam, and was filthy especially underneath the Westinghouse steam pump located just in front of the cab. The pump leaked copious quantities of thick black treacly oil on to the footplate and these deposits had to be scraped, soaked in paraffin, and cleaned away. It was not a pleasant job by any means. However this was a good initiation and in the weeks that followed I found that cleaning the cab, boiler and tender of a locomotive could be quite satisfying work as at the end of the job one could stand back and see what had been achieved. The wheels and side frames proved to be an unpleasant task however as these would often be coated with a hard crust of dirt to be first laboriously scraped away, involving a very time consuming effort.

The only illumination available at the Depot during the hours of darkness was a small paraffin torch. This consisted of a cylindrical body with a protruding wick which gave off nearly as much smoke as it did light. Primitive conditions indeed but the job was always completed. We never had to keep to a strict time table; if we worked hard and finished the engine in good time and to the foreman's satisfaction then we were allowed to adjourn to the cleaners' mess room for a welcome cup of tea. I have never drunk so many cups of tea in my life as I did in my cleaning days.

My first firing job was in the shed limits working with a driver engaged on various duties. Apart from moving engines around for coal, water, and fitters, and also turning on the turntable, we would be required to prepare and dispose of the engines. Disposing of an engine consisted of cleaning or throwing out the fire, raking the ashpan from a pit underneath, and also cleaning out the smoke-box ashes. Many of the engines were not equipped with a dropping fire-grate and the fire would have to be laboriously pulled out through the fire-door and thrown out of the side by means of a long handled fire iron referred to as a long or short "slice". Some of the fireboxes were about ten feet long by five or six feet wide, therefore this was not a very popular task. A fireman always endeavoured to bring his engine to the shed with the thinnest fire possible to make it easier for the shedman. Woe betide a man who brought in a thick fire; he would not rate very highly in the popularity stakes!

Disposing of an engine was a dirty, horrible job, especially on a windy day when you could get smothered with ash.

Preparation was not so bad and consisted of oiling, cleaning and filling headlamps, cracking and trimming coal, topping up with water, checking all fire-irons were aboard, filling the sand-boxes, preparing the fire, and giving the engine a general clean up. (Not every driver and fireman stepped on to an already prepared engine at the start of their shift; some crews had an hour's

*Young railway engine cleaners pause after a game of football during their break time in the grounds of Luther Road School (now Hillside Primary School) in 1946. The use of the playing field adjacent to the Loco Depot was unofficial but the school pupils were on holiday at the time. Left to right (back row): Peter Dennington, Ike Button, Micky Hammond, Donald Adams, Les Driver. Front row: R. Tabor, Jack Savage, "Strawberry" Hart. These men were among the last to commence their railway careers as LNER employees, as in January 1948 the LNER and the other railway companies were nationalised, becoming British Railways, later British Rail.* (Photo courtesy Peter Dennington)

*Fireman seen cleaning his fire on a J15, uisng a long-handled fire-iron known as a slice.*
(Photo by Aubrey Frost, ABIPP, ARPS)

preparation time booked at the beginning of their spell of duty in which they were expected to get their own engine ready.) This type of work was good experience as regards the internal working of a locomotive but obviously it did not help much with actual firing experience.

This started when I had my first firing "turns" on tank engines engaged on shunting duties in one of the local goods yards. I remember my first job was 5.30am Top Yard, this being the name we gave to Ranelagh Road Goods Yard. For the first time I had an engine to look after for eight hours. These yard engines were continuously employed on a three shift 24 hour basis, only going to the shed at weekends for maintenance, boiler-washing and repairs etc. All running work had to be done by the crews who manned them in the yard. This consisted of coaling, watering, firecleaning etc. for which facilities were provided in the yard. The steaming demands of the engine were not very high as they were solely engaged on yard shunting duties with no main line work involved. This was an ideal job for the novice as there was never any reason to be short of steam and one could learn the basics. That day I finished my shift feeling proud that for eight hours I had been responsible for maintaining steam and water on my own engine!

That was how it all started. Eventually days spent cleaning became few and far between and I found myself engaged more and more on firing duties; mostly shed and yard jobs at first but gradually coming into contact with branch and main line work. I mention branch work as this was my first experience of firing on passenger trains.

Ipswich Depot was responsible for four branch lines still being run with passenger services, namely Felixstowe, Aldeburgh, Framlingham and Laxfield. (The Hadleigh and Snape branches were freight only.) These branches had their regular engines and crews stationed at the branch terminus. In the event of sickness or holidays, the branch men were covered by drivers and firemen sent from Ipswich to relieve them and this often involved lodging away from home. We never lodged in the true sense of the word but slept rough in the engine shed cabin or the station buildings. It did not help to be of a nervous disposition on these jobs; a dark night spent deep in the heart of the Suffolk countryside at a branch line terminus with only a flickering oil lamp to keep one company could be very frightening indeed!

This was all part and parcel of our initiation however, and useful experience was gained by being booked on these jobs. These branches, with the exception of Felixstowe, were worked in an old world, leisurely manner. Some of the engines were nearing the end of their lives and were certainly not renowned for their steaming qualities, but as the runs between stations were short, with a little nursing the job could be worked reasonably comfortably.

This opened my eyes to another important point regarding locomotive working, namely a knowledge of the route being worked, or "knowing the road" as we would say. Having this knowledge was invaluable if one had an engine that was not performing well, as one knew in advance where the engine had to be worked hard and where it could be eased down.

To this day, even though I am now retired, I can travel by train for example from Ipswich to Peterborough, close my eyes, and know exactly where I am at any time.

After completing 250 firing turns, I had to undertake my full firing test. This involved a practical trial as well as having to answer questions relating to steam engines, signalling, safety, and rules and regulations. The examination was carried out by District Inspector Bill Slack. After the theoretical part was completed, I and

*Signal gantry near Gippeswyk Park. From left to right: first set of three controlled the exit from the Goods Yard, middle set was for trains approaching the station from the East Suffolk Line, and right-hand set was for trains coming into Ipswich from Norwich. The left-hand signal of each set controlled the entrance to No. 1 platform, the middle signal was for No. 2 platform and the tall, right hand signal applied to the middle or "through" road used by trains not stopping at the station. When approaching these signals, a driver needed to take great care to ensure that the signal taken was the one applicable to his route.* (Photo by Ashley Dryhurst)

another passed cleaner, Johnnie Miller, had to walk from the Loco Depot to the station with the Inspector to join a train for a trip to demonstrate our firing abilities, good or otherwise.

The train selected was a slow passenger train to Norwich which was crewed by Ipswich men. The arrangement was that one of us would fire the train as far as Diss where we would alight and join another slow train coming back from Norwich to Ipswich. We tossed a coin; Johnnie won and elected to go first. The engine was a 4-6-0 B1 Class with a fairly light train. Considering that we were inexperienced with main line passenger work (our previous firing turns being mostly confined to shed, yard and freight trains) Johnnie made a good job of it and I was sure he had satisfied the Inspector as to his firing ability. One incident which occurred still remains in my memory to this day. When we stopped at Finningham there was a small Mission Hall near the platform and displayed on the side of this hall, in large black letters, were the words, "Be Sure Your Sin Will Find You Out". Inspector Slack, with a stern voice, ordered us to get out our notebooks and copy these words down carefully and to bear them in mind at all times! I have often wondered since whether the Inspector was joking or whether perhaps he was of a religious nature.

After stepping off at Diss, we had thirty minutes to wait for the up train from Norwich so we went into the porters' room to make a can of tea, supplying of course the Inspector with one; this was an unwritten rule!

Eventually our train home arrived, the engine this time being a 4-6-0 B12 1500 Class, again crewed by Ipswich men. When we stepped on to the footplate, Fireman Bultitude gave a jump of joy and instantly squeezed himself into a corner of the cab out of the way, knowing he had an easy trip home. I always liked the 1500s although they could be awkward to master as they had a long firebox and a certain technique was required with the shovel to enable the coal to reach the front, or far end, of the firebox. It was impossible to achieve this by simply throwing the coal in and the method adopted was to hit the shovel on the bottom edge of the firedoor. This had the effect of bouncing the coal off and giving it the extra momentum required to reach the front. When we were cleaning in the shed we would often practise this on any convenient engine we could find, and after a while we developed the knack easily. So we left Diss and worked home to Ipswich. We had a light train; the engine was steaming freely, and I had a comfortable trip and was feeling satisfied with myself.

On arrival, we walked back to the Loco Depot, into the room in the general offices. Here Inspector Slack

*Inspector Bill Slack, who conducted the firing test mentioned in the text, seen here (in bowler hat) at the Loco Depot at Ipswich, c 1950. Left to right: Charlie Kemp, two London Inspectors, Inspector Slack, ?, ?, Tony Maile. Sitting: Billy Orris, Alf Pettit.*
(Photo courtesy Tony Maile)

informed us that we had achieved the standard required, shook our hands wishing us well, and departed to catch his train back to Norwich.

The method of allocating firing jobs was always on a strict seniority basis. If one man started his railway career on a Monday, and another man on the Tuesday following, the man who commenced on the Monday would always be considered the senior man. Although stifling initiative to a certain extent, this was a fair system as it stopped favouritism. The ruling applied through all the grades. When a firing turn arose it had to be allocated to the senior passed cleaner on duty at the time. This had financial implications; a passed cleaner's pay was based on the number of firing turns he had completed, so he would want to add to his total as fast as possible.

Often overtime would also be involved, so increasing his payment for that particular turn of duty. The seniority ruling was always strictly applied. In the event of a mistake being made and a man being overlooked, that man could claim the extra money involved and also be credited with the firing turn he should have had. This of course resulted in two men being paid for one job. These mistakes, made by either the running shed foreman allocating an emergency turn, or the list clerk wrongly booking a man on a job, did not arise very often. Too many errors and the man concerned could suddenly find himself invited to a little talk with the Shed Master in his office!

Firemen in this region were required to couple and uncouple their engines to the trains. This involved the actual screw coupling, vacuum or air pipes as applicable, and also steam heating carriage warming pipes in cold weather. The task required a certain knack together with a strong wrist, and it took some practice before it could be perfected. It had to be done quickly as turnround times were sometimes very tight. A good example of this was working three trips on the Felixstowe Branch. First the engine would be attached to the train at Ipswich. Run to Felixstowe Town station; unhook and run round train; couple up at other end. Run to Felixstowe Beach station; unhook and run round train; couple up at other end. Run back to Town Station; unhook and run round train; couple up at other end. Run to Ipswich, unhook. One trip completed with the unhooking or coupling-up operation performed eight times. Three trips would merit twenty-four such operations. On a hot summer's day with an L1 tank engine the Felixstowe job could be quite hectic with the engine to be fired in addition.

To explain in detail a fireman's duties, I will describe working the "Snape Bonus", a job worked by the local goods link which I entered when I was first promoted to regular fireman and had "got my check" as we used to say. The type of engine we had on this job was a J15, 0-6-0. These engines were small but strong and had given good service from the days of the GER. They were employed on local goods and branch work but not used for any long distance working. Occasionally they would be required to haul a heavy train over comparatively short distances. Such an occasion was the last part of the Snape bonus job when they had to work almost to their limits with a heavy train over quite a steep gradient from Woodbridge back to Ipswich.

At the start of the bonus job my driver and I were allowed an hour for preparation which included ten minutes "signing on allowance". This consisted of signing on, observing all late notices applicable to our route telling us of any emergency speed restrictions or signalling faults etc., and getting our engine number for that day. We would then proceed to the oil stores or "tank house" to obtain the oil and tools for our engine. Amongst the tools would be a coal hammer and shovel, bucket, handbrush, large adjustable wrench known as a monkey, various spanners, flaretorch, sealed canister containing twelve detonators and two red flags, water gauge lamp, and a handcloth each.

We also collected three metal oil containers; a large one containing engine oil used for oiling the engine side rods, oil boxes etc., one medium sized container with thick black oil for lubricators and Westinghouse air pump (known as a donkey), and a third small container with paraffin used for filling engine headlamps and water gauge lamp. We then set about preparing the engine, a task I have described earlier. These jobs were shared by the driver and fireman; there was no hard and fast rule as to who did what; we agreed this between ourselves. When the preparation was completed I usually went to the mess room to make a billy can of tea which we would put on a shelf over the firehole door to keep hot as there would be no time for making tea once we had started our trip to Snape. During this bonus job, team work was the order of the day, the driver being the only one who kept to his own job. Whilst engaged in shunting operations at the various ports of call it was the normal practice for the guard to assist the shunter, and the fireman to help the guard with coupling and uncoupling and operation of hand points etc.

During the first part of the journey I was particularly careful not to carry too high a level in the water gauge as the engine had to work quite hard for the climb up Westerfield Bank, and an overfilled boiler could have most unpleasant consequences. Water could be admitted to the cylinders and mixing with the smoke and soot from the firebox could create quite a spectacular dirty rainfall. This, especially on a Monday, the traditional wash-day, would not be greeted with any great enthusiasm by housewives in the gardens below with their lines of Persil whites.

Just before arrival at Snape Maltings Sidings, we crossed the River Alde by means of a precarious-looking bridge consisting of a simple timber framework with the single track laid on top. Looking out over the side of the cab, one could see nothing but water below. Somehow I never felt completely happy when the engine was standing on that bridge.

It was while running down to Snape that I would turn my attention to the state of the fire which would sometimes start to "clinker up". With a tender of good steam coal this would not occur but with some of the poorer grade coal we sometimes had, now would come the opportunity to "take a bit out". Fires had a tendency to clinker up more quickly when engaged on this stop-start type of work than when they were burning bright continuously on a long non-stop journey. Clinker is like a crust, forming on the fire bars and obstructing the air flow through the ash-pan below. This results in a very marked deterioration in the steaming qualities of the engine boiler. By the time Snape was reached I had the clean fire to one side of the firebox, with the clinker the other side ready to be discarded. While the guard was conferring with the shunter we would leave the train and draw up on to the bridge where I would throw the clinker out into the river. The clinker had to be drawn out of the firebox by means of a long shovel-like fire iron we called a slice. I shall always remember the hiss and cloud of steam as the red hot fire hit the water. I sometimes feel I would love to go back there and do it all again.

Back to Woodbridge and then homeward bound to Ipswich I had a busy half-hour ahead of me. With a larger, more powerful engine I could have built up a thick fire and then sat back for a while until it burnt through but these little J15s would not take very kindly to that sort of treatment; if one tried it there would soon be trouble as the steam pressure gauge would soon start to "hang its head". These engines were pressurised at 160 p.s.i. and we liked to keep them as close to that as possible when working heavy. The only way to achieve that was to keep a thin bright fire by firing "light and often". This was the rule with all engines really although we rarely adopted it. With J15s though one had to. The engine had a narrow firebox and I remember well the advice I received from my driver when I first fired one. "Little and often - nine shovelfuls - three up each side - one in each back corner - one under the door."

The front of the firebox was at the far end, the back being at the footplate end which housed the fire-hole

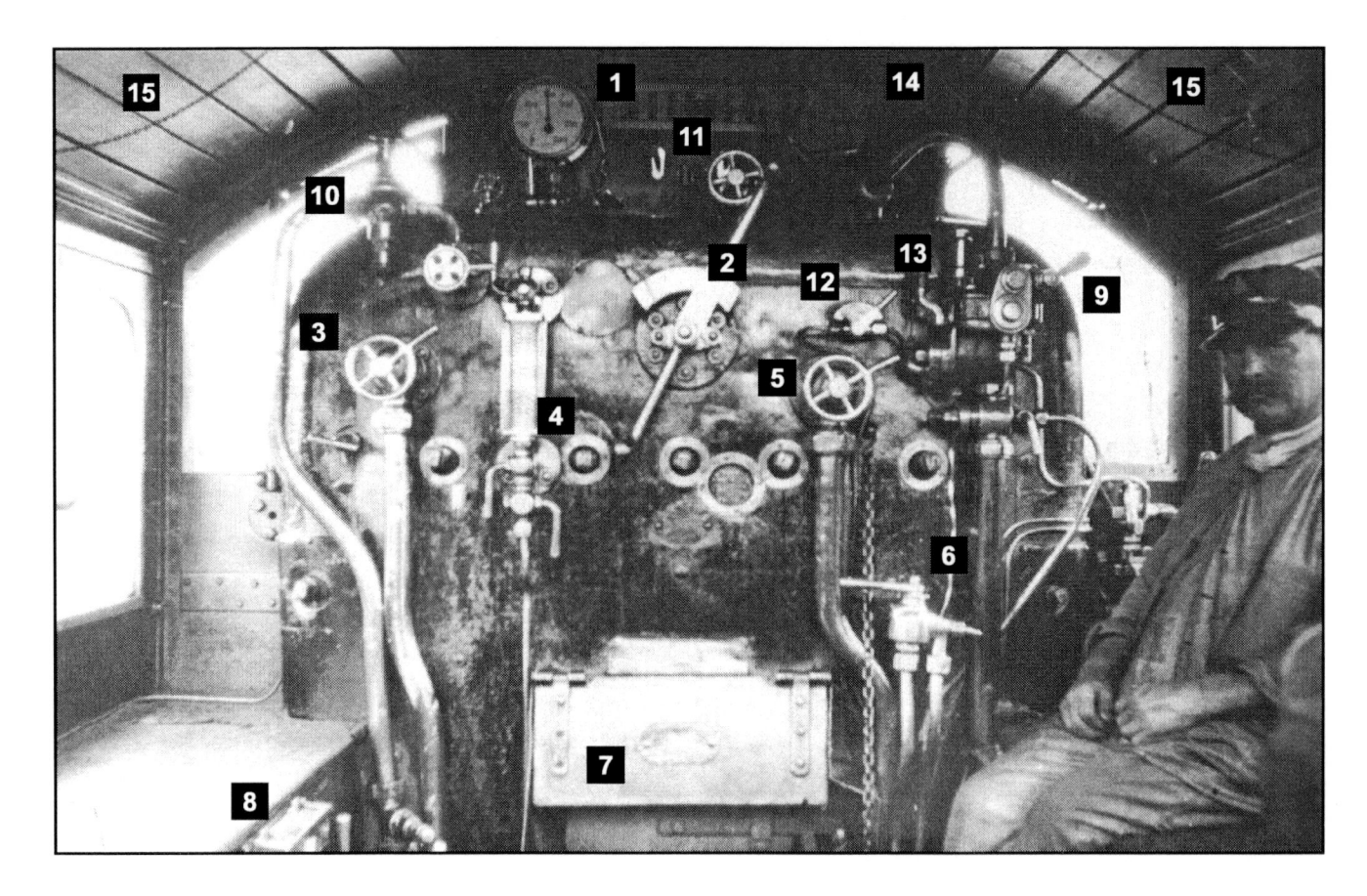

## Main Controls of a Great Eastern Passenger Engine

*The driver pictured is George Pinkney and the photograph is thought to have been taken by his fireman, Ernie Payne.*  (Photo courtesy Richard Pinkney)

1. Boiler Steam Gauge.
2. Main Steam Regulator - admits steam from boiler to cylinders.
3. Left Injector - for transferring water from tender to boiler.
4. Boiler Water Gauge - shows level of water in boiler.
5. Right Injector.
6. Driver's Air Brake Handle.
7. Firebox Door.
8. Oil Box - axle-box lubrication.
9. Vacuum Ejector Handle.
10. Steam Heating Valve and Cock.
11. Westinghouse Pump Control Cock (Donkey).
12. Control Cock for Steam Sanding.
13. Vacuum Train Brake Handle.
14. Vacuum Gauge.
15. Whistle Chain.

door. The "back corners" were each side of the fire door, and to place coal in these required a rather deft flick of the wrist which one acquired with practice. This was important as one could not see the fire below the firedoor and if this part of the grate was starved of coal the result would soon become apparent by a reduction in steam pressure.

Upon leaving Woodbridge we were faced with a very steep climb. There was no chance to "get a run at it" and my driver could not afford to give me any mercy, having to work the engine almost to its maximum to get the train on the move and away up the bank. I was alright at that moment; there was a full head of steam and plenty of water in the boiler. The only problem was to maintain this happy state of affairs. If it was just a question of maintaining steam a fireman's lot would be a happy one, but unfortunately in addition to using steam the engine also required copious amounts of water. This sounds elementary I know but it did make additional problems since to transfer water from the tender into the boiler required the use of injectors. These were worked by live steam from the boiler although some of the larger, more modern engines were equipped with exhaust steam injectors which utilised steam which would otherwise have gone to waste , therefore making no demands on main boiler pressure.

However on our J15 we were not blessed with this aid and every time the injector was operated it used live steam from the boiler; steam that we really could not spare. Apart from this, the cold water from the tender entering the boiler had an appreciable cooling effect with the result that the main steam pressure gauge soon started to "drop back". Only an exceptionally free steaming engine would be man enough to overcome this drop in pressure and there were not many of these about.

This fact brings to mind an unhappy footplate incident. A fireman was on his first main-line firing trip and apparently things were not going very well; the relationship between him and the driver became a little strained to say the least. They had a few words which finished with the fireman exclaiming "Blimey mate, you can't expect to have steam and b- water as well!"

Unfortunately the steam locomotive did require both and this involved quite a bit of scheming if main pressure was to be maintained when the demand was heavy. The object was to fire up and get the steam needle over as far as possible to the 160 p.s.i. mark or "blowing off point", then put the injector on to get some water into the boiler. When the needle dropped to about 140-150, which did not take long, shut the injector off and wait for the needle to "come over" again to repeat the procedure.

This was not quite as straightforward as it may sound. Owing to the heavy demands being made on the engine, the time taken for the pressure gauge needle to "come over" again after the customary "nine shovelfuls around the firebox", and also the water in the boiler being used at an alarming rate, it was not long before there was difficulty keeping the water at a comfortable level. Owing to the severity of the gradients between Woodbridge and Westerfield, there was no opportunity to ease the engine down and have a "shut off and roll". We just had to make the best of a bad job.

Water of course took priority over steam pressure, and if one was to be sacrificed then it had to be the latter. To be taken into account also was the fact that when the engine was working with the main steam regulator open, the water level in the gauge glass tube gave a false reading in relation to the actual amount of water in the boiler. This was because with the regulator open and steam flowing from the boiler through the valves to the cylinders, there was a tendency for the water level to lift, with the result that the water gauge could show three-quarters full whereas the true level could be only half or less. If there was less than half a glass showing, then one did not feel very comfortable, since when the regulator was closed and the water fell to its proper level, it could then become apparent that there was not much water left in the boiler and the level could be approaching danger point.

This point was reached when the top or crown of the firebox became uncovered. In the top of the firebox a fusible lead plug was fitted which, if not covered by water, would melt, allowing a rush of steam into the firebox with the resultant dowsing of the fire and the start of a load of trouble. This had to be avoided at all costs. If matters became very bad, the only alternative would be to stop the train and allow the water and steam to recover. This was called "stopping for a blow-up" and could take several minutes, causing delay and the dreaded task of filling in a "please explain" form upon completion of duty. All footplate men did their utmost to avoid this course of action; humiliation was involved since as soon as word went round the depot the unfortunate fireman had to endure a lot of banter from his workmates even though the incident was often due to circumstances beyond his control. I always managed to complete the Snape Bonus job without this dreaded delay, but many are the times I have breathed a sigh of relief upon finally reaching Westerfield.

Back at the Ipswich shed, we left our engine to be disposed of by the shed staff, and collected together the tools and oil bottles and returned them to the stores. We then made our way to the enginemen's lobby and reported our arrival to the running shed foreman. We were allowed ten minutes for the booking off procedure but if we were on overtime, only the driver booked those ten minutes. This was because he made out the daily ticket describing the day's work, and also reported any problems concerning the engine which would be passed to the maintenance staff. The only time a fireman would have to make a report with his driver would be in the case of their being involved in a mishap, signal irregularity or other extraordinary happenings.

And so the day was over. I made sure, by glancing at the duty list, my next day's working had not been changed for any reason, said cheerio to my mate, made a bee-line to the cycle shed (no cars in those days) and away home to tea. The only snag was that we would have to return the next day and do it all over again!

Looking back, I still consider that the Snape Bonus was the finest grounding a young fireman could have had. I realise that the experience I gained on this particular job was invaluable when I later progressed into the main line goods links with mostly night workings to Whitemoor, Goodmayes, Cambridge, etc. with far heavier trains but larger engines; trains which were easier to work as there was power to spare unlike the little J15s which were taxed to the limit on the Snape run.

Basically, it was text book firing working the Snape Bonus job. A thin, bright, dancing fire was always stated to be the ideal way to fire a locomotive. However as I progressed to different types of engine I found that this was not always the case. Some engines did better with a thick fire built up at the back and sloping toward the front of the firebox. Britannia Class locos had a large square firebox and the technique here was to keep the fire well up in the back of the firebox, not forgetting the back corners of course, as the exhaust of the engine when working heavy would draw fire from back to front of the box which would then need very little feeding.

Steam engines were very temperamental and even two of the same class could have different steaming characteristics. Some engines would do better with the thick heavy fire frowned upon in the text books as being a wasteful and inefficient method of firing, resulting in excessive black smoke and poor combustion, but if one was the fireman on one of these locos and found they responded better this way then one did not worry unduly about books. Having worked on many types of engines, both freight and passenger, I always looked upon each one as an individual and tried to treat it as such.

Another aspect to be considered was the skill of the driver, which could make a terrific difference to the demands placed upon his fireman. Some drivers, although in a minority, would work their engines very hard, resulting in high coal consumption, and these understandably were not very popular with firemen. The majority however were good enginemen, using their vast knowledge of the engine and the route they were travelling to obtain the maximum efficiency from the engine resulting in a far easier trip for the fireman.

A good example of this can be shown by comparing two consecutive evening trips made with a semi-fast train from Yarmouth Southtown to Ipswich. The same loco, a B17 "Sandringham" Class was booked on the train each day but the important point was I had two different drivers. The train consisted of six coaches from Yarmouth with another three being attached at Beccles, these latter coming from Lowestoft. This was a fairly heavy train and the route was steeply graded. After leaving each of our booked stations at Beccles, Halesworth, Saxmundham and Woodbridge, we would be faced with a long heavy climb. Not for nothing was the East Suffolk Branch known as the scenic railway! A non-stop train was by far a better proposition when working over this line as the banks could then be taken at speed. For each station start however a heavy demand would be made upon the engine to get the train away while at the same time climbing and accelerating.

My driver that first evening had a reputation as being on the heavy side and I was to find this was indeed true. When making a start away from a station a driver would have to give his engine nearly full rein, but a skilful driver would ease off when the train was nicely on the move. A heavy driver however never thought of easing off until he was well over the top of the bank. Working full out on a long climb resulted in heavy coal consumption and the demand for a strenuous effort on the part of the poor fireman. This was not necessary. A more considerate driver might take a little longer to climb the bank but he would regain that time on the easier stretches, resulting in far less strain on the engine and fireman. It was said that a heavy driver behaved in that way because he was deaf and unable to hear his engine unless it was really barking!

The first night after leaving Yarmouth Southtown I had a wet shirt by the time we reached Halesworth. On the banks, this particular driver was drawing my fire nearly as fast as I could feed it and I was unable to make much use of my seat on the engine. As we ran into Ipswich Station on time I glanced back and was surprised to see how far back the coal was in the tender. A trip from Yarmouth to Ipswich should not have used such a large amount of fuel. I was sure that the engine, like myself, breathed a sigh of relief when we came off the train at Ipswich.

The following evening was a complete change. I had this time a driver with whom I had not previously worked whose name was Archie Rowe. He was a quiet, unassuming type of man and I liked him from the start.

We left Yarmouth and ran to Beccles with six coaches. This was a level easy running trip but even then I was surprised to see how easily the engine was being worked. I was able to sit down and enjoy the cool evening air and my biggest worry was not to let my fire too low. We ran into Beccles and backed on to our other three coaches.

While waiting for the right-away signal I started to build a thick heavy fire ready for the climb ahead. Starting off, Archie gave the engine her head for a short while but before we had gone very far I saw him wind the reversing lever back which was the method for easing off. We were now running with a smooth rhythmic beat from the exhaust and nothing like the fuss and bother of the previous night, yet still maintaining a good speed. I finished firing up. The steam pressure gauge was hovering on the red mark, the blowing off point, and water was still nicely in the top section of the gauge glass; everything was comfortable. The train and engine was exactly the same as the night before but I could scarcely believe it. The previous night I was firing all the way up and over the bank and now about half-way up I found myself with the opportunity for a sit down. It was easy running down from the top of Beccles bank into Brampton. The engine was still maintaining a nearly full head of steam and I remember thinking to myself, "This is the best trip I have ever had; this is how it should be!" The engine now seemed to be flying with hardly a whisper from the exhaust. We did not stop at Brampton but after running through the station we were faced with another appreciable climb. This was a different proposition however as we were taking it at speed and were half-way up before we really noticed it. I gave the fire another sprinkle around the box and this was enough to take us to our next stop at Halesworth where we ran in dead on time and with a boiler full of steam and water.

The remainder of the trip was performed in this comfortable easy running manner and when we finally ran into Ipswich I once again looked back at the tender as I had done the night before. I was amazed. The coal was still well forward and I was certain that this man had run the train from Yarmouth to Ipswich on less than half the coal used the previous night.

We were dead on time as we had been everywhere. My shirt was still dry and I was sure I could have gone to London and back provided I kept the same driver.

I gradually grew confident in my abilities as a fireman, becoming involved with all types of trains with extensive main line work included. All this was suddenly to come to a close however as I now found myself facing a big upheaval in my life. On 29th March, 1950, I left the railway behind and commenced my eighteen months National Service with the RAF. (This unfortunately was to increase to two years service about six months later!) During my National Service I still had my free and privilege railway travel facilities. My job was held open to me when I returned together with my seniority date which was strictly maintained. I was also kept informed of any major changes which took place. After a few months in the RAF for example I received a letter from Ipswich informing me that I had been promoted to a regular fireman in No. 2 local goods link from a certain date. I had finally got my fireman's check although I was not at the depot to take advantage of it!

Unfortunately, a few months later I received another letter containing not such good news. Owing to a loss of work at the depot I was now demoted from No. 2 goods link, becoming a "fireman put back" although retaining my check and new wage rate.

That was my position when on 29th March, 1952 I left the RAF and returned to "civvie street" and the railway to start again where I had left off two years previously. During my absence there had been a number of new starters in the grade and I was now at the top of the tree owing to my seniority date of 1947 being maintained. This ensured that although I was not in a regular link I was firing continuously on a variety of turns involving extra trains, holiday cover and relief working. This carried on for a few months until I was eventually re-instated as a regular fireman in No. 2 Goods Link. From now on I would be working with the same driver until either he retired or I gained promotion. This could be a mixed blessing of course if neither of you got on very well together.

The one big drawback to gaining promotion was a financial one. With most occupations the obvious incentive to promotion would be an increase in money earned but in our particular case, moving from the top of the passed cleaner link into No. 2 Goods Link resulted in an appreciable drop in earnings. Previously we would have been engaged on a wide variety of work including night freight working with the resultant night rate payment, and also frequent overtime, with its higher rate of pay. On entering No. 2 Goods Link, this would now cease. This link consisted entirely of short distance goods work with no night shift involved at all. Although our basic rate of pay was increased on becoming regular firemen, overall our weekly earnings were much less than we were accustomed to. There were advantages however. The work itself was of a less strenuous nature and our social life was much improved with far more free evenings available. We were rostered on average every other Sunday on engineering working and this helped to boost our pay.

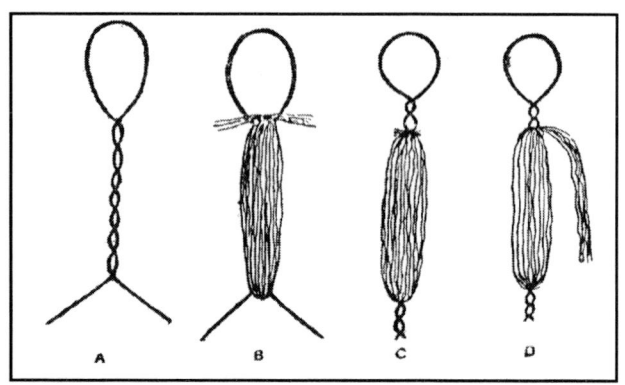

*As part of his driving test, in the days of steam, a footplateman would have to satisfy the examiner that he could make his own oil-trimmings for engine lubrication purposes. Different types of trimmings were used in a locomotive. A worsted tail trimming was used for a bogie axle-box; for a driving axle-box the stem of the trimming would be longer. Ordinary plug trimmings were used for big-ends and coupling rods, although for an eccentric, the top wire ends were differently shaped. Diagram shows the method of making a trimming. The copper wire is twisted (A) and the strands of worsted are passed round it (B) until the required size is obtained. The two ends of the worsted are left at the top. Two or three twists are given to the copper wire at the top and bottom to secure the worsted firmly. (C) shows the ends cut off for a plug trimming, and (D) for a tail trimming.*
(See "Locomotives" by A. Morton Bell)

No. 2 Goods Link was known as the "Old Man's Gang" because the drivers in this link would be older men approaching retirement. Some men would also be in the link for health reasons, others volunteering. The firemen however would all be young men, this being the first link into which they were booked on achieving their fireman's check.

I spent approximately two years in this link. My first driver was Tom Page who retired after a short while. For the remainder of the time, I was with Fred Gosling, one of the best drivers I could have wished for.

My next move was promotion to the "Spare Link" which meant exactly that. Firemen and drivers were rostered as spare for various times over a twenty-four hour cycle to cover vacancies in the other links. Although booked with a regular driver, we would often go several weeks without seeing each other as each would be booked on different turns. My driver in this link was "Tim" Schofield, but I saw little of him. Very often we were not booked on a job for a week but employed on different duties each day. We were required to move two hours either side of our rostered time if necessary, so that if for example a rostered time was 6 am, one could be utilized on any job between 4 am and 8 am. Sometimes we did not know if we were coming or going! Being in this link affected our social life and was not very popular with anyone. After my enjoyable two years in the Local Goods Link this came as a very rude awakening and I breathed a sigh of relief when after a few months I made my next move into the Main Line Goods Link.

I had now entered the "Money Gang". The Main Line Goods was the longest link at Ipswich; to work through all the jobs would take the largest part of a year. A large proportion of the work was night freight working to Goodmayes, Whitemoor, Cambridge, Norwich, etc. with an occasional passenger or mail train working here and there. Good money could be earned although again the social aspect left a lot to be desired.

My first driver in this link was George Robinson with whom I got on very well although he would often refer to me as a "young bounder". He could be difficult to fire for at times however owing to the fact that he sometimes worked the engine a little too easily. On level stretches he would ease the engine back so much that it tended to deaden the fire; a steam engine required a good exhaust to keep the fire bright. It may seem strange that a driver could be too light on his fireman, but certainly George did sometimes make things a trifle awkward for me. He

*Left: Footplatemen on B1 Class engine No. 1228 at Ipswich Loco Depot in 1953. Left to right (top): ?, "Spike" Read; (middle): P. Warne, Smith, Rayner; (standing): ?, Tom Sharland.*

(Photo courtesy T. Sharland)

*Below: Group at Ipswich Loco Depot, c 1953. Left to right: L. Peachey, L. Chambers, E. Rayner, - Smith, D. Brooks, T. Maile, H. Grimwood, S. Read, G. Andrews. Sitting: "Peewee" Johnson.*

(Photo Kelvin Higgins Collection)

was a very good mate though and when he moved out of the link it was with regret that I parted company with him.

My next driver was "Val" Carter but we were only together a short time when a change occurred. It was agreed by all the men in the link to split it into two, namely A and B links as it took such a long time to work through all the turns. My seniority placed me in A link but my driver Val Carter had only just come into the link so therefore he was placed in B link. This meant that I now had another change of driver, finding myself placed with Jack Turner, a jovial character with the largest repertoire of jokes I have ever known anyone to possess.

Jack had only recently come to Ipswich, having previously been driving on the Wickham Market - Framlingham branch line which had just closed for passenger traffic. He had been based at Framlingham which had finished as a depot, with all freight traffic now worked by an engine and crew from Ipswich.

Jack was now experiencing a great change. From jogging up and down on a little country branch line he was now part of the Main Line Goods Link at Ipswich, and he was having a little difficulty in adjusting to his new environment. He had spent several weeks learning all the various routes before taking up his position in what was now the A Goods Link. By a coincidence, the fireman he was placed with upon entering the link was my cousin, Ray Goodchild. Ray was now moving for promotion and I was to take his place. Ray had tried to help as much as possible, but Jack on his own admission was still not very sure of himself. He was not used to night working, and this, coupled with strange large locos and heavy trains, took some time to get accustomed to. During his period of route learning before coming into the link, Jack would have ridden with various drivers who would have told him about speed restrictions, signalling etc. and after a few trips he would be required to sign a route card to the effect that he was competent to work over this particular line. Unfortunately, this route learning took place during the hours of daylight. Working a train at night or during bad visibility was a far different proposition and it would take a man a long time before he was fully conversant with a line by both day and night.

To illustrate this point, one particular night Jack and I were working a goods train from Cambridge to Ipswich. We travelled for a short distance on the main line to Ely and then veered off to the right at Coldham Lane Junction on to the Newmarket line. The track curved sharply and was on a rising gradient. We were proceeding smoothly when suddenly I noticed Jack shutting off steam and starting to brake.

"What's the matter, Jack?" I enquired.

"We've got red lights ahead," he replied.

"We can't have, there's no signals here. The next ones we get are at Fulbourne and that's way ahead as yet."

"Well you come and look if you don't believe me!"

I went over to his side of the cab and sure enough there were three lovely red lights shining brightly in the night sky. They were nothing to do with us however; red lights on factory chimneys are not switched off for passing trains!

One of the few occasions on which I lost my temper with an engine was while firing with Jack Turner. We were working a sharply-timed Ipswich to Whitemoor freight train and going down Higham Bank. That particular night, because neither of the two regular engines kept for this particular job was available, we had a J39 "Standard" 0-6-0 engine which was riding very roughly. (For some unknown reason, footplatemen always referred to a rough-riding engine as a "cab-ranker".) The vibration was so great that utter chaos prevailed on the footplate. Coal was being shaken down from the tender and spilling over the cab floor, the injectors were failing and needed frequent resetting and the firebox dampers had to be wedged open. In addition to this, the fire-irons were constantly slipping forward from their rack at the side of the tender and I was in danger of being hit on the head. While all this was going on, I was required to somehow stand on the footplate and shovel coal. What really incensed me, however, was the fact that my mate was leaning out of the cab window, thinking he was unseen, and laughing his head off.

When the time eventually came that Jack left the link I was really sorry to lose him. He was replaced by driver Harry Holliday who again I got on well with but very shortly I was destined to be moved into the Passenger Link.

At about this time, during the late 1950s, great changes were afoot. British Railways had taken the decision to gradually replace all steam engines with diesel locomotives and these were now beginning to make their appearance, one by one. The process was referred to as "dieselisation". Already, diesel shunting locomotives had replaced the small tank engines and trams in the shunting yards, and in September 1955 diesel railcars started operating between Ipswich and Norwich as part of the standard timetable. The loss of main line steam traction was the beginning of the end as far as firemen were concerned. Over a period of time this grade would cease to exist.

We at Ipswich were at the forefront of this development as the decision was taken that Ipswich loco depot was to be the first to be completely dieselised. The original dark and gloomy loco sheds had previously been demolished and a modern steam depot built in 1953. After years of archaic conditions we were now becoming accustomed to having more modern facilities. The newly-built shed had four tracks running through in place of the original two. It was much wider and longer and could shelter approx. twenty-four engines. There was a brilliantly lit engine inspection pit, coaling plant, wet-ash pits and overhead sand-hoppers. The whole yard was cleverly laid out to facilitate ease of movements. The human need was not forgotten, as in the past, as we now had a brand new administrative block.

This housed on the ground floor the running shed foreman's and roster clerk's offices, a large signing-on lobby, mess rooms for the locomen and fitting staff, and also oil and tool stores. On the first floor was the shedmaster's office and a room that could be used for mutual improvement classes, interviews, etc.. These were situated at one end with a store room at the other. Between the two was a vast area which housed toilets, large wash-hand basins, rows of sinks, and, wonder of wonders, showers! The transformation these improvements made on the morale of the men cannot be described. We were now working in a completely new environment. But after a period of only six years or so, it was to be altered yet again to accommodate the new diesel locomotives.

The shed would be left basically the same but would be fitted with diesel fuel pumps, water pipes, etc.. The coaling plant and wet-ash pits would be dispensed with, and the fitting shops drastically refurbished with new pits, ramps, electrical equipment, etc. to cater for the needs of this new form of motive power. The term loco sheds was long redundant. From the advent of nationalisation these had been called motive power depots (MPDs) but in the future Ipswich was to be known as a diesel maintenance depot. The change-over from steam to diesel was a long drawn-out process and although it happened faster in our area, it would be another five or six years before the last steam engine disappeared from service on the system as a whole.

As with all major technical changes, teething troubles

*Demolition of the coaling tower at Ipswich Loco Depot on 7th December 1961. Three and a half pounds of gelignite were used. The Depot's lighting system was tested after the explosion and was found to be in perfect working order.* (Photo by Reg Farrow)

appeared. Several different types of diesel locomotives were coming into service at this period and the reliability of some of these left much to be desired. A diesel locomotive is basically a power station on wheels. The engine drives the generators that supply the electricity to drive the axle-mounted traction motors. These engines and generators, if used in a factory, would run for very long periods without trouble. When fitted to a railway locomotive however, they are subjected to constantly changing loads and demands, plus vibration. This, coupled with the fact that the drivers and fitters were relatively inexperienced with this new type of traction gave rise to several problems in the early days, and many a time a poor old rusting steam engine would be hastily roused to go out to bring a failed diesel home.

A large proportion of the failures were minor and easily rectified had the drivers had more experience, but it must be remembered that the men were now faced with something that was completely alien to them. For all their previous driving careers with steam they had complete control over their engines. They alone decided how much or how little steam was required to cope with various routes over which they travelled. Now however they had merely to open a power controller after which

*Two Brush diesel-electric locomotives seen in the fitting shops of the rebuilt Ipswich Loco Depot, c 1960.*
(Photo courtesy British Railways)

automatic devices would come into operation in order to cope with the variable power demands. So although a driver would still have to retain his old skills as regards road knowledge and the working of different types of trains, he was no longer the master of his own machine, as he had been in the past.

At this period therefore the morale of the men at the depot was not exactly high. We were faced with a change in our working conditions such as had never before been experienced. Several of the older drivers, quite understandably, viewed the new diesels with apprehension; the firemen even more so as they could plainly see that their grade would gradually be eliminated. Diesel locomotives did not require coal and water, fire-cleaning and turning, and could be in traffic for far longer periods than a steam engine. Thus the spectre of redundancy loomed in the near future and prospects were very uncertain. Promotion which up to then had been steady, now suffered a severe set-back.

This then was the position I found myself in as the 1950s drew to a close, having completed twelve years service working entirely with steam. I had enjoyed those years and I was fully prepared to carry on working with steam for the rest of my career, fulfilling every young boy's dream of becoming an engine driver. But this dream was to be shattered. The mighty steam engine pounding through the countryside, with its smoke, steam, flashing pistons, raucous exhaust, and glow from the firebox lighting up the night sky, was soon to be no more, to be replaced by a faceless diesel looking like an extra carriage attached to the front of the train. We would now be cocooned in the confines of a diesel cab merely operating a controller to deliver power to turn the wheels.

Near perfection had ultimately been achieved in steam loco design, a good example being the Britannia Class, but this had come too late and the engines were soon to be relegated to the realms of history.

I eventually moved into the passenger link as a fireman in 1960. My driver was Bob Tyrrell, a man I was

*J15 engine No. 65389 shunting at Woodbridge on 5th March 1960 before departing for Ipswich on the last official steam working from Ipswich Shed. This engine had been retained for the Snape Branch which closed that weekend and on the previous day had cleared the remaining wagons from Snape.* (Photo by Richard W. Smith)

to remain with for nearly six years, at the end of which time all steam locos had been replaced by diesels. Over this period, our depot was completely dieselised but we often encountered steam locos which were housed at other depots with the result that we would often have a diesel for the outward journey and steam on the return, or vice-versa. The changeover was a long drawn-out process but eventually diesels reigned supreme. The first diesel hauled train I worked had been on July 10th 1959 with Driver H. Holliday and loco No. D5521. The last steam engine I fired was a "Britannia" 70007 *Coeur-de-Lion* on July 15th 1961 with Driver "Spud" Murphy, working a passenger train from Norwich to Ipswich following the failure of the diesel locomotive booked for the job.

Naturally, this changeover had a marked effect on the manning requirements of the depot. There were some redundancies but the grade of fireman was retained for a while even after steam engines had gone from Ipswich, owing to the fact, as previously mentioned, that we were still involved with some steam working. Firemen were eventually designated 'secondmen'; the grade of engine cleaner was a thing of the past. A new entrant now would be classed as a driver's assistant until passed for driving when he became a relief driver, eventually progressing to permanent driver.

Owing to the strict seniority system worked, I was in a reasonably safe position. My next move would have been to acting driver but this would not now come as soon as I had expected owing to a loss of work at the depot.

*Ipswich Loco Depot by night, c 1960.* (Photo Kelvin Higgins Collection)

Thus we entered a new era. Secondmen were gradually eliminated on some jobs, with freight working especially becoming single manned. Rules and regulations had always been based on the assumption that there were two men on an engine at all times. The layout of various sidings and goods yards were such that the driver's visibility was often impaired when engaged in shunting at these sites and therefore a secondman had to be provided. This situation resulted in several disputes amongst the trade unions and management, but eventually single manning became the norm.

Passenger trains, running during the winter period from September to May in the first few years of dieselisation, were required to be double-manned at all times. This was for the purpose of steam heating the carriages. All passenger stock was fitted with steam heating apparatus and the diesels were designed to cope with this demand, being equipped with diesel fired generators installed in the engine compartment, but out of reach of the driver. These heating systems were quite troublesome in the early days. A secondman could sometimes find himself constantly in and out of the engine room restarting a generator which had cut out, or resetting various trips etc.. Sometimes he would even go

*Drivers pictured beside a Brush diesel-electric locomotive while on a diesel instruction course. Left to right: Peter Fletcher, Ron "Butch" Carter, Peter Parsey, Peter Dennington, Charlie Hewlett, Instructor Cyril Broad, Derek Smith.* (Courtesy Peter Dennington Collection)

*Footplatemen, attending a diesel instruction course c 1960, seen outside Ransomes & Rapier's canteen after lunch. Left to right (standing): Peter Dennington, Peter Parsey, Ike Button, Bill Green, Peter "Winkle" Fletcher, Ray Read, Bob Hansen, Charlie Hewlett. (Seated): Derek King, Mr Thomas (Instructor), Derek Smith, Les Driver.* (Photo by Eric Leggett who was also on the course.)

as far as to wish himself back on a steam engine!

During the first part of the changeover period, an appreciable amount of extra work was created due to the fact that all drivers had to be specially trained to operate the new diesel locomotives, resulting in the men being taken off their link duties which had to be covered by spare or acting men. Initially the basic class-room work was taught at Ipswich by an instructor sent down from Stratford, with meal breaks incidentally taken at the now demolished Ransomes & Rapier's canteen. After completion of this basic training, each type of diesel locomotive had to be learnt one by one. The instructors for this purpose were local drivers, one of the first being George Baker, mentioned elsewhere in the book.

My regular driver, Bob Tyrell, would often be taken off for diesel training in these early stages. He would usually be replaced by one of the younger acting drivers, very often not much older than myself. Bob was by now in his last year or two before retirement, and apart from knowing the basics was not, understandably, very interested in extending his knowledge. The younger men realised that the diesels had come to stay and to be the form of traction in use from now on, eventually to be mostly replaced by electrics of course, but that would be a long way ahead. So the younger driver and myself would confer together, pool our knowledge and find out

*Left: Diesel conversion course, left to right: Fred Holland, Ted Barrell, Kenny Allison, Len Southgate, Basil Robinson, Reg Greaves with Instructor Cyril Broad.* (Photo Kelvin Higgins Collection)

*Below: Diesel instruction class. Left to right: Ron Lockwood, "Pussy" Catton, Tim Schofield, Reg Richardson, Harry Daines, "Daddy" Frost, Reg Thompson, Billy Gardiner, Jack Clarke, "Butch" Carter, "Fritz" Oliver, Jack Drake with Mr W. Martin, Instructor from Stratford.* (Photo Tim Schofield Collection)

as much as we could on the intricacies of these new locomotives. I would also have access to my driver's instruction manuals. Being a mere secondman and not yet passed for driving the only tuition I had was on the heating generators. There were different types of these and to learn them we attended a three-day basic course at Stratford with conversion courses back at Ipswich.

And so I worked my last year or two as a fireman/secondman in the passenger link. I eventually lost my driver Bob, to be replaced by Ted Clarke, and finally Harry Carter. The day came at last when I travelled to Stratford to take my test for acting driver. Steam engines were a thing of the past and all thoughts of them had to be put to the back of my mind. The test at Stratford was a theoretical one based on rules and regulations, various forms of signalling, etc. and was quite involved, being viewed by all participants with some apprehension as failure was not unknown. In this event, two more attempts were allowed but anyone failing at the third attempt would be taken out of the line of promotion and downgraded to lesser work. As with the firing test all those years ago, the practical driving test would be undertaken at Ipswich under the eyes of a Norwich inspector. I fortunately passed everything I was expected to and so became a relief driver, the new designation.

Working life would not now be the same. The responsibility was now much greater although having said this, a fireman's job was not to be taken lightly; he would be relied upon by his driver not just for steam and water but also to look for signals which the driver was unable to see from his side of the cab. Ultimately, however, in any serious incident which occurred to them, the driver and not the fireman would be the one who would have to accept responsibility.

I thus said good-bye to my happy firing days and started again on the bottom rung of the ladder as a driver.

By this time we were completely dieselised. On becoming relief driver I now had to learn and be passed out on every type of diesel loco which I would be required to drive. First of all we would have to attend a week's course at Ilford training school. This dealt with the theory of the diesel locomotive in all its intricacies. Engine and generator, basic electricity, cooling and air systems, brakes etc. were all dealt with during the week, at the end of which we came home loaded with

*Ipswich Loco Depot during diesel days. The new engine shed is seen in background at left, with the tank house at centre of photograph. Extreme left is the locomotive washing machine. The controls for this were mounted on the three posts to the right. One of the tall posts had an electronic eye which automatically started the machine on the locomotive's approach. The electronic eye on the second post would stop the machine if the roof of the locomotive had been left open, thus preventing any damage. Fixed to the small post was an override button which the locomotive driver, leaning from his cab window, could press if no washing was required as the locomotive went through. The platforms, seen either side of the line, were intended to be used for hand-washing of the locomotives. In the background, right, can be seen two engine tenders into which lime was put from the water softening plant, ready to be sent to Parkeston for disposal. A third such tender is out of sight.* (Photo by Ashley Dryhurst)

notebooks, pamphlets, diagrams and so on. No shortage of reading material here. As mentioned, this was all theory; we never came into contact with a loco at any time throughout the course. The practical tuition was carried out by our own driver instructors when we attended "conversion courses" at our home depot in Ipswich, or occasionally at Norwich. Every type of locomotive from the humble yard shunters upwards had to be learned and this meant that several weeks or even months could elapse before we had been taught them all. Occasionally this meant that we were unable to take a driving job owing to the fact that we were "not conversant with type of traction".

Attending a conversion course usually involved one day on a static locomotive and two days out on the main line, driving. Although a special empty coach train would sometimes be available for these training trips, this was not always so. Ordinary service trains, both freight and passenger would be utilized. After we had finished the three days, we would still be unable to drive until we were passed as competent by a district loco inspector, just like the old steam firing test all those years ago.

Overall, I feel we had a much easier time with this transition than the older men. We had experience of diesels before being required to drive them, and many of the operating and maintenance problems of the past had been eliminated.

Eventually, with fully signed up traction and route cards, I started on the driver stage of my career. At this time, drivers' jobs were few and far between. We were rostered as secondmen but would be promoted to drive as and when a job arose. Unlike the old days there was very little work at the Depot for trainmen As had been the case on my first outside firing turn, so my first driving turn was Upper Yard shunting. My first main line trip entailed working a special Freightliner to Felixstowe, returning light. I had a young secondman with me and I remember glancing at him occupying the place which I had become accustomed to for so long and realising that I was now in the seat of power! It was a strange feeling; I was not dependent on him for steam and water as in the old days, but being the driver I felt a certain amount of responsibility for him.

One point not mentioned before, but which deserves further explanation, is the practice of being removed from the Main Line Passenger Link and dropping down to the lowly Shunting Link immediately on being passed for driving duties. This gave every indication of being demoted, but there was a perfectly good explanation for this practice. By being employed solely on depot, yard or station duties, a man was always readily available when a driving turn arose. Many times in my early driving days I have worked part secondman, part driver under this arrangement. This system, although unpredictable, added spice and variety to the job. "Never two days the same" we used to say, and unless you were an established regular fireman or driver, this was very true. There could not have been another job quite like that of a locoman.

I eventually achieved the ultimate promotion and became a regular driver. Promotion was on a seniority basis, the vacancy arising owing to the retirement or premature death of an older man, or sometimes additional work being allocated to the depot. The senior acting driver did not always fill the post however, as all vacancies had to be advertised over the region when they arose. A man from another depot, desirous of coming to Ipswich and with a seniority date above that of the local man, could apply and be given the job. The Ipswich man would have to remain in his current link position and await the next vacancy. This obviously caused a certain amount of animosity but had to be accepted as it was the agreed practice under the strict seniority rules to which we worked. When an outstation was closed, the men would usually be offered redundancy or the opportunity to move to another depot in the region. The drivers were nearly always long service men with seniority dates well above those of the men of the depot to which they moved, resulting in men being put back in the line of promotion in order to accommodate them. Ipswich did not suffer too badly from this arrangement. An odd man here and there (foreigners we called them) would appear occasionally to take up a vacancy. When Bury St Edmunds loco depot closed in the 1960s we had a few men from there but we never suffered to the same extent as some depots throughout the system. Norwich in particular was hit very hard by the closure of the M&GN Railway, and had a great influx of men moving there, with the resultant displacement of existing staff. The Depot never recovered from this and several of the acting drivers did not achieve the status of regular driver by the time retirement age was reached.

Following the advent of electric train heating (ETH) all main line passenger locos became single-manned or driver-only (DO). Whereas before the secondman would perform all the coupling and uncoupling of a locomotive, the driver was now relieved on arrival at his destination and all locomotive requirements would be dealt with by the relieving crew. This was a big improvement in working conditions for a driver. He could now step off his train immediately upon arrival and know that he would not be required again until ten minutes before departure time. Before, he had stayed with the locomotive throughout the complete turn-round process. His job now was much cleaner and he received enhanced pay for driver-only turns. The relief crew however were burdened with all the dirty work. This often caused me feelings of embarrassment on arrival at Norwich for the relieving crew often included a secondman who was senior to me both in service and age and was now obliged to play second fiddle through no fault of his own owing to the reasons explained in the last paragraph.

So, I was now a permanent driver; I had got my "check" for the last time. In the several years that had elapsed since I had first been passed out, I had gained experience of driving many types of trains and a brief description of these would appear to be appropriate here. Freight trains, for instance, were of various classifications. Even under modernisation, many of these were still running with restricted braking, and appreciable skill was required when working them. Some trains were loose coupled (no brakes, except on locomotive), some were partially fitted (loco and part train fitted with brakes, remainder loose coupled), and express freight were fully fitted (complete braking throughout). The maximum speed these trains were allowed to travel was dependant upon their stopping

## BR locomotive disc or headlight codes

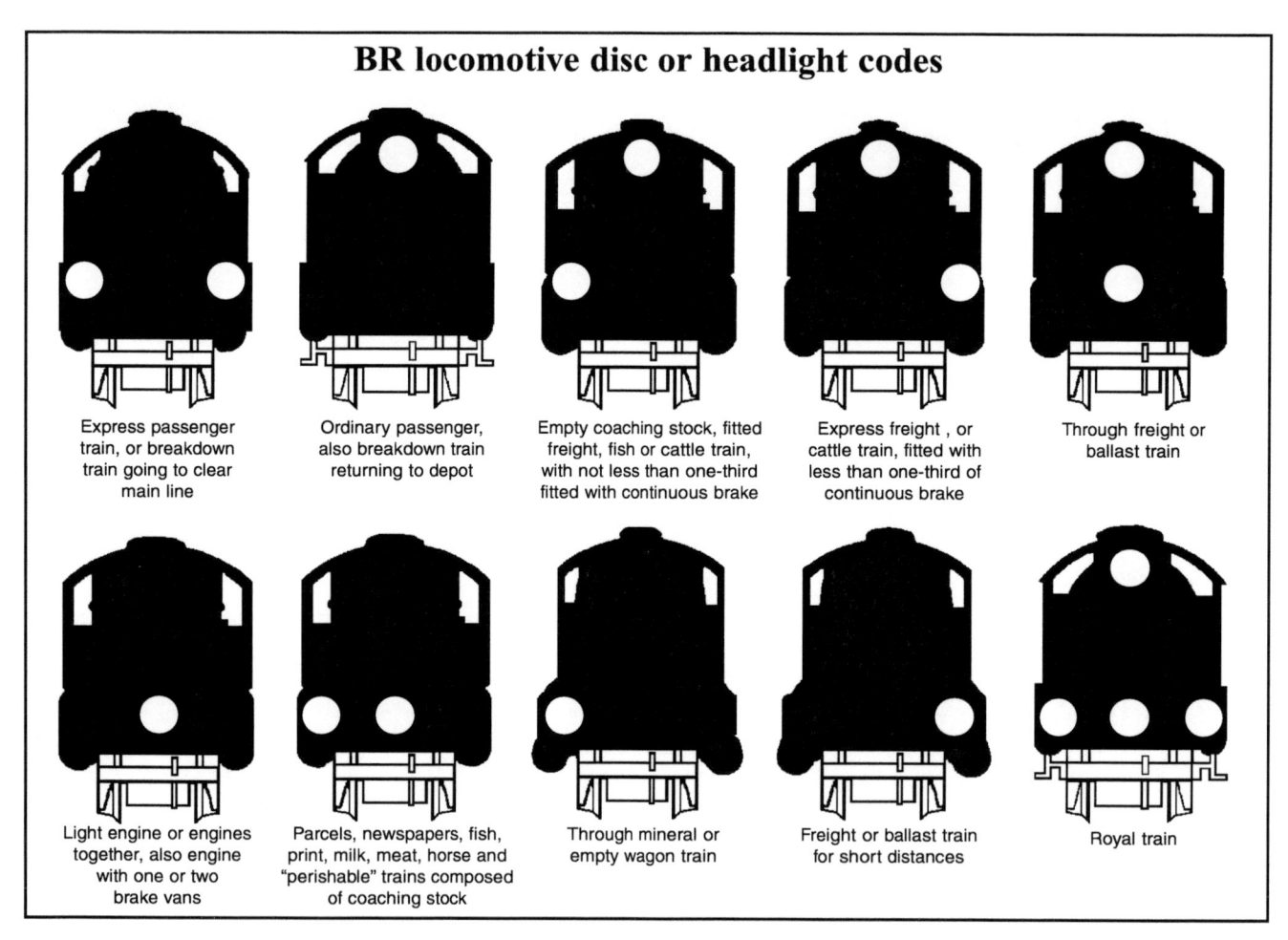

|  |  |
|---|---|
| (lower left + lower right discs) | Express passenger train, or breakdown train going to clear main line |
| (top centre disc) | Ordinary passenger, also breakdown train returning to depot |
| (top centre + lower left discs) | Empty coaching stock, fitted freight, fish or cattle train, with not less than one-third fitted with continuous brake |
| (top centre + lower right discs) | Express freight, or cattle train, fitted with less than one-third of continuous brake |
| (top centre + centre disc) | Through freight or ballast train |
| (lower centre disc) | Light engine or engines together, also engine with one or two brake vans |
| (lower left + lower centre discs) | Parcels, newspapers, fish, print, milk, meat, horse and "perishable" trains composed of coaching stock |
| (centre disc) | Through mineral or empty wagon train |
| (centre + lower right discs) | Freight or ballast train for short distances |
| (top + lower left + lower right discs) | Royal train |

ability. Passenger, mail, parcel and paper trains were braked throughout but there were also different types of these. When I first commenced driving, the vacuum brake system was widely used. The drawback to this, in view of the ever increasing loads and speeds required, was the slow application and release times required with this form of braking. Over a period of time this was dispensed with and replaced with the much quicker and more efficient air braking system. Here was another instance of having to break with the old traditions and acquire a new form of expertise which, apart from some basic tuition, could only be learnt by experience. During the early transition period, locomotives were equipped to deal with both vacuum and air braked trains but eventually the air system became the norm and the vacuum brake passed into obscurity. Exceptions to this were older diesel railcars which were never altered and were vacuum fitted right up to their eventual demise in the 1990s.

Over a period of years, railwaymen had to contend with many alterations and modifications. Most of these were of a minor nature until in the mid 1980s, a major one occurred, namely electrification. The main line from Liverpool Street to Norwich had for some years been electrified as far as Colchester. It was now proposed to extend this in stages all the way through to Norwich. The first stage was to be to Ipswich. Extensive preparation work was required however before this idea could reach fruition. For a start, bridges had to be altered (sometimes demolished and rebuilt) to allow for the extra height required by the overhead wires. Concrete foundations then had to be installed for the masts intended to carry these wires, and finally the wires themselves had to be strung. The track sometimes had to be raised or lowed and re-aligned in order to cater for the higher road speed of 100 mph which would be achieved by the new inter-city trains. For this purpose, preparation trains would be required both day and night, and Ipswich men would be required to man these trains.

By now I was a well-established regular driver, and at this time I was situated in the spare link which covered any additional work. I therefore found myself employed

## Ipswich loco depot to close next month 1968

BRITISH RAILWAYS today confirmed that its locomotive maintenance depot at Wherstead Road, Ipswich (pictured here), will close on May 4.

Fifty-four men have been made the case of the threatened men with BR management.

The result of Sir Dingle's meeting with BR management was not made publicly known. So far there has been no union comment on today's confirmation of the depot's closure, and British Railways have no further comment to make.

*(Courtesy Evening Star)*

extensively working these preparation trains.

The Depot at Croft Street had from 1968 ceased to be a diesel maintenance department. The fitters, electricians, etc. were displaced and the locomen were moved to Ipswich Station which then became the signing-on point. Locomotives were stabled in the old original carriage sidings on the down side of Number Four platform. Fuel and water facilities were provided at the Station for the servicing of the locos. A fitter and his assistant dealt with this and also any minor repair work and examinations that could be undertaken on site. Major repair work could sometimes be dealt with by Colchester but extensive repairs came under the jurisdiction of Stratford.

Following this move, the Croft Street Depot was progressively run down. The carriage and wagon repair shops next to the main line were still in operation but they had also been affected and were at this period working with a much reduced staff and workload. The old loco shed area, covering a large part of the site, was now redundant but was left with full track facilities which were virtually unused. This proved to be an ideal site for the new electrification department. A vast amount of different materials would be required and there was adequate storage space for this purpose. In particular, there was ample provision there for the actual trains to be stabled and loaded. One track, running through the old loco shed, was given a specific use. At the Croft Street end of this track, a large concrete-mixing plant was built adjacent to the line. This was for servicing a special train, consisting of giant yellow drums, known as the "foundation train", its purpose being to transport the concrete needed to fill the previously dug out and prepared foundations for the steel "masts" or vertical supports carrying the overhead cable equipment. This job would take a long while, as there were a lot of holes to fill between Ipswich and Colchester. It should also be remembered that, apart from the main lines, some sidings and yards would also be involved. The foundation train worked during the daytime and came back to the depot at night to be replenished in readiness for the next morning.

The actual track work was undertaken by the engineer's or "ballast" trains, and they were busy day and night throughout the whole electrification project. Other special trains were involved, including those for bridge inspection, steel mast erecting, wiring, and subsequent testing. There were also various types of self-propelled track machines, each designed for a specific purpose. These machines were operated and driven by engineering department men, but in the majority of cases the driver would be unfamiliar with the route and a BR driver would be required to act as his pilotman.

The trains required very careful handling. The foundation, steel or wiring trains, for instance, were quite long and when on site, with men working on them, had to be driven at a very low constant speed (approximately walking pace) which had to be maintained until the driver was told to stop. When driving these, we would alternate between pushing and pulling the train, and this took quite a bit of getting used to, especially as sometimes we would be working on a gradient. At certain times we ran with a little power on, and a light brake application at the same time, in order to keep the speed steady.

Owing to the length of the trains and the curvature of the track at certain locations, communication problems were experienced between the train operators and the drivers, as hand signalling would be out of the question. The problem was overcome by issuing each driver with

*New entrants to the footplate grade seen here, in July 1979, with their driver-instructor Harry Whitman. Left to right: Nigel Driver, Simon Szczepanski, (eventually became a driver, Channel Tunnel Shuttle Service), Instructor Harry Whitman, John Orris and Mark Davies. Unlike the old days, when the job had to be learnt by trial and error, these young men received proper training from the start. Note the yellow high-visibility vests which had to be worn at all times when in vicinity of moving engines and trains.* (Photo Kelvin Higgins Collection)

a mobile radio receiver/transmitter when he took charge of the train. A train supervisor would make himself known to the driver, give him the radio which had to be tested, and the supervisor would be the one the driver took orders from at all times while working on the site.

These jobs were not popular with every driver but I found that moving along at walking pace on a glorious summer's day made a nice change from our normal activities and could be quite enjoyable. We had a secondman with us on all these jobs for protection and look-out purposes, and of course he could be very handy for making the tea. As these trains were out for approximately ten to twelve hours during the day, we would normally be sent relief, although the men on the train worked through. The relief crew would usually arrive by road in an engineers' van in which we travelled back to Ipswich.

During this time, the working timetables had to be amended, as between the morning and evening rush hours, the electrification trains would occupy one of the two main lines. Single line working had to be put into operation, therefore, for the diesel hauled service trains, with the resultant extra time required.

Eventually the work was completed and after exhaustive checking and testing by special trains, the system was given the all clear. Electric trains first ran through from London to Norwich in May 1987. Two years before this, the electrification of the Colchester to Ipswich line had taken place and trains were hauled by electric locomotives from London to Ipswich where they were replaced by diesels for the remaining distance to Norwich, and vice versa.

Electrification, of course, meant that Ipswich men were involved in yet another bout of driver training. The basic electric course lasted three weeks. The first week, in my case, was based at Colchester. We were taught by staff from Ilford Training School plus Stratford instructors, who travelled down for the purpose. This first week was devoted entirely to the infrastructure of the system, namely a description of power generation, supply to the overhead line equipment by various feeder stations, lineside equipment, emergency and safety regulations and a hundred and one other things which took quite a lot of assimilation but which proved to be very interesting.

The second week was devoted to the theory side of the new Class 86 electric locomotives to be employed on the London-Norwich inter-city trains. I say new, as they were to us at Ipswich, but strictly speaking this was not true. These locos had for some years previously been running on the Western Region. All however had been extensively overhauled and refurbished at Ilford Works prior to us receiving them. For years, the older drivers had always maintained that this region never received anything new, only someone's cast-offs. Once again this proved to be the case. To be fair though, a lot of money had been spent on these locos and they were as good as new when they were handed over.

The third week was spent learning to drive the locomotives. For this, we had a special empty coach training train which we ran each day between Stratford and Colchester. On the last day of the three week course

*Loading "foundation train" with ready-mixed concrete at Ipswich Loco Depot, c 1985.* (Photo by Peter Dennington)

*Passenger train approaches Ipswich on the first day of electric working between London and Ipswich, 13th May, 1985.*
(Photo by Les Gould)

we would, if competent, be passed out in both theory and practice by an Ilford traction inspector. From then onwards, we drove these locos as and when required.

Once again, completely new techniques had to be acquired. Both steam and diesel locomotives had, although in different ways, produced their power internally, but now the locos were receiving power from an outside source. This created additional problems, one of which was a "neutral section", which was a short break in the overhead wiring where no power could be obtained.

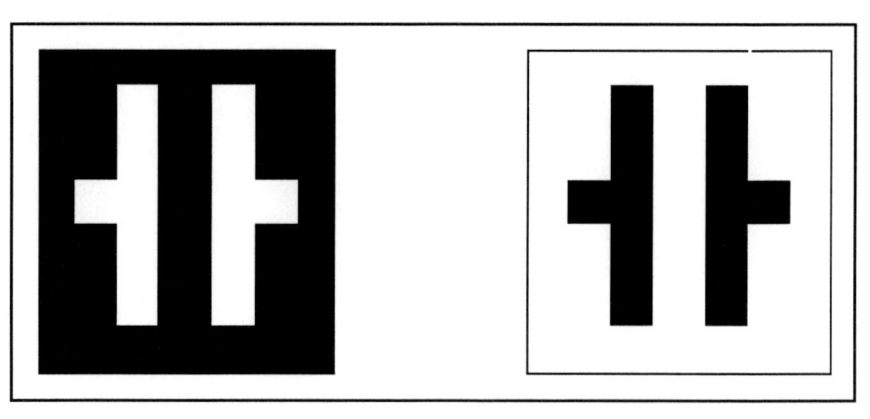

*Drivers' warning signs of neutral sections, (left) the approach, (right) on site.*

There were about nine of these between London and Norwich, and a driver had to bear the position of these in mind all the time. The power on the loco had to be completely OFF when running through these sections otherwise there would be a horrible flash and bang, power would be completely lost and great difficulty experienced in regaining it. Unlike steam and diesel locomotives, power could not be applied or shut off immediately but had to be fed in or taken off gradually, a system known as notching up or down. Therefore, in the case of neutral sections, power would have to be taken off well in advance so that by the time the locomotive reached the section the ammeter would read zero. This could take several seconds, and, when running at the maximum speed of 100 mph, meant that the process had to be initiated a considerable distance before reaching the dead wire section.

Some of these sections, especially in the London area, were situated on lower speed stretches of track where obviously the distance allowed would be less. These running-down points took some getting used to; they could not be taught but were learned by experience, and after a while became second nature. It was still easy to forget however, especially if you were distracted for any reason. I always think that driving electric trains requires just that little extra in concentration.

Now we had yet another set of faults and failures, new regulations and so on with which to contend. We had long ago dispensed with the hard physical side of the job, but the mental aspect appeared to be increasing steadily. I do not wish to imply by this statement that steam men were of low intellect. A high standard was always required of footplatemen, and anyone not up to the mark soon fell by the wayside. With us however, we had already been heavily involved in the railway modernisation process, and now we had many different types of locomotives and multiple units, both diesel and electric, to cope with.

So, with a little experience, we became accustomed to driving the new electrics and we could be forgiven perhaps for thinking that surely this must be the finish. Or was there a boffin lurking somewhere out there, preparing to unleash yet another form of power on our already burdened shoulders. Nuclear perhaps?

We were now in the latter part of the 1980s and at this time I made my final move, which was into the passenger link. After forty years I had now entered the last stage of my career, and all being well, this would be where I would stay until I retired. The passenger link by now was quite different to what it had been in earlier years. Most of the inter-city London-Norwich trains were now worked by Stratford and Norwich men. We did however still work all the East Anglian routes and a fair proportion of cross-country routes to March and Peterborough, etc. We had a different job each week, and with alternating diesel and electric working I was quite content to finish my final years in this link, with no more changes in the offing. This was not to be, however. For some time the old diesel railcars, which had been running since the 1950s and were proving costly to maintain, had been steadily replaced by yet another type of train, namely the Sprinters. These were a modern version of the old railcars, with improved acceleration and a top speed of 75 mph. Some of the earlier railcars underwent a programme of refurbishment to give them another short lease of life until enough Sprinters were built to replace them. Eventually this came about and they were finally broken up and passed into history.

The new Sprinter trains soon became very popular and

in mid-1988, a new cross-country service was introduced with them. The Sprinters, like the railcars before them, were classed as multiple unit trains. They were built as two coach units but could be coupled together to form various combinations of two, four, or six, coach trains. Unlike the old railcars, which had to be coupled or uncoupled manually, this operation was automatically controlled by the driver. A one unit (two coach) train, for example could leave Ipswich and run to Ely. Upon arrival it could then couple to another single or double unit which had come from Norwich, and the whole would then run as one train through to the Midlands. This made for more economical working as coaches could be added or detached to suit passenger demand.

This new service was a great success. Trains ran from Harwich, Parkeston Quay, Colchester and Ipswich right through to Birmingham, Blackpool, Liverpool and Manchester. One train left Colchester in the afternoon to run to Barrow-in-Furness, the longest run of all. Ely, which had always been an important station, owing to its links with Cambridge, Norwich and Kings Lynn, achieved even greater status as it was now an interchange point for this new service to the Midlands and beyond. Passengers for further north, such as York, Newcastle and Scotland, could change at Peterborough and join a train on the East Coast Main Line from London's Kings Cross. Ipswich men worked trains that started from Parkeston & Colchester and most of those from Ipswich, and eventually this work formed the greater part of the Passenger Link at Ipswich.

This Link was by now only a fraction of its original size. The mail, newspaper and parcel train traffic had mostly gone over to road haulage. We had lost our share of electric working with the result that we did not go into Liverpool Street any more. Our work now consisted entirely of rural and cross-country routes. Some Ipswich drivers were not very happy with this arrangement and found the sprinter trains rather boring, considering themselves to be "glorified bus drivers". I myself, now sixty years of age, was quite happy however to be "bored" for the remainder of my time. It was a comedown I suppose after working 100mph electric inter-city expresses and I could well understand their misgivings. But as had been the case back in the steam days and the Old Man's Gang, there were always a certain number of drivers who were quite content to work out their final years in a less-demanding link.

I count myself very fortunate not to have been involved in any serious accidents or mishaps during my railway career. I did however have one hair-raising experience in the early diesel days due to a complete misunderstanding with my driver. At the time I was a secondman in the Passenger Link. I was working with a Spare Link driver on that particular day as my regular mate was unavailable. It was this which led to the misunderstanding.

We were at Lowestoft with a 31 Brush diesel locomotive. It was cold weather and steam heating was in operation. The steam generator for this purpose on a Class 31 was situated in the engine compartment just inside the door from the driver's cab at one end of the locomotive. This was known as No. 1 cab, the other end being No. 2. We were waiting to back on to a train which would come in from Yarmouth and which we would work forward to Ipswich. No. 2 cab was the Ipswich end and would therefore be the operational driving cab for this purpose, No. 1 cab being at the end to be coupled to the train.

The train duly arrived from Yarmouth and we backed on. There was no time to spare on this job as only five minutes were allowed for the turn round and the train was invariably a minute or two late arriving. Station staff were most anxious to get the train away as soon as possible and it was not long before the right-away whistles started to blow. I had completed the coupling-up process but was still down between loco and train as I was having difficulty with a slightly leaking vacuum connection. I heard the whistles but turned a deaf ear. "You wait a minute," I thought "we'll have things right before we go." Sealing the vacuum pipes to my satisfaction I then heard my mate blow the horn, the locomotive lurched, the coupling tightened and, to my horror, the train started to move. I shouted but to no avail as obviously no one could hear me. Panic momentarily gripped me. The obvious thought was to get out but I knew that I could not do it. I would have to duck below the buffers and would never have time to clear my legs. I had to make a quick decision. I hauled myself up and hung over the coupling, managing to rest my feet on the steam heater pipes which were coupled and locked. I thanked my lucky stars that I was of slim build as there certainly was not much room between the diesel and the carriage vestibule. I just had to hang on for dear life, my hope being that the Lowestoft signalman would see me and throw his signals back. That hope was soon dashed however as I realised we were past the signalbox, out on the main line and on our way.

Our first booked stop was Beccles and I wondered if I would be able to hang on for that length of time. I still do not know the answer to that question for fortunately my driver, noticing that the carriage heating gauge had not moved, had a feeling that something was wrong and brought the train to a stand at Oulton Broad South. When he saw me emerge I think he was the more shocked of the two of us.

As I stated previously, this happening was all the result of a misunderstanding between us. When working with my regular driver, we had our agreed ways of working together. When coupling up to trains, he would always wait for me to join him in the cab before moving off. My relief driver on this day however, knowing by his vacuum gauge that I had coupled up to the train, and aware that the steam generator was at the other end cab, had assumed that I had climbed into the rear cab to open the steam line to the train and would rejoin him when the pressure was settled throughout the train. He had therefore immediately taken the right-away signal. This just goes to show how easily accidents can happen. Neither of us was to blame, we had just assumed, wrongly as it turned out, that we knew what the other was doing.

Approximately a year or so before I retired, the cross-country service was drastically reduced, with the result that we at Ipswich suffered a further loss of work. Apart from a train from Parkeston Quay to Birmingham and Liverpool in the morning, and its return at night, other through services were taken off. We did retain one or two jobs but these were simply run as shuttle services to Ely or Peterborough to link up with the through trains from Norwich and Cambridge. Previous to this reduction the service had still retained its popularity and was doing well. Why reduce it, you may ask? The main reason, we found out later, was related to Stansted Airport. It had been decided to introduce a frequent service from the Midlands through to the Airport but the problem was the number of sprinters required to operate this service. Other services were therefore curtailed to provide the full complement needed for this purpose.

We at Ipswich now found ourselves cut back once again and facing redundancies at the Depot. This was a mixed blessing however as a resettlement agreement was offered to drivers aged fifty-five and over. Strict seniority rules still being in force, when there was redundancy at a depot, the younger men would normally be the ones to be displaced. This was not very satisfactory as they were the very men the management wished to retain. It was therefore decided to offer the older men a special resettlement allowance with earlier pension if they wished to retire. I eventually opted for this arrangement as I was by this time in my sixty-second year. Although I was still reasonably fit I decided to call it a day.

BR Management was very good to the men who decided to leave early. A two-day retirement seminar was arranged at the Great Eastern Hotel at Liverpool Street for the drivers and their wives to attend. At this, talks were given regarding finance, income-tax problems, use of leisure time after retirement and so on. A few weeks after retiring, a lunch was held at the Novotel, Ipswich at which the men were presented with a framed certificate in appreciation of their years of service to the railway. Their wives were not forgotten. They were each presented with a bouquet and thanked for their part in supporting their husbands during their railway career, including coping with the irregular hours and having to produce meals at awkward times. The men were given a retirement gift which they were allowed to choose themselves from a list which included clocks, watches, music systems and telescopes. How different from the treatment received by the steam drivers retiring in the early part of this century.

And so in March 1993, after forty-five years service, I finally left the railway. Walking away from Ipswich Station after completing my final turn of duty, I must confess to a strong feeling of nostalgia. I could not help but think back to that cold October morning in 1947 when, as a young lad I first made my appearance, full of apprehension, at the Croft Street Loco Depot and joined the hallowed ranks of Ipswich locomen.

**Trainload Freight**

*Kenneth Freestone*

*On the occasion of your retirement the British Railways Board and Management of Trainload Freight would like to congratulate you upon the completion of ....45..... years service and place on record our high appreciation of the valuable service which you have given to the Railways.*

*We wish you every happiness in the future.*

Tony Huben

*Area Manager*

British Railways Board

---

SA.14/3491

A.R.Ewer
District Motive Power Superintendent

Telephone MARYLAND 4820
Ext. 5393
Telegraphic Address
MOTIVE, RAILWAY, STRATFORD,
LONDON, E.15

Our Reference SA.14/3491
Your Reference

**BRITISH TRANSPORT COMMISSION**

B.R. 32601/4

DISTRICT MOTIVE POWER SUPT.
EASTERN REGION
STRATFORD E.15

29th May, 1956

Driver H.C.Smith,
PARKESTON M.P.DEPOT.

Dear Mr.Smith,

    In accordance with the Rules of the British Transport Commission, you are due to retire from the service of the Railway on attaining your 65th birthday, 30th May, 1956.

    On that date you will have completed 48 years 3 months' Railway service, and I take this opportunity to thank you for your many years of faithful service, and to wish you a long and happy retirement.

Yours faithfully,

R.W.Ward
for A.R.Ewer
DMPS

*Retirement, 1956 and 1993*

# *Diary of a Footplateman*

Footplateman Eric George Leggett's progression from a Cleaner in 1943 to a Driver twenty-three years later in 1966

| | | |
|---|---|---|
| 15th Feb. | 1943 | Joined railway as **CLEANER,** when not quite sixteen years of age. |
| 9th Oct. | 1943 | **PASSED CLEANER** (acting fireman) Check No. 349 |
| 25th March | 1944 | 104 firing turns completed. |
| 23rd Sep. | 1944 | 201 " " " |
| 23rd Nov. | 1944 | 250 " " " |
| 3rd Feb. | 1945 | 313 " " " |
| 7th Feb. | 1945 | FIRING TEST to Diss with Inspector Slack. |
| 24th March | 1945 | 361 firing turns completed. |
| 22nd Sept. | 1945 | 526 " " " |
| 23rd April | 1946 | 686 " " " |
| 16th Nov. | 1946 | **FIREMAN,** Check No. 244, *Old Man's Gang,* with Driver R. Bannock. |
| 17th Nov. | 1947 | *Goods No. 1 Gang* with Driver Dakin |
| 4th Oct | 1948 | *No. 3 Passenger Gang* with Driver C Parr. |
| 17th Oct | 1949 | *Special Link* with Driver Fiddiman |
| 20th March | 1950 | *No.2 Passenger Gang* with Driver T Page. |
| 2nd Oct. | 1950 | *No.1 Passenger Gang* with Driver P Burrows. Engine was 1562 (B12). |
| 27th Oct. | 1952 | " " " with Driver H Browning. " " " " |
| 11th April | 1955 | *Express Passenger Gang* with Driver R Riches. " " 1252 (B1). |
| 24th Oct. | 1955 | *No.1 Passenger Gang* with Driver R Tricker. " " 1564 (B12). |
| 30th Jan. | 1956 | *Express Passenger Gang* with Driver B Southgate. " " 1052 (B1). |
| 12th March | 1957 | Technical Exam with Inspector Mitchell, to be passed for driving duties. |
| 15th March | 1957 | **PASSED FIREMAN** (acting driver), Check No. 179. |
| Mar. onwards | 1957 | *Station Shunting 5.00 am* with Driver J Leaning. |
| | | *Station Shunting 12.35 pm* with Driver A Bloom. |
| | | *Cinders 6.45 am* with Driver H Church. |
| 6th May | 1957 | *Spare Link* with Driver E Button. |
| 20th May | 1957 | Five days training, afterwards passed as driver of Diesel Mechanical Shunting Locomotives, 204 H.P. Drewry and 204 h.p. Hunslett. |
| 17th Nov. | 1958 | *Spare Link* with Driver E Ford. |
| July | 1959 | One week Diesel Training. |
| Aug./Sept. | 1959 | Two weeks " " |
| 28th Nov. | 1959 | First year driving turns completed. |
| 22nd Feb. | 1960 | *Shunting & Loco Link* with Driver R Moore. |
| 21st March | 1960 | One week Diesel Training on Sulzer. |
| 2nd May | 1960 | *Shunting & Loco Link* with Driver S Chapman. |
| 20th June | 1960 | " " " with Driver E Rose. |
| 19th Sept. | 1960 | *Spare Link* with Driver J Bell. |
| Sept. | 1960 | One week training D800 HP Paxman. |
| Oct. | 1960 | Three days Train Heating Boiler Training. |
| Feb. | 1961 | Two weeks Diesel Railcar Training. |
| 14th April | 1961 | Second year driving turns completed. |
| May/June | 1961 | Class 37 Diesel Training. |
| 12th June | 1961 | *Spare Link* with Driver C Broad. |
| Oct. | 1961 | Three days Train Heating Boiler Training, Classs 37. |
| March | 1962 | Four days Diesel Training, Class 40 using locomotive D202. |
| 17th June | 1962 | " " with Driver H Carter. |
| 16th Sept | 1962 | " " with Driver C Broad. |
| 12th Nov | 1962 | Goods Link with Driver P Cole |
| 13th March | 1963 | Third year driving turns completed. |
| 29th April | 1963 | *Spare Link.* |
| 17th August | 1963 | *Passed Fireman Link.* |
| March | 1965 | Three days Train Heating Boiler Training. |
| 4th Feb. | 1966 | **DRIVER,** Check No. 128, *Shunting Link.* |

## *Frederick Charles Salmon (1866 - 1949)*

by Pat Ling, neé Salmon

THE Salmon family lived "Over Stoke" for well over a century before the railway arrived. In consequence, perhaps, several of the menfolk became employees of the railway from its earliest days.

In 1851, Fred's grandfather, William Salmon who lived at 46 Stoke Street, was still a farm labourer but his eldest son William (Fred's father) who was seventeen years of age, was employed as an engine painter.

By 1861 the family had moved to 55 Stoke Street and the Census Return for that address gave William's occupation as platelayer and the occupations of his two sons, William and James, as labourer and fireman respectively.

William junior married Susan Sheppard at St Mary-at-Stoke Church on December 28th 1862, and their first son, William George, was baptized in the same church in 1864, followed by Frederick Charles in 1866. Fred had been born on 4th November, 1866 at 1 Rectory Road and his birth certificate confirms the fact that his father William was indeed a railway labourer.

Four years later in 1871 at 3 Rectory Road, Alice Paternoster was born. Alice was the daughter of Alfred Paternoster, a railway horse driver, and his wife Sarah. Fred was to marry Alice, the girl next door, in 1901.

The 1881 Census confirms that William and Susan Salmon still lived at 1 Rectory Road. Fred was fourteen and had left school and was employed as a gardener's assistant. His father and elder brother were still working as railway labourers. Fred attended St Mary Stoke Sunday School and at Christmas 1881 was presented with a copy of "The Poetical Works of Henry W Longfellow" by the rector, the Rev George Bulstrode, as a reward for regular attendance and general good conduct.

Fred Salmon started his railway career as a cleaner in January 1885. By April 1892 he was promoted to fireman. When he married Alice at St Mary-at-Stoke Church he gave his address as 104 Rectory Road (an address that later in life he would move back to) and his occupation as "Engine Driver". His father's occupation was that of an engine wheel turner employed by the Great Eastern Railway. Alice's family had moved to Little Bealings and her father Alfred was now an agricultural labourer.

Fred and Alice had three children; Ivy born 1902 at 39 Pauline Street, Eva, born 1909, and Fred, born 1911, the latter two born when the family lived at 78 Croft Street. At 74 Croft Street at this time lived Fred senior's brother, William George. This was the house in which their parents William and Susan had lived in 1891, prior to moving to 104 Rectory Road. After the death of Susan Salmon in 1915, Fred and Alice made a final move to that address in Rectory Road. These changes of address, all keeping strictly within the Over Stoke area, clearly demonstrate the requirement for railwaymen to live close by the Loco Depot at Croft Street.

Fred retired from the railway in November 1931 on his sixty-fifth birthday. His official railway record, printed at that time in the LNER Railway Magazine, stated he was promoted to engine driver in January 1907 and that he worked for several years on main line expresses and was located at Ipswich all the time except for short periods at Parkeston and Felixstowe.

When Frederick Charles Salmon died in 1949 aged eighty-two years, his entire life had been spent living "Over Stoke" and for forty-six of those years he had worked on the railway which had also given employment to his grandfather, father, uncle, brother and father-in-law!

Unfortunately the tradition ended there as his son Frederick Stanley spent his working life with Ransomes Sims & Jefferies, and he and his sisters all left the area.

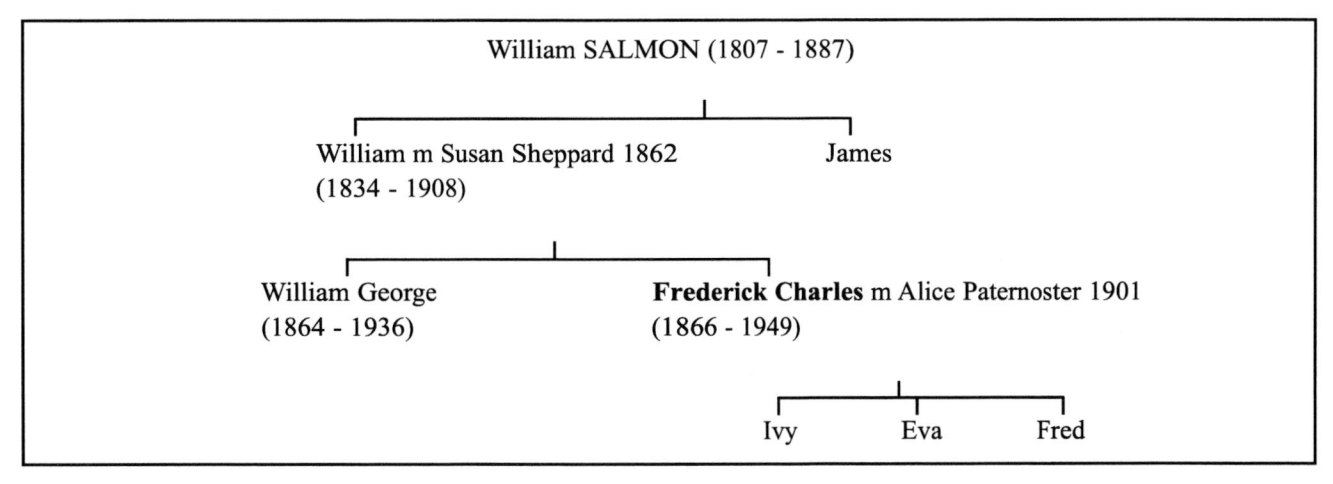

---

William SALMON (1807 - 1887)
├── William m Susan Sheppard 1862 (1834 - 1908)
│   ├── William George (1864 - 1936)
│   └── **Frederick Charles** m Alice Paternoster 1901 (1866 - 1949)
│       ├── Ivy
│       ├── Eva
│       └── Fred
└── James

*Frederick Salmon (nearest camera) when he was a fireman on "Claud Hamilton" Class engine No. 1878, built in 1902.*
(Photo courtesy Pat Ling, née Salmon)

*Frederick Salmon and his wife Alice at their home in Rectory Road, the road in which they had both been born.*
(Photo courtesy Pat Ling, née Salmon)

## George Henry Pinkney

GEORGE Henry Pinkney was born 4th January 1877 at 15 Kemp Street, Over Stoke. His father Charles was a railway labourer who subsequently became an engine driver, as George was to do later. George's own son Philip was to follow the family's railway tradition, thus making three generations of footplatemen.

Young George won a scholarship to further his education but unfortunately was unable to pursue this owing to family circumstances, and so, at the age of fifteen, he started work with the GER as a temporary greaser at Parkeston. That was in 1892. In 1906 George married the daughter of the Ramsey family with whom he lodged at West Terrace, Garland Road, Parkeston. Mary Priscilla Ramsey taught at Parkeston Girls' School. She had been awarded the Royal Humane Society's Testimonial on parchment for having "on the 22nd April, 1892, gone to the rescue of Bertie Ponder, who was in imminent danger of drowning in Parkeston Reservoir, and whose life she courageously saved." Mary's father, Philip Ramsey, was a ship's fireman.

By 1909, George Pinkney had progressed to fireman. Less than ten years later, having moved to Ipswich and living first in Station Street and then at 20 Martin Road, he was driving; initially in the shunting yard, then on goods trains and finally passenger trains - the ultimate goal. When the locomotives of the *North Country Continental* worked from Ipswich through to Manchester, George Pinkney was one of the first drivers on the job, which is described elsewhere. While at work, he always wore bleached overalls, often with a bowler hat.

During the First World War George Pinkney used to run two massive guns from Felixstowe Beach Station to a spot a short distance along the coast. Here they were mounted for action, rails being specially laid for the purpose. Another tough assignment for him was testing certain bridges as a safety measure. He had to drive his light engine at varying speeds across the bridges so the effects could be measured.

*Wedding of George Pinkney and Mary Ramsey which took place at the Wesleyan Chapel, Parkeston, in 1906. George's father Charles, who lived in Rectory Road, Ipswich, is seen left, middle row.*

(Photo courtesy Mrs Rhoda Taylor, nee Pinkney)

George loved his job and was so keen that he was willing to give up his free time to instruct younger cleaners and firemen at Mutual Improvement Classes. Whilst at Parkeston he was vice-chairman of the class held there which was formed in 1909. The object of the classes (mentioned elsewhere in these pages) was to promote a practical knowledge of general locomotive work. The membership was open to drivers, firemen and cleaners. No subject other than locomotive working was allowed to be discussed during class time. The rules stated that no member was allowed to ridicule another on account of lack of knowledge or giving a wrong reply to a question, and anyone disregarding this rule would be fined 6d. Any member attending the class when under the influence of alcohol, or creating a disturbance during class time, would be requested to leave and his name would be erased from the register. When it was known that a member's firing or driving test was imminent then the whole of the class time would be devoted to coaching that person, with a special meeting being called if necessary. While working on the Manchester run, George Pinkney would often take a Mutual Improvement Class during his evening spent "taking rest" at Gorton. Later in life he held classes in his own home at Martin Road; all this for no extra pay, but at the time it was the method the railway companies used for training their drivers and firemen.

An enthusiastic member of the ASLEF, George was branch secretary for twenty-three years. On his retirement in 1942 he was presented with an illuminated address from the Society's Executive Committee, and was praised by its General Secretary. In 1956 he and his wife celebrated their Golden Wedding. The couple worked hard for the Labour Party, and George was one of the founders of the Loco Men's Club in Rectory Road, being a committee member and a former vice-president and president.

George Pinkney died in 1965 aged eighty-eight.

*Illuminated Address received by George Pinkney to mark his retirement in 1942.*

(Courtesy Richard Pinkney, grandson)

*Parkeston infants' class with teacher Mary Ramsey who was later to marry George Pinkney.*

(Photo courtesy Mrs Rhoda Taylor, nee Pinkney)

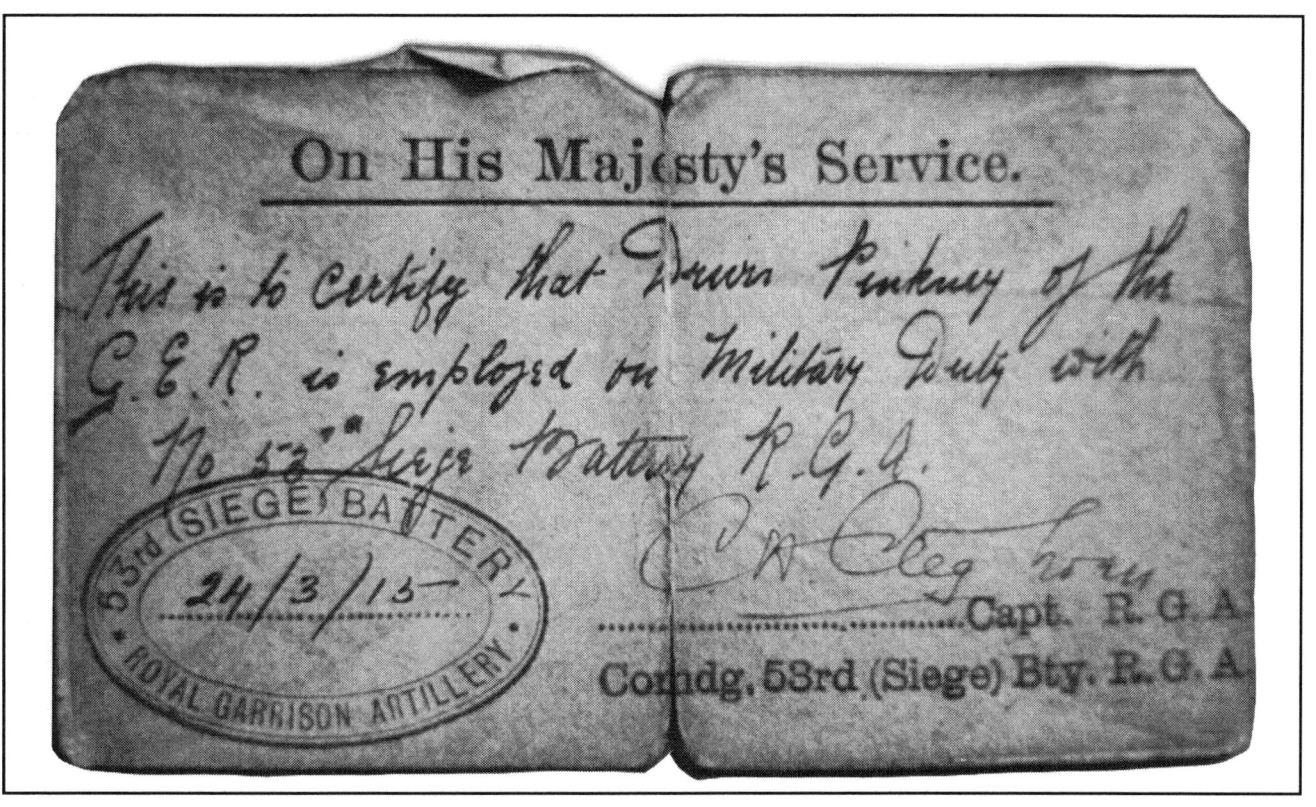

*Driver Pinkney's military pass for use when moving guns at Felixstowe during the First World War.*
(Courtesy Richard Pinkney)

*Group pictured at Ipswich Loco Depot beside LNER engine No. 8523. George Pinkney seen standing far right, wearing bleached overalls.* (Photo courtesy Richard Pinkney)

*Document authorising George Pinkney to retire from the railway, aged sixty-five, in 1942 during the Second World War. Permission had to be obtained under the Essential Work (General Provisions) Order, 1941.*

(Courtesy Richard Pinkney)

*Driver Philip Pinkney, George Pinkney's son. Philip retired from the railway in 1970.*

(Photo courtesy Richard Pinkney)

## William Goddard

WILLIAM Goddard was born on 18th August 1877, the son of Henry and Susan (nee Baldwin) Goddard, of Jarmans Farm, Great Wenham. William left school when he was ten years old to work on the family farm, which in the winter meant stone-picking, and bird-scaring during spring and early summer.

It is not clear how William came to apply to the Great Eastern Railway for a job as an engine cleaner at Parkeston, it being considerably further from Great Wenham than either Ipswich or Colchester. It may have been that at that particular time there was only a vacancy at Parkeston, where after the opening of Parkeston Quay in 1883 much of the labour required came from farms over a wide area and included not only farm workers but also a few farmers, who gave up their land during what was then a period of agricultural depression. William Goddard joined the railway at the age of seventeen in 1894, travelling home when he was able to on his bicycle.

Whilst at Parkeston William, or Bill as he was better known, met Ellen Blake, a local girl whose father worked for the GER as Engine Driver, tending the railway-owned power station boilers and hydraulic accumulators used for working some of the quay side cranes. He and Ellen married on 23rd September 1908 at St Nicholas Church in Harwich and set up home at 29 Parkeston Road, one of the first streets to be built in Parkeston village. Ellen and Bill had four sons and a daughter. In 1913 the family moved to Braintree probably for Bill to gain promotion to fireman or acting-driver, where another son was born, but in 1916 they moved finally to Ipswich and into number 41 Station Street, close to the locomotive depot. Their son William (Bill, junior) applied for a job with the newly established LNER in 1923 but he unfortunately failed an eyesight test and so began an apprenticeship as a carpenter in the Wagon Shops but like most apprentices he was dismissed at the end of his time, a very disappointing end to his railway career. His father however moved on through all the driving links, retiring at sixty-five in 1942. Under the wartime conditions he was given the opportunity to stay on but he declined and for a further six years obtained light work at Ransomes and Rapier Ltd..

Throughout his time on the railway Bill Goddard was known as a very amenable and kindly man by his colleagues and his family. He was one of the founder-members of the Loco Club in Rectory Road. He enjoyed playing cribbage and also working on his allotment near Halifax signal box. He died in 1952 aged seventy-five.

*William Goddard, home from work. (Information and photograph provided by the eldest son Bill, junior, mentioned in \the text, who died aged eighty-eight shortly before publication of the book.)*

# Ernie Gould

ERNIE Gould was born in 1884. He was training to be a pastry chef but decided instead to join the railway, starting at Parkeston in June 1903. He transferred to Ipswich in 1912. At one stage of his railway career Ernie Gould worked the Manchester run, which involved him taking rest and returning with a train the next day. He made good use of his free time in Manchester, however, telling his children later about his many wonderful experiences of hearing the Hallé Orchestra perform there. Ernie Gould retired in 1949.

*Hadleigh Station Master S. M. Ellis congratulating Ernie Gould, who was driving his last train before his retirement in October 1949.* (Photo courtsey Gould Family Collection)

*Express train to London, Liverpool Street, passing Halifax water troughs at Ipswich. The driver is Ernie Gould, who is waving to his younger son Harry, whilst elder son Leslie takes the photograph, c. 1935.* (Photo courtsey Gould Family Collection)

## Robert Ratcliffe

ROBERT Ratcliffe was born at Little Wenham in 1884 and started work at twelve years of age on the land. In 1903 he joined the Great Eastern Railway, engine cleaning at their Colchester locomotive depot. He was married at Ramsey Church in 1907 to Ruby Clarke, of Tyler Street, Parkeston. Ruby's mother, who had lost her husband quite early in life, provided lodgings overnight to Pullman Car attendants in order to make ends meet.

Mr & Mrs Ratcliffe's bill to furnish their first home amounted to £17.18.8d, plus £2.13. 0d for smaller items such as a coal scuttle, oil etc.. The purchases were made from Blomfield & Co. Ltd., St Botolphs, Colchester. They lived for a time at Colchester, then Clacton, before moving to Wherstead Road, Ipswich. Robert Ratcliffe passed through the grades of fireman and driver, eventually retiring from the railway in 1949.

"Bob" Ratcliffe had three daughters, Hetty, Ida and Burston, and a son, John. The son had learnt to fly at Ipswich Airport before joining the RAF in 1939. Sadly Sergeant Pilot John Ratcliffe was reported missing on April 10th 1941, and later confirmed killed in action on that date. He was just twenty-one years of age and about to receive a commission.

During the general strike of 1926, Robert Ratcliffe remembered day-long mass meetings on Cornhill in the centre of Ipswich. There were clashes with the police and two of the strikers were jailed for eight months for assaulting policemen. On one day, twenty-two men were arrested. He recalled how the Government tried to keep the trains running by putting volunteers on the footplate, but without much success. For himself the strike could not have come at a worse time; he had moved into a house at 25 Martin Road a few months previously and had put down all he had as a deposit. When the strike came he did not have much spare cash.

Interested in the Labour movement generally, Robert Ratcliffe became an active trade unionist and was first elected to Ipswich Town Council as a Labour member in 1932. He served as a councillor for 32 years, for the last twelve of which he represented the new Chantry ward. At the time of his retirement from the Council he was Chairman of the Libraries Committee. He held office within the local ASLEF Branch as Chairman and for more than twenty years was Secretary of the Suffolk Federation of Labour Parties.

Robert Ratcliffe and his second wife, Violet Ann, became Mayor and Mayoress of Ipswich in 1957-58. Whilst Mayor, he attended the British Railways Staff Association's first dinner, held in restaurant cars at Ipswich sidings and served by the white-coated dining crew of the 7.55 pm train from Ipswich to London. During his speech he held up to the one hundred

*Robert Ratcliffe (seated first left) in his cleaning days at Colchester Loco Depot in 1904. The tender of the engine in the background bears the number 978 which was one of a class of eighty-two 0-6-0 locomotives designated by the Great Eastern Railway N31 (LNER J14), and built 1888-98. Never so efficient as the ubiquitous J15, all had been withdrawn by 1925.*

(Photo courtesy Ratcliffe Family Collection)

*Robert Ratcliffe pictured with his first wife Ruby, his son John (killed in action during the Second World War), and daughters Hetty, Ida and Burston.*
(Photo courtesy Ratcliffe Family Collection)

assembled guests his union card from 1905, declaring that it was one of his most treasured possessions.

Whilst Deputy Mayor in 1959, Robert Ratcliffe was the guest of BR at a lunch at the Great Northern Hotel, Kings Cross, for Eastern Region staff who had been elected to civic office that year. Among the guests were the Mayor of Great Yarmouth, Mr H. R. Muskett, and the Deputy Mayor of Harwich, Mr C. C. Thurlow.

Robert Ratcliffe frequently contributed items to the local press using the pen-name "Trebor" which was "Robert" spelt backwards. But perhaps his greatest and most lasting achievement was to research and write the four volume "History of the Working Class Movement in Ipswich and District". Unfortunately this only exists in typescript; the hope of publication did not materialize in spite of a preface by the Secretary of the Labour Party, Morgan Philips, in 1947, and a favourable review in 1951 by Vic Feather, then Assistant Secretary of the Trade Union Congress. A copy of the work is deposited in the Suffolk Record Office.

Robert Ratcliffe died, aged eighty-eight, in 1973.

*Robert Ratcliffe in the garden of his Martin Road Home in 1926. Note he is holding his railwayman's metal dinner-box.* (Photo courtesy Ratcliffe Family Collection)

> LONDON & NORTH EASTERN RAILWAY,
> LOCOMOTIVE RUNNING DEPARTMENT.
> SOUTHERN AREA,
> IPSWICH STATION.
> 11th October, 1924
>
> REFER TO
> I.L.R. 3981,
> IN YOUR REPLY.
>
> Driver R. Ratcliffe,
>     IPSWICH.
>
> Trucks on fire between Kelvedon and Witham
> on 21st August last.
>
> Please note that you have been awarded the sum of 10/- for your smartness during the above fire, and this will be entered on next Pay Sheets.

*Driver Ratcliffe's reward for coping with a crisis at work in 1924.* (Courtesy Burston Ratcliffe)

*Bob Ratcliffe on the footplate of an LNER Class F3 2-4-2 tank engine, one of a class of fifty engines built at Stratford Works in 1895, the largest 2-4-2T locomotives built by the GER.* (Photo courtesy Ratcliffe Family Collection)

## Three "Railway" Mayors of Ipswich
### by Kelvin Higgins

THREE locomen, including ROBERT RATCLIFFE (just mentioned) have attained the office of Mayor of Ipswich.

The first to do so was C. W. ENGLISH, who became the Mayor for 1943-44. At the time of his election he lived in Seymour Road, Over Stoke.

Mr English was born in 1878 and started his railway career on the footplate in 1896. He joined the Labour Party in 1920 and was also a founder member of the Loco Club in Rectory Road.

He was first elected on to the Council in 1930 as a representative for Bridge Ward. He served as vice-chairman of the Public Health Committee from 1944-1947.

Renowned for his outspoken, candid but constructive criticism, he was also very active on the Board of Management of the Ipswich and East Suffolk Hospital from 1918 onwards. He died on 5th February 1948, aged sixty-nine.

The term of office of Mayor V. R. FRANCIS was 1965-66. He was born in 1900 and started with the railway in 1917. He resided at 447 Wherstead Road and later 32 Powling Road. Having served on the Council from 1947, he was also a member of the Dock Commission for eight years.

The election of "Bob" Francis (as he was generally known) as Mayor caused some controversy at the time. It had been tradition that the Mayor was elected from the two main political parties on alternate years. 1965-66 should have been the turn of the Conservative representative but the ruling Labour Party decided that V. R. Francis should be Mayor on account of his long service on the Town Council. Mrs M. Keeble would have been the Conservative candidate for the post.

*Robert Ratcliffe, Mayor of Ipswich 1957-58.* (Photo courtesy Ratcliffe Family Collection)

## The Smith family of Bramford and Ipswich
Grandfather, uncle and father of co-editor Richard Smith

### Arthur Smith

ARTHUR Smith was born at Bramford on 30th August 1868. His mother came from Great Cornard and his father had been born in Burstall. They were married at Bramford Church on 29th October 1858 and lived at 136 The Street, Bramford.

Arthur, one of three boys and three girls, attended Bramford School and left when he was twelve to work on the land. He later obtained work at Hitchcock's water and steam mill in Bramford, and at the time of his wedding to local girl Emma Garnham in 1891, Arthur was described as an engine driver, which in fact referred to his job tending the boiler and stationary mill engine for which he possessed a board of trade certificate.

Arthur later worked as a grocer's warehouseman but by 1903 was working for the Great Eastern Railway Company at their locomotive depot at Croft Street in Ipswich where he was employed washing out locomotive boilers, before becoming a storekeeper at some time prior to 1923. He remained there until about 1929 when he had to retire, aged sixty, owing to a serious spinal injury sustained the previous year in an accident which occurred whilst he was on holiday with relatives in the Malvern hills.

Following their marriage Arthur and Emma lived at 1 Cypress Cottages, Bramford Road in Ipswich, where their first three children, Horace, Annie and Eva were born, before they moved across the road to 1 Rose Cottages, (later 394 Bramford Road) where Margaret, Lily and Frederick were born. Just before his accident Arthur had bought a new house in nearby Henniker Road with a large garden which, owing to his injury, he was never able to fully enjoy. He named the house "Burnscroft" which reflected his interest in the Scottish poet and poetry in general. He wrote several poignant poems himself, some on anniversaries of the 1918 armistice, and others on heroic deeds or events of the time such as "The Voyage of the Trevessa's Boats" which made headlines in 1923. It says much for Arthur's parents and his brief schooling at Bramford that he became an intelligent, God-fearing man who was a strong Labour supporter. He was also involved in the work of the "Eastern Star Provident Association", a friendly society established in 1852, holding various offices in the Ipswich Branch including those of Secretary and Chairman.

Arthur Smith died on April 17th 1949 and was buried in Bramford Churchyard with Emma, his wife of over fifty years, who had died in December 1942. Their children all survived them and the two sons, Horace and Fred, both had long railway careers on the footplate (see following pages).

*The Smith Family of Bramford and Ipswich. (Back row): Annie, Margaret, and Daughter-in-Law Ida. (Front): Lily, Eva, Arthur (father), Emma (mother, nee Garnham), sons Horace and Frederick.* (Photo courtesy Smith Family Collection)

*Arthur Smith, standing 5th from left, on engine No. 1813 when it was new at Ipswich Loco in 1910. He was employed there at the time washing out boilers.* (Photo courtesy Smith Family Collection)

*Arthur Smith attending a Hospital Sunday event in Ipswich, c.1912, on behalf of the Eastern Star Provident Association in which he held various posts. In the picture he is standing just right of centre wearing the formal sash (marked with letters BC) of Branch Chairman.* (Photo courtesy Smith Family Collection)

## Horace Smith

HORACE Smith, better known as Horrie, was the eldest child of Arthur and Emma Smith. He was one of the first pupils to attend Springfield School in Bramford Lane, Ipswich, which opened in 1896, and when he left he was presented with a copy of Chambers Dictionary as a prize for science

He started work on his thirteenth birthday with the General Post Office as Telegraph Messenger boy No. 31, and after nine months was promoted to No. 18 and supplied with uniform and boots. He became a postman two years later but received one month's notice in October 1907 after four years service during which his weekly wage had risen from 6s 10d to 9s 8d.

On March 8th 1908 Horrie commenced working for the Great Eastern Railway, cleaning the new motor buses at the garage in Croft Street for twelve shillings a week. To obtain the job, medical and eyesight tests and three references were required. He transferred to the locomotive department as a cleaner on 29th May 1911 to start his career on the footplate. His first trip was to Saxmundham with a goods train in the charge of Driver Button who had begun on the railway in 1892. The engine was No. 882, Class Y14 0-6-0, built at Stratford works in 1890.

In November 1911 Horrie was sent to work at Braintree, where he fired on trains between Witham and Bishop Stortford. Promoted to fireman on 30th October 1914, Horrie transferred to Colchester in the second week of November. His first job was with Driver T. Fisher on a Harwich goods train with engine No. 745, a 4-4-0, rebuilt from one of the 2-4-0 T19 express engines built in 1889. He was allocated to regular shed turning until 1916 when he moved into the goods link, firing to March, Cambridge and London. In 1919 he was promoted to the passenger link and in March 1920 Horrie was passed acting driver. In 1927 he applied for a driving vacancy at Parkeston where he started on August 22nd. Once there he spent four years turning and shunting to the end of 1931 and was then placed in the goods link until the end of the Second World War in 1945. Thirty-four long years after becoming acting fireman he reached the drivers' passenger link. For a time his regular engine was Class B1 4-6-0 No. 1003 *Gazelle*, working all the principal Continental expresses to and from Liverpool Street. This experience was comparatively short lived because of his age, and he joined the Old Man's Gang on 20th September 1948, driving on the Harwich to Manningtree branch, and taking the workmen's trains backwards and forwards between Harwich and Parkeston. Horrie retired on 30th May 1956 aged sixty-five, having completed over forty-eight years on the GER, LNER and British Railways.

*Horace Smith standing beside the bunker of a Class N7 tank engine. He drove these engines on the Manningtree Branch, prior to his retirement in 1956.*
(Photo courtesy Smith Family Collection)

Horrie Smith had married Ida Marion Carrington of Felixstowe Road, Ipswich, at Holy Trinity Church on 25th May 1912, just six months after his move away to Braintree, where they lived until transferring to Colchester some two and a half years later. Horrie and Ida lived in Bergholt Road in Colchester. It was there that Horrie first became involved with the Labour movement, being elected Assistant Secretary of the ASLEF Branch in 1920, later becoming Secretary. In 1922 he was an unsuccessful candidate in the elections to the Board of Guardians for St Pauls Ward, Colchester.

When they moved to Parkeston in 1927, Ida and Horace first lived in Parkeston Road and a year later they moved to a Railway house in Foster Road close to the Quay. Horrie enjoyed life and entertained family and friends with a repertoire of songs often of the Victorian melodrama kind:

"....Cold blew the Blast
Down came the Snow
Nowhere to Shelter
Nowhere to go..........."

He was proficient on accordion, concertina, tin whistle, harmonica and violin. Like his father he liked and wrote poetry. He played steel quoits, bowls and darts for the Parkeston Railway Club where he was a committee member for several years, before holding office as Chairman for ten years during the 1950s and '60s and being elected a life member of the Club.

Ida died 29th June 1960 and Horrie on 22nd September 1972. They had four children, Wilfred, Vera, Len and Thelma.

*(Above) Class T19 2-4-0 engine No. 745, built at Stratford Works in 1889 with 7 ft diameter driving wheels for main line passenger traffic. This was the engine on which Horrie Smith worked his first firing turn after his move to Colchester in 1914. The engine had been rebuilt in 1906 as a 4-4-0, and used for secondary, cross country, goods and branch line traffic. No. 745 was withdrawn in 1933.*
*(Below) Photograph showing a sister engine rebuilt as a 4-4-0. Both pictures were taken at Ipswich Station.* (Photos courtesy Smith Family Collection)

*Horrie Smith (centre) with wife Ida on his right, presiding at a Parkeston Railway Club event in 1951. He was Club Chairman for ten years.* (Photo courtesy Smith Family Collection)

*Engine No. 1003, Gazelle. One of the 410 B1 "Antelope" Class built for the LNER at their Darlington & Gorton Works, also by the North British Locomotive Company and the Vulcan Foundry. The basic design was ready during 1942 in response to Government restrictions on building new passenger engines. B1s handled heavy passenger and fast goods traffic with the widest possible route availability. The last B1 was built in 1952. Gazelle was present at the 1946 Exhibition at Ipswich commemorating the Centenary of the Eastern Union Railway coming to Ipswich. Seen here subsequently at Colchester.* (Photo courtesy Smith Family Collection)

*Horrie Smith in the cab of his regular engine No. 1003* Gazelle *during his time in the Parkeston express passenger link working the Continental expresses. His fireman was Ron Flatt of Parkeston.*

(Photo courtesy Smith Family Collection)

## Frederick Smith

FREDERICK Smith was born at 1 Rose Cottages, Bramford Road, Ipswich on 20th April 1906, the youngest of Arthur and Emma Smith's six children. Fifteen years separated him from his elder brother Horrie and soon after Fred started school Horrie moved away to work at Braintree, so Fred remembered little of his brother living at home.

Fred also attended Springfield School and left when he was fourteen to become an errand boy for Jackson, a well known boot and shoe repairer (or "snob" to use the local vernacular), with a shop on the Norwich Road close to Barrack Corner. Jackson also had a shop in Key Street which Fred Smith served on his trade bike. He was taught the rudiments of boot repairing, experience later put to good use by "soling and heeling" his family's shoes.

At the age of seventeen in April 1923 Fred started work for the newly formed London & North Eastern Railway on the bottom rung as an engine cleaner at Croft Street. He became a passed cleaner (acting fireman) but promotion was slow at Ipswich and shortly after marrying in 1929 he applied for a regular fireman's job on the Kelvedon and Tollesbury Light Railway. This was not forthcoming and he remained at Ipswich. As for many others working on the railway during the Depression, this was a difficult period for Fred. He had just taken on a twenty-year mortgage, from the Ipswich & District Building Society, of £458. 10. 10d, payable at £3 5s per month, for a new semi-detached house, but within two years railwaymen were forced to take a pay cut which caused much concern in a job where promotion could be twenty years away.

Promotion to Driver came on 22nd March 1948, one month short of twenty-five years service, and Fred subsequently passed through the driving links, seeing the end of steam at Ipswich Shed. Diesel shunting engines came early to Ipswich. They were followed by the diesel multiple units requiring driver training and learning new roads for the greater route mileage the new trains were expected to cover. The DMUs, as they were called, heralded the main line diesel-electric locos and further training.

Fred Smith and his contemporaries experienced a revolution on the railways. For years they had contended with the primitive Victorian conditions which prevailed at the Croft Street locomotive depot until it was rebuilt in the early 1950s. They witnessed the wilful destruction of the railway system decreed in the Beeching Report. The footplatemen, in their fifties, had to adapt to new types of motive power which for some meant greater cleanliness and better conditions, but inflicted worry and insecurity for many others. Fred retired on March 9th 1970 after 47 years.

Living on the edge of town, along the Bramford Road, Fred experienced a country boyhood and

*Fred Smith (left) and Second Man (ex-fireman) Fred Ward about to leave Norwich Thorpe with a Liverpool Street express in the mid 1960s. The locomotive is a Class 47 D1583. Loco firemen were re-graded to "second-men" on the introduction of diesels, and their duties included tending the locomotive's oil-fired boiler used for steam-heating passenger trains during the winter months. Eventually steam-heating was phased out, to be replaced by electric train-heating. This heralded the unpopular, single manning of passenger trains, as the driver could now operate the electric heating system unaided.* (Photo courtesy Smith Family Collection)

developed a wide knowledge of birds and other animals. One of the pleasures he always remembered was expecting to enjoy teatime in daylight, after the winter, on St. Valentine's Day. There would be a picnic and primrosing with his mother and sisters up Bullen Lane at Bramford on Good Fridays.

There were lasting impressions of seeing a motor car and, especially, the sight of an early aircraft when the boys ran out shouting "airybuzzer" in case someone should miss this miracle. During the First World War, the family had soldiers billeted with them. This was when fashion expected young men-about-town to sport a silver topped cane, or Swagger Stick, and so at ten years of age young Fred was pleased to be in fashion albeit with imitation silver.

That was until a soldier living with the family enquired as to its purpose. Told of its significance the soldier suggested that the lad was fortunate to have the use of both legs and should have no use for a stick. The cane was smartly put away, a salutary lesson learned!

Like his Father, young Fred memorised poetry at school. He was interested in all things mechanical and became adept at repairing watches, clocks and bicycles. He took a profound interest in his surroundings and at one time kept a rowing boat on the River Gipping, which he later moored Over Stoke at New Cut West.

He cadged rides on the steam barge *Trent River* up to Edward Packard's Bramford Works. He took considerable interest in the ships and sailing barges that frequented the Port. Fred had owned a motor cycle before he married but his first encounter with a car was at the hire car firm, Self-Motoring Ltd, on St. Margaret's Green in the 1930s where he sat in the driver's seat for the first time with the instruction book for company and drove out to take the family for a day trip. He bought his first car in 1951, a 1936 Morris Eight, three years later having a 1952 Morris Minor.

Fred Smith married Ivy Jackaman on Boxing Day

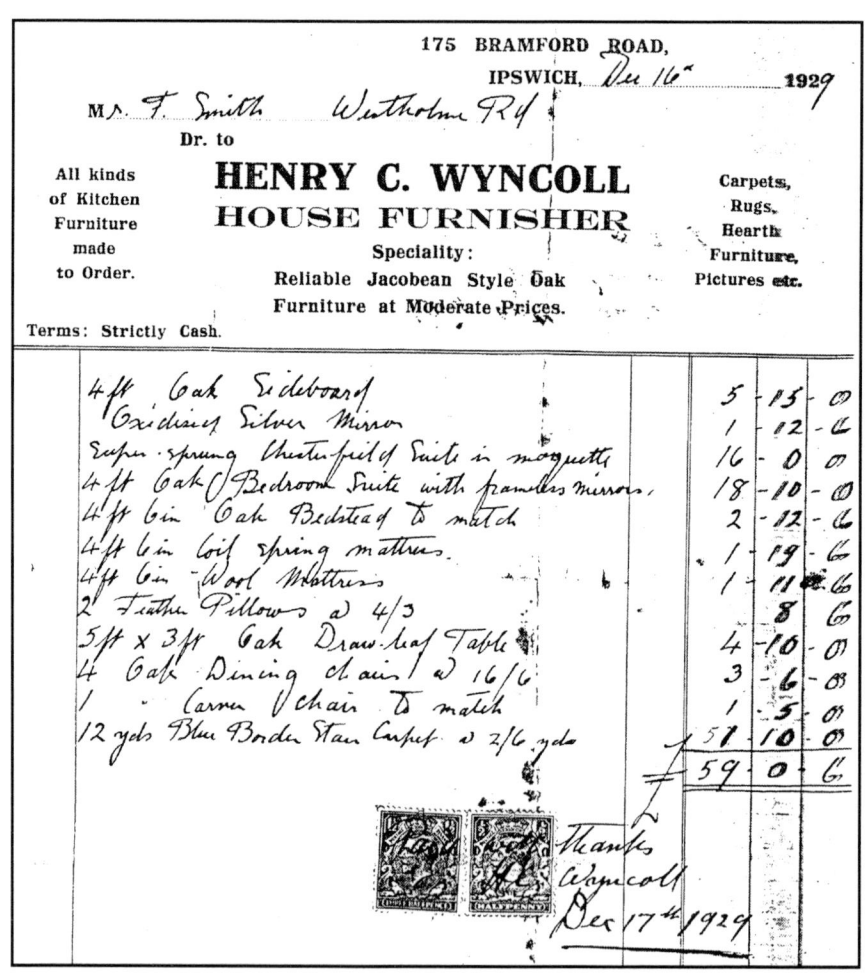

*Fred Smith's receipt for furniture bought on 16th December 1929, two weeks before his wedding. The furniture was adequate for the dining room, the front room and one bedroom. He himself made a chest of drawers and a dressing table. These last two items were a credit to the school carpentry classes held at Turret Lane and attended by boys from elementary schools from all parts of Ipswich.* (Courtesy Smith Family Collection)

1929. Ivy, born 1904, had been brought up in Riverside Road, off the Bramford Road, and before their marriage worked in the village shop at Bramford. Ivy's teenage life had been marked by tragedy. One of her two brothers, serving on the Western Front, died one week after the Armistice. Her mother died in 1920 and her eldest sister in 1921, aged just twenty-one.

After their wedding Fred and Ivy moved into a new semi-detached house off the Norwich Road where several locomen were buying houses. They lived there for forty-one years, moving to Kesgrave after Fred retired. They had one son, Richard. Ivy died in March 1977 after an illness which had taken up much of Fred's time in retirement caring for her. Fred died on 18th October 1982 aged 76.

*Presentation of long service awards at Ipswich Loco Depot on October 17th 1968, at which Fred Smith received a wrist watch. The combined service totals of the five engine drivers pictured amounted to two hundred and twenty-five years. (Left to right): Philip Pinkney, "Don" Burton, S. Parker, Mr I. McIntosh (depot manager), George Rush and Fred Smith.*
(Photo courtesy E.A.D.T. newspaper)

*Fred Smith, with son Richard, on a day trip by train to Cromer, 25th August 1939, during Fred's annual week's holiday. Fred, happily, was not a betting man. He had just assured a good citizen of Cromer that there would be no war. War was in fact declared just nine days later! On Sunday 20th August, the day before his holiday, Fred's diary records that he worked 4.30 pm to 11.45 pm, Felixstowe, firing No.8900* Claud Hamilton.

*Fred and Ivy Smith with their 1952 Morris Minor during a favourite trip to Thetford Forest in 1956.*

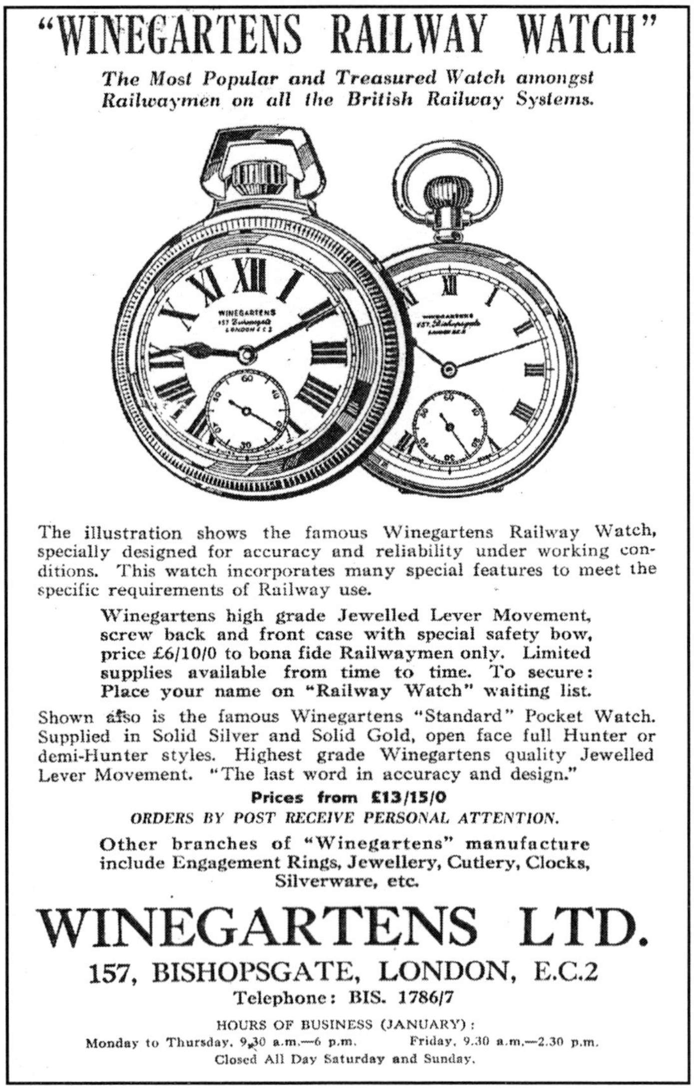

*Above and above left: Two watch advertisements taken from The Locomotive Journal of January 1948. The firm of Winegartens Ltd. was known nation-wide for good quality merchandise, and for the generous discounts given to members of many working organisations especially trade unions. On the back of Ken Freestone's Winegarten "Railway Regulator" watch, bought while he was a fireman, there is a small engraving of a steam engine. Driver Eric Pryke's Swiss-made screw-back lever watch, though similar in design, was purchased not from Winegartens but from Kay & Co. Ltd.. Railway guards were issued with pocket watches but footplatemen were not, having to purchase their own timekeepers. This led to much ill-feeling between the two grades. It was not until the 1980s that drivers were issued with quartz wrist watches.*

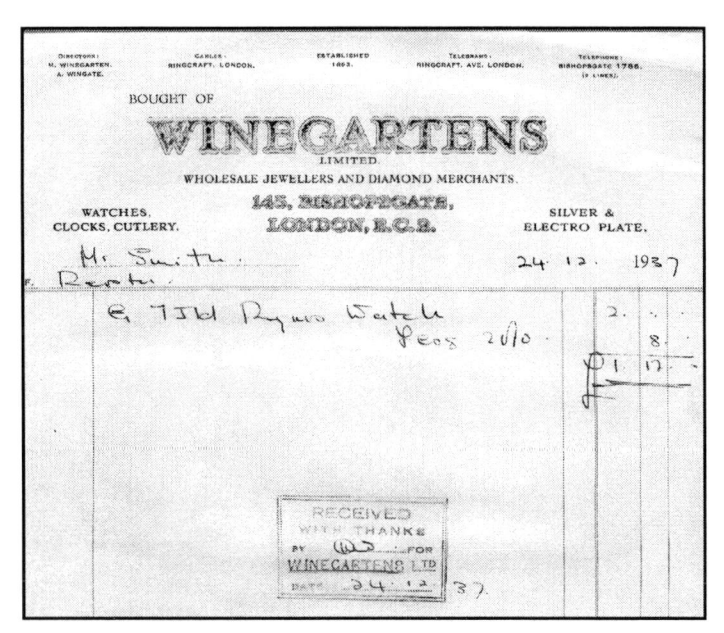

*Left: Receipt for a "Railwayman's Watch" bought by Fred Smith on Christmas Eve 1937 and believed to have been a Christmas present. A discount of 20% was allowed on the production of a "REPTA" card (Railway Employees Privilege Ticket Association) reducing the price from £2 to £1 12s.*

(Courtesy Smith Family Collection)

## George Baker, Senior

GEORGE Baker, senior, was born in 1887 at Bramford, the son of the blacksmith and farrier who moved during the 1890s to Rickinghall, in north Suffolk, to take over a blacksmith's shop situated in the yard of the Cross Public House. Here George helped his father until he was almost nineteen when he joined the Great Eastern Railway at Ipswich as an engine cleaner.

In 1908 he was moved to Framlingham as acting fireman working the branch line until returning to Ipswich just prior to the commencement of the 1914-1918 war. He volunteered for the Royal Artillery in 1915 as a farrier but in 1917 transferred to the Royal Engineers Railway Operating Division (R.O.D). He drove narrow gauge petrol-electric locomotives hauling supplies to the front line at Vimy Ridge, eventually captured by Canadian troops in April during the bitterly

*George Baker, senior (standing left), in uniform during the First World War "somewhere in France" as the chalked writing on the wall behind him explains.*

(Photo Baker Family Collection)

fought Battle of Arras. He then drove steam engines to and from the standard gauge railhead. He was demobbed in 1919 and returned to Ipswich joining the passenger link as a fireman.

George was promoted to driver in the early 1920s following the introduction of eight hour shifts for which additional men were needed, moving on through the shunting link in the twenties, the goods link in the thirties and joining the passenger links in 1940.

During the Second World War in 1944, George and his fireman Cyril Broad were involved in a unique accident at Haughley Junction. An American fighter plane struck the dome of the engine George was driving (a "Claud Hamilton" Class 4-4-0) before crashing into a field, killing the unfortunate pilot. The fireman spotted what was about to happen and pulled George to the cab floor, with the result that George only sustained a cut to his head. George Baker, senior, retired from the old man's gang in November 1952 after forty-six years of railway service. He died in 1969.

George Baker's son, also named George and known as young Ricky, followed his father (old Ricky) on to the railway, becoming an engine driver and diesel instructor. He is mentioned elsewhere in the book. The nickname Ricky reflects the fact that George Baker, senior, spent his childhood and youth in Rickinghall.

*George Baker, senior (left), seen here with Fireman Victor (Bob) Francis, who was later to become one of the Ipswich "railway mayors". The locomotive No. 530 is one of the early Great Eastern Class Y14 (LNER J15) 0-6-0s built at Stratford in 1887. According to the work's plate on the side of the cab, it was rebuilt there in 1916.*

(Photo Baker Family Collection)

## Robert Goodchild

BORN in 1893 at Rushmere St. Andrew near Ipswich, Robert Goodchild left school at twelve and worked on a farm at Tuddenham St. Martin. He joined the Great Eastern Railway in 1909 at the age of sixteen, starting as a cleaner at Croft Street. It meant that he had to lodge in nearby Rectory Road where he was later to make his home.

At that time railwaymen were expected to live within three miles of the depot anyway, because when working early turns they would be knocked up by the "call boy", usually a young cleaner cycling round Ipswich hammering on front doors and bedroom windows, usually to good effect.

In 1956 Robert Goodchild was presented with a gold watch marking over forty-five years service. The speaker at the ceremony recalled that when Robert started his railway career it was considered a good job, a man therefore receiving twenty-five shillings for a 56-hour week. There were few jobs so secure as those on the railways and the employer had no difficulty getting the men required.

Retiring in 1958, after forty-nine years service, Robert witnessed the start of modernisation with diesel locomotives replacing steam.

Robert Goodchild died in 1966 aged seventy-three.

*Robert Goodchild (back row, second left) as a cleaner at Ipswich Loco Depot in 1910.* (Photo courtesy Victor Goodchild)

*Left: Robert Goodchild with his young son Victor at the naming ceremony of* The Suffolk Regiment.
(Photo courtesy Victor Goodchild)

## GOLD WATCHES FOR RAILMEN

Forty gold wrist watches were presented on March 27th 1956 at Southtown Station, Yarmouth, to railwaymen who had each over 45 years' service.

Recipients of watches included: FELIXSTOWE MOTIVE POWER DEPOT, G. H. Ridgeon, engine driver in charge, 46 years; IPSWICH, A. J. Ball, goods guard, 46; B. F. Burns, passenger guard, 45; H. A. Styles, goods guard, 48; IPSWICH MOTIVE POWER DEPOT, L. J. Birch, engine driver, 45; S. W. Gayfer, R/foreman, 45; R. Goodchild, engine driver, 46; R. C. Gooderham, fitter, 45; C. W. Gooding, engine driver, 48; C. E. Skeet, engine driver, 46; A. A. Smith, engine driver, 46; B. E. W. Studd, engine driver, 45; W. L. Thurlow, R/foreman, 46; WICKHAM MARKET, S. A. Templing, signalman, 45.

*Above: newspaper announcement of watch presentation*

*Robert Goodchild with "his" engine, B1 Class 4-6-0 No. 61059.*
(Photo courtesy Victor Goodchild)

# Ernest Payne

ERNEST Albert Payne was born on January 31st 1895 in Old Ford, East London, one of eight children born to Margaret and Charles Payne. Margaret, née Mewse, came from Lowestoft and was in service in London prior to marrying Charles in 1877. Relatively little is known about Charles Payne except that he was born c.1851 on the Isle of Man and came to London labouring, working as a carman (horse driver) and was also employed at Beckton Gasworks, at that time one of the biggest in Europe. In 1896 the family moved to Barking.

The early 1900s were times of extreme hardship. Ernest's two brothers had worked on farms at Rainham and Dagenham but they joined the army in 1903 and 1906 respectively. Father became unemployed, and the family relied on pence from the pawnbrokers, whitening doorsteps and so on. Ernest was a poorly child and was never able to play in the street with other children. He had several spells in hospital and lost time from school.

It was against this background that in 1905 the family moved to Ipswich where Ernest's sister was in service. They lived in Waveney Road off the Bramford Road. Charles Payne did not find work but from the age of thirteen Ernest had various jobs such as milk roundsman, bread roundsman and errand boy. He obtained work as an engine cleaner for the GER at Ipswich in May 1913, being eighteen years old. He became acting fireman when he was almost nineteen and was sent to work on the Mellis to Eye branch. Ernest remained there, working a fifty-four hour week, until May 1915.

The First World War was in progress and he volunteered for the army hoping to join the Royal Engineers and work on their railway operations, but the urgent need was for infantrymen due to the heavy casualty rate and so Ernest followed his two brothers into the Middlesex Regiment.

He was sent to France in March 1916 in time for the Battle of the Somme in which he took part from day one, surviving remarkably without injury. At the end of 1917 he was posted to Catterick for six months officer-training, to be commissioned into the Middlesex Regiment, transferring to a soldiers' training battalion. He was later persuaded to join the new Royal Air Force for flying training and actually underwent several weeks of preparation when the war ended. Ernest then returned to the railway at Ipswich as a fireman.

On August Bank Holiday 1920 Ernest married Muriel Raymer, a near neighbour in Waveney Road. In 1925 they moved to 72 Ranelagh Road, Ipswich, and in 1929 to "West View" along the Hadleigh Road in the

*Fireman Ernie Payne (right) on the footplate with Driver George Pinkney.* (Photo courtesy Richard Pinkney)

Parish of Sproughton, where Ernest lived for the rest of his life. They had three daughters and two sons.

In 1927 and 1928 he was a regular fireman on the *North Country Continental* described elsewhere, becoming a passed-fireman in the early thirties, and a regular driver early in the 1939-45 war.

Ernie, as he was better known, joined the Ipswich and District Railway Company of the Home Guard as Commanding Officer. He moved on through all the driving links and in 1956, as one of the senior drivers, trained on the new diesel multiple units which he drove for his remaining four years of service.

Ernie had held posts with the Ipswich ASLEF branch and served on the Local Departmental Committee. Apart from these and other activities he was a member of his local Parish Council for over twenty years and chairman for twelve.

He served as a magistrate for seventeen years. Ernie also had a good singing voice and one of his great interests was taking part in amateur light operatic society performances and acting.

Ernie Payne died aged ninety-two on September 9th 1987 after an incredibly active and fulfilling life, belying the unfortunate conditions of his early years, for which he was greatly respected.

*Above: Ernie Payne, at the head of the Ipswich & District Railway Company of the Home Guard, marching along Wherstead Road, Ipswich during the Second World War.* (Photo courtesy Mrs Witherley, neé Payne)

*Below: Ernie Payne having words with family pet Danny in the early 1950s.*

(Photo courtesy Mrs Witherley, neé Payne)

Two documents relating to Ernie Payne's army service. Left refers to his commission with the Middlesex Regiment in the 1914-18 War and on the right is a formal letter of thanks for Home Guard service in the Second World War.

(Courtsey Mrs Witherley, neé Payne)

## William and Gordon Barber
(Father and son)

WILLIAM Barber started as a greaser on the railway at Witham in 1913, aged eighteen. After service in the army during the First World War, he transferred to Ipswich where he became a fireman and later driver, retiring in 1960.

William's son Gordon joined the LNER in October 1941 as a cleaner. He had grown up in the Over Stoke area of Ipswich, and both he and his brother were choirboys at St Etheldreda's Church during the 1930s. The church building stood in front of the site which was later to be occupied by the new amenity block and signing-on point for Ipswich railwaymen at Wherstead Road. The church was demolished in the late 1960s.

Gordon Barber became an acting fireman in 1943, a fireman in 1946 and acting driver in 1955. In 1958 he moved to Parkeston and gained promotion to driver. Gordon drove the *Hook Continental* and the *Scandinavian* during the last days of steam and the changeover to diesel locomotives. He progressed through the diesel conversion courses and driving links until his retirement in 1987.

*Right: Gordon Barber, standing in front of the smokebox of engine No. 61570, with Ipswich Driver Frederick George Gibbs.* (Photo courtesy Gordon Barber)

*Gordon Barber standing on the platform at Yarmouth Southtown, c. 1952, with his regular driver at the time, Charlie Parr, who had started with the GER in 1914.* (Photo courtesy Gordon Barber)

## Alfred William Alderton

ALFRED Alderton, always referred to as "Onkie" for some obscure reason, was born 19th May, 1898. His parents had been married at St Mary-at-Stoke Church in 1897 by the Rev Canon Bulstrode and the family lived for a short time at 148 Wherstead Road, Ipswich, before moving further along the road to number 373, a terraced house situated between two public houses; the Live and Let Live and the Lifeboat. Mr Alderton, senior, was a seaman in his younger days, voyaging to Russia in sailing ships. He later spent forty-nine years working at Ransomes and Rapier's Waterside Works, retiring in his seventies.

"Onkie" Alderton began his railway career at Ipswich on November 2nd, 1914 and then worked on the Hadleigh Branch before moving to Stowmarket Station, cycling backwards and forwards to work from the village of Layham. Later he moved to Haughley to be nearer his workplace. He was one of two acting firemen at Stowmarket and he was involved in shunting in the busy yards and sidings there, a job which just prior to his joining the GER was achieved by using horses alone without the aid of steam.

During 1925-26 "Onkie" Alderton decided to transfer to Ipswich Loco Depot in order to gain faster promotion. While waiting for a house to become vacant, he and his family lodged for four months in premises in Commercial Road. This building was the former Ipswich office of the EUR. Here the Aldertons shared facilities with another railway family called Rogers who were also waiting for accommodation to become available. "Onkie" Alderton lived for some time in a house in Bostock Road, near Bourne Bridge, before moving to 30, The Strand, Wherstead.

He was made a driver in 1935, twenty-one years after starting his railway career at Stowmarket. He had the reputation of being a forceful character if provoked. The tale is told of the occasion when he was asked to explain his engine's late running whilst working one of the early morning up trains to London. The fault was with the poor quality coal heaped on the tender, and without more ado "Onkie" filled a bag with the coal dust, marched into the Shed Master's Office, and placing the evidence on the desk, angrily declared, "There's the reason!"

"Onkie" was a great wrestling fan, as was also his regular mate at the time, Frankie Gill. After "Onkie" had attended a wrestling match at the Baths Hall in Ipswich, the younger railwaymen would steer well clear of him the next day as he was wont to demonstrate the latest

*Alfred Alderton as a baby with his parents in the garden of their Wherstead Road home. His father was born at Holbrook in 1872 and his mother, Phoebe (nee Crisp) was born in 1876. The couple had eight children.*

(Photo courtesy Mr & Mrs D. Taylor, son-in-law and daughter of Alfred Alderton)

*Haughley Village where Alfred lived for a while in the house marked with a cross (extreme right).*
(Photo courtesy Mr & Mrs D. Taylor)

wrestling holds and techniques on any unsuspecting cleaner or acting fireman.

He was a very conscientious driver; when his engine No. 61564 went to the fitting shops in 1952 for an overhaul with over 80,000 miles to its credit, he received a letter from Shed Master Richard Hardy thanking him for the interest he had taken in the engine to enable it to go to the fitting shops in such excellent condition. Richard Hardy, who himself would often seize the opportunity to pick up a shovel and fire a steam locomotive, went on to say in his letter that from his own experience of the engine he would not be afraid to tackle any heavy job with it.

In 1956, at the age of fifty-eight, "Onkie" Alderton was trained and passed as a driver of diesel railcars (300 hp AEC type). He was presented with a long service award by British Railways at Norwich Thorpe Station in 1960 and retired in 1963 after forty-nine years with the railway, his career spanning service with the GER, LNER and British Railways.

*"Onkie", as he became known, standing between the wheel splashers (second from cab, hand on rail) of 1500 Class 4:6:0 engine No. 1504 during his early days at Ipswich Loco Depot.*

(Photo courtesy Mr & Mrs D. Taylor)

*"Onkie" firing for Driver "Sweater" English.*
(Photo courtesy Mr & Mrs D. Taylor)

*Alfred Alderton as a driver in later years.*
(Photo courtesy Mr & Mrs D. Taylor)

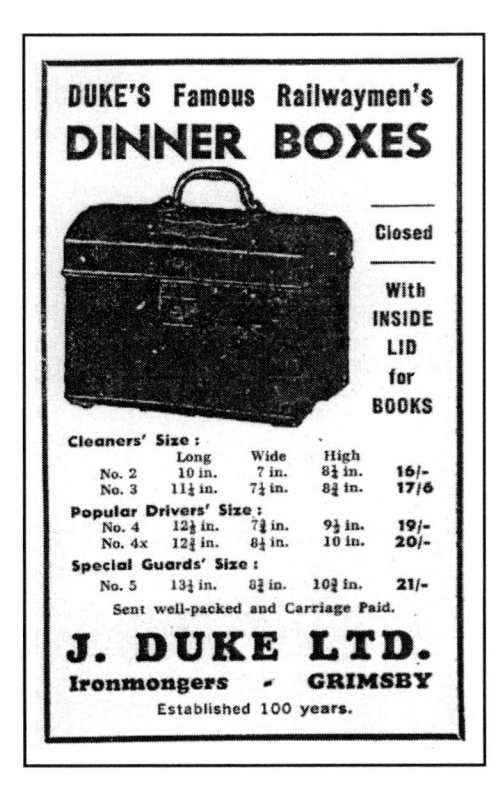

*Alfred Alderton's metal dinner box. The maker's name was G. Hildred, Ironmonger and Tinsmith, Hainton Square, Grimsby. Note the 1948 advertisement from the Locomotive Journal for similar boxes by J. Duke, also of Grimsby.* (Photo by Richard W. Smith)

*Alfred Alderton's GER Pension Supplemental Fund Certificate of Membership. The illustrations changed over the years reflecting more modern types of ships and rolling stock.* (Photo courtesy Mr & Mrs D. Taylor)

## George and Edward Deeks
by Edward Deeks

GEORGE Deeks was born in 1900, in Ipswich. He and his wife Thurza had a family of three girls and two boys and they lived in a small terraced house at 67 New Cardinal Street, off Commercial Road. George Deeks joined the railway on leaving school, starting as a tube cleaner at the Croft Street Depot.

In March 1919, George entered the footplate grade, later becoming a fireman and then an acting driver. His son Edward, as a young boy, remembers his father being knocked up for duty by the "call boys" who tapped on the bedroom window with a long pole. George was interested in sport and played football for the railway team.

The Deeks family were the only "railway" family living in New Cardinal Street and Edward recalls that they were able to go on holiday to places like Great Yarmouth, Clacton and Felixstowe because of his father's train passes.

Edward attended Smart Street School and on his way to or from school would sometimes see his father George at Stoke Bridge driving a tram engine, which reminded Edward of a guard's brake van. This, when under load, had a very distinctive exhaust noise, extremely loud and very harsh. If Edward was lucky and his father's engine was halted at Stoke Bridge, he would be hoisted on to the footplate and given a short ride. On this type of engine the fireman was at one end and the driver at the other. For this reason the fireman had to have a minimum number of firing turns before being allowed to fire the engine as he was working out of sight of the driver.

Edward was proud of his father's work with the railway and loved to hear stories about his jobs and his trips. His father told him about the different engines he fired; the 1500s, the "Clauds", The Suffolk Regiment No. 2845; also the goods engines including the Standards and W.D.s. He would often relate stories about his main line trips to Liverpool Street, Norwich, etc. and the fast freight journeys to Whitemoor.

When George was engaged on light shunting duties at Ipswich Station, his wife would often take Edward and her youngest daughter to Gippeswyk Park near to the main signal box from where they could see their father and wave to him when his engine stopped nearby. Sheffield Wednesday and Bradford City were the names of two of the engines which Edward can remember seeing.

Sadly during the Second World War, George Deeks was caught in the Blitz at Liverpool Street Station and his family remembers him coming home with his head bandaged and suffering badly from shock. He never worked on the main line again. Over a period of time his health deteriorated still further until he was forced to retire in 1948 after being unable to work for some time. The letter he received from the railway read:

> *"I regret to inform you that owing to your state of health it has been necessary to delete your name from the service. I attach Form F.C.4 for you to claim your pension money......It is hoped that you are now making a good recovery and I take this opportunity of thanking you on behalf of the management for your services. Wishing you long life and happiness....."*

George Deeks was forty-eight years of age and he died shortly afterwards.

Edward himself, when about sixteen years old, went to work with the railway as an apprentice fitter at the garage at the foot of Croft Street. From there he went to the Loco Depot, working in the Fitting Shop and then in the Boiler Shop. After a spell there, he became a cleaner in 1948, afterwards doing a few firing turns on goods engines. At the time, the cleaning foreman was known as Clem and in the office was Mr Burrows. Edward played football for the Nicholians' Youth Club in Stoke.

Edward Deeks was eventually called up for National Service and never returned to work on the railway.

*Ipswich Locomotive Depot c 1919. Top (left to right): Stan Chapman, Frank Dale, Ernie Skeels, Arthur English, Ernie Wells, Tom Farrow, Ted Whitehead, Harry Gallington, Bob Tyrrell, Percy Palfrey. Bottom: Len Rodwell, Stan Wells, Tim Ablett, Jack Turner, Albert Elliston, - Pudwell?, Alf Drake and tube cleaner George Deeks (extreme right).*

(Photo courtesy David Cobley)

*George Deeks, gazing from cab window of locomotive No. 2845* The Suffolk Regiment. *Centre is Driver George Baker, senior.*

(Photo courtesy Edward Deeks)

# Don Burton

ERNEST Richard Burton, better known to all his colleagues as Don, was born on 14th December 1905 in East London, the son of a Stratford driver. Don joined the LNER on July 7th 1923 and transferred to Ipswich in February 1926.

During the late 1930s he moved to Maldon for a spell as fireman on the Witham to Maldon branch returning to Ipswich in 1939 where he remained, being promoted to driver in the mid-1940s. He had been an active trade unionist for some thirty years in the Ipswich ASLEF Branch, serving variously as branch delegate to the Ipswich Trades Council and the Ipswich Labour Party.

He was member of the Branch Committee for several years and frequently acted as Vice-Chairman, as well as being a member of the Local Departmental Committee (LDC) which formed the direct link with depot staff and local management. Compulsory participation in Home Guard or Civil Defence units saw Don become a member of L Company, 9th Battalion Suffolk Home Guard, composed of LNER men from the Ipswich area.

As a young man he developed a very strong interest in sailing, becoming an accomplished yachtsman, and in the 1930s he bought a 26 ft barge yacht called *Derry* which had seen better days, having been built by W. H. Orvis of St Clements Shipyard of Ipswich, in 1912. He restored the boat and kept her for nearly 40 years, sailing the East Coast and Thames Estuary into the 1970s.

He originally kept the yacht at Maldon on the River Blackwater which was convenient when he was based at Maldon as a fireman but on his return to Ipswich in 1939 he obtained permission from the authorities to sail her home after the outbreak of war. Permission was given with the comment that his passage would be good practice for the look-outs on the coast. Fortunately no one was trigger-happy and Don brought the *Derry* back to Ostrich Creek and his mooring at the Orwell Yacht Club, where he held various offices within the Club, becoming Commodore in the 1970s.

Another of Don's interests was Modern Sequence Ballroom dancing and he enjoyed regular dances held at St. Bartholomew's Church Hall and the "Gay Nineties" at St Mary Stoke Church Hall, and later on attended the

*Don Burton, (nearest to camera) when firing on the Maldon to Witham Branch just before the 1939-45 war. The driver and guard remain unidentified. The train consists of former Great Eastern carriages converted to conductor-guard working. The engine was a Class F4 2-4-2 tank engine, built at Stratford Works in 1907, from where it worked for many years but is recorded as being allocated to Maldon in 1939.* (Photo courtesy Mrs D. Burton)

*Derry getting underway from Ostrich Creek, about to pass the new Ipswich Power Station and its coal jetty. She was a typical flat-bottomed barge-yacht, 26 ft. in length, but similar to a conventional Thames barge. They were popular with some owners on the East Coast in the early 1900s, though never built in any numbers.* (Photo courtesy Mrs D. Burton)

*Don and Doris Burton, Commodore and Secretary of the Orwell Yacht Club, at the Laying-Up Supper in November 1970 where they had presented the season's prizes. Doris was Secretary for thirteen years and the Commodore's term of Office was for three years.* (Photo courtesy Mrs D. Burton)

Manor Ballroom, all in Ipswich. During this time he met Doris, the lady who was to become his wife. They married on April 1st 1950 and lived just off the Norwich Road in the same house where Don had lodged for fourteen years, before moving to a house along the Wherstead Road within a stone's throw of the Orwell Yacht Club. Doris found herself in an entirely different way of life; knowing nothing about sailing she quickly learned and gained experience, participating in Yacht Club activities and becoming Club Secretary for some years.

Don Burton retired from the railway in 1969 a few months short of his sixty-fifth birthday and with exactly forty-six years service. He and Doris carried on sailing the *Derry* for another five years or so before selling her. Don died in 1986 aged 81.

*Aboard* Derry *in the late 1940s in Ostrich Creek. (Left to right): W. H. (Bill) Whistlecraft, Joe Skinner and Don Burton; all three were locomotive drivers at Ipswich and also members of the Orwell Yacht Club. Joe Skinner drove the last train on the Mid-Suffolk Light Railway on 26th June 1952.* (Photo courtesy Mrs D. Burton)

## Eric Pryke
### Father of co-editor Jill Freestone

ERIC Henry Pryke was born in 1905 at the village of Bramford, just outside Ipswich. His father, Arthur William Pryke, had married Florence Ellen Clover in 1897 at Bramford Church. Eric was one of nine children, two of whom died in early childhood.

His eldest brother Arthur was killed in action in France almost at the end of the First World War. A large framed photograph of the lost son hung on the wall of his parents' home and every Remembrance Day, a poppy would be placed in one corner of the frame, to remain there until the following year. Two of Eric's uncles were also killed in this "War to end all wars." Just two months before he died, Arthur had sent his younger brother a thirteenth birthday card from France which Eric always treasured. The verse read,

*"We all of us have wishes,*
*And pleasant daydreams too. ......."*

Eric followed in the footsteps of his older brothers, attending the village school, becoming a choir-boy at Bramford Church, and, together with his friends, swimming in the River Gipping near the bridge and the old mill. He must have witnessed the fire at Bramford Station in 1911, when a spark from a passing train destroyed the wooden booking office and a platform.

Eric often related in later life how, as a small boy, he had stood with crowds of people in the village street, in the summer of 1912, to gaze in awe at the military funeral of Captain Eustace Loraine, who had been killed in a flying accident over Salisbury Plain. A test pilot for the Royal Flying Corps, he was the elder son of Sir Lambton and Lady Loraine of Bramford Hall. The sight of the soldiers in their splendid uniforms, with tall, fur busbies on their heads, marching in slow-time to the parish church, had a profound effect on all who watched. Nothing like this had been seen in the village before; television was yet to come and the pomp and spectacle of the occasion left a lasting impression on everyone who was there that day.

On leaving school, Eric obtained a gardening job at a large house, "Riverhill" near Henderson's Hill, Bramford. In 1924 however, aged nineteen, Eric decided to become an engine cleaner at Ipswich Loco Depot. His uncle, Harry Clover, already worked on the railway, later becoming a driver on the Maldon Branch. Eric's older sister Florrie had married a platelayer and was employed by the railway company as a crossing keeper at Marlesford on the Framlingham Branch, living in the attached keeper's cottage there.

Eric married Freda Rowland, at St Peter's Church, Ipswich, in 1930. They had met when Freda visited her grandmother who lived at Walnut Tree Place, Bramford. (A young uncle of Freda's, Malcolm Rowland, later became an engine driver on the Braintree Branch.) They moved to Wherstead Road, Ipswich, to be close to Eric's railway work, and had one daughter, Jill, who was to marry fireman, later driver, Ken Freestone. When Ken took early retirement in 1993, the family railway tradition ended, as Jill and Ken's two daughters, Claire and Alison, perhaps not surprisingly, displayed no interest in becoming train drivers.

For many years Eric had an allotment at Maidenhall, close to Halifax Junction, where he grew his own vegetables, together with chrysanthemums and other flowers. He enjoyed reading and was keen on woodwork, making his daughter a wonderful doll's house during wartime from odds and ends; it even had electric lighting!

*Eric Pryke with his seven surviving brothers and sisters, c. 1916. Left to right: (back) Stanley, Eric, Denny, Florrie, Arthur; (front) Margaret (Maggie), baby Fred and Alec.*
(Photo from Pryke Family Collection)

*Arthur Pryke, Eric's father, seen here at the siding at Packard's Bramford factory where he worked for many years.* (Photo from Pryke Family Collection)

During his railway career Eric experienced one frightening incident when driving a train near Manningtree. The engine side rod came adrift, falling downwards and hitting the track before rearing up and piercing the cab floor. Fortunately, both he and his fireman escaped unhurt.

Eric, often referred to as "Prykie" by his friends and workmates, was always very clean and tidy in appearance and his fellow men could never understand how he could appear on a Monday in spotless overalls and shiny boots and manage to maintain this clean state for the rest of the week.

This was not because he was work shy; he had a reputation amongst his firemen as being a man who was always fair and performed his share of the work. He was a conscientious and meticulous driver; woe betide any running shed foreman who tried to get him to take an engine off the shed with a defect.

Like his fellow drivers and firemen, he made many journeys to London during the Second World War, often during bombing raids. These trips were referred to as going "Up Top" (the line to London was always the Up Road) and caused unease to the men's wives and families in Ipswich, especially if the men were late; it was not possible to explain any delay to those back at home as very few people had telephones then.

During Eric Pryke's time on the railway, he not only fired and drove steam engines but was also involved in the momentous changeover from steam to diesel locomotives which was so demanding of the men concerned, especially the older drivers.

Sadly Eric never reached retirement age: he died in 1962 aged fifty-six.

*Eric Pryke as a young engine cleaner, seen standing on the footplate (left) holding a spanner.*
(Photo from Pryke Family Collection)

*Left: Eric's sister Florrie, gatekeeper at Ford Level Crossing, Marlesford, standing beside the crossing gates with her husband Harry Taylor, a railway platelayer, and young daughter Joy, c. 1932.* (Photo courtesy Joy Clements, nee Taylor)

*Right: Eric's uncle, Harry Clover. Born in 1883, he started on the footplate at Ipswich before transferring to Maldon. He is wearing the distinctive GER cap, with a brass "dragon's wing" crest referred to by railwaymen as a "batswing". This cast-off badge from a GER police constable's uniform was in great demand by footplatemen. The emblem (right), initially appearing in a simpler form with fewer points, originated with the Eastern Counties Railway which used the City of London's crest, a dragon's wing, as their device. The GER perpetuated it, using it on wagon tarpaulins, company stationery and china etc.*
(Photo Pryke Family Collection. Crest and information from Ken Leighton & David Barton)

*Eric Pryke with his wife and daughter Jill on The Meare at Thorpeness during a week's holiday at Aldeburgh in 1952. The 'House in the Clouds' is just visible beyond the trees.* (Photo Pryke Family Collection)

## James W. Gilbert

JAMES Gilbert was born 1918 at Shirebrook in Derbyshire. After leaving school, he started work in a textile mill situated three miles from his home, walking there and back each day. Eventually in 1936 he obtained the job of an engine cleaner with the railway at Langwith Junction and after six months was passed for firing duties.

In 1938 Jim, as he was better known, was transferred to Kings Cross owing to a shortage of firemen in the London area. Here his duties were varied and included working on the Metropolitan System, firing on the main line with goods trains and taking empty coaching stock to Grantham.

While at Kings Cross, Jim saw Mr Chamberlain's aeroplane take off for Munich. Hopes of peace were short-lived however and soon he was engaged in blackout preparation at the loco depot, and collecting his gas mask from St Pancras Town Hall.

In July 1939, he received papers recalling him to his home depot at Langwith Junction where he was needed for working the extra coal trains to Sheffield and Immingham for Frodingham Steel Works during the armament build-up. The declaration of war meant the end of social life for the majority of people; long hours of work with only short rest breaks now formed the work pattern for the foreseeable future.

In 1940 Jim married Dorothy Saunders, whose home was at Harleston in Norfolk. They had met while both were on holiday at Great Yarmouth. At about this time, a vacancy was advertised for a fireman on the Aldeburgh and Saxmundham branch line. Jim successfully applied for this and he and his new wife moved to Suffolk. He was somewhat surprised at getting the job so easily but on arrival at Aldeburgh, a small seaside town, quickly realised that no one else had wanted the post owing to the remoteness of the branch line. Jim and his driver at that time coaled their own engines, packed the glands, fitted the wedges in the axle-boxes, and swept the engine-tubes.

He found that the people of Aldeburgh did not rely on a siren; the enemy aircraft were overhead before the siren sounded. Between Aldeburgh and Thorpeness there were guns one side of the railway line and sea the other, and frequent stops were made at Thorpeness for Jim and his driver to sweep glass out of the coaches after the firing of these guns. When the engine water-gauge lamp went out, it was an indication of the engine headlamps having been blown out by the guns' blast.

Jim Gilbert had just been made a driver (the previous

*Jim Gilbert (left) on the footplate at Aldeburgh.*
(Photo courtesy Gilbert Family Collection)

driver having left because of defective eyesight) when the engine shed at Aldeburgh closed in 1956. He transferred to Ipswich, living at 28 Philip Road, later moving across the road to number 29. For a time he was in the shunting link and first he had to learn the various routes, not having done this as a local fireman.

He spent ten years in the goods link, later moving on to the passenger link. For his last years with the railway he was in the rail-car gang. While in this link, he joked that he had every night in bed and dinners at home. Early morning jobs started at 05.00 hrs. and others did not finish until 23.00 hrs. Sometimes a turn involved going to Cambridge and back, then three trips to Felixstowe, with only half-an-hour break which he often had to forgo because of late running.

For several years Jim was an enthusiastic member of the St John Ambulance Movement, taking part in many local first aid competitions as a member of the Ipswich railway team. New regulations required entrants to the footplate grade to be trained in first aid and Jim was made an instructor for this purpose during his final years at Ipswich Loco Depot.

Jim and Dorothy had three children, Basil, David and Margaret. In 1982 the chance arose to take early retirement, or resettlement as it was often referred to, and this Jim did, aged sixty-four. He died in December 1995.

*Aldeburgh signal box, with engine shed in background. Photo shows line where engine was coaled and serviced.*

(Photo courtesy Gilbert Family Collection)

*Jim Gilbert on framing of 2-6-2 tank engine No. 41200 at Aldeburgh in May 1950. This locomotive worked on the Aldeburgh branch during 1949 and 1950. It was one of the last LMS light passenger engines designed by H. G. Ivatt, their Chief Mechanical Engineer. It appeared in 1946 and, together with some small 2-6-0 tender engines, plus a more powerful version of the latter, formed the basis of three of British Railways standard steam locomotives. When LMS No. 1200 first arrived on the branch it still bore the original LMS lettering on the tank sides but with the BR prefix of 40000, added to all ex-LMS engine numbers, it became No. 41200.*

(Photo by D. Pottle)

*J15 engine No. 65447 running round train at Aldeburgh Station.*

(Photo courtesy Gilbert Family Collection)

*Ipswich No. 1 Division Team of the Railway Ambulance Corps. in 1930. Back row (left to right): George Josselyn, Wilfrid Brown, Alf Burgess, Harry Rufford. Seated: Dr. M. McEwan (Hon. Surgeon), George Double, H. Robinson (Supt.). The trophies displayed are The Recreation Cup, The Hodgson Cup and The Individual Cup. Honorary Surgeons of the Ipswich Railway First Aid Class were Dr. G. Ellison (1881), Dr. S. O. Eades (1892 to 1927), and Dr. Malcolm McEwan, followed by Dr. Hugh McEwan, who took over in 1980 after the death of his father aged eighty-five. Percy Wilby, an electrician at the Ipswich Loco Depot and a great railway enthusiast, was secretary during the 1960s and 1970s and it was thanks to him that the Class records were saved from destruction. The documents are now safely stored at the Suffolk Record Office.* (Photo courtesy Wilf Brown.)

*Ipswich Ambulance Class team, Group 2 winners of the Norwich Divisional Competition, in 1973. Left to right: Jim Gilbert, Ken Freestone, Bob King and Betty Crookes.*

(Photo courtesy British Rail)

# Fred Howard

FRED was strictly speaking a Norfolk man, but his railway career was spent at Ipswich, where he became one of the last few Ipswich men to be passed for driving steam engines. His maternal grandfather, Reuben Fysh, was born at Swaffham in Norfolk and worked on the railways in that area until about 1929. Reuben, as a driver, was very much of the old school of GER men who demanded and received respect. Fred's other grandfather, Robert Howard, was a gas engineer at Swaffham and his son Walter (Fred's father) was born there in 1892.

Walter Howard was employed by the GER at Wells-next-the-Sea Station where he became foreman porter. He moved with his wife and family of one girl and four boys to Swaffham in 1929, and then to Framlingham in 1931 to become a guard on the branch, living in the Kettleburgh Road crossing gatehouse on the outskirts of the town.

The traffic on the branch at that time normally consisted of three passenger, and two mixed trains a day. On Saturdays there were regularly up to six additional trucks of pigs, destined for Ipswich bacon factory. In 1937, the family moved to 88A New Cut West, Ipswich. Here Walter continued working as a passenger guard, later becoming carriage cleaning supervisor at Ipswich until his retirement in 1957.

Fred Howard was born in 1923 at Wells and attended school in Wells, Swaffham and Framlingham, leaving school at fourteen to start work in the local Co-op butchery. When the family moved to Ipswich, Fred transferred to the Co-op branch on Foxhall Road. As soon as he was seventeen, in 1940, Fred obtained an engine cleaner's job at Croft Street

In 1941, during the Second World War, Fred volunteered for the services. Having been a sea cadet, he applied to the Navy but was enlisted into the Royal Marines. Following basic and gunnery training he was posted to HMS Roughs Fort (off Felixstowe) where he spent one month on duty and two weeks off, during 1941-42.

The build up to D-Day in 1943 saw Fred posted to Kings Lynn where he joined a crew commissioning a Landing Craft Flak (LCF), which was similar to a landing craft but fitted with several small Oerlikon and pom-pom guns, to work close inshore to help protect the actual landing craft as they made for the beaches. They trained at Invergordon on the Cromarty Firth before sailing south to the Beaulieu River, in February 1944, where much of the preparation for D-Day went on.

*Fred Howard at the controls of a Class 47 diesel locomotive.*
(Photo courtesy F. Howard)

Fred spent the first weeks after the invasion at Arromanches (Sword Beach). As the German Army retreated so the French ports were captured, having been destroyed by the retreating forces.

The Belgian port of Antwerp, however, was taken intact, although it proved to be of no use because 30,000 Germans were dug in on the heavily fortified Walcheren Island which controlled the West Schelde approaches to the port.

An assault by landing craft took place on November 1st, at 7.00 am, the Flak, Gun and Rocket craft escorts sailing in amongst the minefields, to draw the heavy German fire as the infantry and tanks were run ashore. The support craft, of which many had already been sunk, withdrew at 11.00 am after suffering very heavy casualties.

Fred Howard's elder brother Ernest, a pre-war RNVR man, was a lieutenant in command of a landing craft and was awarded the DSO for taking off the survivors of a LCR (Rocket) during the battle. After the landing it took a week to capture the island, and another three weeks to clear the approaches to Antwerp of mines. During the action, Fred was magazine corporal on LCF 36 which was hit below the waterline by an 88mm shell while taking off survivors from LCF 34 which had been hit previously. Several of the crew of LCF 36 were injured, but there were no fatalities and Fred Howard came through unscathed.

Fred came home on leave for Christmas 1944, after which he suffered stomach pains and was taken into hospital at Southampton where he was operated on for appendicitis. He was subsequently sent to holding barracks at Exmouth on light duties, prior to posting to HMS Quebec, a shore establishment near Inverary. It was there that he met Hilda, a Wren cook and they married in 1947 in Hilda's home town of Widnes.

The couple came back to Ipswich to live for a while with Fred's parents, who were then living in Cromwell Street, before moving to their own home in Ainslie Road, where in 1958 they had twins, a girl and a boy. They moved to a new house in Thanet Road in 1961.

Fred Howard had returned to Croft Street early in 1946 as a fireman, and ten years later he was promoted to Passed Fireman, (Acting Driver), and became Driver on 15th February 1960 just after Ipswich had become the first BR Eastern Region depot to convert completely to diesel motive power. Steam engines from March, Stratford and Norwich still required relief at Ipswich and Fred drove a variety of locomotives including Britannias and an ex-LMS Stanier "Black Five"

Always having been interested in union work, Fred held various offices within the ASLEF Ipswich branch from about 1950, becoming a widely respected Chairman of the LDC, and Branch Chairman during the late 1960s and '70s until he retired fifteen months before his sixty-fifth birthday in April 1987.

Since retiring, Fred has pursued his interests in gardening, walking and membership of Chantry Bowls Club. He is also a keen bird-watcher, being a member of the RSPB.

## Ivan Fletton - Apprentice Locomotive Fitter

IVAN Fletton obtained an apprenticeship at Ipswich Loco Depot as a locomotive fitter in 1946. He had been born at Parkeston, the son and grandson of railway employees there. He was discouraged from boilermaking as it was already recognised that there would be no future on the railways for steam engines.

The apprenticeship included general workshop practice, including lathe work, and spending time in the coppersmiths', Westinghouse and millwrights' shops. Apart from the usual fitting and running repairs on locomotives, the work encompassed maintenance of the equipment in the Wagon Shops, such as the vertical steam compressor and the horizontal steam engine which drove the line shaft, and all the machinery linked to that shaft. The wagon shops closed for two weeks holiday in August and the major overhauls were done during that time.

Ivan found that working with the millwright was varied and included steam compressors, loco turntables, and the water supply to, and maintenance of, the water columns at Ipswich station and the goods yard plus the water troughs at Halifax. These troughs filled very quickly after an engine had used its scoop, the amount being recorded by a meter, so it was known exactly how much water each engine had taken. All the water to the troughs and columns was drawn by pipeline from the water softener at Croft Street. The millwright was also responsible for the loco water-supply wells at Framlingham, Haughley, Laxfield and Felixstowe.

Another occasional duty for an apprentice was to meet the senior boiler inspector from Stratford Works off a train from London. The inspector would tell Ipswich the time of his arrival and he always travelled first class in the rear carriage. He was accordingly met, resplendent in a bowler hat, and escorted to the Felixstowe branch train.

Here Ivan recalls his discomfort at the thought of being found seated in a first class compartment with the great man, who never entered into any conversation but always brought a small gift in the shape of a six-inch rule, a pair of pliers, or something similar. The purpose of this particular excursion was to certify that the boilers at the prestige railway-owned Felix Hotel had passed the required hydraulic test.

At the end of Ivan's apprenticeship he decided to try the seagoing life as engineer on a steamship and although a job was available on BP tankers there was very little time off ashore for tanker crews, a fact which was not generally popular with young men. Accordingly he joined the British Railways fleet sailing to the Continent from Parkeston and Harwich. He served on the train ferries SS *Essex Ferry,* MV *Suffolk Ferry* and MV *Norfolk Ferry* and passenger ships SS *Duke of York*, SS *Arnhem* and SS *Amsterdam*.

Ivan spent eight years at sea before coming ashore to become a maintenance engineer at the Sproughton Sugar Beet Factory where he remained for thirty years until retirement. He has since concentrated his skills on building classic working model steam locomotives and steam boats.

*Apprentice fitters enjoying a game of cricket in their lunch break on the playing field of Luther Road Primary School (now Hillside School) adjacent to the Loco Depot, c. 1947. (Left) Ivan Fletton, (right) Albert Whelpton.* (Photo courtesy Ivan Fletton Collection)

# The Men Who Kept The Wheels Turning

*Class B1 engine No. 61059, prepared ready to take part in a publicity drive at Norwich in June 1951, seen here with Ipswich men, left to right: (top) Bill Dunnett, Walter Green, Frank Dowson, Bill Wade, Les Baggott, George Warren, Charlie Dack, John Wardley, Ivan Booth, George Everitt, Les Bloomfield, Ernie Simpson, Jack Clarke, (bottom) Claude Sansom, Cyril Rudland, Bob Elmy, George Mallett, Bill Lovett, Ron Clipstone, Herbert Goddard, Eric Birch, Geoff Weeden, Jack Percy (jun), Jim Boyle, Arthur Percy, Bill Morley, Fred Storey, Jack Cage, Jack Percy (sen).*

(Photo courtesy Ivan Fletton)

## Ipswich Running Shed staff in the days of steam, together with the names of some of those who held the posts.

Shed Master (R. Hardy, Hennessey)
Chief Clerk (Nightingale)
3 Office Staff (A. Cox, W. Cook, S. Bragg, T. Ladbrook, Dedman, Mabel Stapleton)
Telephone Attendant (R. Wright)
List Clerk (E. Rivers)
Time Keeper (Charlie Brunning)
3 Running Shed Foremen on three shifts (Goymer, A. Wilby, W. East, P. Coates, T. Ward, S. Gayfer)
3 Foremen Cleaners (E. Robinson, Smith, Southgate)
30 Engine Cleaners
12 Coalmen on three shifts
2 Ashmen on days (G. Broom)
2 Tube Cleaners (Hearsum, Dowsing)
4 Steam Raisers on three shifts (Aldous, Branch, Stockdale)
6 Boiler Washers on three shifts (Mead, Clayfield, Vincent)
3 Call Boys on three shifts (Brown)
Water Softener Attendant (W. Foulser, F. Foulger)
3 Tank House Men (Sergeant, Doe, Knights)
1 Toolman (C. Seager)
3 Boiler Makers (Winney, Hayward, Cook)
6 Tubers
1 Boiler Foreman (Llewelyn)
Approx. 30 Fitters on 3 shifts (R. Gooderham, S. Peachey, J. Percy)
Footplate Staff

The above information was kindly contributed by Bill Foulser who had various jobs at the Loco Depot during his forty-two years railway service, finishing as a foreman cleaner.

## Examples of job categories in the Carriage and Wagon Shop during the days of steam

Battery attendant
Body-maker & coach repairer
Bosh attendant
Brake fitter's assistant
Carpenter
Carriage serviceman
Chain examiner
Clerk
Coachmaker's assistant
Electrician
Examiner, carriage & wagon
Fitter, carriage & wagon
Foreman, carriage & wagons
Inspector, carriage & wagons
Labourer

Lifter carriage or wagon
Metal machinist
Oil gas filler
Oil gas maker
Oiler & greaser
Oxy-acetylene welder

Oxygen-acetylene welder & cutter
Painter
Painter & acetylene cutter
Plumber
Puncher & shearer
Shop officeman
Shunter & number taker
Smith
Smith's striker
Stationary engineman
Store's issuer
Storeman
Wagon builder & repairer
Wagon repairer
Wagon, horse-box builder & repairer
Wagon fitter
Wheel stamper
Wheel turner
Wheelwright
Wood machinist

## George Higgins
### by Kelvin Higgins (son)

READERS will already be aware that the Ipswich Loco Depot has been occupied by some real characters, famous for outstanding incidents that have entered the locomen's hall of fame. One well known character of the last forty years is a certain George Higgins, responsible for many a tale amongst not only local railmen but also nationally.

When compiling a history it is interesting to learn how people arrived at a given location in the first place. George Higgin's roots probably echo those of several others.

His father, Walter Henry Higgins, was a proud Welshman who made his way to London from the valleys in the early thirties. It was here that he met a genuine Ipswich girl, Ellen Rogers, who had entered service, or, as she liked to put it, became a posh people's maid. They were married, and their son George was born in Kensington on 5th June 1934.

Many years later, George required a passport for a Continental journey. He was informed that he needed his birth certificate, which of course he did not possess. The next step, he was told, was to obtain a copy from the registry office in the place where he was born. The fact that he was born in Kensington meant a visit to the Chelsea Registry Office, extremely famous at that time for the weddings of well known personalities. George therefore set off from Liverpool Street one day to obtain the desired certificate, accompanied by no fewer than twenty of his workmates; just to show him the way you understand. The reaction of the pin-striped staff of Chelsea Registry Office to the sight of twenty or so men, in full railway uniform, marching in and surrounding George at the main desk as he asked for his birth certificate, is best left to the reader's imagination. Those in his company that day included George "Ricky" Baker, Roy Mee, Alan Scarfe, Ray Pearce, Spike Reed and Charlie Hewlett.

Back to the early years, and with the onset of war, George and his parents received a present from Mr Hitler in a bombing raid, and so found themselves evacuated to Ipswich, his mother's hometown, where the family settled down.

George attended Tower Ramparts School. The teachers at that time included Mr Gosling and Mr Heath. George's first job on leaving school was as a counter assistant at the Home & Colonial Stores, but this was AFTER he had attended a successful interview at Marriotts, the builders. All was well as George was informed that he would serve an apprenticeship, THEN he was told this would involve attending night-school. The decision was made; George was not cut out to be a builder!

After a short spell at the Home & Colonial, George joined the railway. His old friend, "Boofer" Knights, had told him of some vacancies at the Loco, and so on 8th August 1950, George signed on as a cleaner for the first time, along with Tony Marsh and R. Duff. His starting wage was £2.5.6d. The foreman was "Ninety" Burrows, but more importantly, his depot master was none other than Richard Hardy. It was he who arranged for George to visit other depots around the country in his quest for engine numbers.

George's shifts in those days were two weeks of afternoons and one week of days. Under-eighteens were not allowed to work nights except on firing turns. George was still cleaning when in August 1952 he was called up for National Service. By this time he had married Kathy (nee Wyatt), and the couple were expecting their first child. George asked for, and expected, a home posting. Upon consideration of this request, and after basic training at Catterick Camp, George was sent to Hong Kong! His son, Kelvin, was born whilst George was en route to this far-flung destination.

George served his two years with the Royal Corps of Signals, and returned to the railway where his place had been kept for him. Under this arrangement, as has been mentioned elsewhere, George retained his original seniority date. He then began his railway career in earnest. His first "mate" on a firing turn was "Pussy" Catton. Other drivers he went with in the fifties were Bill Warnes, Fred Howard, Pat Blake, Edgar Button and Ernie Burroughes. He spent many lonely nights at Laxfield, Aldeburgh and Stowmarket, preparing engines for the morning shift. He regularly slept in the tank-house at Felixstowe Station.

His daughter, Sandra, was born in 1958. By this time George was firing in the Old Man's Gang. From here he progressed into the Goods Gang and then the Passenger Link, still a fireman (or secondman) of course. He was joined on the railway in 1971 by his son, not an unusual occurrence on the railway. A whole host of father/son combinations have worked, and still do, on the footplate. Names that spring to mind include: Bill & John Orris, Bob & Colin Brown, Porky & Matthew Bradbrook, Peter & Peter Parsey, Claude & Ron Holland, Ron Suckling & Alan Tricker and Sam & Steve Scarlett.

George remarried in 1972 to Hazel (nee Leeks). He

*Seen at Ipswich Station (left to right): Bob Brown (father), Colin Brown (son), Charlie Hewlett, Michael Hinton (carriage shunter), and George Higgins himself.*
(Photo courtesy Kelvin Higgins Collection)

was passed to drive in 1975, along with Jack Everson and Charlie Austin. Countless stories exist of George's exploits as a driver but perhaps the most famous is the railcar shunting episode, retold in mess rooms up and down the country.

Whilst semaphore signalling was still in existence at Ipswich, it was the custom to shunt all the early morning railcars in one go. Thus the Felixstowe, Cambridge and Lowestoft trains would all leave the sidings together, stop opposite Gippeswyk Park and then, after the signals were cleared, make their way back into the platform. This manoeuvre required of course three drivers. George, sitting in the mess room one morning, was asked if he could bring out the second of these trains.

"No problem," he said. "Is it ready?"

"Yes," came the reply.

So George jumped aboard and followed the first railcar out. He stopped behind the first unit, took his keys out, and walked through the railcar to the other end. He inserted his keys, and noticing that the unit following him had stopped, albeit quite close, he waited for the "off" ready to follow back into the platform. Five minutes passed; he put his feet up. Ten minutes; nothing happened. Fifteen, then twenty minutes passed. Suddenly George was alerted by a knock on the cab door. It was Driver Alan Scarfe who had taken the first rail car out.

"What's up, George," he asked.

"Nothing," he replied. "When the one in front gets going, I'll follow him."

"But George!" said Driver Scarfe in amazement, "you're a double unit this morning. The unit you're looking at is part of your train"

"Good grief!" said George. "I thought he'd stopped a bit close!"

Double unit it was, although he had not realised this when he took out the railcar. It did not take long for this particular episode to be related all over the Eastern Region. George's place in loco folklore was assured.

George retired in 1995, but he left behind him a legacy of countless stories which have elevated him to almost legendary status.

## Sally Read

ALMOST one hundred and forty years of male domination came to an end in August 1986 when Sally Read became Ipswich's first female locoman, or, to be politically correct, footplate person. After suffering the usual initial bantering, second-person Read settled down and eventually moved to become a driver at London Bridge Depot.

*History in the making. Second-person Sally Read pictured in the cab of a diesel locomotive with Driver Frankie Gill on a Yard pilot turn.* (Photo Kelvin Higgins Collection)

*Sally Read on duty with driver Tony Marsh.* (Photo Kelvin Higgins Collection)

## *Epilogue — The End of the Line and a New Beginning*

by Kelvin Higgins, Driver G. B. Railways (Anglia) at Ipswich

PRIVATISATION of the railways, which had been in State ownership since January 1st 1948, became a reality here in the mid 1990s. It was then that British Rail began dividing the whole system into operating units; not all at once, but gradually. I and my fellow drivers at Ipswich were given a stark choice - we could work either freight or passenger traffic. With a few exceptions, the senior drivers opted for passenger work, leaving the younger men in the freight sector. The long standing 'seniority' yardstick still ruled the day, remember, and thus most of the older men were already placed in the passenger link, making the decision to be taken easier than it would seem.

Now the unthinkable was about to happen; Ipswich depot was to be split into two completely separate sections, and the job preferences marked the start of this process. Shortly after these profound changes had taken place, the freight sector of British Rail was bought out and became known as Freightliner '95. The passenger business, trading as Anglia Railways, remained in the hands of British Rail until 1997 when the Anglia franchise was purchased by G. B. Railways. The important difference between the two companies is that Freightliner '95 is a completely separate private company but Anglia is a franchise which could revert to British Rail or be sold to another company in years to come.

During the past two years (1996-8) the freight drivers have experienced massive alterations to their work practices. Apart from the North Country Continental to Manchester in the 1930s, the majority of duties at Ipswich did not require the enginemen to go beyond the limits of the old Great Eastern Railway, roughly taking in the whole of East Anglia and bounded by Liverpool Street to the south and Cambridge and Peterborough to the west and north. Whereas I, in my younger days with a Freightliner, never ventured further than Stratford, East London, Freightliner drivers have now had to learn the road to Crewe via the old North London Line and on through Wembley, Northampton, Nuneaton and Rugby on the former LMS West Coast main line, and to York, Leeds and Middlesborough over the course of the earlier Great Northern and North Eastern Railways. This has involved resting away from home whilst learning and working over the actual routes, but staying in hotels with standards of comfort far removed from the railway hostels of Stratford and other primitive lodging places known to countless railwaymen of the past. March and Parkeston Quay depots are currently operated by the English, Welsh and Scottish Railway Company for freight working.

The Anglia drivers, myself included, have fared just the opposite. Our current routes go no further than Peterborough, Cambridge, Yarmouth via Norwich, Lowestoft, Felixstowe and Harwich. We drive diesel multiple unit 'Sprinter' type trains developed in the 1980s. A few Anglia men at Ipswich work Intercity trains into Liverpool Street but this is purely voluntary, the majority of senior men opting not to work the 100mph Class 86 electrics into London.

This then is the situation at present. The staff of both Companies, Freightliner '95 and Anglia, still share the same amenity block at Ipswich Station, we still talk to each other (well, most of us do) BUT we are two different depots. What the future holds for us we can only guess, but what is certain is that the past one hundred and fifty years have produced a legacy of the most colourful and individual characters one could ever wish to meet - the loyal and conscientious Ipswich Enginemen!

*Driver Kelvin Higgins leaving Trimley for Ipswich, having just picked up the tablet from the signalman. The temporary signal-box can be seen at left of photograph.* (Photo courtesy Kelvin Higgins)

# APPENDIX I

# *A rough guide to locomotive numbering*

*There is often confusion amongst laymen regarding engine numbers and sequences, more so with the passage of time. The following notes are an attempt to unravel the mysteries.*

The various classes of engine built by, or for, the Great Eastern Railway Company, or indeed any other company, were allocated a sequence, usually a three or four digit number, which had no direct technical bearing on the wheel arrangement or power of a particular type of locomotive, but would nevertheless be identified with a certain class.

The class of a Great Eastern engine was originally known by the works order no. of the first of that type. The small 2-4-0 "Intermediates" were classed T26 by the GER, T26 being the works order no. for the first of the one hundred engines to be built. They were subsequently classed E4 by the LNER. Similarly, the 4-6-0 express passenger engines were designated Class S69 by the GER, that being the order no. for the first one built at Stratford in 1911. They later received the LNER classification B12, and after rebuilding they became B12/3. To complicate matters further, they were generally referred to as "1500s" (fifteen-hundreds) which was the numerical sequence they were given from 1500 to 1580. The LNER then added 7,000 to all ex-GER locomotives. This was to differentiate between the same numbers to be found on engines belonging to other constituent companies, such as the Great Northern and Great Central, which had 3,000 and 5,000 respectively added to their numbers.

Thus the 1500 *et seq* engines became 8500 onwards, and the "Claud Hamilton" 4-4-0s, which commenced at number 1900 (the year they first appeared), changed to 8900. There was an added complication with this latter class as they were originally numbered backwards from 1900 to 1780, giving a total of 121 engines.

In 1946 the LNER instigated a company-wide renumbering scheme which brought together most of the pre-grouping locomotive classes into a specific numerical classification based on wheel arrangements. For example, all pre-grouping 4-6-0s would be numbered between 1000 and 1999. This meant that by happy chance, the ex-GER "1500s" reverted to their old 1500 sequence. The later LNER B17 4-6-0 "Sandringhams" and "Footballers", widely used in East Anglia, were changed from 2800s to 1600s. Thus engine No 2847 *Helmingham Hall* became No 1647.

Nationalisation brought with it the final amalgamation and ex-LNER engines had 60,000 added to them in 1948. Ex-GER engine No. 1500 thus changed to 8500 in 1923/4, went back to No. 1500 in 1946 and in 1948 appeared as 61500. Likewise No. 2847 became 1647 in 1946 and in 1948, with 60,000 added, became No. 61647.

The purpose of setting out these examples of renumbering is to try to explain the complications that can arise after so many years. The same engine can appear in photographs, taken at various times, with three different numbers. Descendants of locomen, finding pictures of great-grandad's engine sporting differing numbers, may well be justifiably confused!

# APPENDIX II

## *Wheel notation*

Wheel arrangements of steam locomotives mentioned in the text, using notation invented by F. M. Whyte (1865-1941) The notation gives from left to right the total number of wheels. (Continental notation cites the number of axles). The leading end of the locomotive is at the left. The central number refers to the coupled driving wheels and the first and last numbers to the leading and trailing uncoupled wheels. The suffix T, e.g. 2-4-2T indicates a tank engine (no tender).

| | |
|---|---|
| 0-4-0 | 2-4-0 |
| 2-2-2 | 4-2-2 |
| 4-4-0 | 0-6-0 |
| 2-4-2 | 0-6-2 |
| 2-6-0 (Mogul) | 4-6-0 |
| 2-8-0 | 4-6-2 (Pacific) |

Electric and diesel locomotive wheel arrangements are expressed by the Continental system which counts the number of axles; the Whyte notation for steam engines cannot be used since it does not distinguish clearly between driving wheels and non-driving wheels.

Driving axles are shown by a letter (A=1 motored axle, B=2 coupled motored axles, C=3 and so on). Carrying wheels are shown by a figure denoting the number of axles. Each bogie or group of wheels is separated from the next by a hyphen. If in a group of driving axles each has its own driving motor, a small suffix "o" is added. When several driving axles are driven from one source, no suffix is used.

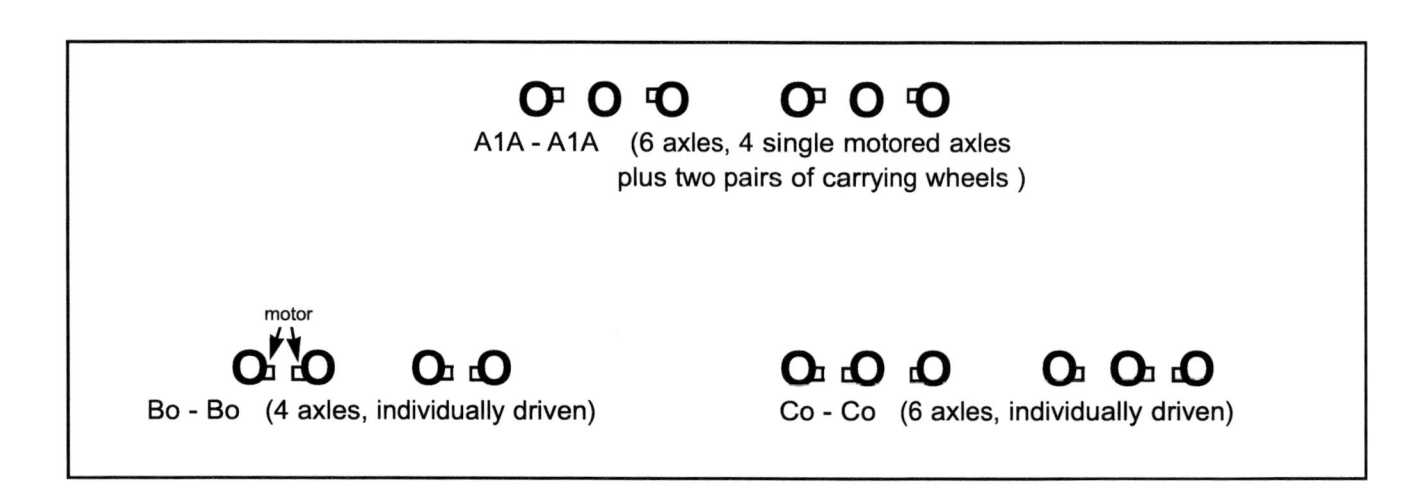

A1A - A1A   (6 axles, 4 single motored axles plus two pairs of carrying wheels )

Bo - Bo   (4 axles, individually driven)

Co - Co   (6 axles, individually driven)

# APPENDIX III

## *Seniority List*

Compiled by Kelvin Higgins

Names of locomen who were at Ipswich Loco Depot for any length of time, together with the date on which they started work in the footplate grade, not necessarily at Ipswich. Promotion was based strictly on this date, referred to as a locoman's "seniority date".

An asterisk (*) indicates that the seniority date of the man is not known but that he was at the Depot during or since that particular time. The list has been compiled from various sources. There may therefore be some discrepancies in the dates and in the spelling for surnames. Some names may be missing owing to the lack of information. Nevertheless, the list contains the names of more than eleven hundred men

| Name | Date | Name | Date | Name | Date | Name | Date |
|---|---|---|---|---|---|---|---|
| Abbott G | 22.03.1948 | Beach D | 30.08.1976 | Brown C | 17.11.1947 | Cherry D | 1949 |
| Ablitt J | 10.02.1919 | Bearcroft K | 1952 | Brown C | 15.01.1962 | Chisnell L | 18.08.1924 |
| Adams D | 14.02.1944 | Beauclerk R | 15.08.1977 | Brown E.N | 06.04.1906 | Chittock A | 08.09.1947 |
| Adams E | 28.02.1944 | Beaumont C | 13.11.1944 | Brown K | 1971* | Chittock K | 24.03.1947 |
| Airey G | 1906* | Beckett C | 07.10.1940 | Brown M.R | 30.12.1893 | Church H | 02.07.1887 |
| Alderton A | 10.04.1920 | Beecroft I | 28.11.1983 | Brown R | 18.05.1936 | Church H | 19.07.1913 |
| Alderton A.W | 02.11.1914 | Beeston R J | 25.06.1917 | Brown R | 14.06.1937 | Churchyard F | 30.05.1891 |
| Alderton F | 19.05.1919 | Beet A | 14.07.1924 | Brown W | 28.01.1899 | Clampen E | 11.09.1920 |
| Aldous R | 1952 | Bell H | 14.04.1941 | Brown W.J | 07.09.1882 | Clark E | 22.08.1949 |
| Aldred G | 28.01.1973 | Bell J | 18.04.1938 | Browning H | 21.05.1917 | Clarke A | 10.08.1901 |
| Allatson R | 1952 | Benham V | 26.01.1925 | Browse E | 03.06.1946 | Clarke A | 1951 |
| Allen A.H | 13.07.1889 | Bennett W. | 05.05.1900 | Brunning C | 24.04.1911 | Clarke D | 23.07.1984 |
| Allington J | 1951 | Benneworth R | 10.08.1942 | Brunning C | 18.05.1936 | Clarke E | 29.03.1926 |
| Allison K | 21.04.1941 | Bennyworth P | 26.01.1948 | Bryan T | 12.02.1945 | Clarke J | 17.07.1939 |
| Allum C | 04.10.1948 | Bensley H | 13.07.1903 | Buckledee W.A | 14.02.1927 | Clarke J | 27.09.1943 |
| Anderson J | 1953 | Betts J.F | 02.06.1917 | Buckles D | 06.04.1942 | Claydon A | 13.03.1944 |
| Andrews G | 12.12.1949 | Biggins J | 18.08.1947 | Bugg P | 29.07.1973 | Clements J | 22.02.1943 |
| Andrews T | 12.08.1974 | Billingham W | 22.09.1947 | Bultitude E | 20.06.1940 | Clements L | 24.07.1939 |
| Annison G | 15.09.1941 | Bilner D | 12.07.1948 | Bunker T | 27.05.1947 | Clements R.A | 06.02.1888 |
| Armes B | 28.06.1948 | Birch L | 17.08.1912 | Burgess R | 07.06.1948 | Closs F | 01.12.1947 |
| Athroll R | 10.07.1944 | Bird E | 1952 | Burman R | 18.02.1985 | Clouting A | 28.11.1983 |
| Atkins | 1949 | Bird W | 18.03.1940 | Burnette W | 01.03.1948 | Clover C | 07.03.1927 |
| Auld R | 20.10.1947 | Bishop E T | 07.12.1914 | Burns R | 16.10.1978 | Clover H | 1913* |
| Austin C | 1950 | Bishop F R | 29.05.1911 | Burroughs E | 28.02.1927 | Clover T | 13.11.1944 |
| Ayden J | 15.07.1907 | Blake H | 04.12.1920 | Burrows F | 09.07.1910 | Coates P.E | 28.04.1924 |
| Aydin D | 29.07.1946 | Blake M | 26.05.1924 | Burrows L | 1960's * | Cobbin C | 28.06.1948 |
| Baker A | 21.02.1944 | Bloom A | 05.01.1920 | Burrows P | 15.09.1947 | Cocksedge F | 28.09.1914 |
| Baker E.G | 06.08.1923 | Bloom R | 27.05.1940 | Burrows P.W | 23.11.1914 | Coe B | 10.05.1909 |
| Baker G | 19.05.1906 | Bloom R | 06.10.1947 | Burton D | 1949 | Cole A | 06.08.1900 |
| Baker G | 08.06.1936 | Bloomfield C | 1949 | Burton E | 07.07.1923 | Cole P | 22.02.1937 |
| Baker G.J | 27.06.1891 | Bloomfield D.W | 26.11.1913 | Butler S.A | 21.02.1927 | Coleman J | 02.11.1914 |
| Baker G.W | 29.01.1917 | Bloomfield H | 13.06.1891 | Button E | 14.11.1891 | Coleman R | 15.05.1916 |
| Baker J | 10.11.1941 | Bloomfield J | 27.06.1977 | Button E.E | 18.08.1924 | Coles W | 20.12.1909 |
| Baker R | 1950 | Bloomfield S | 04.02.1919 | Button F | 09.07.1892 | Colls M | 12.01.1948 |
| Baldry S | 19.01.1948 | Blyth J | 07.01.1946 | Button I | 28.02.1944 | Collyer M | 06.08.1946 |
| Baldwin J | 17.02.1926 | Blythe A.E | 01.02.1915 | Buxton P | 20.05.1940 | Columbus P | 13.10.1947 |
| Ball D | 1952 | Bond M | 28.11.1983 | Calver J | 16.06.1914 | Condur C | 02.05.1979 |
| Balls D | 1960's * | Bond P | 09.04.1974 | Calver W | 26.04.1948 | Cook K | 25.02.1974 |
| Banham W | 08.03.1948 | Boreham A | 1913* | Canham A | 03.11.1947 | Cook K | 1971* |
| Bannock R | 07.04.1900 | Bottomley R | 21.06.1937 | Canham T | 1949 | Cook P | 20.09.1978 |
| Barber C | 22.03.1948 | Boulton G | 27.07.1878 | Card D | 24.09.1974 | Cook S | 16.06.1980 |
| Barber E.A | 13.08.1923 | Boulton G | 30.05.1979 | Carden W | 09.02.1948 | Cook T | 1906* |
| Barber G | 27.10.1941 | Bowden C | 09.02.1948 | Cardwell G | 1951 | Coomber D | 08.08.1949 |
| Barber K | 1971* | Bowman J | 04.12.1924 | Careswell A | 10.08.1942 | Coombes K | 06.06.1983 |
| Barber L | 14.08.1986 | Bradbrook B | 30.10.1950 | Carr A | 08.06.1979 | Cooper A | 27.06.1977 |
| Barber R | 1950 | Bradbrook M | 06.06.1983 | Carr K | 15.07.1946 | Cooper B | 1951 |
| Barber W | 28.07.1913 | Bradbrooke E | 1907* | Carr R | 08.10.1945 | Corston E.A | 07.01.1888 |
| Barker H | 04.02.1919 | Bradbrooke F | 1907* | Carraccio N | 1949 | Cotterell T | 29.07.1973 |
| Barlow N | 1971* | Bradley M | 1971* | Carter B | 29.12.1900 | Cotton W | 07.10.1940 |
| Barnard G | 07.07.1896 | Bradley R | 28.06.1948 | Carter E.V | 25.08.1923 | Cousins D | 20.05.1974 |
| Barnard J | 1846 | Bragg A | 12.02.1946 | Carter H | 14.08.1911 | Cox G | 07.04.1986 |
| Barnby J | 23.10.1944 | Braithwaite D | 09.10.1982 | Carter H | 06.07.1936 | Cox M | 1960's * |
| Barnes C.E | 31.01.1900 | Brame S | 12.02.1946 | Carter H | 07.08.1939 | Crabbe K | 1950 |
| Barnes H | 22.03.1926 | Brett A.W | 12.07.1937 | Cassin W | 08.08.1949 | Crabtree A | 24.01.1938 |
| Barnes S | 28.07.1924 | Brill C | 22.04.1946 | Catchpole A | 20.10.1947 | Cracknell A | 29.01.1940 |
| Barnett G.E | 01.03.1915 | Brittall M | 1949 | Catchpole J | 23.08.1937 | Cracknell D | 23.02.1948 |
| Barrell E | 08.12.1914 | Broad C | 21.06.1937 | Catling B | 26.04.1948 | Cracknell R | 13.06.1887 |
| Barrell E | 23.06.1921 | Broad D | 14.10.1940 | Catling R | 19.09.1944 | Crane R | 1912* |
| Barringham A.J | 27.02.1972 | Broad H | 21.09.1912 | Cattermole C | 13.04.1942 | Crapnell D | 29.07.1946 |
| Barton R | 14.08.1909 | Brooks A | 16.07.1917 | Catton W | 29.07.1929 | Creasey F.C | 21.10.1912 |
| Bass G A | 28.03.1927 | Brooks D | 1952 | Chambers L | 1951 | Creasey R | 26.01.1942 |
| Bates F | 14.10.1945 | Brooks R | 1949 | Chaplin R | 28.06.1919 | Crisp R.A | 16.08.1920 |
| Battle F | 02.02.1948 | Broom B | 03.05.1948 | Chapman S | 11.03.1940 | Crisp.D | 01.04.1946 |
| Baybutt H | 16.06.1913 | Brown A | 18.02.1985 | Chenery R | 1950 | Cross C.W | 07.08.1897 |

# IPSWICH SENIORITY LIST

| Name | Date | Name | Date | Name | Date | Name | Date |
|---|---|---|---|---|---|---|---|
| Cuckow T | 26.01.1948 | Edgar D | 26.06.1979 | Garrard A.W | 08.10.1887 | Hammond G | 01.07.1974 |
| Cullum B | 1953 | Edwards A | 15.01.1979 | Garrard C | 01.02.1943 | Hammond G.W | 11.07.1903 |
| Curtis F | 04.03.1919 | Edwards C | 1971* | Garrard L | 11.10.1937 | Hammond J | 06.07.1942 |
| Curtis H | 21.08.1909 | Edwards G | 14.07.1986 | Garrett W | 15.03.1879 | Hammond M | 16.10.1944 |
| Curtis K | 31.07.1945 | Edwards J | 15.03.1971 | Garwood J | 1952 | Hancock N | 29.09.1947 |
| Curtis W F | 01.10.1904 | Edwards J | 23.01.1978 | Gates A | 21.06.1943 | Hansen R | 03.08.1943 |
| Cutting G | 13.08.1984 | Eley F | 06.03.1944 | Gayfer C | 11.02.1888 | Harding F | 1906* |
| Dakin F.W | 16.08.1887 | Eley L | 16.06.1924 | Gayfer H | 23.03.1926 | Harkins C | 14.02.1977 |
| Dakin T | 06.09.1915 | Eley R | 14.10.1946 | Gayfer S | 10.06.1912 | Harlott A | 30.04.1984 |
| Dakin T | 25.08.1923 | Elmer J.R | 05.02.1917 | Gee D | 12.06.1944 | Harlott D | 12.08.1974 |
| Dakin W.B | 07.02.1927 | Elvin R | 19.04.1948 | Gee M R | 02.09.1946 | Harman J | 1950's * |
| Dalby R | 02.03.1884 | Emmerson P | 12.04.1943 | Gibbs A | 16.06.1980 | Harris A | 26.01.1984 |
| Dalby R | 1906* | Emmett G | 09.04.1979 | Gibbs D | 05.10.1942 | Harris J | 04.04.1977 |
| Dale F.H | 24.09.1919 | Emmett R | 09.02.1953 | Gibbs F.G | 16.11.1914 | Harsum L | 17.03.1941 |
| Dale J | 09.08.1937 | Enfield A | 10.02.1919 | Gibson A | 06.10.1947 | Hart J | 12.06.1945 |
| Dale W | 03.11.1924 | English A | 13.01.1920 | Gibson G | 06.07.1936 | Harvey R | 14.02.1950 |
| Dalton A | 1912* | English C.W | 04.07.1896 | Giddings G | 19.11.1919 | Haste F.W.H | 24.06.1905 |
| Darby A | 18.05.1944 | English E | 14.03.1927 | Gilbert J | 30.03.1936 | Hatch A.J | 17.09.1904 |
| Darton F | 09.11.1942 | Essex R | 26.04.1984 | Gill F | 03.03.1941 | Hawes G | 18.07.1910 |
| Davey R | 1960's * | Everett C | 18.05.1936 | Girling B | 1952 | Hawes L | 31.01.1944 |
| Davies M | 11.06.1979 | Everett F | 20.03.1893 | Girling G | 24.04.1944 | Hawthorn J | 22.03.1926 |
| Davis E | 23.06.1919 | Eversfield F | 18.09.1920 | Girling G | 01.12.1947 | Haylock F | 06.07.1936 |
| Davis R | 1947 | Everson J | 11.04.1950 | Girling S | 28.04.1941 | Hayward C | 06.02.1915 |
| Dawson A | 1917* | Eves F | 05.07.1890 | Gladding S | 1951 | Hayward R | 16.06.1980 |
| Daynes H | 14.09.1939 | Faiers K | 26.01.1984 | Gladwell H | 31.01.1944 | Hazell E | 05.08.1929 |
| Death J | 23.10.1944 | Fair A | 15.06.1943 | Glover | 17.02.1947 | Hazlehurst G | 19.03.1981 |
| Death S | 26.07.1948 | Fair E | 26.01.1948 | Goddard W | 08.05.1897 | Head F | 13.08.1892 |
| Deeks G | 10.03.1919 | Farrow G.E | 31.03.1919 | Godfrey H | 29.02.1904 | Hearsum A | 06.06.1881 |
| Deeks E | 26.01.1948 | Farrow R | 07.02.1944 | Godfrey T | 1947 | Heffer E | 17.07.1916 |
| Dell A | 15.07.1985 | Farrow S | 25.08.1947 | Goldspink E | 22.05.1944 | Heffer W | 04.04.1891 |
| Dennant A | 17.05.1920 | Farrow T | 19.02.1919 | Gooch C.J | 23.06.1919 | Herod A | 07.09.1942 |
| Dennant A.J | 24.06.1893 | Fearn B | 1951 | Good F | 15.12.1941 | Hewlett C | 20.09.1943 |
| Dennant B | 1913* | Fenn S | 12.02.1945 | Goodchild E | 12.01.1918 | Hibbert P | 14.07.1924 |
| Dennant G | 09.05.1914 | Fenning E.G | 11.08.1923 | Goodchild R | 05.06.1911 | Hicks W | 14.01.1946 |
| Dennant H.G | 06.03.1897 | Fenning R | 1906* | Goodchild R | 05.02.1945 | Higgins G | 08.08.1950 |
| Dennington P | 06.03.1944 | Fiddiman W | 12.07.1915 | Goodchild S | 04.12.1944 | Higgins K | 15.03.1971 |
| Denny R | 1950 | Fieldsend G | 27.11.1922 | Gooderham D | 1952 | Hines F.G | 05.05.1924 |
| Derrett A | 18.02.1985 | Fillis E | 1950 | Gooding C | 02.12.1911 | Hines R | 08.05.1944 |
| Deverson A | 01.07.1946 | Finbow E | 03.02.1941 | Gooding T | 14.06.1937 | Hitter E | 20.03.1944 |
| Dewhurst A | 30.04.1984 | Finch F | 18.02.1918 | Gooding W | 1949 | Hobbs-Hurrell J | 1952 |
| Dewing G | 07.06.1948 | Finch R | 29.03.1943 | Goodings N | 24.10.1945 | Hogger R.W | 17.10.1896 |
| Dickerson N | 28.07.1902 | Finch R | 03.11.1947 | Goodwin J | 16.09.1891 | Holland A | 1971* |
| Doling D | 29.07.1946 | Finch W.E | 27.07.1895 | Goole A | 1907* | Holland C | 09.07.1945 |
| Doling W | 02.09.1946 | Fisher A | 02.06.1913 | Gosling C.T | 30.01.1909 | Holland F | 28.09.1942 |
| Donovan D | 1966 | Fisher C | 04.09.1978 | Gostling F | 12.07.1910 | Holland R | 23.06.1978 |
| Dorwood N | 14.02.1972 | Fisher D | 13.09.1954 | Gotts P | 14.07.1947 | Holliday H | 29.03.1920 |
| Double B | 16.07.1923 | Fisher K | 30.04.1979 | Gould E | 22.06.1903 | Hollier W.J | 11.04.1927 |
| Double H | 28.08.1920 | Fisher N | 15.07.1985 | Goward N | 16.06.1980 | Hollingsworth L | 17.10.1910 |
| Downing C | 1906* | Fisk A | 15.07.1985 | Graham C | 23.07.1984 | Hollingsworth W | 01.09.1924 |
| Dowson G | 01.11.1943 | Flack I | 29.12.1947 | Gray C | 25.01.1926 | Holman | 10.02.1941 |
| Drake A | 18.03.1919 | Flanlan D | 05.04.1948 | Graystone F | 13.10.1924 | Holmes M | 01.04.1985 |
| Drake A | 17.06.1940 | Fletcher P | 20.09.1943 | Greaves R | 25.11.1924 | Holton R | 22.09.1947 |
| Drake J | 10.07.1939 | Fletcher R.A | 28.02.1944 | Green A | 14.04.1947 | Hood.R | 09.11.1914 |
| Drane A.W | 26.05.1919 | Flowers R | 23.02.1948 | Green B | 1960's * | Hook M | 10.05.1948 |
| Drane G | 12.11.1891 | Folkard W.G | 24.06.1893 | Green D | 1971* | Hooks C | 25.04.1978 |
| Drayton V | 1918* | Ford E | 28.02.1927 | Green E | 01.03.1948 | Hovells H | 26.02.1941 |
| Drew L | 23.08.1937 | Foreman A | 09.06.1883 | Green G | 02.04.1974 | Howard A.J | 20.07.1895 |
| Driver H | 23.09.1940 | Foreman R | 1949 | Green W | 20.03.1944 | Howard F | 22.08.1940 |
| Driver L | 21.02.1944 | Foster J.S | 11.03.1911 | Greenacre P | 17.08.1942 | Howard F.P | 06.01.1912 |
| Driver N | 11.06.1979 | Fowkes A | 05.11.1979 | Greer W | 10.07.1920 | Howard K | 13.03.1944 |
| Driver R | 14.06.1948 | Fox W | 13.12.1937 | Griffiths D | 07.01.1946 | Howe E | 27.01.1912 |
| Duff R | 1950 | Fox.W | 04.06.1892 | Grimsey A | 08.02.1915 | Howell R | 05.04.1926 |
| Dunlop T | 01.03.1948 | Francis V.R | 02.04.1917 | Grimwood H | 1949 | Howes W.W | 30.06.1924 |
| Dunnett E | 14.12.1914 | Freestone K | 13.10.1947 | Gummerson E.G | 30.09.1924 | Hubbard C | 01.05.1920 |
| Dunnett R | 19.04.1926 | French E | 1950 | Gunther F | 19.10.1920 | Hubbard S | 06.01.1919 |
| Dunnett W | 28.11.1896 | Frost A | 14.02.1927 | Gurney N | 13.05.1940 | Hudson R | 31.03.1941 |
| Dunstan R | 1976 | Frost G | 02.06.1900 | Gurr O | 1950 | Hudson R | 31.03.1947 |
| Dunster L | 15.12.1947 | Galligton H | 10.11.1919 | Haggar E.W | 21.09.1903 | Huggett H | 27.06.1977 |
| Dunston R.J | 20.10.1920 | Game D | 01.04.1985 | Haggar H | 13.04.1889 | Hughes A | 28.11.1983 |
| Durrant S | 25.08.1923 | Gant R | 1966 | Haggar S | 1906* | Hullis A | 20.09.1943 |
| Dutton F | 05.05.1924 | Gardiner P | 1977 | Haggar W | 22.01.1940 | Hullis C | 17.11.1947 |
| Eastbury R | 01.03.1948 | Gardiner W | 17.07.1939 | Hales P | 1907* | Humphrey G | 05.02.1946 |
| Easter A.G | 15.09.1924 | Garnham H | 01.12.1919 | Hall S | 20.03.1911 | Humphreys D | 1889 |
| Eaton P | 1960's * | Garnham W.A | 27.07.1914 | Hall W | 05.11.1945 | Hunnibell A | 1912* |
| Eaton R | 26.01.1948 | GarnhamJ | 17.04.1944 | Hames W | 12.07.1943 | Hunt L | 16.10.1944 |
| Eaton T | 1960's * | Garrard A | 1971* | Hammond D | 31.03.1941 | Hunt S | 18.08.1924 |

# IPSWICH SENIORITY LIST

| Name | Date | Name | Date | Name | Date | Name | Date |
|------|------|------|------|------|------|------|------|
| Hurn P | 09.04.1974 | Law J | 20.11.1944 | Merchant S | 1867 | Overett C | 18.02.1985 |
| Hurst W | 24.03.1919 | Laws D | 1951 | Messenger J | 01.04.1985 | Owen W | 27.03.1944 |
| Hutchinson C.H | 17.01.1914 | Leah E.W | 14.02.1927 | Miller D | 04.09.1939 | Pack A | 08.11.1891 |
| Hutchinson S | 17.09.1986 | Leah W.H | 09.05.1892 | Miller I | 29.10.1945 | Page J | 10.11.1941 |
| Iddon T | 29.12.1947 | Leaning J.F | 23.09.1912 | Miller J | 14.07.1947 | Page R | 1949 |
| Iris R | 03.07.1922 | Leeds G | 08.04.1940 | Millett R | 1952 | Page T. | 17.04.1909 |
| Isom G | 1966 | Leeks E | 08.09.1947 | Milliard M | 1965 | Palfreyman B | 1952 |
| Jackaman W | 20.06.1910 | Leeks F | 21.09.1943 | Milligan O | 17.06.1940 | Palgrave W | 18.10.1948 |
| Jacobs J | 08.07.1946 | Leeks H | 19.02.1940 | Mills F | 18.04.1938 | Pallant E | 24.01.1926 |
| Jacobs T.C | 09.06.1919 | Leggett C.W | 26.08.1915 | Mills S | 11.08.1903 | Palmer D | 14.06.1948 |
| James A | 09.09.1946 | Leggett E | 15.02.1943 | Mills W | 31.05.1948 | Palmer D | 1953 |
| James P | 28.11.1983 | Leggett L | 1909* | Minns G | 1950 | Parker C | 16.11.1914 |
| James R | 12.01.1925 | Leggett R | 30.04.1945 | Minns R | 10.05.1948 | Parker S | 06.08.1923 |
| James W | 10.07.1939 | Leighton B | 12.12.1949 | Moggs F | 1910* | Parmenter B | 1960's * |
| Jarrold L.C.A | 02.11.1914 | Lemon P | 1971* | Mole T | 18.05.1936 | Parr C | 09.11.1914 |
| Jay P | 09.08.1920 | Lenney F | 12.06.1899 | Moore G | 03.11.1947 | Parrish R | 26.02.1940 |
| Jaye F | 21.02.1944 | Leonard W | 01.03.1926 | Moore P | 14.08.1986 | Parsey P | 17.01.1944 |
| Jaye L | 31.03.1947 | Lette S | 1984 | Moore R | 29.01.1940 | Parsey P | 14.03.1978 |
| Jenkins W | 20.10.1941 | Lewis G | 1913* | Moores R | 03.05.1926 | Partridge G | 1949 |
| Jessop J | 20.03.1944 | Licence H | 08.02.1927 | Morgan J | 27.02.1978 | Partridge M | 28.08.1911 |
| Jessop M | 15.01.1979 | Lightfoot R | 1952 | Morley A | 24.09.1951 | Pawsey H.G | 29.09.1924 |
| Johnson C | 1952 | Lillyman A.N | 21.02.1927 | Morley R | 01.02.1919 | Paxman E | 20.01.1913 |
| Johnson F | 29.07.1893 | Lincoln G | 30.10.1885 | Morling J | 01.09.1947 | Payne E | 23.06.1913 |
| Jonas F | 04.07.1935 | Lindley W.W | 13.08.1923 | Morrow D | 01.04.1985 | Payne G | 19.11.1945 |
| Jones L | 12.04.1948 | Ling H.C | 13.08.1923 | Mortimer D | 1960's * | Peace S | 27.05.1940 |
| Jones R | 1950 | Llewellyn P | 1983 | Mortimer P | 1950 | Peachey F | 25.08.1923 |
| Jordan L | 18.12.1944 | Lloyd E | 1949 | Moutell W | 13.12.1898 | Peachey L | 07.08.1951 |
| Jordan R | 04.09.1945 | Lloyd L | 24.05.1948 | Moyes F | 20.09.1884 | Pearce A | 01.04.1985 |
| Josselyn T | 04.06.1917 | Locksmith F | 12.12.1908 | Moyes F | 02.05.1910 | Pearce J | 06.03.1909 |
| Kape E.E | 01.11.1913 | Locksmith T.H | 16.11.1914 | Moyse R | 15.01.1941 | Pearce R | 20.08.1951 |
| Keeble A | 1950 | Lockwood | —.12.1946 | Mudd A | 06.06.1944 | Pearce R | 27.02.1978 |
| Keeble R | 15.03.1948 | Lockwood R | 14.06.1937 | Mulley P | 08.04.1947 | Peck B | 1950 |
| Keeble S | 28.11.1983 | Lockwood W | 06.03.1917 | Mulley R | 05.04.1948 | Peck S | 1947 |
| Keeble W | 1908* | Loose R | 08.08.1939 | Mullin H | 19.05.1924 | Percy H | 08.11.1891 |
| Kemp A.E | 29.03.1902 | Lord G | 18.05.1948 | Mullitt C | 23.08.1937 | Perkins R | 01.01.1983 |
| Kenny R | 1971* | Lowe | 30.12.1946 | Mullitt R | 22.04.1940 | Perryman F | 15.04.1940 |
| Kenworthy D | 28.02.1944 | Lown G | 16.06.1941 | Mumford B | 1952 | Petch W | 1912* |
| Kerridge F | 23.05.1910 | Lucas R | 1952 | Munnings S | 1907* | Pettingale A | 27.09.1915 |
| Kerslake R | 18.05.1948 | Lucas R.C | 29.10.1898 | Murphy G | 14.03.1927 | Pettingale H | 1906* |
| Kidby A | 24.05.1943 | Lynch F | 09.02.1948 | Murton B | 1965 | Pettitt A.G | 14.07.1924 |
| Kidd G | 27.09.1943 | MacDonald W | 1880 | Mutimer E.W | 24.02.1912 | Philips H | 26.04.1948 |
| King C.E | 07.04.1900 | Maguire D | 22.09.1947 | Mutimer W | 19.01.1914 | Phillips A | 03.08.1920 |
| King D | 24.04.1944 | Maile T | 15.08.1949 | Nash N | 09.08.1937 | Phillips K | 22.02.1943 |
| King E H | 25.09.1944 | Mallion T | 16.01.1984 | Neal I | 14.05.1979 | Pickering F | 09.02.1888 |
| King F | 02.06.1941 | Manley J.M | 27.02.1906 | Nestling J | 07.07.1947 | Pickess A | 1907* |
| King G | 09.04.1974 | Mann F.W | 20.08.1923 | Newman A | 11.10.1902 | Pickess D | 26.10.1942 |
| King J | 01.04.1985 | Mann W | 23.01.1909 | Newman C | 1906* | Pierpoint K | 14.10.1940 |
| King O | 18.03.1940 | Manning R | 14.07.1924 | Newman R | 22.02.1941 | Pigg R.N | 04.11.1924 |
| King T | 11.11.1940 | Manning W.A | 16.11.1914 | Newman W.B | 07.03.1927 | Pinfold D | 1952 |
| King T | 26.03.1979 | Mansfield F | 07.08.1920 | Newman W.J | 19.05.1924 | Pinkney C | 01.11.1904 |
| Knight M | 30.04.1984 | Markham J | 1906* | Newson C.C | 25.08.1913 | Pinkney G.H | 30.04.1892 |
| Knight P | 14.08.1986 | Marsden D | 27.06.1977 | Nibloe O | 1909* | Pinkney P | 05.05.1924 |
| Knights A | 13.08.1951 | Marsh T | 08.08.1950 | Nicholls F | 03.09.1894 | Pipe A | 06.10.1947 |
| Knights E | 13.07.1942 | Marsh W | 01.03.1948 | Nicholls R | 14.06.1937 | Pitt J | 01.12.1947 |
| Knights R | 1949 | Martin E | 21.02.1944 | Nicholls W | 27.07.1912 | Pizzey F | 28.07.1883 |
| Knights W | 1916* | Martin J | 17.11.1947 | Noble T | 29.08.1920 | Plant J | 01.02.1943 |
| Lacey C | 04.04.1977 | Martin W | 12.07.1879 | Noble W | 1950 | Plumb K | 26.10.1942 |
| Lacey W | 1918* | Martin W | 1912* | Nock F | 15.11.1919 | Podd S | 09.06.1947 |
| Lacy H | 09.05.1919 | Maskell M | 1950 | Nock F W | 02.07.1923 | Pollard J | 18.03.1946 |
| Laing R | 1960's * | Mattin F | 28.09.1901 | Norman K | 25.08.1985 | Poole K | 01.07.1974 |
| Lait E.E | 12.03.1892 | Mattin N | 1977 | Norris D | 1953 | Poole S | 03.03.1975 |
| Lamb H | 14.09.1888 | Maxim L | 17.03.1941 | Norris L | 03.05.1926 | Pooley R | 29.12.1947 |
| Lancaster I | 31.07.1945 | May M | 1960's * | Notley P | 06.10.1947 | Porter D | 1974 |
| Lancaster M | 02.04.1973 | May R | 1951 | Nudds A | 08.08.1950 | Porter J | 1950's * |
| Lancaster R | 09.02.1942 | Mayes D | 22.03.1943 | Nunn A | 16.06.1941 | Potter D | 01.04.1985 |
| Land R | 1971* | Mayhew G | 01.04.1922 | Nunn W | 13.12.1887 | Potter G.W | 15.01.1906 |
| Lane D | 1954 | Mayhew W | 29.07.1907 | Nuttall B | 27.11.1922 | Potter J | 26.04.1948 |
| Larkin A | 1966 | McCarthy D.A. | 29.01.1921 | O'Hare N | 1971* | Potter M | 1966 |
| Last J | 31.08.1895 | McDonald W | 19.07.1937 | O'Keefe L | 1971* | Potter W | 16.06.1887 |
| Last K | 16.11.1942 | McGann F | 05.10.1943 | O'Neill W | 1950's * | Pottle D | 26.06.1944 |
| Last R | 13.12.1947 | McKie A | 21.10.1946 | Oliver E | 1934 | Pratt D | 1952 |
| Last S | 24.02.1919 | McWade L | 17.03.1941 | Orris G | 02.12.1946 | Prentice J | 1964 |
| Last V | 10.05.1948 | Meckiff C | 02.07.1907 | Orris J | 11.06.1979 | Preston J. (1) | 01.04.1946 |
| Latter T | 04.10.1909 | Mee E | 29.01.1940 | Orvis A.B | 15.01.1913 | Preston J. (2) | 15.09.1947 |
| Laughlin L | 22.03.1943 | Mee L | 27.05.1940 | Osbourne B | 05.04.1948 | Prince-Wright N | 1977 |
| Laughlin R | 31.08.1903 | Melville | 27.01.1947 | Osbourne E.G | 09.07.1892 | Prior R | 26.02.1940 |

# IPSWICH SENIORITY LIST

| | | | | | | | |
|---|---|---|---|---|---|---|---|
| Pritchard L | 18.11.1946 | Saunders V.C | 03.10.1908 | Stannard E | 08.07.1887 | Ward F | 22.12.1941 |
| Pryke E.H | 12.05.1924 | Savage J | 20.03.1944 | Stannard H.R | 16.03.1903 | Ward F.C | 15.06.1912 |
| Pugh R | 09.01.1945 | Scarfe A | 23.07.1951 | Stannard V | 11.09.1944 | Ward R | 15.07.1985 |
| Pulham E | 1906* | Scarfe M | 19.08.1974 | Steele B | 01.03.1948 | Warden E | 1909* |
| Pulkam H | 26.02.1921 | Scarfe P | 1950 | Stephenson A | 12.04.1915 | Wardley J | 20.03.1944 |
| Pye A | 30.03.1948 | Scarlett A | 12.04.1915 | Stephenson C | 15.08.1949 | Warne A | 1960's * |
| Pywell J | 01.02.1919 | Scarlett J | 25.06.1945 | Stevens H | 22.02.1915 | Warne P | 1950 |
| R Potter | 27.05.1947 | Scarlett S | 17.11.1941 | Stevenson F | 27.01.1941 | Warnes W.G | 18.01.1915 |
| Ramsey E | 03.07.1886 | Scase J | 01.03.1948 | Stevenson H | 1950 | Warren C | 12.07.1943 |
| Randall E | 28.06.1937 | Schofield A.C | 11.08.1923 | Steward R | 27.07.1939 | Warren R | 21.08.1939 |
| Rands E | 13.10.1947 | Schofield H.A | 07.03.1910 | Stiff R.T | 14.07.1924 | Warren W.B | 03.11.1913 |
| Ratcliffe R | 29.06.1903 | Schofield J | 29.01.1887 | Stopher | 30.12.1946 | Waspe G | 10.11.1941 |
| Ratcliffe W | 10.08.1912 | Scott J | 14.12.1903 | Storey R.J | 18.09.1945 | Waterman R.W | 03.09.1923 |
| Rattle W | 26.05.1919 | Scoulding E | 23.06.1947 | Story H | 03.07.1882 | Waters C | 31.12.1951 |
| Rattle W | 28.07.1924 | Scrivener J | 1947* | Stowers J | 22.01.1941 | Watson B | 05.07.1920 |
| Rayner E | 08.08.1950 | Scrivener N | 18.02.1985 | Strutt R | 1912* | Watts | 1949 |
| Rayner G | 05.05.1947 | Self F | 08.03.1943 | Studd B | 30.09.1912 | Webb E | 1906* |
| Rayner L.H | 28.06.1915 | Sewell W | 02.09.1946 | Studd B | 26.01.1948 | Webb H | 08.04.1947 |
| Read R | 06.09.1943 | Sharland C | 03.05.1948 | Studd C | 18.04.1938 | Webb P | 28.02.1944 |
| Read S | 1950 | Sharman F | March 1926 | Studd D | 1949 | Webb W | 07.01.1946 |
| Read S | 14.08.1986 | Sharp R | 1965 | Studd R | 12.11.1945 | Webber B | 18.05.1948 |
| Reed S | 15.03.1937 | Sharpe A.J | 1964 | Sturgeon F | 1950 | Webster J | 1949 |
| Reid D | 1971* | Sheldon N | 07.05.1946 | Suckling R | 26.04.1948 | Welch F.S | 19.07.1899 |
| Reynolds E | 10.08.1895 | Shemming R | 10.07.1944 | Swallow A | 1960's * | Welham J | 02.06.1919 |
| Richards G | 29.07.1954 | Shutt H | 02.10.1896 | Symonds | 1949 | Wells E | 31.03.1919 |
| Richards R | 23.07.1984 | Simmons C.E | 16.08.1884 | Symonds A | 1952 | Wells S | 31.03.1919 |
| Richardson R | 28.12.1937 | Simpson E | 23.06.1941 | Szczepanski S | 11.06.1979 | Welsh F | 1913* |
| Richardson W | 25.04.1938 | Simpson W | 1946* | Tabor R | 12.02.1945 | Welton A.E | 11.04.1903 |
| Riches R.G | 15.02.1915 | Skeels A | 17.03.1919 | Talbot A | 17.06.1940 | Welton K | 28.08.1946 |
| Ridgeon G.H | 02.03.1912 | Skeet C | 01.07.1911 | Talbot C H | 23.08.1920 | Westgate W | 28.02.1944 |
| Ridley G | 04.01.1943 | Skene A | 03.06.1940 | Talbot E | 22.09.1947 | Weston J | 14.08.1920 |
| Risby A.R | 21.03.1927 | Skinner J | 19.02.1940 | Talbot J | 27.06.1977 | Weymouth L | 29.03.1897 |
| Rivers T | 01.03.1937 | Slee P | 29.07.1973 | Talbot S | 22.09.1924 | Whent N | 1960's * |
| Rivett H | 1949 | Smales G | 07.12.1922 | Talman M | 14.08.1986 | Whistlecraft W.H | 04.08.1923 |
| Roadd R | 11.04.1944 | Smith A | 1952 | Taylor C | 31.08.1903 | White N | 13.05.1946 |
| Robertson C | 24.03.1941 | Smith A.A | 26.08.1911 | Taylor D | 1916* | Whitman H | 06.10.1941 |
| Robinson B | 29.04.1940 | Smith C | 02.06.1919 | Taylor H | 04.08.1912 | Wilding E | 16.10.1944 |
| Robinson D | 26.03.1979 | Smith D | 20.03.1944 | Taylor J | 14.01.1941 | Wiles G | 20.08.1951 |
| Robinson F | 14.07.1888 | Smith E | 15.03.1948 | Taylor W | 19.05.1919 | Williams K | 20.10.1947 |
| Robinson G | 1919 | Smith E.E | 12.04.1897 | Theobald H | 11.01.1909 | Williams L | 1947* |
| Robinson H | 09.06.1906 | Smith F.A.W | 13.08.1923 | Thirkettle E | 1906* | Willsmore J.A | 20.08.1923 |
| Robinson P | 14.12.1942 | Smith G | 1952 | Thompson B | 17.03.1941 | Willson J | 23.10.1944 |
| Robinson R | 09.07.1917 | Smith J.H | 01.04.1922 | Thompson R | 27.07.1939 | Wilson T | 19.01.1959 |
| Robinson T | 1949 | Smith M | 08.10.1945 | Thompson R | 20.10.1947 | Winney G | 31.07.1891 |
| Rodgers P | 26.07.1937 | Smith P | 24.05.1943 | Thorpe F.W | 30.11.1914 | Winney W.C | 03.11.1913 |
| Rodwell L | 21.04.1941 | Smith R | 03.03.1947 | Thorpe I | 21.06.1943 | Wood D | 08.08.1944 |
| Rolfe G | 07.10.1929 | Smith R.R | 09.08.1915 | Thorpe P | 23.02.1948 | Wood P | 28.04.1947 |
| Rolfe P.S | 22.07.1913 | Smith S | 1971* | Thurlow W | 26.11.1910 | Woodard A | 23.06.1947 |
| Rose E | 01.04.1940 | Smith W | 1966 | Topple S.E | 25.08.1923 | Woodcock C | 13.09.1904 |
| Rose H | 15.03.1943 | Smith W | 29.12.1947 | Towler A | 17.02.1919 | Woodgate B | 14.07.1894 |
| Rose R | 1950 | Smith W | 1950 | Trenter A.V | 23.11.1914 | Woods J | 21.02.1927 |
| Rose S | 19.05.1913 | Sole G | 03.01.1938 | Tricker A | 01.07.1974 | Woods K | 05.06.1944 |
| Ross B | 18.02.1946 | Southgate A | 1912* | Tricker G W | 03.03.1919 | Woodward W.E | 15.09.1924 |
| Rowe A H | 18.01.1915 | Southgate A.E | 02.10.1916 | Tricker R | 29.10.1917 | Woolhert E | 02.06.1941 |
| Rowland C | 29.11.1943 | Southgate B.G | 25.05.1915 | Tricker R J | 21.12.1920 | Woolnough R | 23.06.1978 |
| Rowland M | 23.08.1920 | Southgate G | 14.05.1904 | Trout F | 19.01.1925 | Wright E | 14.06.1948 |
| Rudge | 1953 | Southgate L | 14.09.1942 | Tuck R | 1964 | Wright G | 04.08.1924 |
| Rudge P | 1952 | Southgate P | 21.03.1910 | Tuke F | 16.06.1894 | Wright R | 1909* |
| Rudland D | 27.06.1977 | Southgate R | 12.01.1942 | Tunstall B | 1913* | Wright R | 19.08.1946 |
| Rumbellow A J | 29.04.1907 | Southgate T | 01.07.1974 | Turner A.J | 26.07.1919 | Wroth F | 17.06.1905 |
| Rumsey F | 15.01.1912 | Spall H.H | 11.08.1924 | Turner C.W | 05.07.1884 | Wroth V.W | 29.06.1920 |
| Rumsey H | 11.07.1896 | Sparke H.E | 04.01.1915 | Turner W | 09.07.1910 | Wroth W | 16.09.1882 |
| Rumsey R | 1952 | Sparrow E | 08.03.1944 | Tweed B | 11.08.1923 | Wyard N | 04.03.1940 |
| Rumsey W | 27.07.1912 | Spence J | 21.01.1941 | Tweed J | 1950 | Young D | 22.01.1926 |
| Runnacles H.C | 23.09.1912 | Spencer P | 1950 | Tyrell R.B | 11.11.1919 | Young J | 1960's * |
| Rush G | 11.08.1923 | Spencer R | 1960's * | Versey W | 02.07.1923 | Young S | 19.04.1977 |
| Sadler E | 1912* | Spencer W | 1952 | Viney G.F | 24.10.1908 | | |
| Sadler E.G | 13.03.1897 | Spiers D | 17.01.1944 | Votier G | 25.08.1947 | | |
| Sadler H.S | 14.09.1901 | Spooner V | 1906* | Vyse J | 01.12.1947 | * At Ipswich during or since the date shown. | |
| Sadler J | 05.07.1879 | Spooner W.G | 22.10.1898 | Wade M | 07.02.1977 | | |
| Salmon F.C | 19.01.1885 | Spurling C | 1917* | Wagstaff | 1954 | | |
| Sansom C | 30.10.1906 | Spurling N | 17.11.1947 | Waite J | 18.08.1947 | | |
| Sapsford R | 13.09.1920 | Squirrell D | 1949 | Walford A | 24.02.1919 | | |
| Sargent G | 06.10.1947 | Staff R | 1949 | Walker F | 08.06.1942 | | |
| Saunders A F | 27.07.1912 | Stammers H | 1907* | Walker R | 16.03.1942 | | |
| Saunders T | 26.07.1897 | Stanley H | 1941* | Walker W | 03.05.1948 | | |

## Sources and further reading

| | |
|---|---|
| Aldrich, C. Langley. | *The Locomotives of the Great Eastern Railway* - Aldrich (1955) |
| Allen, C. J. | *The Great Eastern Railway* - Ian Allan (1955) |
| | *The London & North Eastern Railway* - Ian Allan (1966) |
| Bell A. | *Locomotives,* (Volumes I & II) - Virtue & Company Ltd. |
| Bishop, Peter. | *The History of Ipswich - 1500 years of Triumph & Disaster* - Unicorn Press (1995) |
| Clarke, R. H. | *A Short History of The Midland & Great Northen Railway* - Goose & Son (1967) |
| Comfort, N. A. | *Mid-Suffolk Light Railway* - Oakwood Press (1963) |
| Cross, Dennis. | *Suffolk Railways - A Portrait in Old Picture Postcards* - S. B. Publications (1993) |
| Cross, R. L. | *The Living Past - A Victorian Heritage* - Borough of Ipswich (1975) |
| Fellows, Reginald B. | *Railways To Cambridge* - Oakwood Press (1948) |
| Fincham, Paul. | *Ipswich in Old Picture Postcards* - European Library (1986) |
| Glyde, John. | *The Moral, Social & Religious Condition of Ipswich (1850)* - Republished S.R. Publishers Ltd. (1971) |
| Gordon, D. I. | *A Regional History of the Railways of Great Britain, Vol 5: The Eastern Counties* - David and Charles (1968) |
| Greenstock, Harry. | *Go On and Prosper* - Edited by Percy Reboul, BXL Plastics Ltd (1981) |
| Grimsey, B. P. | *Monograph on the Parish of St Mary Stoke* (c 1886) |
| Hawkins, Chris & Reeve, George. | *Great Eastern Railway Engine Sheds Part 2* - Wild Swan Publications (1987) |
| Hilton, H. F. | *The Eastern Union Railway, 1846 - 1862* - (1946) |
| Ipswich Engineering Society. | *The History of Engineering in Ipswich* - W.S.Cowell Ltd. (1950) |
| Jackson, Alan A. | *The Wordsworth Railway Dictionary* - Wordsworth Editions Ltd.(1997) |
| James, Trevor. | *Ipswich Inns, Taverns and Pubs* - Fuller-Davies Ltd. (1991) |
| | *Ipswich, Old and New* - B. J. Books (1989) |
| | *Ipswich, Years of Change 1956 - 1966* - Trio Books (1988) |
| Joby, R. S. | *Forgotten Railways: East Anglia* - David & Charles (1977) |
| Kindred, David. | *Around Ipswich in Old Photographs* - Allan Sutton (1991) |
| | *Ipswich: A Second Selection* - Allan Sutton (1993) |
| | *Ipswich Revisited* - Sutton Publishing Ltd. (1996) |
| McKillop, Norman. | *The Lighted Flame Nelson* - (1950) |
| Malster, Robert. | *Ipswich, Town on the Orwell* - Terence Dalton Ltd. (1978) |
| | *Ipswich, A Pictorial History* - Phillimore & Co. Ltd. (1991) |
| | *Suffolk Transport* - Sutton Publishing Ltd. (1997) |
| Malster, Robert & Jones, Bob. | *A Victorian Vision, The Building of the Wet Dock* - Ipswich Port Authority (1992) |
| Moffat, Hugh. | *East Anglia's First Railways* - Terence Dalton (1987) |
| Nock O.S. | *Great British Trains* - Pelham Books (1985) |
| Paye, P. | *The Mellis and Eye Railway* - Oakwood Press (1980) |
| Pevsner, Nikolaus. | *The Buildings of England - Suffolk* - Penguin Books (1961) |
| Redstone, Lillian. | *Ipswich Through the Ages* - East Anglian Magazine (1948) |
| Scarfe, Norman. | *The Suffolk Landscape* - Hodder & Stoughton (1972) |
| Suffolk Record Office. | *Ipswich Remembered, 1 - 4* |
| Thompson, Leonard P. | *Suffolk Coaching Days* - Peake Publications (1966) |
| Thorne, Robert. | *Liverpool Street Station* - Academy Editions (1978) |
| Woodgate, Patricia & James, Trevor. | *Ipswich, Past and Present* - Countryside Books (1986) |

Parish registers of St Mary-at-Stoke Church, Ipswich
Minutes of the Ipswich Branch of the ASLEF
GER and LNER Magazines (various)
Railway Magazine (various 1954-62)
Journals of the Great Eastern Railway Society
Directories including Pigot, White and Kelly of various dates
Sale catalogues (various)
Wymer, J.J. *Palaeolithic Sites of East Anglia* (1985)
Exhibition catalogue *The River Orwell* (1959)
*British Railways in Peace & War* British Railways Press Office for GWR, LMS, LNER, SR & London Transport (1944)
Working Timetables, LNER & British Railways
*Ipswich Scrapbook, Volume 8 - St Mary Stoke* John Glyde (Suffolk Record Office)
Robert Ratcliffe. *The History of the Working Class Movement in Ipswich & District* 4 volumes, typescript (Suffolk Record Office)
*Jubilee of the Ipswich & Suffolk Freehold Land Society* Ipswich (1899)
Historical Manuscripts Commission. Ninth report (1883)
Isaac Johnson's map of pipeline leading from Stoke Hall, 1792 (Suffolk Record Office)
Tithe map, 1840 - St Mary Stoke (Suffolk Record Office)
Route of possible EUR line, surveyed by Bruff, 1844 (Suffolk Record Office)
White's map of Ipswich 1867 (Suffolk Record Office)